18-50

The Waite Group's®
Discovering
MS-DOS ®

Second Edition

The Waite Group's®
Discovering
MS-DOS®

Second Edition

Kate O'Day and Harry Henderson

SAMS

A Division of Macmillan Computer Publishing
11711 North College, Carmel, Indiana 46032 USA

International Standard Book Number: 0-672-22772-x
Library of Congress Catalog Card Number: 91-61352

From the Waite Group, Inc.:
Development Editor: *Scott Calamar*
Managing Editor: *Joel Fugazzotto*

From SAMS:
Editor: *Sam Karnick*
Copy Editors: *Mary Ella McNeary, Andy Saff*
Cover Design: *Ron Troxell*
Production Assistance: *Martin Coleman, Sandy Grieshop, Betty Kish, Michele Laseau, Howard Peirce, Tad Ringo, Bruce Steed*
Indexer: *Susan VandeWalle*
Technical Reviewer: *Dan Derrick*

Printed in the United States of America

To Seamus Matthew Mercer Hursh——who, waiting patiently for his trip to the beach or to see the latest movie, has no choice but to be part of the "computer generation." This book's for you!

Kate O'Day

To Lisa, who showed me how rewarding writing could be.

Harry Henderson

Overview

Preface   *xv*

Acknowledgments   *xvii*

About the Authors   *xix*

Introduction   *xxi*

1 This Is a Computer System   *1*

2 This Is an Operating System   *11*

3 Getting MS-DOS Off the Ground   *19*

4 System Insurance   *37*

5 Minding Your E's and Q's   *61*

6 Editor's Choice   *89*

7 Getting the Files in Shape   *121*

8 Shifting into High Gear   *149*

9 Mixing Up a Fresh Batch   *193*

10 You Can See the Forest for the Trees   *227*

11 Plumbing Techniques   *277*

12 What's on the Menu?   *305*

13 Tooling Around DOS   *337*

Appendix   *379*

Index   *387*

Contents

Introduction
   Let Me Introduce You to MS-DOS   **xxi**
   Welcome MS-DOS Users   xxiii
   What You Need to Use This Book   xxiii
   What's in Discovering MS-DOS   xxiv

1 This Is a Computer System   **1**
   What Is a Computer System?   3
   Hardware   3
      Central Processing Unit (Microprocessor)   5
      Memory   5
      Storage Devices   7
   Software   8
      Application Programs   8
      Programming Languages   8
      Operating Systems   9

2 This Is an Operating System   **11**
   What Does an Operating System Do?   13
   History of MS-DOS   15
   Which Version of MS-DOS Do You Need?   16
   What MS-DOS Means to You   17

3 Getting MS-DOS off the Ground   **19**
   First Things First   21
      Do You Have a Hard Disk?   21
      Installing MS-DOS   22
      Save the MS-DOS 4.0 or 5.0 "DOS Shell" for Later   22
   If the Boot Fits . . .   23
      You Are Now Entering MS-DOS Airspace   24
      Playing It Safe with Your Hard Disk   25
      What's This About Time and Date?   26
      Setting the Time and Date   26
   How Does That Data Get in There?   26
      Entering Data into the Machine   27
   How To Set the Calendar and Clock   28

Boot Temperature (Cold Versus Warm)   30
Who's on the Passenger List?   31
     Listing All the Files   32
     Stop the Action!   32
     Listing a Specific File   34
Starting with a Clean Slate   35

4 System Insurance   37

Disks and Disk Drives   39
The Nature of Disks   41
     You Can Look, But You Better Not Touch   42
     Righting the "Write" Stuff   44
     Better Living through Labeling   44
     Differences with 3 1/2" Disks   45
How Is That Data Stored on the Disk?   47
Getting the Disk Ready to Be Used   47
     How Many Drives Do You Have?   48
     Filling in the Blank Spaces   48
     Using the FORMAT Command   50
     Signed, Sealed, and Delivered   52
Writing the Insurance Policy   53
     Clarifying the Beneficiary   54
A Written Guarantee   56

5 Minding Your E's and Q's   61

What Is an Editor?   63
Safety in Numbers   65
You ASCII Me and I ASCII You   66
As Easy As...   67
     Short and to the Point   68
     Current Events   68
Getting into the Act   69
     Open Sesame   70
     Putting Thoughts into Words   72
     Final Curtain   73
     Going over Your Lines   74
Revising the Script   76
     Looking at the First Draft   76
     Getting the Right Line   77
     Adding New Parts   78
     Eliminating Unneeded Characters   80
     Major Revisions   84

6 Editor's Choice

89

A New Edition   91
Eeek! A Mouse In the House?   93
Ready for a Screen Test?   94
    Take It from the Top   95
    Stage Left, Stage Right   96
    Rolling the Credits   98
    What's Next on the Menu?   102
    Let's Have a Little Dialog   104
Send It to Rewrite   106
    Take It Away   108
    The Cutting Room   110
    Searching for Fame and Fortune   112
Finishing Touches   115
    A Little Help from Your Friends   116
    Customizing the Edit Program   118
    It's A Wrap   119

7 Getting the Files in Shape

121

What Exactly Is a File?   123
What's in a Name?   124
Official Rules and Regulations   125
    Avoiding Hyperextension   128
    Set Specific Goals   129
Commands, Inside and Out   130
    Internal and External Commands   131
The Great American Novel   134
Reviewing What You Wrote   135
Where Is the Carbon Paper?   136
    May the Source Be with You   138
    Being Redundant   139
A Rose by Any Other Name   142
Wiped Out   144

8 Shifting into High Gear

149

Let Your Fingers Lead the Way   151
    Text and Graphics Screens   157
    The Numeric Keypad on the Regular PC Keyboard   157
    The Numeric and Cursor Pads on the Enhanced Keyboard 158
The Editing Express   159
The Functions at the Junctions   160
Exercising Control   166

Dealing with a Full Deck 167
Some Old Friends Revisited 170
Reorganizing the Filenames in Your Directory
with MS-DOS 5.0 173
Getting On-line Command Help in MS-DOS 5.0 176
Putting a Label on a Disk 180
Changing the Disk Label 182
Making a Bootable (System) Disk 182
Making New Acquaintances 185

9 Mixing up a Fresh Batch 193

What Are Batch Files? 195
Creating a Batch File from Scratch 196
A Choice of Cooking Methods 198
How Do You Use a Batch File? 199
Starting a Batch File 199
Solving a Problem with a Batch File: FORMAT Revisited 201
Stopping a Batch File 203
Adding More Ingredients 204
Commands in Batch Processing 208
You Can CALL On Me (Chaining Batch Files) 221
Putting It on Automatic 223

10 You Can See the Forest for the Trees 227

Directly on the Path in Front of You 229
Getting to the Root of the Matter 232
Subdirectories and Pathnames 234
Special Path Markers 235
Getting Back to Your Roots 239
Keeping Current 241
Finding the Right Home for a File 242
Blazing New Trails 246
The Path of Least Resistance 249
Taking a Shortcut 250
Climbing Around in the Tree 252
Watching Out for the Wildlife 254
A SUBSTitute for Lengthy Pathnames 261
Better Forest Management: Pruning and
Grafting with XCOPY 262
Jogging Along the PATH 265
Supplementing PATH with APPEND 267
Organizing Your Hard Disk 267
Hard Disk Insurance with the BACKUP Command 269
Using Batch Files to Simplify Backup 273
The RESTORE Command 273

11 Plumbing Techniques   277

Diverting the Flow   279
Redirecting Standard Output   280
Redirecting Standard Input   281
    The Trans-DOS Pipeline   281
Filtering the Flow   283
    To FIND and SORT Still MORE   294
The DOSKEY to Command Performance   296
    Recalling Previous Commands   297
    Editing Commands   299
    Using More Than One Command at a Time 300
    Holy Macro, DOS Man!   301

12 What's on the Menu?   305

Getting Started   307
Playing the Shell Game   308
Climbing the File Tree   309
    Menus and Options at Your Command   312
    Let's Have a Dialog   314
    I've Got a Little List . . .   314
Working with Files   317
    Doing the Chores, DOSSHELL Style   318
    A Handy Helper   319
Working with Multiple Directories and Files   322
    Using Path names with DOSSHELL   323
    Working with More Than One File   324
    Where's That File?   325
Running Programs from DOSSHELL   327
    Getting Prompt Service   327
    Running a Program from the File List   328
    Using the Program List   328
    Adding Your Own Program Groups   329
    Adding Programs to a Group   331
    Switching Between Programs   333
    Associating Data Files and Programs   334

13 Tooling Around DOS   337

It Slices, It Dices . . . Introducing Utility Packages   340
    Norton Utilities   340
    PC Tools   342
Making Backup Easy   345
The Doctor Is In   347
Recovery Room   350
    Backing Up Directory Information   350
    Restoring Erased Files   352

Restoring Accidentally Formatted Disks 353
Revving Up Your Disk 358
Device Drivers 358
Cache-ing in on Speed 360
Buffing Up Your BUFFERS 361
Speedy Navigation with FASTOPEN 362
Defragmentation 364
Interleaving 365
Tools for File Management 366
Where's That File? 366
Where's That Letter About... 367
What Does "gb99zrkl.txt" Mean, Anyway? 368
Devising with Devices 370
Speaking in Tongues 370
Using Your Resources 372
FILES 372
FCBS 372
LASTDRIVE 372
STACKS 373
Thanks for the Memories 373
Memory Lane 374
Which Kind of Memory Should You Use? 375
Freeing Up More Memory 377

Appendix
Error Messages

379

Device Error Messages 381
Additional Error Messages 383

Index

387

Preface

MS-DOS is the powerful disk-operating system developed by Microsoft for use with IBM PC-compatible microcomputers. It provides the instructions that enable your PC to manipulate files, handle interactions between the computer and the user, and manage peripherals such as printers and modems.

Today's typical PC user is not interested in programming. With the wealth of applications programs on the market today, users can survive nicely without learning much about the software "heart" of their systems. But by learning to use the power of MS-DOS, you can increase the ease with which you use your system. Certain procedures can be streamlined, information can be stored and accessed rapidly, and MS-DOS shortcuts can make using a computer easier than ever. You can also use MS-DOS utility commands to speed up the performance of your system.

In *Discovering MS-DOS* you will embark on an exciting and educational voyage of discovery to the most popular disk-operating system for microcomputers today. MS-DOS provides your computer with the instructions that make it perform its amazing feats, from running a spreadsheet program to writing letters to playing games and watching the stock market. While most users barely scratch the surface of their systems, *Discovering MS-DOS* will show you how to master this powerful software tool, expanding the usefulness of your system in a way that is both informative and fun.

This book differs in several ways from many books on MS-DOS and other operating systems. First, you don't need a computer background to read it. Second, it is written in the belief that computer concepts don't have to be complicated or boring. They can be presented in an entertaining way and still be instructive. Third, when you have finished this book, you will find that in addition to having had fun reading it and working the examples, you will have learned how to employ the power of MS-DOS in the daily use of your PC.

This completely revised Second Edition follows the same user-friendly, comfortably paced approach as the original edition. It adds the latest MS-DOS commands and features through version 5.0, preparing you for the DOS of the 90s. The new topics include Edit, an easy-to-use text editor that replaces the old EDLIN program; the DOSSHELL program that helps you manage your files and programs; new MS-DOS version 5.0 utility programs; and third-party utilities from PC Tools and Norton Utilities. We have paid particular attention to helping you get the most out of MS-DOS on today's powerful hard-disk-equipped desktop powerhouse while not forgetting the humblest PC with a single floppy disk drive.

Discovering MS-DOS begins with a description of what a computer is and why it needs an operating system. You then learn how to start your system from a floppy or hard disk, how to handle floppy disks, and how to get information into and out of your system. You are then given a choice of EDLIN or, if you have MS-DOS version 5.0, the new Edit program. Using these tools, you can create your own text files. The files you create are then used to help you practice file management. Then you move into high gear and learn about the power of the keyboard—function keys and keystroke combinations that make everyday tasks easier. Next you learn how to use batch files to automate repetitive tasks and increase your productivity. The real power of MS-DOS is then revealed in the tree-structured directories and pathnames and the advanced features of redirection, piping, and filtering. To this is added the power and versatility of the MS-DOS version 5.0 DOSKEY program, which lets you reuse old commands and create new custom command combinations. Next, MS-DOS version 5.0 users are introduced to DOSSHELL, a "graphical user interface" that simplifies many file-management tasks and lets you run commands and programs from menus using the keyboard or a "mouse" pointer. The final chapter looks at a variety of utility programs you can use for backing up your hard disk, recovering lost data, improving hard-disk performance, and using your PC's memory efficiently. An appendix explains the most common error messages in MS-DOS, and suggests possible solutions. A reference card provides a handy summary of MS-DOS commands.

The authors are uniquely equipped to guide you on this exciting journey to MS-DOS mastery. Kate O'Day has used MS-DOS on a variety of microcomputers, and has been involved in development of training programs and user orientation. This background has helped her identify the areas where users new to the world of computers and MS-DOS in particular have the most difficulty. Harry Henderson, contributing author to many Waite Group MS-DOS books, brings this experience to the updated coverage of MS-DOS features, choosing those most important to the new MS-DOS user, and suggesting further paths to take as your experience grows. We hope that you will not only learn about this important part of your microcomputer system, but enjoy yourself along the way.

Kate O'Day
Harry Henderson
The Waite Group

Acknowledgments

The Waite Group would like to thank Harry Henderson for doing a wonderful job revising this book. Thanks to Kate O'Day for her contributions to the first edition. Thanks, too, to Peter Weverka and Sam Karnick for their diligent editing of this project. Finally, thanks to Bob Johnson for his cartoons, which help illustrate that learning computer concepts can be entertaining.

Trademarks

All terms mentioned in this book that are known to be trademarks or service marks are listed below. In addition, terms suspected of being trademarks or service marks have been appropriately capitalized. SAMS cannot attest to the accuracy of this information. Use of a term in this book should not be regarded as affecting the validity of any trademark or service mark.

IBM is a registered trademark of International Business Machines.

Lotus 1-2-3 is a trademark of Lotus Development Corporation.

MS-DOS, Microsoft Word, and Microsoft Windows are registered trademarks of Microsoft Corporation.

Norton Utilities is a trademark of Symantec.

PCTools is a trademark of Central Point Software.

SideKick is a registered trademark of Borland International, Inc.

About the Authors

Harry Henderson has contributed to numerous books on computer languages and operating systems for The Waite Group, Waite Group Press, SAMS, and other publishers. He also works with his wife, Lisa Yount, writing school textbooks and trying to avoid tripping over cats. Some of the books he has coauthored include *Understanding MS-DOS*, *The Waite Group's UNIX Communications*, and *The Waite Group's Tricks of the MS-DOS Masters*.

Kate O'Day has a master's degree in educational technology. She has authored user's guides for the Sharp PC-5000 and Panasonic Sr. Partner personal computers, as well as software manuals for Koala Technologies and the Rolm Corporation. She also writes employee training programs, user orientation modules, and marketing presentations for the computer industry.

Introduction
Let Me Introduce You to MS-DOS

- Welcome MS-DOS Users
- What You Need to Use This Book
- What's in *Discovering MS-DOS*

Introduction
Let Me Introduce You to MS-DOS

Welcome MS-DOS Users

This book is about using your computer system. It is written especially for new computer owners. To read, use, and enjoy *Discovering MS-DOS,* you don't have to know a thing about MS-DOS, operating systems, or even computer terminology. The only thing you need to know right now is that MS-DOS is the operating system that comes with your computer. (Later, we'll tell you more about what an "operating system" is.)

You may have some doubts that you really know what a computer system is. You may be a little unsure of what a computer system does. And you're all but sure that you don't know how to operate a computer system. Relax, you've come to the right place. Together we're going to explore MS-DOS, and this guided tour will stop at all major points of interest. At the end of this journey, you're going to be a confident and experienced MS-DOS user.

This book is particularly about MS-DOS, one of the most popular operating systems used in microcomputers today. MS-DOS is available for a wide variety of computers, ranging from laptops and self-contained portables to full-sized desktop computers. Any "IBM-compatible" computer can use MS-DOS. (The IBM PCs, ATs, and PS/2s themselves use a special version of MS-DOS called PC DOS.) Although there are slight differences in the way MS-DOS works on different computer models, most of the things you learn in this book will be applicable to any MS-DOS system.

Discovering MS-DOS employs a well-known educational technique: "learning by doing." Computer folks call this the "hands-on approach." Whichever term you prefer, this book is not only descriptive; it also presents examples and exercises for each aspect of MS-DOS. You will "get your feet wet" typing information into the computer and seeing the results of your labor. These projects are designed to help you really understand the information being discussed.

What You Need to Use This Book

To use this book, you need a personal computer equipped with a keyboard, monitor, and the MS-DOS operating system. You also need at least one floppy disk drive. Two are preferable. If you also have a hard disk, you will find that it's faster and more convenient to use than floppy disks, but a hard disk is not required for any of the activities you will master in this book. (For Chapters 6 and 12, you will also find it convenient to have a "mouse" pointing device connected to your computer, but again, it is not required.)

Users of all versions of MS-DOS can learn from this book. Many of the important MS-DOS features and concepts date back to versions 2.0 and 2.1. However, *Discovering MS-DOS* also covers a number of important and useful features that are available only with MS-DOS versions 3.0 and higher. (You will need MS-DOS 4.0 or later to work with the examples in Chapter 12, and MS-DOS 5.0 to use Chapter 6. Even if you don't have one of these later MS-DOS versions, however, we recommend that you read through these chapters to learn about important new features.) If we don't specify the minimum MS-DOS version for a particular feature, you can assume that it is available starting with MS-DOS 2.0. (MS-DOS version 1.0 is obsolete.)

If you have the previously described equipment, an MS-DOS disk, and a willing mind, you're ready to begin this adventure.

What's in *Discovering MS-DOS*

If this is your first experience with computers, the layout of this book is designed especially for you. You just start with Chapter 1, "This Is a Computer System," and don't look back. In Chapter 1, you will get an introduction to computer systems. Then in Chapter 2, "This Is an Operating System," you will gain some knowledge about operating systems in general. You will begin using your operating system in Chapter 3, "Getting MS-DOS Off the Ground." If you are already familiar with the components of a computer system and understand what an operating system is and does, you can go directly to Chapter 3. Chapter 3 will also show you how to install MS-DOS so that it is ready to run on your system. You may have to do this if you have just bought a brand-new computer.

Chapter 4, "System Insurance," shows you how to protect your investment in MS-DOS by explaining how to care for and make copies of your floppy disks. Chapter 5, "Minding Your E's and Q's," lets your creativity shine through; it explains the operation of the EDLIN line-editing program that comes with MS-DOS. With this program, you can write letters, memos, and other short documents and make changes and corrections as you go along. All the EDLIN commands are explained here for you. Chapter 6, "Editor's Choice," introduces the new Microsoft full-screen text editor that comes with MS-DOS 5.0. If you have this new version of MS-DOS, you can skip Chapter 5 and learn how to use this easy-to-use editor rather than EDLIN, although it doesn't hurt to be familiar with both. Chapter 7, "Getting the Files in Shape," expands your understanding of MS-DOS by leading you step-by-step through file creation and naming, and basic commands involving files. You will learn how to look at a file, copy a file, rename files, and erase files.

In Chapter 8, "Shifting into High Gear," the real power of the keyboard and the function keys is described. You will learn techniques to speed up the process of entering and changing data as well as how certain key combinations can enhance your use of your system. Chapter 9, "Mixing Up a Fresh Batch," will make your routine use of MS-DOS even handier. You will learn what batch files are and how they can make your job easier. You will see how to program your system to perform many functions automatically.

After you have learned all the interesting things your MS-DOS-equipped system can do for you, Chapter 10, "You Can See the Forest for the Trees," will show you how to organize your information files into easy-to-use directories and how to rapidly access the data you have so carefully arranged. Chapter 11, "Plumbing Techniques," shows how to make your system direct, sort, and find data and files in such a way that you will wonder why you waited so long to acquire your computer. If you have MS-DOS 5.0, you will also learn how to use the new DOSKEY utility to create easy-to-use command shortcuts. Chapter 12, "Of Mice and Shells," introduces the use of the menu-driven "DOS shell," available starting with MS-DOS 4.0. This facility makes it even easier to select files and programs you want to work with. Finally, Chapter 13, "Tooling Around DOS," will show you how to use some of the more advanced MS-DOS features and third-party utility programs to get the most out of your PC. You'll get tips to make backing up your hard disk quick and painless, speed up hard-disk performance, and use your application programs efficiently.

By moving through the chapters in sequence, you will gradually build on your growing knowledge of MS-DOS. The chapters are best read in order. Of course, after you have finished this book, it will be a valuable reference tool. For quick, concise reference, we have included a pull-out DOS Reference Card at the end.

So fasten your seat belts, and let's begin!

This is a Computer System

1

- What Is a Computer System?
- Hardware
  - Central Processing Unit (Microprocessor)
  - Memory
  - Storage Devices
- Software
  - Application Programs
  - Programming Languages
  - Operating Systems

1 This Is a Computer System

What Is a Computer System?

A microcomputer system can range from a "laptop" computer you can carry in your briefcase to a small "portable" machine you can store under an airplane seat, to a desktop or stand-alone "tower" system with fancy graphics capabilities and three printers. Most likely, your machine falls somewhere in between. MS-DOS is available for almost all these machines and many more that fall inside the broad definition of "computer system."

This book will help make your learning experience more enjoyable. But you may sometimes be confused when our discussion or illustrations do not match your specific computer layout. Since MS-DOS is available for many types of computers, our discussion will deal with general definitions and components of computer systems and generic elements of MS-DOS. If at times you are confused about specific names, displays, keys, or messages, check the manual that the manufacturer packages with your system.

In this chapter, we are going to take a look at the parts of your computer system, both inside and out. This discussion is just to get you started on the road to building a "computer vocabulary." These are "terms" that help make operating MS-DOS easier. Don't worry about knowing these words; no memorization is necessary.

Your computer system is made up of many different components. The machine parts are called hardware. This includes your keyboard, disk drives, and monitor. You can connect peripherals (additional hardware) to your machine through specialized ports or connectors (the places where they "plug into" your machine). One typical peripheral is a printer.

The part of your computer system that makes this hardware perform is called software; it controls the operation of your machine. If you have been using your computer at all, you may already be acquainted somewhat with one type of software—your MS-DOS operating system. Other types of software include application programs (for example, word processors, games, accounting packages) and utility programs (for example, the PC Tools and Norton Utilities programs to be introduced in chapter 13). Software also includes programming languages such as BASIC and C that you can use to create your own application programs.

Hardware

One of the advantages of MS-DOS is the ability of many different models of machines to operate with this system. This simply means that MS-DOS is the operating system that "controls" how the computer performs its work. Because many types of computer systems run MS-DOS, you can choose the specific system you want and still use the most popular operating system on the market.

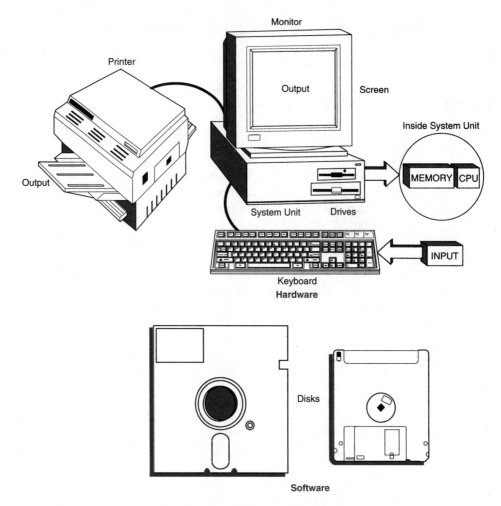

Fig. 1-1. Hardware and software.

Your computer system may be an easy-to-carry laptop or a specialized worksta-
tion which is part of a large office networking system. Still, every system has several
common features.

Information that is fed into the computer is called "input." Most often this input
comes from you. You will use a keyboard to type in your entries. Another increasingly
popular input device is the "mouse," which we will discuss in Chapters 6 and 12. The
information that comes from the computer to you is called "output." Messages and
results are displayed on a monitor or screen.

You can get a permanent record of computer output by connecting a printer
to your computer. Printers range from inexpensive and quite capable dot-matrix
types to faster and sharper (but more expensive) laser printers.

When the computer is not actually using some information, that information
is put into "storage." Computers use floppy disks or hard disks to store data.

Inside every microcomputer is a "microprocessor." This "chip" is what makes your computer do the things it does so well. Also inside the machine is some "memory." Let's explore the inside of the machine first.

Central Processing Unit (Microprocessor)

The "brains" of your computer are contained in the central processing unit (CPU). CPUs vary in size, speed, and the amount of work they are capable of performing. The CPU is the workhorse of your computer. MS-DOS makes the most of the common CPUs used in today's personal computers. But the design and technology of CPUs are growing at a rapid rate, and, as more and better CPUs are developed, there will be enhanced versions of MS-DOS to take advantage of the latest advances in technology.

Memory

The computer has two types of memory, each with very specific characteristics.

Random Access Memory (RAM) is memory that is used by the computer to hold the information it is currently working on. Information in RAM changes as you edit and enter data. It is very important to remember that RAM is transient. Things stored in RAM are only temporary; when you turn off the machine, RAM is wiped clean.

This means that before you turn off your machine you must transfer to storage on a floppy or hard disk any data in RAM that you wish to use again. Application programs, which come on their own disks, or information that you do not alter and already have on a disk do not need to be returned to storage at the end of a working session.

Read Only Memory (ROM), on the other hand, is permanent. It is actually contained in hardware on your CPU. ROM contents are determined by your computer manufacturer. In most IBM PC-compatible computers some of the detailed instructions that MS-DOS uses to carry out its tasks are loaded from ROM when the system is turned on.

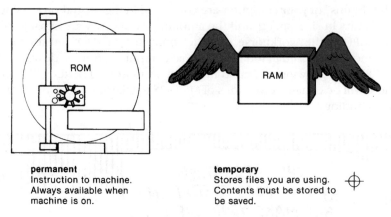

permanent
Instruction to machine.
Always available when
machine is on.

temporary
Stores files you are using.
Contents must be stored to
be saved.

Fig. 1-2. ROM and RAM.

The amount of memory in your computer is measured in bytes. Each byte contains eight bits. A byte can be thought of as one character (such as a letter, "a," or a numeral, "1"). As I enter this text on my word processor, it takes six bytes to store "MS-DOS" (actually eight, if you count the quotation marks).

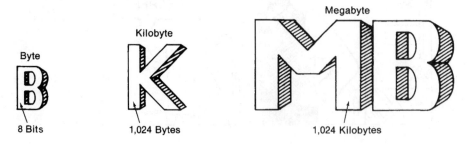

Fig. 1-3. Bits, bytes, K, and M.

Computer memory is often described in terms of K, as in "I know where I can get some additional K real cheap!" K is shorthand for kilobytes, which means 1024 bytes. You may have seen the claim "expandable to 640K." This means the total computer memory of that system would be 640 times 1024 or 655,360 bytes. Most systems sold today come with at least 640K and often 1024K. 1024K is called a *megabyte*, meaning "a million bytes." (Actually a megabyte contains 1024 x 1024 or 1,048,576 bytes.) The more advanced systems can be expanded to 8 megabytes or more. While some application programs require large amounts of memory (or work better with more memory), MS-DOS itself works fine with 512K or even less.

Storage Devices

Nearly all computer systems use disk drives to read and write information to storage. There are two kinds of drives: floppy disk drives and hard disk drives.

Floppy disks (sometimes called "diskettes") are small disks coated with a magnetic material to contain information. The information is stored as tiny "spots" of magnetism. You insert these disks into disk drives. Your system may have one, two, or several disk drives. Today's PCs use either 5 1/4" floppy disks or the newer 3 1/2" hard-shelled disks; in fact it is convenient to have one disk drive of each size. Although different types of computers often use the same size disks, you may not (generally) interchange disks full of data between machines that use different operating systems. This is because operating systems place information on disks in different ways. (Besides MS-DOS, other examples of operating systems include UNIX, OS/2, the Macintosh System, and CP/M.) Hard disk drives can be built into your machine or they can be external "peripherals." The hard disk inside such a drive is not removable. The advantages of hard disks are that they can store much more information than floppy disks and they are faster than floppies. However, they are also more expensive. Hard disk prices have fallen dramatically in recent years, however, and many machines now come with a hard disk as standard equipment.

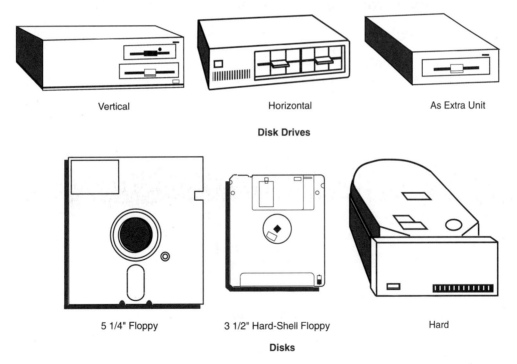

| Vertical | Horizontal | As Extra Unit |

Disk Drives

| 5 1/4" Floppy | 3 1/2" Hard-Shell Floppy | Hard |

Disks

Fig. 1-4. Storage devices.

As mentioned earlier, disks store programs and data that you are not actively using. Information is read from the disk into the computer's RAM (temporary) memory. As you need more information, the drive retrieves it from your disk. When you are finished working, the information is sent back to the disk for storage.

These are the basic terms associated with hardware that will help you understand using MS-DOS.

Understanding a few terms that apply to software may prevent confusion when you venture inside your friendly computer store. A quick definition of these terms will boost your computer confidence considerably.

Software

According to experts on computer buying, when choosing a computer system you should first find the software you want and then buy the computer to fit the software's specifications. That's how important the software is in a computer system. You want convenience and ease of use in the system hardware, but if the software does not do what you want, you really have nothing but an easy-to-use white elephant.

Application Programs

A program that does something for you is an "application program." Some of the most common types of application programs are word processors (e.g., WordPerfect or Microsoft Word) and integrated (multiple-use) packages (e.g., Lotus 1-2-3 or Framework). Games are also considered application programs, although your boss may disagree!

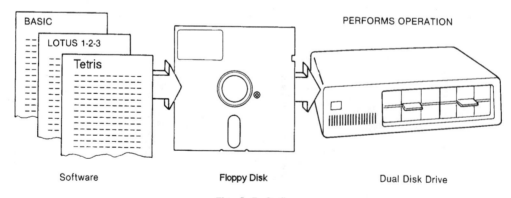

Software   Floppy Disk   Dual Disk Drive

Fig. 1-5. Software.

Programming Languages

Another type of software lets you write instructions, in the form of programs, for your computer. This software is known as a programming language. You use these languages to design your own "application" programs. Your computer probably uses the BASIC programming language. BASIC may be contained inside ROM memory, or you may have it on your operating-system disk. Other programming languages commonly used on microcomputers include C and Pascal.

Operating Systems

Yes, your operating system is a type of specialized software. The operating system manages all the disk input and output operations of your computer. It's also in charge of some of the operations involving the screen, printer, and other devices. You are an important part of the input and output system, because you are the originator and receiver of this input and output. How well you, the information, and the machine all work together is the secret of an effective operating system. In Chapter 2 you will learn about the "secret life of MS-DOS."

This first chapter has served several purposes. For those of you unfamiliar with computers, it defined some useful computer terms: hardware, software, memory, storage, and input and output. Along the way it introduced most of the parts of your computer system that are used in the operation of MS-DOS.

This Is an Operating System

2

- What Does an Operating System Do?
- History of MS-DOS
- Which Version of MS-DOS Do You Need?
- What MS-DOS Means to You

2 This Is an Operating System

This chapter explains what an operating system is, what it does for the computer, and what it can do for you. It also takes a brief look at the evolution of operating systems, the history of MS-DOS, and the unique position of MS-DOS in the operating-system world of today.

When you first encountered the term "operating system," it was probably in the small print of an advertisement or part of an eager salesperson's technobabble. Among all those other incomprehensible terms, such as "RAM," "ROM," "modem," "expandability," "peripherals," "RS232," and "CPU," its significance may have escaped you. Computer advertising may seem at times to be based on several thoughts: that a lot of information is better than a little, double-talk or jargon is a virtue, and the longer and more obscure the word, the better.

But the concept of an operating system is not really complex or confusing. Let's start with definitions from the *Random House Dictionary of the English Language*:

> *Operate*. 1. To work or perform a function, like a machine does. 2. To work or use a machine.

Well, that's pretty clear. The term "operate" has to do with performing machine-like actions.

> *System*. 1. A complex or unitary whole. 2. A coordinated body of methods or a complex scheme or plan of procedure.

So, an operating system is a coordinated body of methods or a plan of procedure for controlling machines. MS-DOS, the operating system in your computer, organizes the information that goes into and comes out of the machine, and it controls how the parts of your computer system interact. The operating system runs the computer.

What Does an Operating System Do?

As you read in Chapter 1, a computer system is a collection of hardware, machine parts, and software (the instructions that tell the computer how to perform the actual computing operations).

You use the hardware, such as the keyboard, disk drives, monitor, and printer, to coordinate data. Hardware provides the tools to type in data, feed data to or from a floppy disk or hard disk, receive data from other machines, or print it on the printer.

By itself, however, the computer's hardware doesn't know what to do. Software, usually in the form of programs, gives instructions to the computer. Software tells the computer what to do, at what time, and with what data. Without software, the hardware is as useless as the abandoned shell of a 1965 Mustang convertible. It's beautiful but powerless.

The main function of the operating system is to manage the information you enter into, store in, and retrieve from your computer.

In the course of its work, the operating system acts as an interface between you, who understand what you would like to happen to the data you type in, and the mechanics of the computer, which demand that instructions be in a very detailed form that can be "understood" by the hardware. Let's see how MS-DOS responds to this challenge (see fig. 2-1).

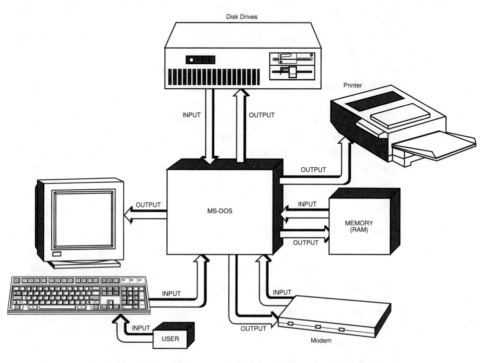

Fig. 2-1. Managing files is DOS's main job!

The major responsibility of the operating system is to keep all the incoming and outgoing information in order. MS-DOS accomplishes this task by storing information in files. Computer files are no different from paper files; both hold a collection of related data. For example, a list of names and phone numbers or a letter you have written with your word processing program are both files. You give each file a name, and the operating system does the rest, storing the file where it can find it quickly, updating the file when you enter new information, and even eliminating the file when you don't want it anymore. Computers may not be terribly interesting to converse with, but they are very good file clerks.

If this idea of a master program still seems a bit obscure, let's compare it to something equally complex in everyday life. Suppose that instead of speaking of a DOS ("DOS" is an acronym for disk operating system), we were speaking of an ATC (air traffic controller). This ATC is in charge of all operations at a major international airport.

The controller is responsible for coordinating the overall traffic flow. He or she is constantly aware of which planes are coming in, which runways they'll land on, their speed, and their arrival gates. The controller must make sure that those runways and gates have been cleared for landing. This person must also know the relative position of each plane waiting to take off, and which flight path it will follow as it ascends. The controller must often make quick decisions so that all planes arrive and depart on schedule.

Listening to the conversation in a control tower is like landing on another planet. You know that the instructions being passed back and forth are in English, but it's hard to believe these people are conversing sensibly. It might sound something like this:

"United 9er9er 7 heavy, clear for take-off on 2-1-left. You're number 3 behind the company."

You can't really understand it, but obviously it's working.

Well, the operating system is like that controller. It monitors all the incoming and outgoing activity of your computer system. Just as the controller is in constant contact with the position of every plane in the air or on the ground, the operating system knows the location and size of all the files currently in its memory or stored on its current disk. And like the controller, the operating system constantly updates all of its information according to changing conditions.

The controller's job is to make sure that each plane scheduled to come into the airport does indeed arrive and each plane scheduled to leave does disappear into the wild blue yonder. Again, the operating system does much the same thing for your computer programs and data files. It loads them, makes sure that they start executing, and when one is finished, the operating system makes room for the next.

This kind of organized control system sounds like a pretty handy helper to have, whether you are navigating the skies over Chicago or attempting to get your accounting software to run. But just as the first "air traffic controller" was probably someone standing alongside the runway waving a flag, the MS-DOS operating system also evolved from a simple way to run programs to a sophisticated and very capable control system.

History of MS-DOS

MS-DOS packed quite a bit of history into its first decade of life. In July of 1981, Microsoft purchased the rights to 86-DOS, an operating system developed by Seattle Computer Products. In secret they began working with IBM, adapting this system to be used as the PC DOS operating system for IBM's personal computer (the IBM PC).

Microsoft released its version of the operating system (MS-DOS) to the general public in March of 1982. Soon, numerous companies that had been developing their own copies or "clones" of the IBM PC snapped it up for their own use. In February 1983, an enhanced version of MS-DOS, version 2.0, appeared. This version included tools for organizing information on hard disks, which were still small and expensive but were starting to become popular.

In 1984, version 3.0 of MS-DOS was released. This version was developed mainly to allow people to connect larger hard disks, the new smaller 3.5" floppy disk drives, and other new kinds of hardware to their computers. With additional software, 3.0 also enabled PCs to be linked together in networks for sharing programs and data.

More and more people began to use PCs, and many of them wished computers were easier to use. In 1988, Microsoft gave MS-DOS a "new look" with version 4.0. Users could now select the programs and files they needed without having to type in their names. Finally, in 1991 Microsoft came out with version 5.0, which made MS-DOS even easier to use. With this version users can take advantage of the more powerful PCs of the 1990s.

Which Version of MS-DOS Do You Need?

If you have bought some applications programs for your PC, you may have noticed the "fine print" that talks about MS-DOS versions. For example, the package might say, "Requires IBM PC/XT/AT or PS/2 or compatible, MS-DOS version 3.0 or later." Nearly all PCs sold today come with MS-DOS 3.3 or later, and if they don't, a recent version of MS-DOS is offered as an option. (It isn't *really* "optional," of course, since you need the operating system in order to run your computer.) If you're given a choice of versions, get version 5.0. Remember that the IBM PC DOS sold with IBM machines has the same commands and functions as "generic" MS-DOS, and the material in this book applies equally to both.

If you have inherited an older PC, however, you may have an earlier version, such as MS-DOS 2.11. Much of the material in this book applies to MS-DOS 2.0 or later, but some newer programs won't run with these older MS-DOS versions. At any rate, if your MS-DOS is earlier than version 3.0, it's a good idea to upgrade to the latest version so you can take advantage of all the new features. This is easy to do: you just buy the new version and install it by following the instructions in its manual.

You can identify your MS-DOS version by looking at the title of its reference manual or the labels on the distribution disks. (You can also type VER once MS-DOS is running, and the version number will be displayed.) Keep your version number in mind as you read, and we'll point out any features or functions that require you to have a certain version (or later) of the operating system.

Sometimes the screen displays or messages that MS-DOS shows will vary from one version to another. Most of these variations are minor and shouldn't concern you, but we'll point out any significant differences.

What MS-DOS Means to You

Every computer needs an operating system, but the fact that your computer uses the MS-DOS operating system brings you some extra advantages. Since the operating system is the interface between you and your computer's operation, you want it to be easy to use. MS-DOS more than fills this bill. Most of the operations you want to accomplish can be performed with a few, easy-to-understand commands, so it is easy to learn enough to get around. And, as you will see in Chapter 12, MS-DOS versions 4.0 and later even include menus from which you can select programs and files, as well as on-line help that explains each operation. Yet, while it is easy to learn the basic commands, MS-DOS also incorporates some very sophisticated and complex functions in its structure. As your computer knowledge grows, so will your appreciation of MS-DOS's capabilities.

One of the biggest advantages of MS-DOS is its popularity. Because MS-DOS is the chosen operating system of so many personal computer manufacturers, software programmers have responded with a deluge of application programs. This means you can usually find the programs you want right away, and they will work with no modifications on your machine.

This chapter discussed the concept of an operating system. It told you that MS-DOS manages files to keep track of the information put into the computer. It traced the growth of MS-DOS and explained some differences between MS-DOS versions. Finally, it summed up the advantages that MS-DOS gives you as a computer user. In the next chapter you'll start actually using MS-DOS on your PC.

3

Getting MS-DOS
off the Ground

- First Things First
    - Do You Have a Hard Disk?
    - Installing MS-DOS
    - Save the MS-DOS 4.0 or 5.0 "DOS Shell" for Later
- If the Boot Fits . . .
    - You Are Now Entering MS-DOS Airspace
    - Playing It Safe with Your Hard Disk
    - What's This About Time and Date?
    - Setting the Time and Date
- How Does That Data Get in There?
    - Entering Data into the Machine
        - Understanding Instructions.
        - Some Common Misconceptions.
        - Correcting Mistakes.
- How To Set the Calendar and Clock
- Boot Temperature (Cold Versus Warm)
- Who's on the Passenger List?
    - Listing All the Files
    - Stop the Action!
    - Listing a Specific File
- Starting with a Clean Slate

3 Getting MS-DOS off the Ground

Now that you are familiar with the basic facts about computer systems and know that MS-DOS helps operate your system, it's time to put two and two together and begin computing. You probably agree that this sounds like a good plan, but you may have no idea about how to begin. Well, just as a pilot approaches takeoff in a logical step-by-step fashion, so you are going to follow a simple routine for your "pre-flight checklist."

First, make sure that your machine is properly set up and ready to go. (Your computer vendor's user manual should give you all the necessary instructions, but don't be afraid to ask your dealer or a knowledgeable colleague for help.) Second, sit down at the controls. Just as the cockpit of an airplane may seem intimidating to you, so may the intricacies of actually being in command of your computer.

But using MS-DOS is very simple. In this chapter you will learn how to "boot" your system and install MS-DOS on a floppy or hard disk if necessary, and practice entering MS-DOS commands at the keyboard. Two commands are introduced in this chapter—the DIR (directory) command and the CLS (clear the screen) command. So put on your captain's hat, and let's get off the ground.

First Things First

To begin using your computer, you must "boot" the system. This does not mean you deliver a sharp kick to the backside of the machine! The term is derived from "pulling oneself up by the bootstraps." In computerese, *boot* means getting the machine ready to accept your instructions.

This sounds very simple, but logically it creates a Catch-22 problem. How can the machine start if the instructions it needs to begin are located inside the machine (which you can't get to until the machine starts)?

This problem is solved by a handy little program called, you guessed it, the "bootstrap loader." This small program, located in ROM (that's the part of memory that is permanent), is the first thing the computer reads when the power is turned on. The bootstrap contains one simple directive—"Start reading the instructions on the disk in drive A." That's all MS-DOS needs to get up and running.

Do You Have a Hard Disk?

If your system comes with a hard disk (a fast, built-in disk drive that holds large amounts of data without the need for individual floppy disks), the programs and other files that make up the operating system may already be stored on the hard disk. Most dealers set up a new machine so that it is ready to run MS-DOS. If you're borrowing someone else's PC and it has a hard disk, MS-DOS will probably be ready for you as soon as you turn on the machine. We'll go into more details about hard disks in Chapters 10 and 13; for now, just think of the hard disk as another place where MS-DOS can store files. Remember that except where noted otherwise, you don't need a hard disk to use this book.

If your system has a hard disk, don't put a disk in drive A when you turn the machine on. When the bootstrap loader discovers there is no disk in drive A, it will look on the hard disk and load MS-DOS from the hard disk.

If the lights for the floppy and hard disk drives come on, the motor whirs, and you see a message such as "Insert system disk in drive A:", then MS-DOS has not yet been installed on your hard disk; see the next section.

Installing MS-DOS

Installing MS-DOS means setting up a floppy or hard disk that contains all the programs and files that MS-DOS needs in order to start up and perform its functions. In addition to a user's manual, the MS-DOS package contains one or more floppy disks filled with the MS-DOS programs and files. When you install MS-DOS, you are basically copying these files to working disks (if you have floppy disk drives only) or to the hard disk.

The procedures for installing MS-DOS can be quite different for the various versions of the operating system, but we won't fill up this book by repeating the necessary instructions for each version. Simply follow the instructions given in your MS-DOS manual (usually found in a section entitled "Getting Started" or something similar). MS-DOS versions 4.0 and 5.0 make installation easy. If you have one of these versions, simply insert the disk indicated in the manual (usually labeled "Install") into your machine and start it up. The installation program will run automatically. It will explain what it is doing, let you choose among various options, and tell you which disks to put in and when. For now, just accept the options that MS-DOS suggests; after reading Chapter 13, you may want to "fine-tune" some of these options further.

Save the MS-DOS 4.0 or 5.0 "DOS Shell" for Later

Unless you tell it otherwise, versions 4.0 and 5.0 of MS-DOS set up your hard disk so a special interface program called a *DOS shell* will run automatically each time you start the system. Chapter 12 will introduce you to DOS shells, which simplify your work with MS-DOS considerably. For now, though, if you are installing MS-DOS 4.0 or 5.0 to a hard disk, select "no" when MS-DOS asks you whether to set up the shell. That way you can read the chapters of this book in order and learn how to type in commands in the traditional way. This knowledge will help you get more out of the shell when you come to it later. (If you are installing to floppy disks, MS-DOS will prepare a separate disk that starts the shell. Once the installation is complete, use the disk marked "Startup" to start the system. Later, when you want to try the shell, start the system with the disk marked "Shell.")

For now we'll assume that you've followed the instructions in your manual and installed MS-DOS if necessary. Be sure you have in a convenient location the user guide supplied by your computer system's manufacturer, as well as the user guide that came with your version of MS-DOS. You probably won't need to use these manuals often, because this book gives complete guidance for operating a "generic" MS-DOS system. But because not everyone has the same system, there may be slight differences in the way systems run, how keys are arranged on the keyboard, and how the messages are worded and appear on the screen. If things seem a little different to you, just consult the appropriate user's guide.

If the Boot Fits . . .

Now you're ready to start using MS-DOS. Don't put any disks in the floppy disk drives if you do have a hard disk; just start the computer, and MS-DOS will start automatically.

If your system does not have a hard disk, pick up the startup disk you prepared when you installed MS-DOS. (If MS-DOS was already installed by someone else, look for a disk that says "boot disk" or "MS-DOS system disk" or something similar.) This disk contains your operating system; it is the key to your computer's operation.

Insert the startup disk in disk drive A. If you have a question about "which end is up" on the disk or "which drive is A," consult your user guide. Every computer sage will recount a favorite story about trying to get something to work for hours, using all kinds of imaginable procedures, only to discover that the disk was in wrong or was in the wrong drive. Except with the new 3.5" disk drives, you must be sure to close the drive door after inserting the disk; you can't get any information from a disk unless the door is closed. (See fig. 3-1.)

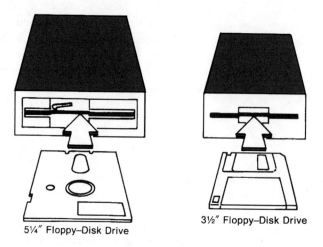

5¼″ Floppy–Disk Drive   3½″ Floppy–Disk Drive

Fig. 3-1. Inserting a floppy disk.

ˋNow, whether you are booting from the hard disk or a floppy disk, you're ready to fire her up. But where's the "on" switch? This is another question for your user's guide, but the switch is probably on the side or back of your machine. Turn on the power and wait patiently.

It takes a few seconds for the machine to "wake up and stretch." Then several things happen at once. You'll hear some whirring sounds as the cooling fan comes on, and you may be startled by a short electronic "beep." Then a small line will start flashing on the screen. Good, this is the first sign of life! This line is the cursor, a small marker that indicates your place on the screen. Your cursor may or may not flash, and it may have some shape other than an underline. More about the cursor in a moment.

You will also notice the drive's indicator light (usually red) flashing on and off. You can hear the drive moving when the light is on. All of this is quite normal. Your machine is just doing some self-checking and getting ready to receive instructions. (If none of the above occurs after a minute or two, check whether the machine is plugged in.) Figure 3-2 summarizes these procedures.

You Are Now Entering MS-DOS Airspace

When the activity stops, there may be some unfamiliar-looking messages that have to do with commands and functions that MS-DOS was set up to perform automatically. What you see will depend on your MS-DOS version and on how you answered the questions asked by the installation program. Chapter 9 will show you how to create your own "batch files" containing various automatic commands. For now, ignore these messages and just look at the last line of characters shown on the screen. If you don't have a hard disk, the symbols should look something like the following:

```
A>_
```

or

```
A:\>_
```

If you have a hard disk, the screen will probably display as follows:

```
C>_
```

or

```
C:\>_
```

The underscore (_) shown here represents the cursor, which will probably be blinking on the screen. On some systems the cursor is a little square of light. The cursor is MS-DOS's way of saying "I'm ready! Tell me what you want to do!" Just remember that when you see A> or C>, you're dealing directly with MS-DOS.

Floppy Disk Systems   **Hard Disk Systems**

Fig. 3-2. Booting checklist.

Playing It Safe with Your Hard Disk

If you have a hard-disk system and you're now looking at the C> or C:\> prompt, play it safe for now. While you're learning how to use MS-DOS you don't want to make a mistake that erases or changes data on your hard disk. So, find a copy of your MS-DOS "system" or "startup" disk (not the original one that came in the package), and put it in drive A. (To make a copy of your system disk, see the instructions in your MS-DOS user manual.) Now type:

```
C:\>A:<Enter>
A:\>
```

(The symbol <Enter> means "press the key marked Enter on your keyboard." The "Enter" key is usually an oversize key to the right of the "home row" on the keyboard. On some keyboards it is called "Return" or marked with a large arrow. As you'll see, you press Enter to send your commands to the computer.)

You've just told MS-DOS that you want to work with the disk in drive A. (MS-DOS changes the prompt to A:\> to remind you which drive it is using.) Now, while MS-DOS will run its commands and programs for you from the speedy hard disk, any files you work with will be on the floppy disk in drive A. Any mistakes you make won't cause any permanent damage to your programs or data. By the time you get to Chapter 10, you'll be able to work safely with the hard disk.

What's This About Time and Date?

Nowadays just about all PCs have a little clock built in. This clock tells MS-DOS the current date and time so that it can keep track of your files. (Later, you will see why MS-DOS does this.) If you have installed version 3.3 or later, MS-DOS will automatically set the time by reading the built-in clock, so you don't have to worry about keeping the time or date current. Even though you won't have to set the date, you should still read the next section, to learn more about entering information into the computer.

Setting the Time and Date

If you have a version of MS-DOS earlier than 3.3 and another user hasn't already set up any automatic MS-DOS commands, don't worry. This just means that each time you start the system, you'll have one more step before you're airborne. You'll see a message that looks something like the following:

```
Current date is Tues 1-1-1980        The date may be different.
Enter new date: _
```

Note that the cursor is now after the word "date." The cursor indicates the spot where the next incoming piece of information will appear on the screen. In this case, it means that when you type in a new date, it will be placed directly after the colon.

How Does That Data Get in There?

If you see this message about a date, it means that the computer is waiting for some specific information. Now is the moment of truth. You will use the keyboard to enter data into the computer. Sometimes your entry is in response to a request such as the "enter new date" statement. Sometimes you initiate the interaction with a request of your own.

Entering Data into the Machine

Understanding Instructions. At first, deciphering how, what, and when to enter information may seem mysterious. But there is no secret to deciphering the instructions in this book because herein lies your "official code breaker."

Symbol	Meaning
`A:\>Format another? (Y/N)`	Information within the screen in black type is supplied by the computer.
`A:\>format b:`	Information within the screen in blue type is supplied by you. When you type your entries, be sure to include all punctuation and leave blank spaces where indicated.
`< >`	These brackets indicate a key on the keyboard (other than the letter or number keys).
`<Enter>`	The <Enter> key is your signal that you have finished typing in an entry. YOU MUST PRESS THE <Enter> KEY BEFORE THE COMPUTER CAN RESPOND TO YOUR COMMANDS OR INSTRUCTIONS. The <Enter> key may appear on your keyboard as <RETURN> or <↵>.

Some Common Misconceptions

To the computer, each key means a different character. You must not type the "l" (lowercase L) if you really mean the "1" (number one). The same is true of the "0" (number zero) and the "O" (uppercase O).

The spacebar on your computer does more than move the cursor across the screen. It also sends a message to the computer—"Make this a blank space." If you want to move along a line without inserting blank characters or erasing existing characters, use the right-arrow key <→>.

Correcting Mistakes

Since you are just beginning your exploration of the computer, it's natural that you will make mistakes (especially if you're also new at typing). So double-check your entries before you press the <Enter> key. If you find a mistake, just use the <Backspace> key (it may look like the following: <←>) to erase characters until you back up to the error. Then retype the entry. No white-out or smudged copies here!

If you can't get the keyboard to accept your data, or you've lost track of what is going on, just press <Esc> (the Escape) key. If all else fails, turn off the machine and take it from the top.

Take a moment to find these keys on your keyboard (see fig. 3-3 for examples).

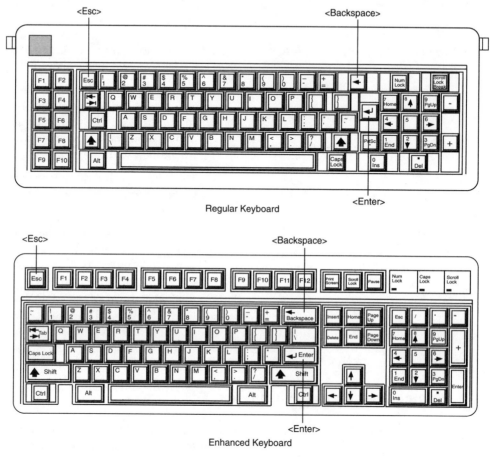

Regular Keyboard

Enhanced Keyboard

Fig. 3-3. Position of <Esc>, <Backspace>, and <Enter> keys on keyboard.

How To Set the Calendar and Clock

If you got the message to "enter new date," this is the way the screen looks now:

```
Current date is Tues 1-1-1980
Enter new date: _
```

The date you see on the screen will not be today's date. Let's say that today is August 1, 1990. This is the new date you want to enter. You can enter the date in a variety of ways:

```
8-1-90
08-1-90
8/1/90
08/01/90
```

Whichever method you use to enter the date, the key thing here is to separate the parts of the date with hyphens or slashes. Notice that you don't enter the day of the week, just the numeric equivalents of the month, day, and year. Enter the date now:

```
Current date is Tues 1-1-1980
Enter new date: 8-1-90<Enter>
```

Immediately after you enter the date, MS-DOS returns the current time and asks you if you want to enter a new time:

```
Current time is 0:00:46:08
Enter new time:_
```

At this point, the computer is really in the Twilight Zone—no hours, no minutes, and what you see will vary with the DOS version and machine configuration. But "time stands still for no machine," so enter the current time now. Our current hypothetical time is 9:30 in the morning. Here are the various ways you could enter the time:

```
9:30:00.0
9:30:0
09:30:0
9:30
```

Your computer follows the international standard of the 24-hour clock (sometimes called "military time"). This means that the hours from midnight to noon are indicated by 0-12. After noon the hours go from 13-24 (midnight). You can enter the time according to the precise hours, minutes, seconds, and tenths of seconds, but for most applications the hour and minutes suffice nicely. When entering the time, separate the hour, minutes, and seconds with a colon (:). If you do add tenths of seconds, they are preceded by a period.

Starting with MS-DOS version 4.0, you can use the more common AM/PM system of time. That is, you can enter

```
9:30a
```

for 9:30 in the morning, or

```
9:30p
```

for 9:30 in the evening. (You can still use the 24-hour system if you wish.)
Now enter the time:

```
Current time is 0:00:46.08
Enter new time: 9:30<Enter>
```

Easy, fast, and precise! Your clock and calendar are now right on the mark. And you did very well with your first computer encounter! After a while, setting the date and time will become second-nature to you. (In Chapter 9, we'll show you how to have the time and date set automatically by MS-DOS.)

Pilot To Control—Help!

What we have been describing is the ideal sequence of events when setting the time and date. But what happens if you follow the instructions (you think perfectly), and the following message appears on the screen:

```
INVALID DATE or INVALID TIME
```

or

```
ok
```

There is nothing to worry about; just try the entry again. You probably put a period where you need a slash or some such. If you get a message that just says "ok," however, you will have to boot the system again.

Boot Temperature (Cold Versus Warm)

When you insert the operating-system disk and turn on the power, you are performing a "cold" boot (i.e., starting the machine from a "power off" position). There is another kind of boot that occurs when you are already working on the machine (the power is on), but you want to start over again from the beginning. This is called a "warm" boot. You might perform a warm boot if you enter the wrong date or get the "ok" message described in the previous section. To warm-boot the system, press the <Ctrl> key, and while holding down <Ctrl>, press the <Alt> and <Del> keys. This action brings you back to the "enter the date" message if your date is not set automatically (see fig. 3-4).

"COLD BOOT"

Your machine is turned off. Insert the operating system disk and turn on the power.

"WARM BOOT"

Your machine is already in use. Press the <Ctrl> <Alt> <Del> combination.

Fig. 3-4. Cold boot versus warm boot.

Keeping Everything Under Control

You will find that the <Ctrl> key is a device of many uses. It is never used alone, but always in conjunction with other keys on the keyboard. In some ways, <Ctrl> is like a master toggle switch. When used with another key, it changes the message that key sends to the computer. Whenever you use <Ctrl> you must press and hold down this key while pressing another key or keys. All keys are released together.

Who's on the Passenger List?

You are now flying in MS-DOS airspace—as indicated by the A:\> prompt—and there should be no turbulence. In response to this prompt you are going to give MS-DOS your first *command*. Commands are nothing more than instructions to the operating system. They consist of short words or abbreviations that tell MS-DOS to perform specific actions. Right now you want to find out what's on your disk.

The DIR Command

Use: Displays a general disk directory or lists information about a particular file

Examples:
```
dir
dir command.com
```

The DIR command (short for DIRectory) lists information about files on a specific disk. Files, or collections of related data, are the way MS-DOS keeps track of where information is stored. All the files on your system disk come ready-made from MS-DOS. You will learn how to create your own files in Chapter 6. You use the DIR command to see the names of all the files that are on a disk or to find out if a single file is located on a particular disk.

Listing All the Files

If you booted from a floppy disk, your system disk is already in drive A. If you booted from a hard disk, you should have "played it safe" as explained earlier, by putting a system disk in drive A and changing to the A:\> prompt. Let's use the DIR command to see what files are on the disk in drive A. When you enter a command you can use either upper- or lowercase letters (don't forget to include all punctuation and blank spaces). Enter this command now:

```
A:\>dir<Enter>
```

MS-DOS responds with a listing of the files. But if you are viewing the "typical" operating system disk, you may be feeling a slight panic. Did the entire screen fill up and then move on quickly to another screen? No one can read that fast! What do you do now?

Stop the Action!

There is a simple explanation for this phenomenon. MS-DOS presents information to you one screen at a time. This is fine if the disk contains only a few files; after they are listed the display stops. But when a disk contains many files, they cannot all fit on the screen at the same time, and the display will *scroll*. Scrolling means that as the screen is filled with information, new data is added to the bottom of the display as old data rolls off the top. This does make it very difficult to read. There is, however, a simple way to freeze the screen and stop the scrolling action.

To stop scrolling, press and hold down the <Ctrl> key and then press the S key. Release both keys together. In some systems you stop scrolling by holding down <Ctrl> and pressing the <Num Lock> key.

Try using the DIR command to list the disk contents again. If your display is more than one screen long, freeze the scrolling action by using the <Ctrl>S combination:

```
A:\>dir<Enter>
<Ctrl> S
```

Press any key (<Enter> is a good one to use) to resume scrolling. When the display is finished, the screen will look something like this:

```
SHARE    EXE     13388 06-07-90    2:24a
SMARTDRV SYS      6866 06-07-90    2:24a
UNFORMAT EXE     11879 06-07-90    2:24a
```

```
AUTOEXEC BAT        24 08-21-90    4:35p
CONFIG   SYS        22 08-21-90    4:35p
         36 File(s)      609782 bytes
                          29696 bytes free
```

The exact names and numbers do not matter and will vary according to the files included on your system disk and the disk's size and capacity. The information on the screen describes the files on the operating system disk. Let's look at the pattern in which the files are listed:

```
Volume in drive A is STARTUP
Volume Serial Number is 1515-83AB
Directory of A:\

COMMAND  COM      41035 06-07-90    2:24a
FDISK    EXE      54380 06-07-90    2:24a
FORMAT   COM      27131 06-07-90    2:24a
ANSI     SYS       9119 06-07-90    2:24a
COUNTRY  SYS      12820 06-07-90    2:24a
DOSKEY   COM       4518 06-07-90    2:24a
DRIVER   SYS       5286 06-07-90    2:24a
HIMEM    SYS      10560 06-07-90    2:24a
KEYB     COM      10334 06-07-90    2:24a
KEYBOARD SYS      49282 06-07-90    2:24a
MOUSE    COM      31833 06-07-90    2:24a
PARTDRV  SYS       2112 06-07-90    2:24a
SETVER   EXE       7994 06-07-90    2:24a
SYS      COM      12064 06-07-90    2:24a
4201     CPI       6404 06-07-90    2:24a
4208     CPI        720 06-07-90    2:24a
5202     CPI        370 06-07-90    2:24a
DISPLAY  SYS      16088 06-07-90    2:24a
EDLIN    EXE      14121 06-07-90    2:24a
EGA      CPI      49068 06-07-90    2:24a
EMM386   EXE      61010 06-07-90    2:24a
FASTOPEN EXE      12307 06-07-90    2:24a
GRAFTABL COM      10033 06-07-90    2:24a
GRAPHICS COM      19230 06-07-90    2:24a
GRAPHICS PRO      21227 06-07-90    2:24a
JOIN     EXE      17991 06-07-90    2:24a
LCD      CPI      10703 06-07-90    2:24a
NLSFUNC  EXE       7344 06-07-90    2:24a
PRINTER  SYS      18978 06-07-90    2:24a
RAMDRIVE SYS       5719 06-07-90    2:24a
REDIR    EXE      27822 06-07-90    2:24a
SHARE    EXE      13388 06-07-90    2:24a
SMARTDRV SYS       6866 06-07-90    2:24a
```

```
UNFORMAT EXE      11879 06-07-90    2:24a
AUTOEXEC BAT         24 08-21-90    4:35p
CONFIG   SYS         22 08-21-90    4:35p
        36 File(s)      609782 bytes
                         29696 bytes free
A:\>_
```

If you are looking at the first page of the directory listing, you may see a short statement about the volume label and (for DOS version 4.0 or later) a serial number. Ignore this statement for now. This mystery will be unraveled in Chapter 8.

The body of the listing is divided into five separate columns. Column 1 gives us the name of the file. For example, COMMAND, FDISK, and FORMAT are files listed in column one. These names identify the contents of the file. Column 2 is an extension of the file's name. EXE and COM tell us what types of file they are. Pay no attention to these particulars right now. The science and art of filenaming are detailed in Chapter 7.

Column 3 tells us how big the file is. File size is measured in bytes. Depending on the kind of file, each byte can represent a character (such as a letter of the alphabet), a small number, or a part of a larger number. As you can see, the COMMAND file takes up 41035 bytes on the disk. Columns 4 and 5 tell us the date and time that the file was last updated (this is the type of information that is supplied when you or MS-DOS set the time and date at the beginning of a computer session).

Finally, MS-DOS performs a little housekeeping chore. It reports the total number of files on the disk, the total number of bytes used by all of these files, and the space available on the disk for new files. This information will be very useful to you later, when have to find out whether a file will fit on a particular disk. Versions of MS-DOS earlier than 5.0 don't give the total number of bytes used by the files, just the total number of files and the bytes available.

That's a lot of information from one small three-letter command!

Note that when MS-DOS is finished performing the DIR command, it returns you to the operating system. You know this has happened when you see the DOS prompt A:\>.

Listing a Specific File

In addition to listing all the files on a disk, DIR can also tell you if a specific file is on a particular disk. To get this information, enter the command followed by a "filename." Although you already know the contents of your system disk, let's assume that you are trying to find a file named "command.com." Enter the DIR command, leave a blank space, and then enter the name of the file:

```
A:\>dir command.com<Enter>
```

Note the period between the first part of the name, "command," and the second part, or extension, "com".

MS-DOS replies:

```
Volume in drive A is STARTUP
Volume Serial Number is 1515-83AB
Directory of A:\

COMMAND  COM     41035 06-07-90   2:24a
     1 File(s)        41035 bytes
                      29696 bytes free
```

And there it is—all the same information listed in columns one through five, as they describe this particular file.

If the file you request is not on the disk, MS-DOS returns this message:

```
File not found
```

Sorry, try again. Either you never put the file on this disk or you are looking at a different disk than the one you thought you were using.

Well, now you are reaping the fruits of your labors (either a DIR of the entire disk or a DIR of the COMMAND.COM file). But how do you remove this information from the screen so that you can look at a different display of information? Our next command provides the answer.

Starting with a Clean Slate

The CLS Command

Use: Clears all information from the screen

Example: cls

As you use your computer more and more, you quickly realize that a lot of the information you display is for temporary use only. In other words, you don't need to save the information after you have seen it. And with mistakes and changes of mind, you can fill up a screen pretty quickly. For instance, in the previous use of the DIR command, you displayed all the files on your system disk. You don't really need this information once you have looked at the listing. You have no special reason to save it. The CLS (CLear Screen) command is a handy way of ridding the screen of all the stuff you are tired of looking at. Try using CLS now to empty the screen:

```
A:\>cls<Enter>
```

Like magic, the screen is cleared. After you execute the CLS command, the cursor moves to the upper left-hand corner of the screen and waits for the next entry. This corner is sometimes called the cursor's "home" position.

CLS affects only the information currently on the screen. It does nothing to data in memory or to information stored on disks. The corollary is that it also saves nothing. Use CLS only when you don't need the information on the screen.

Okay, time to take a breather. You've really come a long way in one short session! In this chapter you've learned how to insert your system disk into the disk drive, and you may have gone through the process of installing MS-DOS on your hard disk. You've learned how to perform cold and warm boots. You've learned some simple rules for entering data into the machine and gotten your "feet wet" by entering your first MS-DOS commands. The DIR command allowed you to display the listing for a disk, and <Ctrl>S showed you how to freeze that display. The CLS command cleaned up your screen when you were finished looking at the displayed information. And you thought this was going to be tough!

In the next chapter we will take a closer look at a piece of computer technology that helped spawn the personal computer revolution—the floppy disk!

System Insurance

4

- Disks and Disk Drives
- The Nature of Disks
    - You Can Look, But You Better Not Touch
    - Righting the "Write" Stuff
    - Better Living through Labeling
    - Differences with 3 1/2" Disks
- How Is That Data Stored on the Disk?
- Getting the Disk Ready to Be Used
    - How Many Drives Do You Have?
    - Filling in the Blank Spaces
    - Using the FORMAT Command
    - Signed, Sealed, and Delivered
- Writing the Insurance Policy
    - Clarifying the Beneficiary
- A Written Guarantee

4 System Insurance

There is a precaution that most of us take as a matter of course whenever we acquire something we want to protect or safeguard. We take out insurance, whether for our health, our house, or that new car we have waited so long for. We automatically insure these things. And then, if the unexpected happens, we are protected.

Well, your newly acquired operating-system disk falls into the category of "valuable things you would be lost without." The sad truth is: no operating-system disk, no computer operation. In this chapter you will learn how to take out this insurance at no additional cost to you (except the cost of a floppy disk). In other words, you will make a backup copy of your operating-system disk. By using this backup in your everyday computing, you always have the original to fall back on if your disk should suffer damage or be misplaced.

MS-DOS versions 4.0 and later make a working copy of the operating-system disks as part of the installation process. You use the copy rather than the original disks to start the system each day; therefore, your original disks are protected from wear and tear. Even if you are using MS-DOS 4.0 or 5.0, however, it doesn't hurt at all to learn how to make backup disks, since you will also want to make backup copies of disks containing the documents, spreadsheets, and databases you work with every day.

It is staggering to think of how much information is stored on each magnetically coated piece of plastic. Detailed instructions about how the computer is to receive input, manage files, deliver output, and operate its equipment are all there on your operating-system disks.

Before you actually insure this precious commodity, let's take a closer look at what makes up a disk.

Disks and Disk Drives

Just as the size, speed, and capabilities of computer hardware have undergone a remarkable technological evolution in the last three decades, so have the methods for storing the programs and data the computer needs to operate. Early methods for storing programs and data included punch cards, punched paper tape, and magnetically coated drums. Eventually, magnetic disks were developed, with data stored as magnetically coded patterns in an arrangement somewhat like grooves on a phonograph record. Magnetic disks proved much more convenient than easily-torn tape or stacks of cards that often ended up being out of sequence. All the early disks were permanently attached to the disk drive, like the hard disks used in PCs today. (This chapter will discuss only floppy disks; we will discuss hard disks in detail in Chapters 10 and 13.)

As minicomputers and, later, microcomputers were developed, it became clear that they needed a reliable data-storage system. Hard disks were very expensive; besides, users needed a way to exchange programs and data with each other. The solution was the floppy disk drive with its removable disks. The first type of removable disks were 8" in diameter. Because they were flexible, they were termed floppy disks. Constructed of thin, plastic mylar and surfaced with a magnetic coating, these disks stored information on only one side. Typically, the 8" disk held 50K-100K bytes of information.

"Floppies" rapidly got smaller and became capable of holding more and more information (see fig. 4-1). Modifications of the reading "heads" of the disk drive allowed both sides of the disk to hold data. Today, "minifloppies" (5 1/4" in diameter) are used for most systems that operate using MS-DOS, although "microfloppies" (3 1/2" in diameter) are becoming increasingly common.

The capacity of 5 1/4" disks varies according to the disk's design. Some disks (single-sided) record on one side; these are obsolete, but they can still be used by your PC. Today's double-sided disks use both sides to store data. In addition, the amount of information on the disk depends on how tightly the magnetic particles are packed together. The first disks, also now obsolete, were "single density." Today the standard disk packs data in double density. The standard double-sided, double-density disk can contain about 360K bytes of information.

Many PCs are also equipped to use "quad density" 5 1/4" disks. These disks store 1.2 megabytes of data—four times as much as the standard double-density disk.

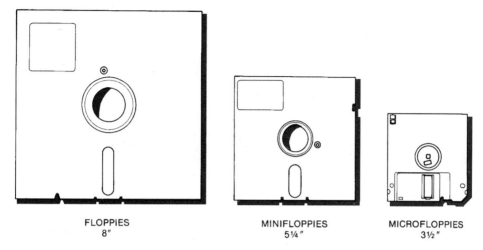

FLOPPIES
8″

MINIFLOPPIES
5¼″

MICROFLOPPIES
3½″

Fig. 4-1. Floppy-disk evolution.

An increasingly popular alternative to 5 1/4" floppies is the 3 1/2" disk. These "microfloppies" are held in a rigid, rather than flexible, sleeve. Like the 5 1/4" floppy, the microfloppy is also available in two different formats: double density, holding 720K, and high density, holding 1.44 megabytes. How data gets put on disks is covered later in this chapter. For now, the only thing you need to know about your disks is what type your computer uses. Check your user's manual to find out what types of disks you should buy.

The Nature of Disks

Whatever their size, "sidedness," or density, all disks have several features in common. This discussion will describe the most common features found on 5 1/4" floppy disks and then look at the newer 3 1/2" format (see fig. 4-2).

Disks usually come stored in convenient boxes (save these for storing your disks). Inside the carton, each disk is nestled inside a paper envelope. This is the disk's storage jacket. You should put this paper jacket on the disk whenever you're not using it.

The disk is completely enclosed inside a square plastic protective jacket. The actual shape of the disk is round. This protective jacket is permanent and should never be removed. In fact you won't be able to remove it unless you use a sharp instrument like a knife or scissors (or an errant dog develops a taste for it). If the disk does not appear square in shape, something dreadful has happened to the protective jacket (and probably to any information that was on the disk).

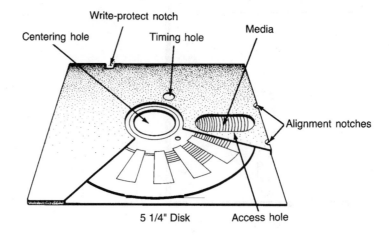

5 1/4" Disk

Top View

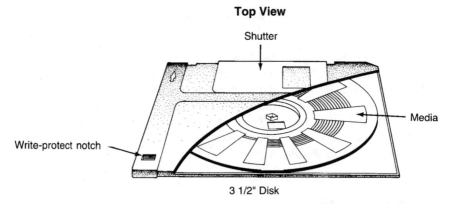

3 1/2" Disk

Bottom View

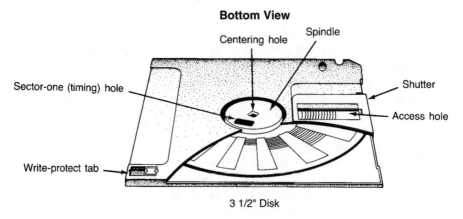

3 1/2" Disk

Fig. 4-2. Features of disks.

You Can Look, But You Better Not Touch

There are three areas where the recording surface is exposed on the disk (see fig. 4-3). Take care not to put your fingers (or anything else) on these sections. One exposed area is around the centering hole of the disk. The disk drive uses this area to make sure that the disk is in the right place before it begins operation. The timing or indexing hole is just off to the side of the centering hole. It too is used to align the disk correctly.

The third area is an oblong opening along one edge of the disk. This area serves as a "window" used by the drive to read and write data onto the surface of the disk. As the disk revolves, the special heads within the disk drive (just like the heads on a tape recorder) code the magnetic surface with information that contains the pattern of your data. It is especially important to keep this window free of all dirt or dust. Imperfections in this window can be transferred to the drive heads and damage your drives, as well as your disks.

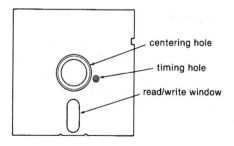

Fig. 4-3. Exposed surfaces on a floppy disk.

Righting the "Write" Stuff

Along one edge of the disk, you will see a distinct square cut-out indentation. This is the write-protect notch. A very clever design feature, this small space may save you from a fate worse than death—erasing vital information by inadvertently writing over it.

New information can overwrite, or erase, previous information. But before the computer writes to a disk, it checks this notch. If the notch is covered, the disk is "write-protected," that is, it cannot receive new data. If the notch is open, the disk is fair game for both reading and writing (see fig 4-4).

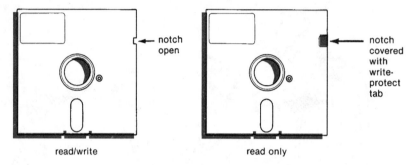

Fig. 4-4. Write-protect notch.

When you want to make sure that the contents of a disk will not be altered, cover this notch with one of the write-protect tabs included in your box of purchased disks (there will be several oblong tabs stuck on one sheet; they are usually silver or black). These pieces of adhesive foil or paper seal off the notch and prevent any new information from being written to the disk. If you decide later that you don't need the data on the disk, you can remove the write-protect tab and reuse the disk for new data.

You may notice that some disks, especially those containing application programs, have no write-protect notch. Another form of free insurance for you! If you can't write to the disk, you don't run the risk of altering or destroying the program.

Better Living through Labeling

Also in your carton of purchased disks, you will find a packet of adhesive labels (they come in many colors and usually have lines on them). These are content labels, used to identify each disk (see fig. 4-5). These labels can save you hours of frustration. Without labeling, most disks look distressingly alike, as you may discover late one evening as you sit among piles of unidentifiable disks looking for the one you "put down for just a minute." (See Commandment 7 of "The Ten Commandments of Disk Handling and Usage" in the next section.) How much information you put on these labels is up to you, but it should be clear enough so that you'll know what's on your disk when you pick it up next month or next year.

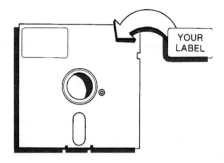

Fig. 4-5. Labeling.

Differences with 3 1/2" Disks

The 3 1/2" microfloppy disk has most of the features of its larger cousin, but some of the features work a little differently. As you saw in an earlier illustration, a sliding shutter covers the disk's exposed surface when the disk is not in use—more insurance against damage! This shutter slides back when you insert the disk in the drive.

A 3 1/2" disk can also be write-protected, but instead of putting a tab over the write-protect notch, you simply move a little slider in the corner of the disk to expose the write-protect hole. When the hole is open, no data can be written to the disk. To make the disk writable again, just move the slider so that the hole is covered.

The 3 1/2" inch disk first became popular in laptop computers, where space is at a premium. While most desktop PCs come with 5 1/4" drives as standard equipment, many sold today have both 5 1/4" and 3 1/2" drives, for maximum versatility. (You can also buy an add-on drive for an existing PC.) The 3 1/2" disk has several advantages over the 5 1/4" disk: the 3 1/2" disk is more compact, yet holds more data and is harder to bend, scratch, or physically damage (although both are equally vulnerable to magnetism). Their only real disadvantages are that some software packages provide only 5 1/4" disks (although you can usually request 3 1/2" disks) and a person with whom you want to exchange files may not have a 3 1/2" drive.

All this talk of "do this" and "don't do that" may have you wondering if you will ever have the courage to pick up a disk, let alone use it in your computer. But fear not, ye of little faith; a concise tract to peaceful coexistence with your disks follows. (Commandments 2, 6, 8, and 9 are less applicable to 3 1/2" disks.)

The Ten Commandments of Disk Handling and Usage

1. Thou shalt not rest heavy objects upon thy disk surfaces. Such objects include reference books, instruction manuals, and the omnipresent elbow.

2. Thou shalt not eat, drink, smoke, nor comb thy hair around thy disks. These seemingly simple activities of daily life can cause great havoc when they deposit impurities upon the surface of a disk. Thou shalt always be on guard against the "coffee cup demon."

3. Thou shalt not bend, staple, paper-clip, or mutilate thy disks by rough handling or improper storage.

4. Thou shalt protect disks from the common forces of creation. This encompasses the peril of destruction by sunlight or exposure to acts of high temperature and/or humidity.

5. Neither X-ray machines (including those at the airport inquisition), telephones, nor any other source of magnetic energy shalt thou let come near thy disks. (Beware the magnetic paper-clip dispenser.) These "fields of force" can wreak havoc with thy disks' good intentions.

6. Keep thy fingers to thyself. Thou shalt handle thy disks by the edges only, and gently.

7. Acknowledge the individuality of thy disks by proper labeling. When transcribing said labels, use only a felt-tip pen, for pencils and ballpoints do damage thy disks. Unlabeled disks carrying precious information have been known to succumb to the destructive prowess of the FORMAT command.

8. Store thy disks with honor. Specifically, refrain from resting thy disks on their sides, or crowding them too closely into a closed space.

9. When not in use, clothe thy disks properly. Thou shalt always return thy disks to their storage jackets.

10. Know that the responsibility for thy disks rests upon thy shoulders. Disk loyalty and performance is directly related to thy loving care and devotion.

How Is That Data Stored on the Disk?

MS-DOS is a careful and efficient manager, so when it stores information on a disk it does so in an orderly, logical way. Before any information can be put on a disk, the disk must first be prepared by using the FORMAT command (discussed later in this chapter). Your blank disk, fresh from the box, is like a newly paved running track—one large, unmarked surface. The first thing that FORMAT does is divide this area into specific tracks. The tracks run in concentric circles around the disk, much like the painted lanes that mark boundaries for runners on a running track (see fig. 4-6).

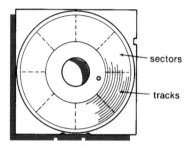

Fig. 4-6. Tracks and sectors.

The tracks are divided into small sections called sectors. This division makes storage and retrieval of your data faster and more efficient, because MS-DOS knows just what track and sector holds each file. Having this information is equivalent to knowing a friend's house number; it makes finding him more efficient than wandering aimlessly up and down the street. The amount of data stored in a sector is dependent upon your computer system. The lower-density 5 1/4" and 3 1/2" MS-DOS disks divide the disk into 9 sectors per track. High-density 5 1/4" disks have 15 sectors per track, while high-density 3 1/2" disks have a whopping 18 sectors per track. Normally, each sector can hold either 512 or 1024 bytes.

The first section of the first track on every disk is reserved for storage of the operating system. Thereafter, as data is written to the disk, it is stored on a first-come, first-served basis. You do not have to remember the order in which you store data on the disk; MS-DOS keeps track of that for you.

Getting the Disk Ready to Be Used

It's easy to prepare your disks for use. Don't let this new challenge make you nervous. After all, you already know how to handle disks, and how they go into your disk drive (remember how well you executed the DIR command). But a little planning can make things easier for you as you perform this procedure. Be sure to have the following tools ready:

❏ The computer, up and running

❏ Your computer instruction manual

❏ The system disk

❏ Several new blank disks

Your blank disks should be the right size for your drive (5 1/4" or 3 1/2"). You should also check whether your drives are designed for regular (double) or high-density (quad) disks; check your system's user manual if you're not sure. If the drive is designed for high-density disks, use high-density disks for now.

The instructions for the following MS-DOS commands are given in terms of the "typical" MS-DOS system. Do you have a typical system? To find out, answer the following question.

How Many Drives Do You Have?

When asking questions and giving responses to commands, MS-DOS assumes that you have two disk drives, "A" and "B." Operating with at least two drives is the most efficient method for MS-DOS because it simplifies transferring information from one disk to the other and makes giving instructions easier. With two drives, MS-DOS can easily differentiate where the information is "coming from" and where it is "going to."

The operating system is quite set in its ways on this point, so much so that even if you have a single drive, MS-DOS pretends you have two. It always issues instructions in terms of drive "A" and drive "B." How can single-drive owners use this system? Well, you just have to participate in some chicanery yourself.

One easy way to do this is to think of your disks as "drives." That is, one disk represents drive "A" and the second represents drive "B" (see fig. 4-7.) When the displays tells you to do "x, y, and z" with the disk in drive A, you use the first disk. When you need to do "x, y, and z" with the disk in drive B, you remove the first disk and insert the second disk before performing the action. Both the operating system and you are happy, and no one is any the wiser.

With these preliminaries out of the way, you're ready to prepare some new disks. To accomplish this task, you will call upon the FORMAT command.

Filling in the Blank Spaces

The FORMAT Command

Use: Readies a disk to receive data

Example: `format b:`

The FORMAT command is designed to divide up the disk specifically for use with MS-DOS. That's why your friend who has an Apple Macintosh probably won't be able to read your disks. (Some new Mac models can read MS-DOS disks.)

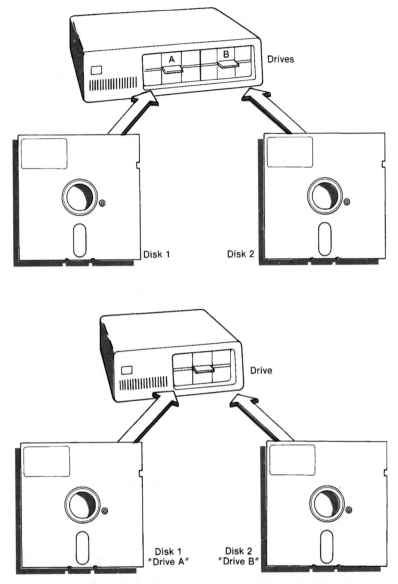

Fig. 4-7. Two drives versus a single drive.

The FORMAT command is used in several situations. Here are the most common:

❏ The first time you use a disk

❏ When you want to erase an entire disk (be careful here)

❏ When you want to change the already existing format of the disk (for instance, to use it on a different type of machine)

Using the FORMAT Command

You fit into the first category right now, so let's begin breaking in this command. Step one is to insert your operating-system disk into drive A. (Single-drive owners should see the discussion at the beginning of this section.) Put your new blank disk in drive B. If the machine isn't already running, turn it on and let it cycle though the boot. Enter the time and date if you are asked for them. The computer will signal its readiness to accept commands, by displaying the MS-DOS prompt:

```
A:\>
```

A Note for Hard Disk Users

Remember that for now you aren't using the hard disk for anything other than running MS-DOS. So even if you booted MS-DOS from your hard disk, put a system disk in drive A. Type A:<Enter> if necessary, to change to the A:\> prompt. (If you're not sure whether your disk in A is a system disk, you know how to find out, right? Use the DIR command to see whether the disk contains files such as COMMAND.COM and FORMAT.COM.)

Now you are going to tell the operating system to FORMAT the disk in drive B (see fig. 4-8). YOU MUST INCLUDE THE LETTER "B" IN YOUR COMMAND OR ELSE YOU MIGHT DESTROY YOUR SYSTEM DISK. Enter the command:

```
A:\>format b:<Enter>
```
Make sure to include the space between the command and the drive specifier, and the colon after the letter "b".

Now watch the screen. It answers your command with this response:

```
Insert new diskette for drive B:
and press Enter when ready...
```

(Versions of MS-DOS earlier than 3.0 say "strike any key" rather than "press Enter.") You have already put a new blank disk in drive B, so press Enter.

The drive will click and whirr, and the indicator light will go on and off. Do not interrupt this process; just let the machine do its work. The operating system lets you know what is going on by displaying this message:

```
Formatting...
```

MS-DOS keeps you informed of its progress. MS-DOS versions earlier than 4.0 tell you which "head" (side) and cylinder (both sides of a track) are currently being formatted, but this information isn't particularly useful. Version 4.0 and later tell you what percentage of the disk has been formatted, which gives you a much better idea of your progress. Formatting usually takes several minutes, so be patient.

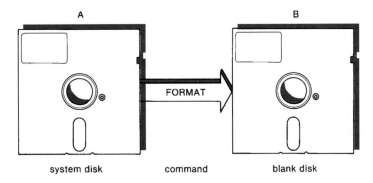

Fig. 4-8. The FORMAT command.

With MS-DOS version 4.0 or later, you'll now be asked for a *volume label*.

```
Volume label (11 characters, ENTER for none)?
```

This is an "electronic label" that will be displayed every time you list the directory of that disk. Volume labels can be useful as an additional way to identify disks quickly. Enter up to eleven characters—for example, "systemdisk" or "practice" (without the quotes)—or press <Enter> if you don't want to use a volume label.

When the formatting is completed, MD-DOS tells you so:

```
Formatting...Format complete

362496 bytes total disk space
362496 bytes available on disk
```

MS-DOS versions 4.0 and later provide some additional "techie" information about "allocation units," but you can ignore it. These versions of MS-DOS also assign a *serial number* to the disk, but this isn't particularly useful, either.

```
Format another (Y/N)?
```

Note that you may have considerably more bytes available on the disk than shown here, depending on the capacity of the drive in which you formatted the disk. The total disk capacity won't matter now, but in Chapter 9 you will learn more about formatting disks of different sizes and capacities.

Let's take a moment to look at the messages MS-DOS is giving you. First you are told that the formatting of the disk has been completed. Then the total number of bytes on the disk is given. Since formatting has not put any information on the disk but has only divided up the space, the amount of total disk space and the amount available on the disk are the same.

You must now make a decision. Do you want to format any additional disks? If you answer "Y," you will be instructed to insert another disk in drive B. It's a good idea to format several disks at a time. Then, when you desperately need a disk to put the crowning touches on some masterful project, you won't have to stop, insert your system disk, and format a disk. As long as you're here, go ahead and format several disks now.

Good for you! Everything is moving along smoothly, and you now have several pristine disks eagerly awaiting use. When you're tired of formatting, just answer "N" to the "Format another" question, and you will be returned to the MS-DOS prompt.

Signed, Sealed, and Delivered

But you're not quite finished. Be sure to label those disks. (Label the disk with a physical label, regardless of whether you added an electronic label during formatting.) This label can be quite short or rather long, just make sure that its meaning is clear to you. One simple label consists of the letter "F," or the word "formatted," followed by the date. This label leaves lots of room for you to fill in the contents of the disk as you store information on it.

One note of caution in using the FORMAT command. When you tell MS-DOS to format, you are indicating that this is a new, blank disk. FORMAT, then, ignores any information already on a disk; it merrily lays down new track and sector divisions. This can be useful if you want to erase an entire disk. Just use FORMAT and *voila!* Everything is gone. But naturally this situation can also backfire. If you FORMAT a disk that contains something you really want, or desperately need, there is no way to get the data back using ordinary MS-DOS commands. (Chapter 13, however, describes some commercial utility programs that can recover data even from a formatted disk. If you *do* accidentally format a disk, don't save any files to it. Put it aside until you read Chapter 13. That chapter will also discuss some features of MS-DOS version 5.0 that can help you recover data.)

This danger of formatting the wrong disk only reiterates the importance of labeling all disks. Keep this fact in mind whenever you use the FORMAT command:

FORMAT TREATS EACH DISK AS BLANK; IT WILL ERASE ANY INFORMATION ON THE DISK.

Occasionally, when you format a disk you will receive a different message. It will look something like this:

```
Bad sector on track xxx
```

or

```
xxxxx bytes in bad sector
```

If this message appears, do not continue to use the disk. There is probably some manufacturing fault with the disk (and possibly with the entire carton of disks). Return these disks to your dealer and request a refund or replacement.

Writing the Insurance Policy

Now, before you do anything else, you are going to make that insurance copy of your system disk. This copy will be an exact duplicate of the original disk. You do not want to add or delete any information. Whenever you want to copy an entire disk (produce an identical twin, as it were), you use the DISKCOPY command.

The DISKCOPY Command

Use: Makes a duplicate of an entire disk

Example: `diskcopy a: b:`

Normally, before transferring any information to a disk, you must prepare it using FORMAT. But in the case of the DISKCOPY command, the exception proves the rule. DISKCOPY automatically formats the disk as it makes the duplicate copy. Therefore, the same precautions exist as when formatting a disk:

DISKCOPY ERASES ANY PREVIOUS INFORMATION ON THE DISK YOU ARE COPYING TO.

It's important to distinguish between DISKCOPY and COPY (an MS-DOS command that will be introduced in Chapter 6). DISKCOPY can only make an exact copy of all the files on the disk. When you want to copy only part of the files on a disk, you use the COPY command.

DISKCOPY versus COPY

DISKCOPY	COPY
Automatically formats disk	Needs a formatted disk
Copies entire disk	Copies only designated files

Now let's make DISKCOPY jump through some hoops. If your system disk is not already there, put it in drive A. Insert an unformatted, blank disk in drive B (or a formatted disk whose information is no longer needed). (If your A and B drives are of different sizes—for example, A is a 5 1/4" drive and B is a 3 1/2" drive—you can't use DISKCOPY to copy disks from drive A to drive B, because the disks have different formats and capacities. You can use COPY, however. For this exercise, use only the drive for the size of disk you want to work with, and see the box on "Copying Disks With Only One Drive" in the next section.)

Before you enter the DISKCOPY command, take a close look at the exact wording of the example:

```
diskcopy a: b:<Enter>
```

This DISKCOPY command tells MS-DOS to copy the entire contents from the disk in drive A to the disk in drive B. Of course, the instructions are in a kind of shorthand, so this is probably not readily apparent to you. MAKE SURE TO ENTER THE COMMAND IN THIS EXACT ORDER. OTHERWISE, YOU MAY ERASE YOUR ENTIRE SYSTEM DISK.

How can this happen? Well, as DISKCOPY transfers the information, it wipes out anything previously on the disk. So when you are using this command, you must be sure to indicate clearly where the information is coming from and where it is going to.

Clarifying the Beneficiary

The disk that holds the original information is your source disk. It contains the information you want to copy. In this case, the source disk is your system disk, currently in drive A.

The disk that receives the copy is your target disk. It is the destination of the information you are copying. Your target disk (as yet empty) is currently in drive B (see fig. 4-9).

A

SOURCE
information to be copied

B

TARGET
holds copied information

Fig. 4-9. Source and target disks.

Copying Disks With Only One Drive

Remember what was said earlier about MS-DOS letting you use one disk drive as both A and B? If you have only one disk drive (or only one drive of a particular size), give the DISKCOPY command as follows:

```
diskcopy a: a:<Enter>
```

or

```
diskcopy b: b:<Enter>
```

depending on which drive you are using. MS-DOS will ask you for the SOURCE disk, then the TARGET disk, then the SOURCE disk again, and so on until the diskcopy is completed. Just be careful not to get the SOURCE and TARGET disks mixed up. It's a good idea to write SOURCE and TARGET on the disk labels before you begin. You might also want to write-protect the source disk before copying. (Chapter 3 explained how to do this.)

It's wise to become familiar with these terms; they are used in the instructions MS-DOS uses to perform copying commands. You'll see an example now as you execute DISKCOPY:

```
A>diskcopy a: b:<Enter>
```
 Include the blank spaces and colons.

MS-DOS gives you a reminder:

```
Insert source diskette in drive A
Insert target diskette in drive B
Strike any key when ready
```

Well, that couldn't be much clearer. You already have the source and target disks in place, so press any key.

The operating system now performs the same sequence of events that accompanied the FORMAT command, with the added bonus of copying the contents of the disk at the same time. Again the drives will whirr and the indicator lights will flash on and off. When the light under drive A is lit, information is being read from the system disk. When the light under drive B comes on, information is being written to this disk. DO NOT ATTEMPT TO OPEN THE DRIVE DOORS OR REMOVE ANY DISKS WHILE THE DRIVE LIGHT IS ON.

During this process, this message will be on the screen:

```
Copying 9 sectors per track, 2 side(s)
```

Depending on the type of disk your system uses, your message may read a bit differently (it may refer to the number of tracks being copied). But in any case, MS-DOS tells you when the DISKCOPY command has finished copying the disk:

```
Copy complete
Copy another diskette (Y/N)?
```

At this point you are offered an option. In the same way that you can use FORMAT repeatedly without retyping the command, you can also use DISKCOPY to make more than one duplicate of the source disk. If you answer "Y" to MS-DOS's query, you are instructed to insert a new target disk in drive B and start the copying process with a keystroke. If you answer "N" you are returned to the system prompt. Here is a chance for you to exert your individuality. If you want to be doubly protected, make an extra copy of your "insurance" disk. If you want to live dangerously, don't!

Now you are all set. You have taken out an insurance policy on your system disk (properly labeled, of course). You can take your original system disk and store it in a dry, safe place. Keep your backup system disk and your newly formatted disks handy; you will need them in the next chapter.

DISKCOPY is the first MS-DOS command you have encountered that requires the use of two disks, one in each drive. Many MS-DOS commands rely on this kind of "transfer" of information from one disk to another. It is important that you understand exactly how MS-DOS identifies which drive to find the information "on" and which drive to transfer the information "to." You inform MS-DOS as to which is the "source" and which is the "target" through the use of drive indicators.

A Written Guarantee

After you complete a command, MS-DOS returns you to the system prompt:

```
A:\>
```

You are now back under the control of the MS-DOS operating system. (That is, MS-DOS is ready for your next command.) Besides being the system prompt, the A:\> symbol gives you another important piece of information. It informs you that the system is working off the A drive. The system expects that any information you request or store will be on this drive. So this "A" is also a drive indicator. (If you've been booting from a hard disk, you know that "C" is the drive indicator for the hard disk.)

In order to keep track of where it is working, MS-DOS uses the concept of a "current" drive. The current drive is the one represented by the drive indicator. This is also called the "default" drive because, unless you tell it otherwise, MS-DOS will always look for information or store information on the current drive (see fig. 4-10).

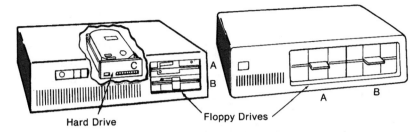

Fig. 4-10. Drive indicators.

Take, for example, the DIR command. Suppose that you want a listing of the disk in drive A. You ask for this information by entering the command, followed by a drive indicator. Drive indicators in commands are separated from the command by a space, and must be followed by a colon:

```
A:\>dir a:<Enter>
```

This command produces a listing of all the files on the disk in drive A. But you may be mumbling to yourself, "That's not the way I got a listing of the system disk." You are absolutely right. This is how you entered the DIR command in Chapter 3:

```
A:\>dir<Enter>
```

You did not include any drive indicator. These two versions of the DIR command produce the same listings because of the "default drive" feature of MS-DOS. The A:\> system prompt tells you that A is the current drive; therefore, when you enter a command without any drive indicator, it lists the files on the disk in the current, or A, drive.

This default feature is very handy when you are working extensively with one disk. But it does have its drawbacks. You can cause some pretty weird and unwanted file changes if you neglect to include a drive indicator in a command. It does no harm to include a drive indicator; therefore, when in doubt, write it into the command. Even if the operation involves only the current drive, it doesn't do any harm to include the default indicator in your command. Specifying drive indicators is always a good idea when you are transferring information from one disk to another, just as an extra measure of protection.

You can issue commands to be performed on the disk in other drives without changing the current drive. Suppose that you have your system disk in drive A and a disk holding some data files in drive B. You want to see a directory of the data files. To do this you include the drive indicator in the command:

```
A:\>dir b:<Enter>
```
The command is followed by a blank space, then the drive indicator followed by a colon.

The screen displays the listing of the files on the disk in drive B. After the listing you will be returned to the system prompt.

```
A:\>
```

The current drive is still A, because you have only taken a "peek" at the files on the disk in drive B. When you issue your next command, MS-DOS will look for the information or write the information to the disk in drive A, because this is still your current drive.

Current Drive

The A:\> prompt indicates the current drive.

There will come a time when you will be working extensively with the disk in drive B (or the hard disk, drive C). When this is the case, it can become a bit inconvenient to keep including the drive indicator in every command, but there is a simple solution: change the current drive. To make drive B the current drive, just enter the drive indicator in response to the system prompt:

```
A:\>b:<Enter>
```

The new current drive will appear as the system prompt:

```
B:\>
```

Don't get confused; this new indicator is still the MS-DOS system prompt; it does not mean that MS-DOS is not operating. It's just that your definition of system prompt has expanded. The MS-DOS system prompt is now seen to be the indicator of the current drive followed by >. So both A:\> and B:\> are MS-DOS system prompts.

Now that you have changed the current drive, what would be the result of the following command?

```
B:\>dir<Enter>
```

If you answered, "A listing of the files on the disk in drive B," give yourself two gold stars. B is now the current drive, and you did not include a drive indicator in the command; therefore, MS-DOS automatically performs the command on the disk in drive B.

If you are still a bit confused about when to include a drive indicator, think of it this way. The computer can only do what you tell it to. Including drive indicators is like making a will; you can only make sure that the goodies go to the right recipients if you make your wishes known (preferably by writing them down). If you tell MS-DOS that drive A is the current drive, it will return to that drive after every command until you tell it differently. It will also perform the entered command on the data in the current drive unless you tell it to go to another disk. Be patient with the computer; it does many things quickly, but in reasoning abilities (or mind-reading abilities) it rates a fat zero!

To return to A as the current drive, enter the drive indicator in response to the B:\> prompt:

```
B:\>a:<Enter>
```

The current drive is A again:

```
A:\>
```

As you become familiar with other MS-DOS commands, the significance and use of drive indicators will become clearer, especially when you move into the more advanced MS-DOS commands in Chapter 7.

This completes the sales pitch from Mutual of MS-DOS. The theme of this chapter has been protecting yourself. This process includes using and handling your disks wisely (it is your data!) and making sure that you back up your original system disk. (It's your computer!) In addition, you have moved into the realm of actual "doing-something-with-a-disk computing." You've used FORMAT to prepare your disks and DISKCOPY to make your insurance copy. Finally, you have begun to see more of the inner operations of MS-DOS by learning the basics of source and target disks and the current-drive indicator.

Minding Your E's and Q's

5

- What Is an Editor?
- Safety in Numbers
- You ASCII Me and I ASCII You
- As Easy As...
  - Short and to the Point
  - Current Events
- Getting into the Act
  - Open Sesame
  - Putting Thoughts into Words
  - Final Curtain
  - Going over Your Lines
- Revising the Script
  - Looking at the First Draft
  - Getting the Right Line
  - Adding New Parts
  - Eliminating Unneeded Characters
  - Major Revisions

5 Minding Your E's and Q's

Computers, no matter what their fancy names or reputed powers, are simply machines for organizing information. Information management is also the ultimate purpose of software packages and programming languages; they are tools to help you arrange, classify, and use the data in your computer. But before you can use your computer to organize data, you have to put in its memory the information you want to work with.

Most of the information you enter into the computer is in the form of "text," or combinations of numbers, letters, and punctuation marks. MS-DOS keeps track of data by placing it in files. (You were introduced to files when you used the DIR command in Chapter 3.) These files, or groups of related data, are the meat and potatoes of using your computer. MS-DOS is a very efficient file organizer. In Chapter 7 you will learn how to name files and give MS-DOS commands to manage your files.

First, however, you must learn how to create files. Included in the MS-DOS operating system is a special program named EDLIN. EDLIN (EDit LINes) is a text editor, and its sole purpose is to help you create and edit files.

What Is an Editor?

EDLIN belongs to the category of computer-software tools called "text editors." Editors are used to create new files and add, delete, or revise text in existing files. Editors can also move text around inside a file or transfer information from one file to another.

There are two types of editor: full-screen editors and line editors. A full-screen editor displays files so that the entire screen is filled with text (usually 23 lines at a time because this is the capacity of most personal-computer displays). Full-screen editors that go beyond basic text editing and let you boldface or underline text, select a different typeface or font, or use other special features are called "word processing programs." In a full-screen editor or word processor, each full screen is like a window, displaying a specific section of your entire file. Getting around in a full-screen editor is quite simple. You use special keys or a "mouse" to move the cursor to the part of the text you want to work with. (Using a mouse pointing device will be discussed further in Chapters 6 and 12.) With a full-screen editor, you have complete freedom of movement with your cursor, and you can move different parts of your text (lines or whole paragraphs, for example) into the window with one or two keystrokes. To make changes in the text, you type directly into the window.

Two Types of Editor

Full-screen Editor	Line Editor
Displays entire screen	Displays designated block of lines
Edits anywhere on-screen	Edits within one line
Sophisticated editing features	Limited set of commands
Adds special characters	Uses ASCII codes
Longer loading time	Built-in and compact
May use lots of memory	Doesn't take up much memory
Can be expensive	Free with MS-DOS
Good for large files	Good for small editing jobs

EDIT, A Full-screen Editor for MS-DOS 5.0 or Later

Microsoft started including a full-screen text editor called, appropriately, "EDIT," with MS-DOS version 5.0. Chapter 6, "Editor's Choice," is devoted to EDIT. If you have MS-DOS 5.0 or later, we recommend that you read Chapter 6 and consider making EDIT your tool of choice for creating and revising text files. EDIT is even easier to use than EDLIN; however, because every version of MS-DOS includes EDLIN and only the latest version has EDIT, it wouldn't be a bad idea for users with MS-DOS 5.0 to skim through the rest of this chapter and learn about EDLIN. That way, if you find yourself sitting at a PC that doesn't have EDIT or your favorite word processor, you can still get the job done.

EDLIN is a line editor. Line editors are more limited than full-screen editors and a bit more difficult to use. Each line of text is handled separately. Every line of text is identified by a line number. You use these line numbers to create your own "window."

Before you can perform any command using a line editor, you must define the exact location where the operation is to occur. Then you enter instructions to move to this section and display the specified part of the text document. Only then can the editing changes be made. For this reason, using the line editor can be time-consuming.

Actually, using a line editor is not as complicated as it sounds, but these extra steps can slow you down and be frustrating until you become familiar with the EDLIN commands. If most of your work on the computer will be with large files, you should consider purchasing a word processing program. For smaller jobs, EDLIN is just fine.

Safety in Numbers

In the last chapter you learned about the importance of making "insurance" copies of disks containing valuable programs or data. One nice touch of the EDLIN editor is that it comes with a built-in safety device, for which you will thank the designers of EDLIN more than once during your computing experience. This feature is the automatic creation of a backup file whenever you modify an EDLIN file. This backup has the same name and contents as your text file, but is identifiable by a three-letter addition to the filename. Not surprisingly, this extension is .BAK. When you list your files using the DIR command, you will see these "insurance" files listed with the .BAK extension. Look at the files below, for example. The first three are text (.TXT) files, and the second three are their backup (.BAK) files.

```
Volume in drive A has no label
Volume Serial Number is 1B1E-17E0
Directory of A:\

BILLS     TXT    46976    3-8-90    12:00p
SCORES    TXT      468    3-8-90    12:00p
LETTERS   TXT     3392    3-8-90    12:00p
BILLS     BAK    45568    3-8-90    12:00p
SCORES    BAK      148    3-8-90    12:00p
LETTERS   BAK    33792    3-8-90    12:00p
        6 file(s)     130344 bytes
                      193024 bytes free
```

Backup files are essential in helping you recover data if a problem occurs while you are in the middle of an editing session.

Imagine that you have worked long and hard to create a file and are just about ready to call it quits. But, horror of horrors, you experience a power blackout due to massive use of air conditioners in the next state. Of course, your computer goes off, and with it go all of the changes and modifications you have been patiently entering for the last hour. (They were in transient RAM memory.) Well, EDLIN can't miraculously recover those changes, but it can help you "cut your losses." Because your original file still exists in the .BAK version, you will lose only the modifications entered during this current editing session.

EDLIN has another built-in safety feature: it won't let you edit a file with a .BAK extension. If you could get into the backup files and randomly make changes to this last version, you wouldn't have that pristine copy when you needed it. To use a backup file, you must first give the file a new name, removing the .BAK designation. (In Chapter 7 you'll learn how to use the RENAME command to do this.) Once the file is no longer the backup, you can begin the editing process all over again (sigh).

What's in a Backup File?

An EDLIN .BAK file contains:
A duplicate version of the latest text in a file, not including changes made in the current editing session.

Use a .BAK file:
Whenever you lose the contents of an EDLIN file, you must first rename the file extension.

Of course, if anything happens to your disk, your insurance is cancelled because both the original and backup files are stored on the same disk. It's a good practice to have "reserve" copies of your files on separate disks. (In Chapter 4 you learned how to make a backup copy of a whole disk with the DISKCOPY command. In Chapter 7 you will learn how to use the COPY command to make copies of individual files.)

Although EDLIN is not as efficient and comprehensive as some full-screen editors, there are some advantages to using it rather than a word processing program.

One is that EDLIN is free; it is built-in as part of MS-DOS. Another advantage is that some word processing programs make subtle changes to the text files. These are not changes you can see, but internal changes usually involving modification of the way the file is stored. These changes and discrepancies can be a problem if you try to use a word-processed file with another program, want to share a file with someone who has a different editor, or try to display the file using the MS-DOS TYPE command. These word-processed changes can cause the display of the file's contents to resemble some as-yet-undiscovered language.

You ASCII Me and I ASCII You

To eliminate some of these problems, most ordinary text files are stored in a format known as an ASCII file. ASCII (American Standard Code for Information Interchange) is a specific code scheme which the computer uses to recognize the letters, numbers, and punctuation marks that make up a text file. ASCII files contain their text information in exactly the same format as it is entered. When displayed, ASCII files make perfect sense.

ASCII is the most widely used format for computer files, and it is used by most personal computers. One big advantage of entering your data in ASCII code is that these files can be used by many types of programs. Using ASCII increases the flexibility of your data files. EDLIN enters and stores files in ASCII code.

In addition to the letters, numbers, and punctuation marks you enter into an ASCII file, there are a few characters that MS-DOS itself adds to help format the text in a way it can easily understand.

MS-DOS indicates the "end of each line" by inserting two characters—the carriage return and the line feed. These characters carry the message "stop this line and move down to the next line."

At the conclusion of each file, MS-DOS inserts a marker to indicate the "end of the file." This character is "Ctrl Z," often written with a caret (^) to indicate the control key (^Z). These special punctuation characters are hidden from view; you do not see them when you display or print out ASCII text files.

What's in an ASCII File?

An MS-DOS ASCII file contains:
The text of a file
End-of-line characters
The end-of-file character (^Z)

Use ASCII format for:
Text files
Source code for programs
Batch-processing files

ASCII text files are used in three main areas of data entry—text files, written source code for programs (source code means the way the programs look as you type them in), and batch-processing files. (Batch processing is covered in Chapter 9.) When you create files with EDLIN, you are joining this ASCII club and making your files as useful as possible. But now, on to the nitty-gritty of actually using EDLIN.

As Easy As...

Because EDLIN is a line editor, it identifies all information in terms of line numbers. You do not enter these line numbers as you enter text; they are automatically supplied by EDLIN. Line numbers are only reference points within the file; they are not part of the data contained in the file. For example:

```
1: This is the first line of text.
2: You do not enter the line number as part of the file.
3: The numbers are supplied automatically by EDLIN.
```

Lines within the file are numbered in sequence. When new lines are inserted or lines are deleted, EDLIN renumbers the lines automatically. But it doesn't show you the renumbering until you ask to see the file again. This situation is a bit confusing at first.

Suppose that you want to add a line at the beginning of an existing file (you'll learn how in just a minute). This file is about computer history, and right now the first line reads:

```
In the beginning there was ENIAC...
```

When you create or display this file using EDLIN, the first line appears as follows:

```
1: In the beginning there was ENIAC...
```

But you have decided to change your opening. Now you want the first line to read: "And on the eighth day She created computers." This is how your file would appear after the insertion:

```
1: And on the eighth day She created computers.
2: In the beginning there was ENIAC...
```

Thereafter, if you wanted to modify "In the beginning there was ENIAC...", you would need to refer to it as line number 2.

Short and to the Point

EDLIN receives its instructions from you in the form of commands. Commands are indicated by one-letter abbreviations. Many commands also require that you indicate which line or line numbers are to be affected by the command. The format of EDLIN commands is simple. First you enter the beginning line number, then the ending line number (when line numbers are present they are separated by commas), and finally the single letter abbreviation indicating the command. Here are some examples of EDLIN commands:

FORMAT OF EDLIN COMMANDS	
1D	Delete line 1
1,9L	List the file starting with line 1 and ending with line 9
4I	Insert a new line before line 4
E	End the editing session

Each EDLIN command is discussed in detail in this chapter.

Current Events

Inside EDLIN, the current line (the line you are working on or the last line you modified) is indicated by an asterisk after the line number and preceding the text on that line. If line 2 is your current line, it appears as follows:

```
2:*In the beginning there was ENIAC...
```

Using the current line as a marker can help you move through your file more quickly. For instance, to make modifications to your current line you do not have to enter the current line number. Instead you enter a period:

.D   Tells EDLIN to delete the current line.

You can use the current line in place of a starting line number as a "short cut" to get to a new location. To do this, you indicate the new location relative to the current line using a plus or minus sign and a number:

+35   Refers to the line that is 35 lines after the current line.

-54   Refers to the line that is 54 lines before the current line.

Until you become more familiar with EDLIN, use the actual line numbers to get to the line you want. Later you might find using the current line useful for faster movement in a large file.

In addition to serving as a marker of the current line, EDLIN also uses the asterisk as a command prompt. When EDLIN is waiting for a command or for you to enter some information, the asterisk appears on the far left of the screen and is not associated with a line number. When the asterisk is located after a line number, it is indicating the current line.

Two Uses of the Asterisk

```
2:*In the beginning there was ENIAC...  * indicates the current line.

*                                        * indicates that EDLIN is
                                           waiting for input.
```

Okay, with this brief introduction to line numbers, commands, and current lines you are ready to begin using EDLIN.

Getting into the Act

In earlier chapters you learned the advantages of "doing it yourself." Each use of MS-DOS commands becomes easier when you participate in the learning. Up until now you have been learning the fundamentals, and this book has encouraged you to take part. Because this book is based strongly on the "immersion" theory of learning, you are now going to take this participation one step further. Not only will you be learning through practice, you will be doing it in the guise of a series of "personae," each designed to demonstrate an important aspect of MS-DOS. No costumes or Academy-award performances are required; just use your imagination to star in these scenarios.

Your first role will not take you far from home. In this scene you are an overworked, underpaid, harried worker who is definitely in need of some time-saving organization. Sound familiar?

Every Friday you leave the office with fresh determination to accomplish all those chores you have been putting off. Every Monday morning you wonder, "Where did the weekend go?" Well, all this is about to change. As the owner of a new personal computer, you are about to get organized. In fact, that was one of the reasons you bought your computer in the first place. On this early Friday evening you begin by making a list. Here's how it looks:

CHORES
Jody's soccer game, 9:00
Chad's Little League game, 12:00
Go to grocery store
Mow lawn
Put up hammock
Dog to vet
Get flea collar for dog!
Tennis with Annie, 2:00

Open Sesame

To begin this play, you must get your computer set up and ready to "run." Take your system disk (the write-protected backup version of your system disk), insert it in drive A, and turn on the computer. (If you have a hard disk, just turn on the computer without putting a disk in. EDLIN should already be included with the other MS-DOS programs on your hard disk.) If you are running MS-DOS from a floppy disk, use the DIR command as follows to make sure that this disk contains the EDLIN program:

```
A:\>dir edlin.com <Enter>

Volume in drive A has no label
Volume Serial Number is 1B1E-17E0
Directory of A:\

EDLIN        COM  14121   3-8-90    12:00p
             6 file(s)     14121 bytes
                           29696 bytes free
```

(If you are using MS-DOS version 5.0 or later, the EDLIN file will be named EDLIN.EXE rather than EDLIN.COM, so you should use the command DIR EDLIN.EXE to verify that EDLIN is on the disk.)

Next take a formatted disk with plenty of space available and put it in drive B. (If you are running MS-DOS from a hard disk, you can put your formatted disk in either drive A or drive B. In order to be consistent with the following examples, we recommend that you use drive B if you have two floppy disk drives.)

As you contemplate creating your first file, you may find yourself in a quandary; what should you call this new creation? In the interest of time, let's call it "chores."

With that decided, you're ready to begin. To create a file, EDLIN needs two facts: the name of the program and the name of the file.

Is the A:\> prompt on the screen? The A drive should be your current drive if you are running MS-DOS from a floppy disk. (Hard disk users will see the C:\> prompt, indicating that C is the current drive. When we show the A:\> prompt in our examples, you hard-disk users should remember that you will be seeing C:\> instead.)

You are going to create this file on the diskette in drive B, so you must include the drive indicator (b:) in the command:

```
A:\>edlin b:chores <Enter>
```

EDLIN responds promptly with the following:

```
New file
*
```

Well, so far so good. Yes, this is a new file. The asterisk (*) is the EDLIN prompt, and tells you that the program is waiting for further instructions.

EDLIN returns this "new file" message after it searches the disk in the indicated drive and does not find an existing file with the entered filename. In other words, since there is no "chores" file on the disk in drive B, it assumes this is a new file.

EDLIN'S OPENING SPEECHES	
If EDLIN displays:	**It means:**
New file	There is no file by this name on the designated disk.
End of input file	The file has been loaded into memory.
*	The file is too large to fit into memory; memory is filled to 75% of capacity. The remainder of the file is still on the disk.

If you enter the name of an existing file, EDLIN reads this file into memory, and then returns the following message:

```
End of input file
```

There is only one instance in which you do not receive a message from EDLIN in response to entering a filename. It occurs when your file is so large that not all of it can fit into the computer's memory at one time. When this is the case—and it is unlikely that a beginner would have files this large—EDLIN reads in as much of the file as can fit, reserving 25 percent of the memory. EDLIN operates with this 25 percent "safety reserve" at all times. If this situation should occur, EDLIN will simply display the asterisk prompt (*) with no additional message. Later we will show you how to make more space within memory and move data around when your file is very large.

In the present case, EDLIN has given you the * prompt and is awaiting your command.

Putting Thoughts into Words

Now you are ready to enter your list of chores into the file. To inform EDLIN that you want to begin entering text, enter the letter "I." As in MS-DOS commands, you can use upper- or lowercase letters to enter commands; you will probably want to use lowercase, since they are easier to type.

"I" stands for "insert text into the file." In this case, you are inserting text into a new, empty file. As you might suspect, you also use the I command to insert information into existing files, but first things first:

```
*i<Enter>
```

EDLIN accepts your instructions and presents you with the first line number. The entire screen now looks like this:

```
New file
*i
        1:*
```

Begin to type in your list. The first line of your file is your title, "Chores." You must indicate the end of every line by pressing the <Enter> key. Each time you press the <Enter> key, EDLIN will automatically supply a new line number for the next entry.

```
1: Chores <Enter>
2:
```

If you make a typing mistake and discover it before pressing <Enter> to start a new line, just use the <Backspace> key to erase the incorrect characters and type the rest of the entry again. (Soon we will show you how to go back and change text on a preceding line.)

Entering Information into an EDLIN File

Text and commands may be in upper- or lowercase.

Use <Enter> to indicate the end of each entry.

Command format: starting line number, ending line number, command.

Correct mistakes with <Backspace> before pressing <Enter>.

This is quite a list, but now that you're organized, think of how much more efficient you will be. When you have entered all the items, you will have nine lines of text. EDLIN will be waiting for line 10. The file looks like this:

```
 1: Chores
 2: Jody's soccer game, 9:00
 3: Chad's Little League game, 12:00
 4: Go to grocery store
 5: Mow lawn
 6: Put up hammock
 7: Dog to vet
 8: Get flea collar for dog!
 9: Tennis with Annie, 2:00
10:*
```

After you have entered the last chore, you are ready to exit from the "insert" mode. To return to "command mode" (where EDLIN is ready to receive commands rather than text), you press <Ctrl>C (the Control key and the C key at the same time. When you do this, EDLIN puts the symbol ^C on the screen. <Ctrl>C and ^C mean the same thing). On a few computers you may have to press <Ctrl><Break> (the Control key and the Break key simultaneously) instead. Remember that you must hold down the <Ctrl> key while you press the other key. Both keys are released together. Enter this <Ctrl>C combination now in response to the prompt for line 10:

```
    10:^C
*
```

The asterisk, which has been keeping track of the current line, returns to the prompt position at the far left. You are now back in "command" mode.

Final Curtain

There is one more step to take before leaving the EDLIN program completely. You must tell EDLIN that this is the end of the file. And, logically enough, you do that by using the E (END) command.

The E (End) Command

Use: Indicates the conclusion of an editing session

Example: e

When you finish entering text in an EDLIN file, you must first exit the "insert" mode (using <Ctrl>C) and then give the end-of-file signal to EDLIN by entering the E command. End the "chores" file now:

```
*e <Enter>
```

When you enter this command, EDLIN returns control to the operating system (indicated by the `A:\>` prompt).

```
A:\>
```

IN AND OUT WITH EDLIN

These are the steps to take to go into EDLIN and return again to MS-DOS at the completion of the EDLIN program.

`A>`	Start out in operating system
`edlin filename`	Call the EDLIN program
`i`	Enter the "insert" mode
`lines of text`	Enter the content of the file
`^C`	Exit the "insert" mode
`e`	Exit the EDLIN program
`A:\>`	You have returned to the operating system

Well, bravo! Your debut as an EDLIN operator gets rave reviews. To verify that your role was as successful as it seems, take a look at your completed "chores" file.

Fine, you'd love to, but you are looking at an `A:\>` prompt. Where is your EDLIN file? Why, stored safely away on the disk, of course. Use `DIR` to check for the presence of "chores." Remember that you designated this file to be on drive B when you entered the original filename. Don't forget to include the drive letter now that you are looking for the file:

```
A:\>dir b:chores <Enter>
```

No surprise, there is your "chores" list on the directory.

```
Volume in drive B has no label
Volume serial number is 1B2C-23F0
Directory of B:\

CHORES          175   12-17-90      8:50a
             1 File(s) 90 bytes
                   29786 bytes free
```

Going over Your Lines

There are two ways to check the contents of an EDLIN file. The first requires the use of the MS-DOS TYPE command, which will be discussed in full in Chapter 6. Here is a sneak preview of TYPE. Enter this command and watch what happens:

```
A:\>type b:chores <Enter>

Chores
Jody's soccer game, 9:00
Chad's Little League game, 12:00
Go to grocery store
Mow lawn
Put up hammock
Dog to vet
Get flea collar for dog!
Tennis with Annie, 2:00
```

There is your file, exactly as you entered it. But notice one thing. There are no line numbers. That's because line numbers are not part of the data in EDLIN files; they are simply reference points to use when editing or creating EDLIN files.

The second way to see the contents of your file is to use the EDLIN L (List) command. There will be more about this command a little later in this chapter. Right now you are going to learn about another way to lower the curtain on an editing session.

The Q (Quit) Command

Use: Ends an EDLIN editing session without saving any changes

Example: q

In addition to the E command, there is another way to end an editing session using EDLIN: you can use the Q (Quit) command. Choose the Q command when you want to stop editing but don't care about saving the new file or any changes you have made to an existing file. The Q command does not write your file back to the disk; it simply cancels the current editing session.

You might want to stop a session because you find that you don't really want to make any changes, or because things have become very mixed up, and you just want to throw this session away. This is the time for the Q command.

Don't confuse the E (End) and the Q (Quit) commands:

E is for END,
Save for the next day.
Q is for QUIT,
Toss this #%&* thing away.

EDLIN provides a safeguard to prevent the loss of changes that you really intended to keep. When you enter the Q command, EDLIN asks:

```
Abort edit (Y/N)?
```

This is your last chance. A "Y" response sends the information entered in this editing session into the nearest black hole. An "N" response lets you continue with the edit.

Revising the Script

Now that you have created a file and seen it safely put away, it's time to learn how to make changes in an EDLIN file. Floppy disk users: make sure that your system disk (containing the EDLIN.COM file) is in drive A, and the disk containing your "chores" file is in drive B. Now ask for the file:

```
A:\>edlin b:chores
```

Since the file named "chores" already exists, EDLIN responds with the appropriate message:

```
End of input file
*
```

The asterisk prompt indicates that EDLIN is waiting in the command mode. It's ready to make any required modification. There is one problem, however—where is the text of the file?

You must remember that EDLIN moves one step at a time. All you requested was access to the file. Now EDLIN is waiting to find out which part of the file you want to see. You have to issue a command to look at your file.

Looking at the First Draft

The L command allows you to look at a file (or a section of a file) while the EDLIN program is in operation (TYPE lets you look at the contents from MS-DOS). As with many EDLIN commands, LIST requires the use of line numbers so that EDLIN can find the correct location in the file. As discussed earlier, EDLIN commands follow this pattern: starting line number, comma, ending line number, letter of the command (some commands require additional information).

The L (List) Command

Use: Lists the contents of an EDLIN file

Example: 1,9L

Following this pattern, enter the L command to display the "chores" file:

```
*1,9L <Enter>

    1: Chores
    2: Jody's soccer game, 9:00
    3: Chad's Little League game, 12:00
    4: Go to grocery store
    5: Mow lawn
```

```
6: Put up hammock
7: Dog to vet
8: Get flea collar for dog!
9: Tennis with Annie, 2:00
*
```

The command told EDLIN to list lines 1 through 9 of the file. If you enter the L command without any line numbers, EDLIN lists 23 lines, eleven above and eleven below the current line number. (The asterisk indicates that line 1 is the current line, which makes sense because you have just opened the file.) Displaying the section immediately surrounding the current line makes working with large files easier when you want to see an overview of the section you are editing. Because "chores" is so short, you could have entered "L" without a line number and the entire file would have been displayed. Longer files require that you limit your range of line numbers to 23, since this is the maximum number of lines that can be displayed at one time.

There are other ways to use the L command. The L command with one line number lists the 23 lines starting with that line number, no matter what the current line number is. For example, *43L would list from line 43 through line 65.

Getting the Right Line

Okay, as the weekend moves closer it's time to get those chores in order. Glancing over your list, you detect a few minor conflicts. You decide that while you can definitely go to the soccer game at 9:00 and, barring excessive overtimes, make the Little League game at 12:00, there is no way you can play tennis at 2:00 and get anything else done. So you make a quick call: "Sorry Annie, how about a bit of twilight tennis?" It is forecast to be in the high 90s tomorrow afternoon, so Annie quickly agrees: "Tennis at 7:00."

Now it's time to update your file. To edit a specific line within an EDLIN file, enter the line number in response to the asterisk prompt. This command has no letter of the alphabet; simply enter the single line number. Your tennis match is on line 9:

```
*9 <Enter>
```

EDLIN immediately displays a copy of that line in its current version. You are then offered a seemingly blank line, preceded by the same line number.

```
9: Tennis with Annie, 2:00
9:*
```

This new line will contain the edited version of the current line. To update your list, you want to change the time of this appointment to 7:00. For now, type in the line again, changing the time. (There are some nice shortcuts you can use in editing lines in EDLIN files. You will learn about these tricks in the section on special keys in Chapter 8.)

```
         9:Tennis with Annie, 7:00<Enter>
    *
```

This is all EDLIN shows you; it doesn't show you the correction right now. To see how changes affect the contents of an EDLIN file, you must use L to list the file again.

```
    *1,9L <Enter>

        1: Chores
        2: Jody's soccer game, 9:00
        3: Chad's Little League game, 12:00
        4: Go to grocery store
        5: Mow lawn
        6: Put up hammock
        7: Dog to vet
        8: Get flea collar for dog!
        9: Tennis with Annie, 7:00


    *
```

Sure enough, tennis with Annie is now scheduled for 7:00.

If you don't want to make any changes in a line once you have called for it, press <Ctrl>C. The line remains unchanged, and you are returned to the * prompt.

Adding New Parts

Of course, once you sat down and started thinking about it, you remembered another thing that you really wanted to do this weekend—go to the computer store and get that hot new game your son was telling you about. Well, let's add it to the list. To add new lines, use the I command, the same one you use to create a new file.

The I (Insert) Command

Use: Inserts new lines into an EDLIN file

Examples: i
                4i
                #i

You have to give some more information to EDLIN when you use the I command to insert new information into an existing file. You must tell EDLIN where to insert the new line. You indicate the line number before the line where you want to make the insertion.

Because your list shows you going out to the grocery store anyway, why not put the computer store right above the grocery store on our list? As with other EDLIN commands, you enter the line number first and then the command. You want to insert this new line before line 4:

```
*4i <Enter>
```

The screen displays the line number and waits for the new line:

```
4:*
```

Now type in your addition:

```
4: Go to computer store <Enter>
```

EDLIN will continue to supply you with new line numbers for insertions until you exit the "insert mode" by pressing <Ctrl>C.

```
    5: ^C
*
```

Calling for a listing with the L command displays the changes:

```
*L <Enter>

     1: Chores
     2: Jody's soccer game, 9:00
     3: Chad's Little League game, 12:00
     4: Go to computer store
     5: Go to grocery store
     6: Mow lawn
     7: Put up hammock
     8: Dog to vet
     9: Get flea collar for dog!
    10: Tennis with Annie, 7:00

    *
```

The new line has been assigned line number 4, and all the remaining items on the list have been moved down one line number. There are now a total of ten items on the list.

Sometimes you may want to add new information at the end of a file. This presents a problem, because no line number currently exists that you can insert before. EDLIN solves this problem by providing the number-sign (#) symbol. Using # in conjunction with an editing command means, "Do this operation at the end of the current file in memory." If you had wanted to add the store trip to the end of the file, you would have entered this command:

```
*#i <Enter>
```

In response to this command, EDLIN presents a line number that is one higher than the current total number of lines in the file:

```
11:*
```

You would then type in the new line or lines. EDLIN keeps supplying line numbers after every <Enter>. But you don't want to duplicate this item on your list, which is long enough as it is. So just press <Ctrl>C to tell EDLIN you have finished entering new information. Line 11 will remain blank and will not be included in the file. If you are skeptical, check your file using the L command. If the line did somehow sneak in there, the next command tells you how to get rid of it.

Eliminating Unneeded Characters

Looking over your list, it seems like things are beginning to pile up. And after all, this is the weekend; you deserve some time off. Maybe you can get the kid next door to mow the lawn and put up the hammock. Then you can relax in the yard after your tennis game. You're in luck; the kid agrees to do those chores (for a fair price, of course). You can eliminate two things from your list.

The D (Delete) Command

Use:	Deletes lines from an EDLIN file
Examples:	86d
	1,5d

To delete lines in EDLIN, you enter a starting line number and an ending line number. In effect, these two line numbers mark the boundaries of a block of information you want to eliminate. This block concept is useful for performing several commands in EDLIN. A block can also be only one line, in which case the starting and ending line numbers are the same and need be entered only once.

First double-check the line numbers of the items you want to delete by displaying the file with the L command:

```
*L <Enter>

    1: Chores
    2: Jody's soccer game, 9:00
    3: Chad's Little League game, 12:00
    4: Go to computer store
    5: Go to grocery store
    6: Mow lawn
    7: Put up hammock
    8: Dog to vet
    9: Get flea collar for dog!
   10: Tennis with Annie, 7:00
    *
```

In the current version of the file (since you added the computer store), "Mow lawn" and "Put up hammock" are line numbers 6 and 7. To delete these lines, enter this command:

```
*6,7d <Enter>
*
```

And they are banished, to trouble your conscience no more. To check to see that they are really gone, use the L command:

```
*L <Enter>
```

Here is your new revised listing:

```
1: Chores
2: Jody's soccer game, 9:00
3: Chad's Little League game, 12:00
4: Go to computer store
5: Go to grocery store
6: Dog to vet
7: Get flea collar for dog!
8: Tennis with Annie, 7:00
*
```

You'll notice that in this new listing your original items 6 and 7 are now deleted and the remaining items have been renumbered. You're doing pretty well, considering that you haven't left the house yet and you've already cut the entire list down to 8 chores.

COMPARISON OF INSERT AND DELETE

Insert		Delete	
i	Begin a new file	d	Delete the current line
6i	Insert a new line 6	6d	Delete line 6
	Line 6 becomes line 7		Line 7 becomes line 6
#i	Add new lines at end	1,6d	Delete lines 1 through 6
			Line 7 becomes line 1

The S (Search) Command

Use:	Searches for a string in an EDLIN file
Examples:	1,8sdog
	1,8?sdog

Often when you are using EDLIN, you want to find a specific place in a file by searching for a particular word or pattern of characters within the file. In computerese, a group of characters (whether or not they make up an English "word"), is called a string. You might, for instance, want to edit a section of a file dealing with the string "Christmas," or you might want to check whether you changed all occurrences of "Strong And Sons" to "Strong And Associates" in a letter. To do this you use the S command.

In addition to the string, which tells EDLIN "what I should search for," the S command also needs to know "where should I search for it?" You give EDLIN this information by indicating the starting and ending line numbers of the "block" to be searched.

Since you have made several modifications to your "chores" file, you want to make sure that the trip to the vet is still on the agenda. You want to search the entire file (lines 1 through 8) for the string "dog."

The S command follows this pattern: line number to begin the search, a comma, line number to end the search, the S command, and then the string to search for. Enter the S command to find your dog:

```
*1,8sdog <Enter>
```

EDLIN begins searching at line 1 and reports the first match:

```
    6: Dog to vet
*
```

If you want to continue the search for other occurrences of "dog," enter the S command again:

```
*s<Enter>
```

EDLIN displays the next match:

```
    7: Get flea collar for dog!
*
```

When you enter S without any new "string," EDLIN uses the last string it was told to search for.

There is one catch with the S command. It only finds exact string matches. If dog appeared in our file as Dog or even DOG or as part of another word, DOGMA, these instances would not be reported by EDLIN.

Each time you enter the S command, EDLIN continues searching for "string matches" until it reaches the last line number entered. If it does not find the string, it sends this message:

```
Not found
```

There is a variation of the S command which allows you the option to continue searching after each occurrence of the string without reentering the S command. To do this "global" search, insert a question mark (?) in the initial S command. Try looking everywhere for your dog:

```
*1,8?sdog <Enter>
```

Note that the question mark is entered before the S command. Because you included a ? in the S command, EDLIN asks you whether this is what you were looking for or if you want to continue searching:

```
    6: Dog to vet
O.K.?
```

If you answer "N," EDLIN continues to search for matches. A "Y" answer indicates this is where you want to be, and the search ends.

The R (Replace) Command

Use:	Replaces a string in an EDLIN command with another string
Examples:	`1,8rdog^Zdog and cat` `1,8?rdog^Zdog and cat`

The R command is related to the S command in that it too goes through the file searching for the specified pattern. R, however, allows you to replace every instance of your pattern with new information.

As you are reading over your list you get a revelation. The cat needs a shot too, and she certainly needs a flea collar. To put this information on your list, you must search through "chores" for "dog" and replace it with "dog and cat" (see fig. 5-1).

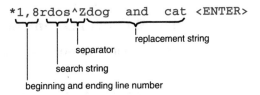

Fig. 5-1. Example using the R command.

The beginning line number is followed by the ending line number. Then comes the R command preceding the string to be searched for. The R command requires one additional piece of information: the replacement string. A ^Z character separates the two strings. The R command automatically replaces every occurrence of the old string with the new string.

```
      6: Dog and cat to vet
      7: Get dog and cat flea collar!
   *
```

As with the S command, you can use a question mark (?) with the R command. This symbol is useful if you are not certain that you want to replace every occurrence of the string. When you include a question mark in the command, EDLIN asks if you want to make the replacement:

```
*1,8?rdog^Zdog and cat <Enter>
      6: Dog and cat to vet
O.K.?
```

Use "Y" to approve the replacement and instruct EDLIN to continue with the search. It then displays the next occurrence of the string:

```
      7: Get dog and cat flea collar!
O.K.?
```

If you answer "N" to this query, no replacement occurs in this line, but the search continues until the ending line number is reached.

These commands—Insert, Delete, Search, and Replace—are useful editing tools when you are dealing with small changes in just a few lines. But there are times when you will need to make changes involving large sections of a file. These require additional EDLIN commands.

Major Revisions

You use the M command when you want to move a block of information to a different location within the file. Because you want to accomplish all your "car-related" chores at one time, you decide to move the "animal items" right up there with the store items. It's much more efficient to have your list in neat, chronological order.

The M (Move) Command

Use:	Moves blocks of information within an EDLIN file
Example:	6,7,4m

The M command requires beginning and ending line numbers which define the block to be moved. You must also indicate the place you want the block to be moved to. Just as with the I command, you indicate the line number before which you want the items to appear. Since the vet is farther away than the computer store, and, after all, efficiency is the name of the game, you move lines 6 and 7 to before line 4.

```
*6,7,4m <Enter>
   *
```

Note that in addition to the comma separating the beginning and ending line numbers, you must also put a comma between the ending line number and the line number indicating the new location.

Now you have modified your list a lot. Time to see what the newest version looks like:

```
*L <Enter>

    1: Chores
    2: Jody's soccer game, 9:00
    3: Chad's Little League game, 12:00
    4:*Dog and cat to vet
    5: Get dog and cat flea collar!
    6: Go to computer store
    7: Go to grocery store
    8: Tennis with Annie, 7:00
    *
```

Looks like a full, but satisfying, day.

The C (Copy) Command

Use: Duplicates lines within an EDLIN file

Example: 2,4,7c

Another useful way to move lines around inside an EDLIN file is with the C command. Just like the M command, the C command requires three line numbers: the starting and ending block line numbers, and the line number before which the copied lines should appear.

In our "chores" file, you don't really have a need to put duplicate lines elsewhere in the file, but for practice let's copy lines 2 through 4 and put them before line 7:

```
*2,4,7c <Enter>
*
```

The resulting list looks like this:

```
*L <Enter>

    1: Chores
    2: Jody's soccer game, 9:00
    3: Chad's Little League game, 12:00
    4: Dog and cat to vet
    5: Get dog and cat flea collar!
```

```
 6: Go to computer store
 7: Jody's soccer game, 9:00
 8: Chad's Little League game, 12:00
 9: Dog and cat to vet
10: Go to grocery store
11: Tennis with Annie, 7:
 *
```

The three copied lines appear twice in the list: in their original location as lines 2, 3, and 4 and as new lines 7, 8, and 9. But this makes no sense, so delete lines 7, 8, and 9:

```
*7,9d <Enter>
*
```

All right, take a third curtain call. You have passed your opening-night performance with nary a forgotten line or missed cue. The lucky character in this play can now take Sunday off, and you deserve a rest too.

The remaining EDLIN commands require two files or one very large file, so you won't actually perform these commands right now. Be sure to read through the description of these three commands, however, so that you will be familiar with their capabilities when you need to use them.

The T (Transfer) Command

Use:	Moves lines from one EDLIN file to another
Example:	`8tb:schedule`

T is yet another line-moving EDLIN command, but in this case it moves lines of text from one file to another, not to different locations within a file.

Let's consider a hypothetical situation in which you would use this command. You have another file on the disk in drive B entitled "schedule." This file contains a list of appointments you want included in your "chores" file. You want to merge these two files.

You are going to add the contents of "schedule" to the "chores" file right before your tennis engagement, which is line number 8. The T command requires you to give EDLIN the following pieces of information: the line before which you want the text from the other file to be transferred, the drive containing the disk that holds the other file, and the filename (with its extension if necessary) of the other file. The T command for merging these files looks like the following:

```
*8tb:schedule<Enter>
```

The contents of "schedule" now appear in the "chores" file, located immediately before line 8. But what about the schedule file? Is it gone? No, not to worry. The file that is transferred is not changed in any way. The T command simply copies the text from the other file into your current file; it does not remove the text.

The W (Write) Command

Use: Writes lines to a disk from a file in memory

Example: `2222w`

As mentioned earlier, you may at some point be working with EDLIN files so large that they exceed the 75 percent memory capacity EDLIN allocates for file size. In this case you will need to work with your file in parts.

You know when an entire file is not in memory, because EDLIN does not return the "End of input file" prompt after you load the file. Instead only the asterisk appears.

To access the part of your file that is still on the disk you must first clear out some space in memory. This is the function of the W command. To use W, enter the number of lines to be written back to the disk, followed by the command:

```
*2222w<Enter>
```

In response, EDLIN writes the first 2222 lines back to the disk. If you enter W without any line numbers, EDLIN writes back lines until memory is 25% full.

The A (Append) Command

Use: Writes lines from a disk into memory

Example: `2222a`

After you have made room using the W command, you want to transfer the next section of your file into memory. The A command adds new text to the EDLIN file currently in memory. This command also uses the specified line number as a total count of lines to be moved. To add 2222 lines to the file, enter the following command:

```
*2222a<Enter>
```

If you don't specify any line numbers here, EDLIN automatically fills memory up to its 75 percent working capacity.

It is unlikely that you will be using the W and A commands in the near future; they are required only for editing very large files.

Well, strike the set and call it a wrap. That's EDLIN in it's entirety. Although a lot of information was presented in this chapter (and much of it may seem intimidating to you right now), don't worry. EDLIN is just like acting; after a while you have your stage directions down pat, and you can get on with the show. In this chapter you have learned what an editor is and how to use the MS-DOS EDLIN editor. In addition to creating a new file, you now know how to use all the EDLIN commands: E, Q, L, I, D, S, R, M, C, T, W, and A. If you can make a word out of that, go to the head of the class!

Users of MS-DOS 5.0 can now go to the next chapter to learn how to use the new MS-DOS full-screen editor. If you have an earlier version of MS-DOS, you will probably want to skip the next chapter and go directly to Chapter 7, which explains lots of fascinating facts about files and how to use MS-DOS commands to manage the files you create and edit with EDLIN.

Editor's Choice

6

- A New Edition
- Eeek! A Mouse in the House?
- Ready for a Screen Test?
  - Take it from the Top
  - Stage Left, Stage Right
  - Rolling the Credits
  - What's Next on the Menu?
  - Let's Have a Little Dialog
- Send It to Rewrite
  - Take It Away
  - The Cutting Room
  - Searching for Fame and Fortune
- Finishing Touches
  - A Little Help from Your Friends
  - Customizing the Edit Program
  - It's a Wrap

6 Editor's Choice

Many people think of computers as tools for "number crunching." Actually, the most work done on personal computers involves words, not numbers. Think of all the information you have to keep track of in your business and personal life: shopping lists, "to-do" lists, schedules, reminders, and other notes. Now think of the various forms of written communication: "while you were out" messages, quick notes, memos, letters, and reports. Of course, the need to work with words isn't confined to business settings; you may use your PC at home for writing letters, sending out invitations, and making lists of household chores, or your kids may use it to do their homework.

Equipped with the appropriate software, your PC is a superb tool for keeping track of written information and communicating with words. With a *word processor* you can write letters, reports, and books. Most of today's word processors are powerful but rather complicated. They come with commands for specifying margins, headers, footers, fonts (typefaces), and other details about text layout and printing. The most sophisticated word-handling programs are those used for *desktop publishing*, which involves the complete layout and typesetting of documents such as brochures, advertisements, and books.

This book cannot teach you how to use all the sophisticated word processing and desktop publishing packages available today, but this chapter can be an important first step. We will show you how the MS-DOS text editor, Edit, can help you create useful text documents, such as lists and letters. The Edit program is available starting with MS-DOS version 5.0. If you have an earlier version, we suggest that you browse through this chapter anyway. What you learn about Edit and other new MS-DOS features might make you decide to upgrade your MS-DOS to version 5.0. We should also note that text-editing programs similar in design and function to Edit are available with many programs, including Borland's SideKick, Central Point Software's PC Tools, and others. You can use these programs without upgrading your MS-DOS version.

A New Edition

If you read Chapter 5 and learned to use EDLIN, you know that EDLIN is a text-editing program. Specifically, it is a *line editor*, a program that works with text line by line. As such, it has distinct disadvantages. For example, if you run EDLIN to type in a list of ten items and then decide you want to change item 7 from "wash the car" to "walk the dog," you must first tell EDLIN that you want to work with line 7 and then type in a replacement line that has "walk the dog" in it.

Actually, you probably won't remember where the text you want to change is, so you'll have to list lines 1 through 10 on the screen, look for the right one to change, and then give the appropriate command. This process quickly becomes tedious if you have many changes to make in your document.

The Edit program, unlike its older cousin EDLIN, is a *screen editor* rather than a line editor. With Edit, you see a full screen's worth of your document, which makes it much easier to read and revise your text. Instead of having to specify line numbers, you simply move the cursor to the place where you want to make changes or additions. Instead of having to remember commands such as EDLIN's E, Q, L, I, D, S, R, M, C, T, W, and A (whew!), you can choose commands from lists, or menus, that are always available.

You will find that Edit is very easy to learn. Here are some things that Edit is good for:

- ❏ Making notes for future reference

- ❏ Writing short letters and memos

- ❏ Making all kinds of lists

- ❏ Writing batch files (see Chapter 10)

- ❏ Revising your AUTOEXEC.BAT or CONFIG.SYS file (see Chapters 9 and 13)

- ❏ Browsing through ASCII text files such as the "readme" files that often come with software packages

Edit, like EDLIN, uses ASCII (American Standards Committee for Information Interchange) text files. ASCII is a set of standard text characters that can be understood by MS-DOS and most software programs. Files created by Edit and EDLIN are often called *pure ASCII* files because they don't contain the invisible formatting characters that word processors usually add to ASCII files to make boldface, underline, italics, paragraph-boundaries, and other more sophisticated formatting specifications.

In fact, Edit gains important advantages by using pure ASCII files. Because the AUTOEXEC.BAT and CONFIG.SYS system control files must be pure ASCII, you can use Edit to create or revise these files without having to worry about messing them up with unsavory characters. Similarly, batch files (see Chapter 10) must also be in pure ASCII, as must the source code for programs in BASIC and other languages.

On the other hand, because Edit uses pure ASCII and doesn't include any formatting capabilities, it is not the best choice for making long reports or documents that require special layouts, type styles (such as bold, italic, and underline), or fonts. For such projects you will need a full-fledged word processor. What is especially nice, though, is that most of what you will learn in this chapter about moving the cursor, inserting and deleting text, using menus, and using the mouse will be applicable to word processors as well as to Edit.

Eeek! A Mouse In the House?

You may have heard that many "big cheeses" operate their computers today by using a pointing device called a *mouse* to interact with their software. You don't need a mouse to use Edit, but having one makes some operations easier. If you have a mouse, be sure to follow the installation instructions in your mouse manual. Usually a program called MOUSE.COM or MOUSE.SYS is run at start-up from the AUTOEXEC.BAT or CONFIG.SYS file, respectively. This program enables your software to receive instructions from and respond to the mouse. Note that you can use a mouse only with software that has been designed to use it, but many of today's programs support the mouse, including both Edit and the DOSSHELL program discussed in Chapter 12.

As shown in figure 6-1, a mouse is a small rectangular box that slides across the surface of your desk. As you move the mouse, a pointer (often shaped like an arrow or a little box) moves in the corresponding direction on the screen. Pushing the mouse directly toward the rear of your desk moves the pointer toward the top of the screen, while pulling it toward the front of your desk moves the pointer toward the bottom of the screen. It only takes a few inches of mouse movement to reach any part of the screen.

The mouse comes with two (sometimes three) buttons for making selections. How the buttons function depends on the software you're using. In Edit, only the first (leftmost) mouse button is used. Pressing the button once is called *clicking*. Clicking is the mouse equivalent of pressing <Enter> on the keyboard. Clicking the button with the mouse pointer over the name of a menu (a list of commands) opens the menu. Clicking the mouse while the pointer is over a particular item on a menu selects that item—in other words, it gives that command to the software.

Pressing and holding down the mouse button while you are moving the mouse is called *dragging*. With Edit and most word processors, you drag the mouse to select or highlight a block of text you want to delete or move. You can also drag the mouse to move a small rectangular slider along the *scroll bar* that runs along the edge of a text window to control which portion of your text appears in the window. Don't worry if these mouse techniques sound rather abstract now—we will illustrate them for you soon.

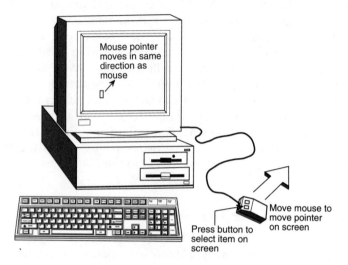

Fig. 6-1. Using a mouse.

Throughout this chapter we will first give the instructions for performing each operation with the keyboard and then the corresponding instructions for performing the operation with the mouse. If you don't have (or don't wish to use) the mouse, you can skip over the mouse instructions. We do suggest, however, that you at least try using the mouse. Most people do get the knack of using a mouse in about five minutes, and they never look back!

Ready for a Screen Test?

By now you know that in each chapter of this book we ask you to take on (what we hope is) an interesting persona or role. Today you will be a writer. You're trying to make a business of writing, starting out part-time. One day, while watching TV and trying to sneak past a bad case of writer's block, you get this crazy idea for a TV show. "Well, maybe not *too* crazy," you think to yourself. You decide to write a letter to your brother, who is a bigwig at a TV studio. Who knows? Perhaps this will be the start of something big!

Naturally, you want to write the letter on your new PC. You have MS-DOS 5.0, so you decide to kill two birds with one stone; you'll write the letter while learning how to use Edit.

Take It from the Top

To use Edit, you must have the files EDIT.COM and QBASIC.EXE on your current disk (hard disk users can run Edit from their hard disk as usual). To start Edit, simply enter its name at the MS-DOS prompt:

```
A:\>edit<Enter>
```

In the middle of the first screen you see (shown in figure 6-2) a box bearing the title "Welcome to the MS-DOS Editor." This is called a *dialog box*. Edit and many other modern programs use dialog boxes both to give you information about your current task and to ask you what you want to do next.

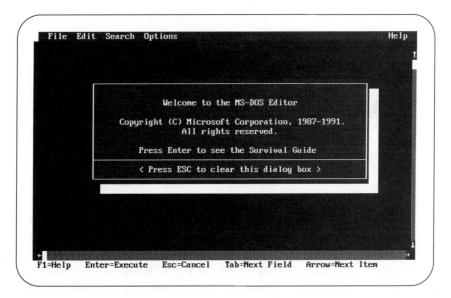

Fig. 6-2. Edit's opening screen.

Here you have two choices. You can press <Escape> to clear the screen or you can press <Enter> to see a "Survival Guide," some screens summarizing the essentials of using Edit. Since you will be learning how to use Edit step-by-step in this chapter, you can skip over the Survival Guide for now. Instead, press <Esc> (referred to as ESC in the dialog box) to clear the screen.

Figure 6-3 shows the important parts of the Edit screen. Along the top of the screen is the *menu bar*, with the words "File," "Edit," "Search," "Options," and—on the far right—"Help." As you will soon see, you select menus, or lists of commands, from the menu bar. Below the center of the menu bar is the name of the file currently being edited. Since you don't have any text yet, the file is called "Untitled."

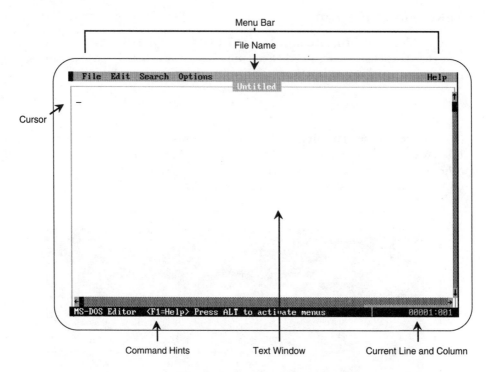

Fig. 6-3. Blank edit screen.

Look at the bottom of the screen. Here, Edit provides some helpful information about how to proceed. You are told that you can press <F1> for Help or press <Alt> to activate the menus. The information you see on the bottom line will vary with the command or function you are performing. This information is *context-sensitive*—it is designed to help you with whatever task you are trying to perform at the moment. Context-sensitive help is increasingly common in modern software.

In the center of the screen is the *text window*, in which you will enter the text of your letter. The small flashing line in the upper left corner of the text window on your screen is called the *cursor*. As you have seen when entering MS-DOS commands, the cursor marks the place where your next text character will be entered.

Stage Left, Stage Right

Now you're ready to start writing your letter. Just type in the lines shown in figure 6-4. (If you come across any spelling errors, type them as is—we'll correct them later.) Press <Enter> at the end of each line to move to the next one. Unlike word processors, Edit doesn't perform *word wrap*—it doesn't move the cursor and the word you are typing to the start of the next line when you reach the right margin. This lack of automatic formatting is one reason why Edit isn't suitable for long documents that you have to revise extensively. Be sure to skip a line between paragraphs. To skip a line, simply press <Enter> at the start of the line without typing any text.

If you make a mistake and catch it before you reach the end of the line, you can use the <Backspace> key to fix it. Later you will learn how to revise text anywhere on the screen.

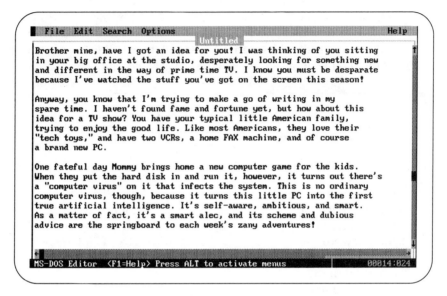

Fig. 6-4. Entering text.

Now that you've entered some text, you can practice moving the cursor. You can move the cursor anywhere in the text window and reach any part of your file to make insertions, deletions, or other changes. The cursor should now be just after the word "adventures" at the end of the text. Press <Up Arrow> to move the cursor up one line and place it under the letter *n* in *and*. Press <Left Arrow> and the cursor moves left to the *a*. Press <Right Arrow> to move the cursor back to the *n*. Note that moving the cursor doesn't actually change the text in your file.

You can also move left or right a whole word at a time. Press <Ctrl> <Right Arrow> and the cursor moves to the end of *and*. Press <Ctrl><Right Arrow> again to move the cursor to the start of the next word to the right, which is *dubious*. Repeatedly pressing <Ctrl><Right Arrow> moves the cursor to the right, one word at a time. Similarly, pressing <Ctrl><Left Arrow> moves the cursor to the start of the current word if it isn't there already. Repeatedly pressing <Ctrl> <Left Arrow> moves the cursor one more word to the left each time.

Keyboard Review

If you have trouble finding any of the keys mentioned in this chapter, please review Chapter 3. This chapter describes the standard and enhanced PC keyboards. Users of enhanced keyboards can move the cursor with the arrow and scrolling keys on either the numeric keypad or the separate cursor pad.

With the mouse it is even easier to move the cursor. Simply move the mouse until the mouse pointer (the small rectangle) is where you want the cursor to be; then press the left mouse button to place the cursor there.

It's time to summarize the key combinations we have discussed so far. Throughout the chapter we will use boxes like the following one to give you a handy reference to key combinations and procedures for accomplishing various tasks with Edit. To keep things simple, we aren't listing all the possible key combinations. You can use the on-line help (discussed later) to get a complete list.

Moving the Cursor

... from the Keyboard

To move the cursor	Press
Up one line	<Up Arrow>
Down one line	<Down Arrow>
Right one character	<Right Arrow>
Left one character	<Left Arrow>
Right one word	<Ctrl><Right Arrow>
Left one word	<Ctrl><Left Arrow>
To the start of the line	<Home>
To the end of line	<End>

... with the Mouse

To move the cursor	Action
Anywhere in the text window	Move pointer to desired position and press left mouse button.

Rolling the Credits

Now that you've got the hang of moving the cursor, let's add some more text to the letter. Move the cursor to the end of the text, press <Enter> twice to start a new paragraph, and type in the last paragraph, which is shown in figure 6-5. (Again, don't worry about spelling errors.)

Did you notice that as you added the last paragraph, some of the existing lines of text disappeared at the top of the screen? As you probably remember from Chapter 3, the movement of text off the screen as more text is added is called *scrolling*. This text has not been lost. There's an important difference between the listing of a DIR command, for example, scrolling off the screen and the text scrolling in Edit. With DIR and most MS-DOS commands, you can't go back and look at text that has scrolled away. With Edit, however, all the text is still in memory, and you can go back to it at any time. But to do so you need to learn how to use the scrolling keys.

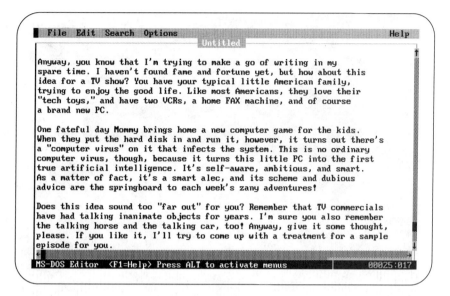

Fig. 6-5. Adding more text.

Press the <Pg Up> key, and you'll see that the beginning of your letter is still in memory. <Pg Up> moves "one page up" toward the beginning of the file. (A *page* here means one screenful of text.) Now press the <Pg Down> key, and the text moves one page down toward the end of the file. The cursor ends up where it began, at the end of the last paragraph. <Page Up> and <Page Dn> are very useful for "browsing" in a file, reading it a screen at a time, and perhaps going back to review previous material. You can jump directly to the beginning of the file by pressing <Ctrl><Home> or go to the end of the file with <Ctrl><End>. The latter key combination is especially handy if you are adding to a set of notes or a list.

You can scroll text with the <Up Arrow> and <Down Arrow> keys, too. Pressing <Up Arrow> when the cursor is on the top line of the screen scrolls the text one line at a time toward the beginning of the file. Similarly, pressing <Down Arrow> when the cursor is on the bottom of the screen scrolls the text one line at a time toward the end of the file.

With the mouse, you control text scrolling with the *scroll bars* at the right and bottom sides of the text window, as shown in figure 6-6. The scroll bar on the right side of the window controls upward movement (toward the beginning of the file) and downward movement (toward the end of the file).

Note the little arrows at the top and bottom ends of the up-and-down scroll bar. To scroll the text one line at a time toward the beginning of the file, move the mouse pointer until it is over the top arrow, and press the left button. Each time you press the button, another line of text scrolls into view. The bottom arrow works in exactly the same way, except that when you move the pointer over it and press the button, the text scrolls one line at a time toward the end of the file.

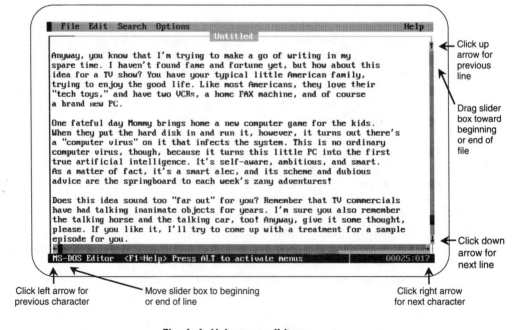

Click up arrow for previous line

Drag slider box toward beginning or end of file

Click down arrow for next line

Click left arrow for previous character

Move slider box to beginning or end of line

Click right arrow for next character

Fig 6-6. Using scroll bars.

By the way, it's awkward to have to say, "Move the mouse until the pointer is over the top arrow, and then press the button." Experienced mouse users simply say, "Click on the top arrow." From now on, when we say to "click on" something, we mean, "Move the mouse until the pointer is over that something, and then press the left button."

Scrolling Text

... from the Keyboard

To Scroll	Press
Up one screen	\<Pg Up>
Down one screen	\<Pg Dn>
To the beginning of the file	\<Ctrl>\<Home>
To the end of the file	\<Ctrl>\<End>
Up one line	\<Up Arrow> (with the cursor on the top line)
Down one line	\<Down Arrow> (with the cursor on the bottom line)
Left one character	\<Left Arrow>
Right one character	\<Right Arrow>

... with the Mouse

To Scroll	Action
Up one line	Click on the top arrow of the right scroll bar.
Down one line	Click on the bottom arrow of the right scroll bar.
Left one character	Click on the left arrow of the bottom scroll bar.
Right one character	Click on the right arrow of the bottom scroll bar.
To approximate position in file	Drag the slider box on the right scroll bar.

Now look at the main part of the scroll bar between the arrows, and you will see a small dark square. This is the *slider box,* and it lets you move quickly to an approximate location in the file. You move it by putting the mouse pointer over the box, then pressing the mouse button and keeping the button down. Now, as you move the mouse, the slider moves in the same direction. Experienced mouse users call moving the mouse while holding the button down *dragging.* For example, they would say, "Drag the slider box up or down." As you move the slider up, the text scrolls toward the beginning of the file; as you move the slider down, it scrolls toward the end of the file. The position of the slider box is proportional to the location of the cursor in the file. That is, if the slider box is two-thirds of the way down the scroll bar, then the current cursor position will be about two-thirds of the way through the file.

The scroll bar at the bottom of the text window works in the same way, except that it scrolls to the left or right. You use this scroll bar when a line of text is too long to fit on the screen. The arrow at the left scrolls one character at a time toward the beginning of the line, while the arrow at the right scrolls one character at a time toward the end of the line. Dragging the slider box to the left moves the cursor toward the beginning of the line; dragging it to the right moves it toward the end of the line. Press <Left Arrow> on your keyboard to scroll toward the beginning of a long line or <Right Arrow> to scroll toward the end. Press <Home> to go directly to the beginning of the line and <End> to go (you guessed it!) to the end.

We don't recommend entering text lines that are too long to fit on the screen. Finding and working with text in long lines is difficult, and many printers have trouble printing lines longer than 80 characters. Edit's lines can be up to 255 characters long, but this feature is mainly for the benefit of BASIC programmers. Many older BASIC programs include very long lines.

What's Next on the Menu?

Now that you've entered a fair amount of text, it's a good idea to save the file. To do so you must select the Save option from the File menu.

As you saw earlier, the *menu bar* runs along the top of the text window. To select a menu, press the <Alt> key and then the first letter of the name of the menu you want. Press <Alt>F to select the File menu. This done, a list of commands is displayed in a pull-down menu, as shown in figure 6-7.

To select a command in an open menu, press the highlighted letter of the command you want. Here you press "S", since it is the highlighted letter for the Save command. Note that the highlighted letter is not always the first one. You can also select a command by pressing the <Up Arrow> or <Down Arrow> key until the command you want is highlighted, and then press <Enter>.

Note that Edit gives you a brief description of the currently highlighted command at the bottom of the screen. For a quick review of each command, press the <Up Arrow> and <Down Arrow> keys to move the highlight on the menu, and look to the bottom of the screen to read the message pertaining to each command.

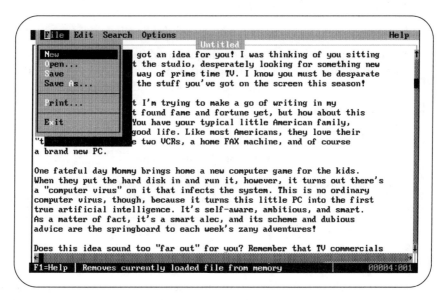

Fig. 6-7. The `File` **menu.**

Commands on the File Menu

Command	*Purpose*
New	Clears out memory and starts a new file
Open	Loads a file from disk
Save	Saves the current file to disk, using the current filename
Save As	Saves the current file to disk under a different name
Print	Sends the current file to the printer
Exit	Leaves Edit and returns to the MS-DOS prompt

You can also open menus and select commands with the mouse. To open a menu, click on the menu name. To select a command from an open menu, click on the command name or drag the mouse to the command name, and then release the button.

Opening Menus and Selecting Commands

... from the Keyboard

To select	*Action*
A menu	Press <Alt> and the first letter of the menu name.
A command in an open menu	Press the highlighted letter in the command name, or highlight the command with the arrow keys and press <Enter>.

... with the Mouse

To select	*Action*
A menu	Click on the menu name.
A command in an open menu	Click on the command name, or drag across the command name and release the mouse button.

Let's Have a Little Dialog

Once you've selected the Save command, Edit needs to know what name you want to give your file. Like most modern programs, Edit uses a *dialog box* to request this information. Figure 6-8 shows the dialog box for the Save command.

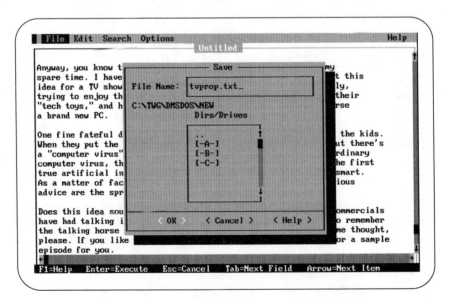

Fig. 6-8. Dialog box for the Save **command.**

Each dialog box is divided into a number of separate areas. Here, the first area is a *text box* with its own cursor. Text boxes appear whenever you have to type in some text. Usually, as in this case, the text is a filename. Below the File Name text box is a *list box* that lets you choose from a list of items. Here you use the list box to specify which disk drive and directory you want to use for saving your file. Finally, there are three *command buttons*: < OK >, < Cancel >, and < Help >. Selecting a command button and pressing <Enter> executes the operation. For example, selecting the < OK > button saves the file to the filename in the text box.

But let's not get ahead of ourselves. You've just opened the dialog box and the File Name text box is ready for your input. Type in a name for your letter. In our example, we used "tvprop.txt," which stands for "TV proposal." (You don't have to use the .txt extension, but it is a useful convention for identifying ASCII text files.) Remember that filenames are limited to eight characters plus the three-character extension. The < OK > command button at the bottom of the dialog box is already highlighted. We can simply press <Enter> to execute the save operation. That's it! You've now saved your file to the current disk under the name you specified.

But suppose you wanted to use a different disk. Or perhaps you decide you don't want to save the file yet. Once you have saved a file to disk, the Save command no longer displays the Save dialog box. It simply saves the file to the name you gave previously. This feature lets you quickly save and update your file on disk as you work.

As you know from Chapter 4, however, it is a good idea to have an "insurance copy" of your file on a different disk. To make a different copy of the current file, you use the Save As command.

Select Save As from the File menu. To do this, press <Alt>F and then "A" for Save As. Let's assume that the current drive is A but you want to save the file to drive B. Press <Tab> to move to the Dirs/Drives list box. Press <Down Arrow> until the B drive is highlighted. You have now told Edit to use the B drive. Press <Shift><Tab> to return to the File Name text box, and type in a name. We'll use "tvprop.bak" because this is a backup copy.

Finally, press <Tab> until the < OK > command button is highlighted (the brackets around it appear in white), and press <Enter> to complete the operation. You have now saved a backup copy of your letter on drive B and a copy of the original on drive A.

When you save the current file under a particular filename, that name ("tvprop.bak" in this case) becomes the "current" name—the name under which the Save command will now save the file. You don't want to work directly with your backup file—leaving it untouched during the session allows you to go back if you decide you don't like the changes you've made. To return to your original file and continue working, simply choose Save As again and save the file again as "tvprop.txt."

In dialog boxes, use <Tab> to move forward through the various areas and <Shift><Tab> to move backward. Another way to select an area of a dialog box is to press <Alt>, which highlights letters in the names of most of the areas, and then press a highlighted letter to select the area you want. In a text box, type in the text you need. In a selection box, use the arrow keys to highlight the item you wish to select. To execute the operation, use <Tab> or <Shift><Tab> to highlight the

⟨ OK ⟩ command button, and press ⟨Enter⟩. The ⟨ OK ⟩ button is highlighted when the dialog box appears, so you don't usually have to select it. To abandon the current operation without completing it, select the Cancel button and press ⟨Enter⟩.

As you might expect, you can also use the mouse in a dialog box. To work in a particular area of the box, simply click there with the mouse. To choose an item in a selection box, click on the item with the mouse. To execute a command, click the appropriate command button. It's fast and easy!

Working with Dialog Boxes

To:	*Do the following:*
Select an area of a dialog box	Press ⟨Tab⟩ to move forward or ⟨Shift⟩ ⟨Tab⟩ to move backward; or press ⟨Alt⟩ and the highlighted letter of the area name; *or* click with the mouse.
Select an item from a list box	Highlight it by pressing the ⟨Up Arrow⟩ or ⟨Down Arrow⟩ key; *or* click item with the mouse.
Select an item from an option box	Press the arrow keys to mark the option with a bullet; *or* click between the parentheses with the mouse.
Select an item from a check box	Press ⟨Tab⟩ to move to the desired item, and press ⟨Spacebar⟩ to put a check near it; *or* click in the check box with the mouse.
Enter text	Type text in the text box.
Execute a command	Select ⟨ OK ⟩, ⟨ Cancel ⟩, or ⟨ Help ⟩ command button by pressing ⟨Tab⟩ or ⟨Shift⟩⟨Tab⟩, then press ⟨Enter⟩; *or* click on the command button with the mouse.

Send It to Rewrite

So far so good. We need to add some more text to our letter, however. It needs addresses, a salutation, and a closing. Move the cursor to the beginning of the letter and press ⟨Enter⟩. Note that pressing ⟨Enter⟩ at the start of a line moves it and all subsequent lines down one line, leaving an empty line at the start of the letter. You can use this empty line to type in your addresses and salutation; use the text in figure 6-9.

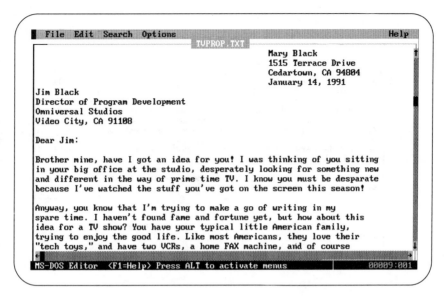

Fig. 6-9. Adding addresses and salutation.

Note that the return address is indented uniformly to the right. You use the <Tab> key to indent text. By default, each time you press <Tab> you move eight characters to the right. Press <Tab> six times to set up the indention, and then type "Mary Black" (or your own name if you wish) and press <Enter>. Instead of moving to the beginning of the next line, the cursor moves to the next line and lines up under the "M" in "Mary." This *auto-indent* feature is very handy for typing addresses and other indented text. When you have completed the four indented address lines, press <Enter> and then press <Home> to override the auto-indent and return to the left margin. You can now type the address and the salutation.

Now go to the end of the file and add the closing, "Fondest regards, Mary," as shown in figure 6-10. Don't forget to press the <Tab> key six times to indent and align the closing and the name.

Indenting Text

To:	*Do the following:*
Set up an indention	Press <Tab> until you reach the position you want.
Type indented text	Type each line and press <Enter>.
Return to left margin	Press <Enter>, then <Home>.

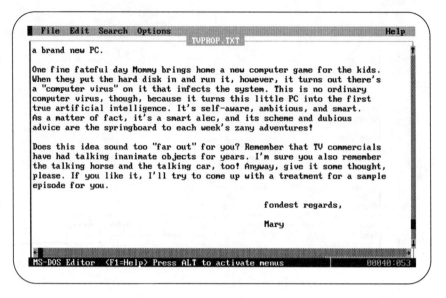

Fig. 6-10. Adding the closing.

Take It Away

Now might be a good time to proofread your work. Do you see any errors in spelling or word usage? Well, if you're a good proofreader you may have noticed in the accompanying illustration that the word "desparate" at the end of the third line of the body of the letter should be spelled "desperate." As a budding professional writer, you don't want to get a reputation for sloppy spelling, so let's fix this error.

Making corrections is simple. First, move the cursor to the area of your text that you want to revise, using the cursor movement keys discussed earlier. In our case, move the cursor to the first "a" in "desparate" (see figure 6-11). Now press <Delete> to remove the incorrect letter, and then press "e." That's it—you've now corrected the error.

If you continue proofreading, you may notice some other mistakes. For example, the third paragraph of the letter contains the phrase, "put the hard disk in and run it." Whoops! We meant to say, "put the floppy disk in and run it."

Move the cursor to the beginning of the word "hard" and press <Delete> four times to remove the word. There's also another, faster way to delete a word: press <Ctrl>T to delete the word all at once. Now type in the word "floppy."

By default Edit is in *Insert mode*, which means that any text you type is inserted automatically at the cursor, pushing existing text to the right to make room. Sometimes, however, it's handy to type over existing text rather than deleting and inserting it. The <Ins> key on your cursor or numeric keypad toggles Edit between the Insert and Overtype modes. Once you press <Ins> the characters you type will replace (type over) the existing characters. Press <Ins> again and you are back in Insert mode, and new text will be inserted rather than typed over existing text. To remind you which mode you are in, Edit changes the cursor from an underline to a little box when you are in Insert mode.

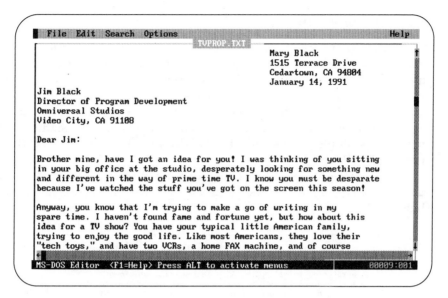

Fig. 6-11. Making a correction.

The mouse is also useful for making corrections. Simply click on the text where you want to make a change, and use any of the correction keys we have discussed. As you will soon see, you can also use the mouse to select text for deletion or other operations.

Making Corrections

To:	*Do the following:*
Start a correction	Move cursor to start of the text you want corrected; *or* click on the text with the mouse.
Delete characters	Press <Del> for each character you want to delete.
Delete a word	Press <Ctrl>T.
Delete a whole line	Press <Ctrl>Y.
Delete the rest of the current line	Press <Ctrl>Q, Y.
Insert text	Type the text at the cursor.

Now, finish your proofreading, and make any other necessary corrections.

The Cutting Room

Sometimes you want to make large revisions to your text. For example, you might decide to change the order of paragraphs or of items in a list. A text editor is especially useful because it allows you to put down your thoughts and later reorganize your ideas. Edit lets you select text—a word, line, paragraph, or more—and then delete the text, move it to another location in your file, or copy it elsewhere in your file.

To get some practice in selecting and manipulating text, start by adding the new paragraph (beginning with "Here's why") shown in figure 6-12. (Part of this paragraph is highlighted; we'll explain why shortly.) Note that this paragraph includes a bulleted list with four items, each starting with the letter "o" to represent the bullets. Type in the text, indenting with <Tab> and <Spacebar> to create the bulleted list.

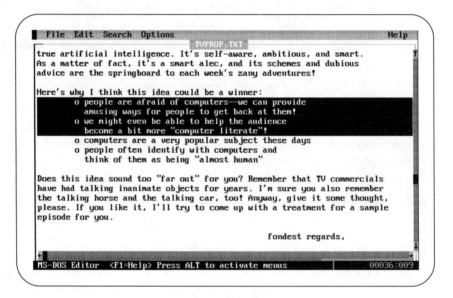

Fig. 6-12. Selecting text.

Suppose that after looking over the list you see that the first two items should be placed after the last two, and you decide to move them. But before you can move or otherwise manipulate text, you must select the text you want to work with. To select text, use the cursor keys to move to the start of the text, or click with the mouse at the start of the text. With the keyboard, select text by holding down the <Shift> key while pressing the appropriate arrow key. In this case, once you have put the cursor at the start of the first line in the list, hold down the <Shift> key and press <Down Arrow> three times, and then release <Shift>. The first two list items (four lines of text) will be highlighted as shown in the illustration.

To select text with the mouse, click on the beginning of the text, drag the mouse to the end of the text, and release the mouse button.

Selecting, Moving, Copying, and Deleting Text

To:	Do the following:
Select text	Move the cursor to the beginning of the text; or click there with the mouse. Hold down <Shift> while moving the cursor to the end of the selection, or drag mouse to the end of the selection.
Move selected text	Choose Cut from the Edit menu or press <Shift><Del>. Move the cursor where the text is to be inserted; Choose Paste from the Edit menu, or press <Shift><Ins>.
Copy selected text	Choose Copy from the Edit menu or press <Ctrl><Ins>; move cursor where the text is to be copied; Choose Paste from the Edit menu, or press <Shift><Ins>.
Delete selected text	Press <Del>.

You've now selected the text. You use the Edit menu to choose operations to perform on the selected text (see figure 6-13). Because you want to move the selected text, you will perform two operations: first Cut, then Move. Choose Cut from the Edit menu; the selected text disappears. Now move the cursor down below the last item in the list, open the Edit menu again, and choose Paste. The text now reappears in the new position, as shown in figure 6-14.

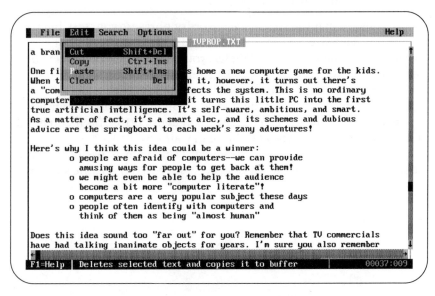

Fig. 6-13. The Edit **menu.**

It is important to remember that Edit holds only one piece of cut text at a time. If you cut some text and want to move or copy it rather than just discard it, perform the "paste" operation before cutting more text.

You may have noticed some shortcut keys to the right of each item on the Edit menu. You can speed up your text revision by learning to use these shortcut keys. Figure 6-14 shows the revised text.

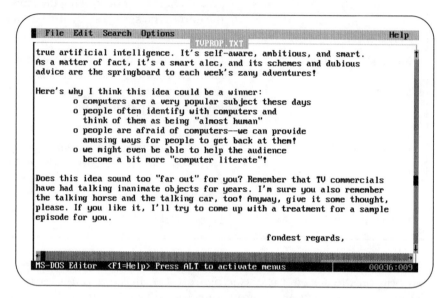

Fig. 6-14. Text has been moved.

Searching for Fame and Fortune

Sometimes you may want to change a word or phrase in your text, but you're not sure where it is. Likewise, you may want to find a particular topic, but you've forgotten where it is in your document. Edit lets you search for a string of text or replace one string of text with another. A *string*, remember, is computerese for a group of characters such as a word or phrase.

For example, let's find the phrase "computer literate" in our text. To do this, open the Search menu, which is shown in figure 6-15. This menu has three items. Choose Find to find a word or phrase in your text. Repeat Last Find repeats the search for the last string you specified. (This item is useful for finding several identical phrases in your text.) Choose Change to replace one string with another.

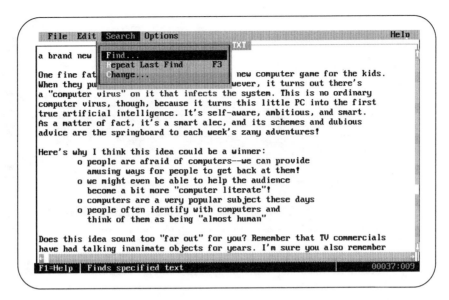

Fig. 6-15. The Search **menu.**

Choose Find, and you will see the Find dialog box shown in figure 6-16. Type "computer literate" into the text box. This is your search string, the phrase that the program will look for in your document. Note the two check boxes in the dialog box. Match Upper/Lowercase lets you conduct a case-sensitive search—that is, to look for phrases with upper- and lowercase letters identical to those in your search string. If you check this box, "computer literate" won't match "Computer Literate." You usually won't want to use this option. The other check box, Whole Word, lets you match a string only if it is a whole word, not part of another word. For example, if you were searching for just the word "compute," you would check this box to keep the program from matching "computer."

Here you don't have to check either box, so simply press <Enter> to perform the search. Since "computer literate" is in our text, the phrase is found and highlighted as shown in figure 6-17.

The Change item on the Search menu works similarly, except that you specify both a search string and something to replace it with. This is handy when you want to make a "global change"—that is, replace many occurrences of one word or phrase with another. Figure 6-18 shows the dialog box for the Change item.

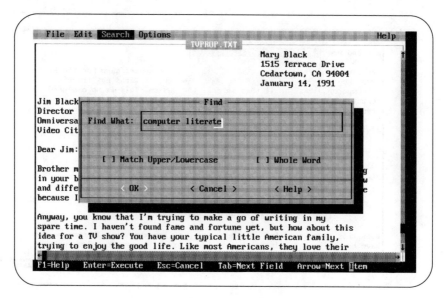

Fig. 6-16. Find **dialog box.**

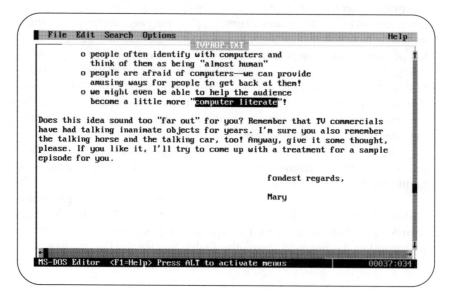

Fig. 6-17. Text found by a search.

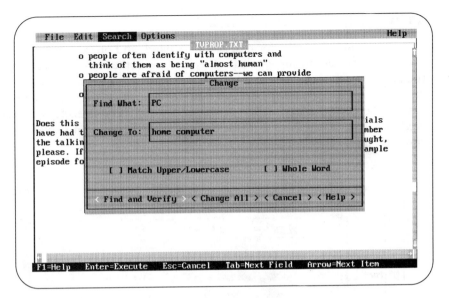

Fig. 6-18. Change **dialog box.**

Two command buttons help you to perform this operation. The Find and Verify command (located at the bottom of the dialog box) has the program stop at each occurrence of the search string and asks you whether you want to change it. Alternatively, the Change All command changes all occurrences without consulting with you. Be careful with this option!

Finding and Changing Text

To:	Do the following:
Find a string in text	Choose Find from the Edit menu, and type the string into the dialog box.
Repeat the last search	Choose Repeat Last Find from the Edit menu; or press <F3>.
Change one string to another	Choose Change from the Edit menu.

Finishing Touches

Your letter is now complete—you might want to save it to disk for future reference. There are still a few more things about Edit that are useful for you to know; probably the most important is how to get help.

A Little Help from Your Friends

Edit offers you help in the form of key, command, and procedure summaries. For example, consider the Change dialog box you saw in the last exercise. Suppose that you are confused about how to use this box. Simply press F1, and Edit will show you the Help screen for the Change dialog box (see figure 6-19). As you can see, you are given a brief but clear explanation of what you should do with each part of the dialog box. Similarly, if you have a menu open, press F1 to get an explanation of the currently highlighted menu item.

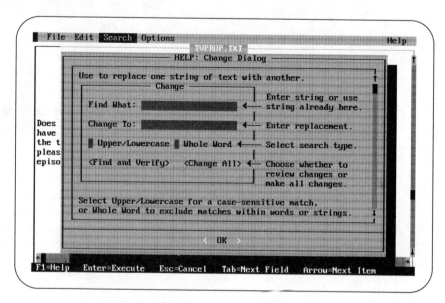

Fig. 6-19. Help for Change **dialog box.**

If you haven't used Edit for a while or you're simply at a loss over how to proceed, you can press F1 while the menu bar isn't active, and you will get general help for using Edit in the form of a "Survival Guide" (see figure 6-20). It summarizes the use of menus and commands, and tells you how to get more help.

As the Survival Guide explains, you can choose one of the highlighted topics, "Getting Started" and "Keyboard," by moving to it with the <Tab> or <Shift><Tab> keys and pressing <Enter>, or by clicking on the topic with the mouse. Select the "Keyboard" topic.

Take a look at the Keyboard help screen shown in figure 6-21. Note that it is further broken down into topics that represent categories of keys. Select Cursor Movement Keys. The Cursor Movement Keys help screen tells you how to move the cursor around the screen with your keyboard (see fig. 6-22).

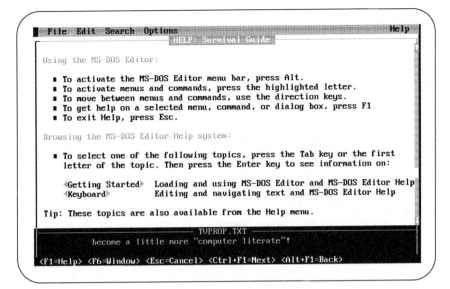

Fig. 6-20. Survival guide.

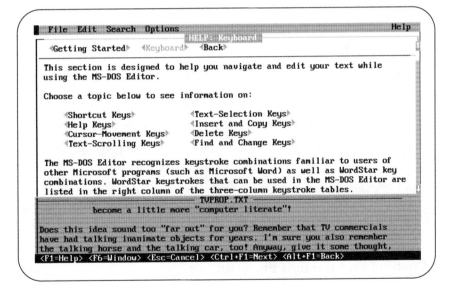

Fig. 6-21. Keyboard help screen.

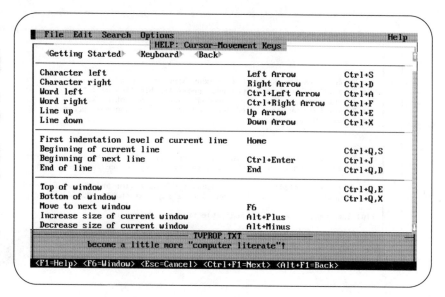

Fig. 6-22. Cursor Movement Keys help screen.

Getting Help

To get help on:	*Use:*
A highlighted menu item	F1 when the menu is open
A dialog box	F1 when the dialog box is open
General procedures	F1 when menu bar is not active
Using the editing keys	Choose Keyboard help or "Survival Guide" from the Help menu
A topic on a help screen	<Tab> or <Shift><Tab> and <Enter>, *or* click on the topic with the mouse

---

Customizing the Edit Program

You can change some aspects of the way Edit works. For example, you can change the colors Edit uses to display text. To do so, choose Change Colors from the Options menu. Look at the dialog box, and press F1 to get an explanation of its operation.

You can also specify filenames or command switches when starting Edit. If you know the name of the file you want to work with, give the filename following the word Edit on the MS-DOS command line, as in the following:

```
A:\>edit tvprop.txt<Enter>
```

If you have an EGA or VGA display, you may want to add the /h switch when starting Edit. This switch tells Edit to use as many screen lines as can be handled by the display (normally 43 for EGA and 50 for VGA). The text may be a bit harder to read, but you'll see more of it at one time on your screen.

It's a Wrap

Well, we've come to the end of our tour of Edit, and you deserve a tangible reward for your efforts. If you have a printer connected to your computer, turn it on, and choose Print from the File menu. You will see the Print dialog box, which has two check boxes: Selected Text Only and Complete Document. The Selected Text Only option prints only text that you have selected with the selection keys. This option is useful when you want to make a copy of part of your document, such as someone's address or a bibliographical reference. Usually, however, you will use the Complete Document option, which is the default. Press <Enter> to select this default, and the printer will produce a complete copy of your letter.

We're sure that you've passed your "screen test" with flying colors. You'll soon be a pro at creating and revising text files (though we can't guarantee that you'll become an award-winning TV scriptwriter). Now that you're creating files, it's time to move on to the next chapter, where you'll learn how to organize and manage all those files!

Getting the Files in Shape

7

- What Exactly Is a File?
- What's in a Name?
- Official Rules and Regulations
    - Avoiding Hyperextension
    - Set Specific Goals
- Commands, Inside and Out
    - Internal and External Commands
- The Great American Novel
- Reviewing What You Wrote
- Where Is the Carbon Paper?
    - May the Source Be with You
    - Being Redundant
- A Rose by Any Other Name
- Wiped Out

7 Getting the Files in Shape

Now you're ready to run the full mile and find out "everything you ever wanted to know about files." You've done your stretching exercises by learning the DIR and CLS commands. You've mentally prepared yourself by studying about disks and becoming acquainted with the FORMAT and DISKCOPY commands. And you've taken a practice lap by creating a file with EDLIN or EDIT. You're ready for the MS-DOS marathon!

What Exactly Is a File?

The term "file" is not unknown to you. You've been working with files for a while now. You listed files with DIR, copied files with DISKCOPY, and created files with EDLIN or EDIT. In this chapter you will learn about the intricacies of naming files and how to use MS-DOS to manage your files. First a quick summary.

A file is a group of related data, stored together in one location. *File* is not a term restricted to the high-tech world of computers—you use files every day in a variety of ways. When you stack all your phone bills in one pile, you're creating a file. When you add a memo to a project report at work, you're expanding a file. When you delete from your address book the names of people who moved away ten years ago, you're updating a file.

Computer data files perform this same organization and storage function, but they happen to reside on disks (see fig. 7-1). When DIR displays the contents of a disk, it details the information about each file—its filename, its size in bytes (remember that each byte represents one character in a text file), and the time and date the file was created or last modified. To MS-DOS all data is part of one file or another.

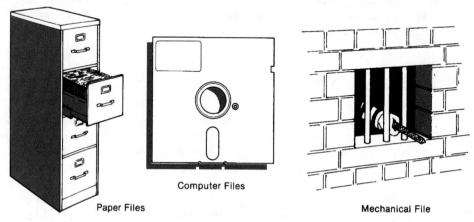

Paper Files   Computer Files   Mechanical File

Fig. 7-1. Types of files.

Of course, "file" is also a verb, as in filing your income tax or filing it away in the "to be done" drawer, or even "filing your way to freedom," but in this discussion, file is a noun and defines a collection of related data.

What's in a Name?

To be created, stored, and retrieved, files must be named. Otherwise how would MS-DOS differentiate among the thousands of files it has to keep track of? And how would you know what was in each of those files? To alleviate confusion, MS-DOS has established a very simple rule.

The Golden Rule of Filenaming

Each file on a disk must have a unique name!

The reasons for this rule are pretty obvious to anyone who has been blessed with a common name such as Mary or John, or Smith or Johnson. Someone calls out a name and you, along with five or six other people, questioningly point at yourself or hesitantly raise your hand. Well, the same is true of your files. If more than one had the same name, MS-DOS would be totally confused. You have to be very specific.

Here is another example of the necessity for unique names. Imagine a group of participants all milling around at the beginning of a track meet. If the announcer calls over the loudspeaker, "Racers to their marks, please," confusion reigns. Which racers for which race to which marks? This problem is solved by adding specific information that clarifies the instructions: "Attention participants in the 400-yard dash: racer 2 report to lane 1, racer 4 report to lane 2, racer 6 report to lane 3, and racer 8 report to lane 4." Adding specific identifications clears up ambiguities and assures that everyone is in the correct location.

Here's how this same confusion might happen within DOS. One of the commands you will learn about in this chapter is COPY. Typing the command as follows will drive MS-DOS toward a nervous breakdown:

```
A:\>copy<Enter>
```

Copy what, from where, to where? In just a second you'll see how to enter this command with all the necessary information.

Official Rules and Regulations

When you assign each file a unique filename, all these problems are laid to rest. Now both you and MS-DOS know exactly which file is to be created, modified, operated upon, or stored away. A filename must follow this pattern:

filename.extension

The filename can be one to eight characters. An optional extension, not exceeding three characters, may be added to the name. When you give a filename an extension, use a period to separate the extension from the filename itself.

Filenames must follow one additional rule. They must be made up of valid characters. MS-DOS makes this pretty simple:

Valid Characters for Filenames

Letters of the alphabet

Numbers one through zero

Special characters: $ # & @ ! % (_)

The exact list of special characters may vary slightly, depending on the version of MS-DOS on your machine.

In general, the following symbols may not be used in filenames:

Invalid Characters for Filenames

. (period, except to delineate an extension)

: (colon)

- (hyphen)

/ (slash)

? (question mark)

< (less than)

> (greater than)

\ (backslash)

¦ (vertical bar)

* (asterisk)

These symbols have special meanings in MS-DOS and are misinterpreted if included in a filename.

Also, some perfectly legal names are already taken; they belong to important files used by MS-DOS to perform its commands and functions. For example, the FORMAT command you learned earlier is actually run by a program file called FORMAT.COM or FORMAT.EXE (depending on your version of MS-DOS). While you *could* use a name like FORMAT.COM for your own files, you wouldn't want to because you might wipe out the program and not be able to use it any more. You ask, "Does that mean that I have to memorize the names of all the special MS-DOS files so that I won't accidentally use their names for my own files?" No, not really. Program and system files normally end with extensions like .COM, .EXE, and .SYS. If you avoid using those extensions for your own files, you shouldn't have any problems.

Another group of special names to avoid using consists of device names. These are abbreviations that MS-DOS uses to refer to specific pieces of computer equipment such as the printer or the screen. If you use these combinations of characters in filenames, MS-DOS gets confused. Again, this list may vary from system to system. To be really sure about filename limitations, check your computer's user's guide.

Reserved Filenames and Device Names

Special Filenames and Device Names

4201.CPI	COMP.EXE	EDIT.COM	GRAPHICS.PRO
4208.CPI	CON:	EDIT.HLP	HIMEM.SYS
5202.CPI	COUNTRY.SYS	EDLIN.EXE	JOIN.EXE
ANSI.SYS	DEBUG.EXE	EGA.CPI	KEYB.COM
APPEND.EXE	DISKCOMP.COM	EMM386.EXE	KEYBOARD.SYS
ASSIGN.COM	DISKCOPY.COM	EXE2BIN.EXE	LABEL.COM
ATTRIB.EXE	DISPLAY.SYS	FASTOPEN.EXE	LCD.CPI
AUX:	DOSKEY.COM	FC.EXE	LINK.EXE
BACKUP.EXE	DOSSHELL.VID	FDISK.EXE	LPT1:
CHKDSK.EXE	DOSSHELL.INI	FIND.EXE	LPT2:
COM1:	DOSSHELL.EXE	FORMAT.COM	LPT3:
COM2:	DOSSHELL.HLP	GRAFTABL.COM	MEM.EXE
COMMAND.COM	DRIVER.SYS	GRAPHICS.COM	MODE.COM

MORE.COM	PRINT.EXE	RECOVER.EXE	SMARTDRV.SYS
MOUSE.COM	PRINTER.SYS	REDIR.EXE	SORT.EXE
MSHERC.COM	PRN	REPLACE.EXE	SUBST.EXE
NLSFUNC.EXE	QBASIC.EXE	RESTORE.EXE	SYS.COM
NUL:	QBASIC.HLP	SETVER.EXE	TREE.COM
PARTDRV.SYS	RAMDRIVE.SYS	SHARE.EXE	UNFORMAT.EXE
			XCOPY.EXE

Seems like a pretty formidable list, huh? Well, believe it or not, by the time you finish reading this book you will know, and even be intimately acquainted with, at least half of these names.

Except for the special cases listed above, you can name your files almost anything. Here are some sample filenames:

    bills
    scores
    games
    letters

Just for convenience and to make typing them in easier, this book always shows filenames in lowercase letters. When you use filenames in commands, you can enter them in either upper- or lowercase. In this book, filenames referred to in the text are enclosed in quotation marks (" "). Don't include the quotation marks when using the filename in MS-DOS commands.

A FILE BY ANY OTHER NAME

DAN DISK AND HIS DISKETTES

Avoiding Hyperextension

A three-character extension in any filename is optional. Extensions are useful for clarifying or categorizing the contents of a file. Assume, for example, that you have a file named "letters." If you put all your letters in this one file, not only would it be very large, it would also be extremely difficult to use. Each time you wanted to look at a specific letter, you would have to search through the entire file. By subdividing this file into three smaller files with identifying extensions, you can save yourself a lot of time and trouble:

letters.bus	These are your business letters
letters.sue	These letters are of a more personal nature
letters.tax	Legal correspondence concerning tax shelters

At first glance it would seem that these three files violate the sacred uniqueness rule for filenames. All the files are named "letters"! But the extension, as a part of the filename, can be the differentiating factor. Sometimes it is even desirable to use similar filenames to group related files together. However, be prudent in doing so, because too many similar filenames can cause you confusion.

Although you can use any valid character in an extension, a loose sort of convention has grown up among software designers to give certain types of files certain extensions. A few extensions are mandatory because they tell MS-DOS what to do with a file. For example, .BAS refers to a file that is written in BASIC source code. All BASIC files must have this extension. MS-DOS recognizes files with a .BAT extension as "batch files." (Batch files are discussed in Chapter 9.) Here are some of the most frequently used filename extensions:

.BAK	A backup copy of a text file
.BAS	A BASIC source-code file
.BAT	A batch-processing file
.COM	An executable program in memory-image format
.DAT	A general data file
.EXE	An executable program in relocation format
.TXT	A text file from a word processor

Many software packages have their own special file extensions. Microsoft Word, for example, uses the extension .DOC for its text files, and Lotus 1-2-3 uses the extension .WKS for its spreadsheet files.

Don't worry if you don't understand these explanations. As you work more with application programs, you will soon recognize extensions that are important to you. Meanwhile, the most important rule of naming files is to assign a name that makes sense to you. Although you can use many special symbols in filenames, what good is a file when you can't remember what's inside it?

Pop Quiz on Filenames

What's wrong with these filenames?

(Cover up the answers on the right-hand side of the page)

ZZ;#9HUH.YUK   This is a legal filename, but what's in it?

MYOWN/.TEXT   Two things are wrong here: the slash (/) is an illegal character, and there are too many characters in the extension.

FASTNOTES   A filename can have only eight characters.

COPY.BAS   Unless this is a BASIC program, you may run into trouble.

DING.BAT   This is a perfectly valid filename, and I'm sure you'd remember what you put in it!

Set Specific Goals

The name of a file is made up of the filename (up to eight characters) and the optional extension (up to three characters). But when you use a filename in a command, MS-DOS must have one more piece of information—which drive contains the disk that holds the file? You direct MS-DOS to the correct drive by including the letter of the drive (the drive indicator a: or b:) in the filename. You were introduced to this concept in Chapter 4 when you learned about the "current" drive and source and target disks.

Here's a quick review on drive indicators:

A:\>dir a:games   The drive indicator is optional because A is the current drive (as shown by the A prompt).

A:\>dir games   Produces the same results as the previous command.

A:\>dir b:games   The drive indicator is mandatory because the file is not on the disk in the current drive.

B:\>dir a:games   The same situation in reverse.

A:\>format b: Drive indicator is mandatory for MS-DOS to perform the operation on the correct disk.

A:\>diskcopy a: b: When you transfer data from one disk to another, it is a good idea to include both drive indicators.

Because you are going to use the COPY command later in this chapter, learning to use drive indicators takes on added significance. These three elements of a filename—the name itself, the optional extension, and the drive indicator—make up a file specification.

File Specification

drive indicator: + filename + .extension (optional)

And that's all you really need to know about naming files. This is one area where you can let your imagination run free; just remember a few special rules (see fig. 7-2).

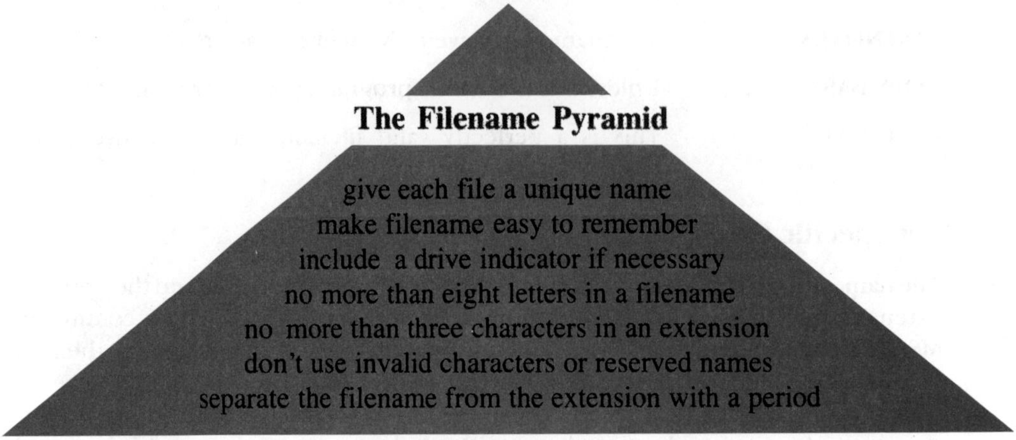

The Filename Pyramid

give each file a unique name
make filename easy to remember
include a drive indicator if necessary
no more than eight letters in a filename
no more than three characters in an extension
don't use invalid characters or reserved names
separate the filename from the extension with a period

Fig. 7-2. The filename pyramid.

Now that you've conquered filenaming, it's time to expand your routine a bit. Breathe deeply and jump into the command workout.

Commands, Inside and Out

Just as "file" was familiar to you from earlier chapters, so is the term "commands." You've been issuing commands since your first DIR experience. But now you are going to expand on that knowledge.

Command is another word that is not restricted to computer use. Any of you who have been in the army or have suffered through dog-obedience courses with lovable Rover know about commands. Commands are simply clear and comprehensible instructions.

Commands in MS-DOS are instructions to the computer. As mentioned earlier, MS-DOS, while true and loyal, is rather stupid. It can only understand instructions when they follow a preordained pattern. The commands you give MS-DOS must be very specific. Fortunately for users, MS-DOS commands make sense in English, too. It's pretty simple, now that you have used them a few times, to remember that DIR stands for DIRectory, and CLS stands for CLear the Screen, while FORMAT and DISKCOPY are self-explanatory. You'll find the commands in this chapter just as clear and concise.

Internal and External Commands

Some commands are resident in your computer's RAM (transient) memory whenever you are operating under MS-DOS control, that is, whenever you are responding to the MS-DOS prompt A:\>, B:\>, or C:\>. These commands are called internal because they are inside the machine's memory, ready for use whenever you are operating in MS-DOS. The following list shows the most commonly used MS-DOS internal commands.

Internal Commands	
COPY	Makes copies of files
DATE	Sets or displays the date
DIR	Displays a list of files
ERASE (DEL)	Eliminates a disk file
RENAME	Changes a file's name
TIME	Sets or displays the time
TYPE	Displays the contents of a file

The internal commands in your version of MS-DOS may include other commands. Check your user's guide for the internal commands associated with your system.

The important thing to remember about internal commands is that you can use them any time after you have booted your system, without reinserting your system disk (see fig. 7-3). For instance, you might be running a program off the disk in drive A—for example, a word processing program. You have finished with the file, which is on the disk in drive A, and you want to copy it to drive B. After exiting the word processing program, you return to the MS-DOS system prompt. Your word processing program is on disk 1, now in drive A. The file you want to copy is also on disk 1. Disk 2 is in drive B. It contains text files and is the target disk for your newly completed file.

Because COPY is an internal command, you can use it without removing your word processing disk from drive A. The command is in memory, available for use regardless of which disks are in the drives. Use caution, however; there is more to copying files. Before you copy anything, read the section on the COPY command later in this chapter.

Most MS-DOS commands do not make their home inside RAM memory, which means they are not available when you are "in" MS-DOS. These "external" commands must be loaded from the operating-system disk when you need them. To use these commands, you must either be able to access the external commands from a system disk in drive A or be running MS-DOS from a hard disk (see fig. 7-4).

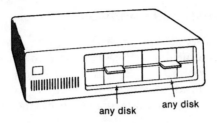

Boot system with MS-DOS disk.
Internal commands are always available.

Fig. 7-3. Using an internal command.

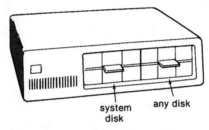

Boot system with MS-DOS disk.
Must have system disk in drive A
for external commands.

Fig. 7-4. Using an external command.

When you enter a command, MS-DOS first checks whether the command is internal. If the command is not found, MS-DOS goes out to the system disk to find and load the command. If it is not on the disk, or you don't have a system disk in the drive, MS-DOS sends you a nasty error message such as

```
Bad command or file name
```

FORMAT is an example of an external command. In the hypothetical example above (word processing disk in drive A, and data disk in drive B), you may occasionally find yourself in a bit of a pickle. You want to transfer the file on disk 1 to a new disk, disk 3, but first you need to FORMAT a disk to receive the data.

Since FORMAT is an external command you must have a system disk in a drive to make use of this command. (That is why you should have several formatted disks handy at all times.) To execute the FORMAT command, you must first remove your word processing disk and insert the system disk. Only now are you ready to use the FORMAT command. (Of course, you'd better also remove the data disk from drive B and insert a new blank disk before entering the FORMAT command, or you can say goodbye to the data currently on the disk in drive B.)

Easier External Commands for Hard Disk Users

If you are running MS-DOS from a hard disk and your system has been properly set up, MS-DOS will always look on the hard disk for external commands. This means you can run external commands just as easily as internal commands, and you never have to worry about not having a system disk in drive A.

If you *do* get a "bad command or filename" error message and you are running MS-DOS from a hard disk, make sure that you haven't misspelled the name of the external command or program. If the error message repeats, see the discussion of the PATH command in Chapter 10 for the remedy to your problem.

Before you begin studying specific commands in detail, here are some helpful hints for entering all MS-DOS commands:

❑ Wait until you see the MS-DOS prompt (A:\>, B:\>, or C:\>) before entering a command. The prompt means DOS is ready and waiting.

❑ When a command requires a filename to operate, be sure to include all the necessary parts of the file specification (drive indicator, filename, and extension).

❑ Use a blank space to separate different parts of a command.

`format b:`	Leave a space between command and drive indicator.
`copy olddata b:`	Leave spaces between command, filename, and drive indicator.

❑ You can enter commands in either upper- or lowercase.

❑ When commands don't work, check your typing. Is the command correct, did you leave the appropriate spaces, did you spell the filename correctly? Are you trying to use an external command without inserting the system disk?

❑ End each command with the <Enter> key.

This chapter covers four MS-DOS commands: COPY, TYPE, ERASE, and RENAME. They are all internal commands. But before you start copying, typing, erasing (especially erasing), and renaming files, you need a file to use with these commands. So let's put your EDLIN skills to work and create a new file.

Put your backup system disk in drive A. Make sure that it contains a copy of the EDLIN.COM program. The file you create will also be located on this system disk.

The Great American Novel

Time to take on a new identity. In this chapter you are playing the role of a writer just embarking on a literary career. You are using your new personal computer to write your first work. Your book text will be contained in a file called "novel." Using EDLIN, enter the text of this file. (If you have MS-DOS 5.0, you might want to use the new EDIT program instead of EDLIN to write your "Great American Novel." See Chapter 6 for a tutorial on how to use EDIT.)

The first line of text is the title of this work, "EVEN MONEY":

```
A:\>edlin novel<Enter>
New file
*i <Enter>
        1:*EVEN MONEY<Enter>
```

As EDLIN returns new line numbers, enter the remainder of the text. You're only going to get through the opening paragraph in this session.

```
2:*There was a 50-50 chance the world would end today.<Enter>
3:*It was down to just the three of us now.<Enter>
4:*The "Stranger" kept watching the darkening sky.<Enter>
5:*Finally he saw the signal.<Enter>
6:*Tossing the quarter in the air, he laughed "Call it"...<Enter>
7:*
```

Press <Ctrl>C to exit the "insert" mode.

```
7:^C
```

Now give EDLIN the end-of-file command:

```
*e<Enter>
```

The system prompt tells you that MS-DOS is now back in control:

```
A:\>
```

If you want to, you can use DIR to verify that the file is on the disk.

```
A:\>dir novel<Enter>

 Volume in drive A has no label
 Directory of A:\

NOVEL              242 08-27-90  11:16a
        1 File(s)        242 bytes
                       29786 bytes free
```

Are you anxious to see your work in print? Well, let's use a new MS-DOS command to see the contents of this file. You had a preview of this command in Chapter 5.

Reviewing What You Wrote

The TYPE Command

Use:	Displays the contents of a file
Example:	`type novel`

TYPE is a very straightforward command. Used with a filename, it displays the contents of the file (see fig. 7-5). The text of the file must be in ASCII format, or you'll have a tough time deciphering it. If you missed it earlier, ASCII file format is discussed in detail at the beginning of Chapter 5. EDLIN and EDIT create files in ASCII code, so you will have no trouble reading your "novel":

```
A:\>type novel<Enter>
```

The file contents appear (without line numbers):

```
EVEN MONEY
There was a 50-50 chance the world would end today.
It was down to just the three of us now.
The "Stranger" kept watching the darkening sky.
Finally he saw the signal.
Tossing the quarter in the air, he laughed "Call it"...
```

Not bad for a beginner.

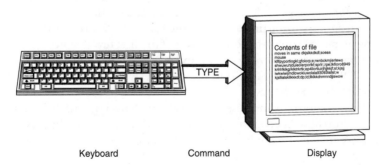

Keyboard   Command   Display

Fig. 7-5. The TYPE command.

By including a drive indicator in the TYPE command, you can view files on other disks. Suppose that you had created "novel" on the disk in drive B. This, then, is how you would ask to see the file:

```
A:\>type b:novel <Enter>
```

Since you don't currently have the file on the disk in B, this command will not work. But how do you go about making a backup of this copy to put on another disk?

Where Is the Carbon Paper?

In today's world of information proliferation, rarely do you make just an original of anything. From term papers to tax forms, it's always smart to keep a copy. When the documents are on paper, you type multiple copies or, more likely, run down to the friendly copy machine.

Copies are useful for many reasons. They are handy if two or more people are referring to the same document. They allow you to share information that might not otherwise be available to someone else. They provide a record of interaction between two companies or communication between two people. But by far the most persuasive argument for copies is that they provide "insurance" in case something should happen to the original. (This subject was discussed in some detail in Chapter 4.)

All these reasons for making copies hold true for your computer files, too. It is just as easy to copy a computer file as it is to copy a paper file, but you don't need any extra copying equipment. All you need is another disk. How important are copies? Let's pick up on the saga of "EVEN MONEY."

Much as you would like it, you can't earn a living as an unpublished author. Therefore, your writing times are squeezed between the demands of the office and the need for sleep. Naturally, this time is precious to you. Late one evening, you start to work on some changes that your agent has suggested. After hours of work, you have incorporated the revisions into the text. But the very next day your agent phones and says, "Scratch those changes; there may be a question of libel involved."

Unfortunately, while you were editing the work, you entered and exited the EDLIN program several times, so even the EDLIN backup file no longer contains your original version. You do have a printout of the first few chapters, but to put it on the computer requires entering lots of text again. MORAL OF ACT 1: MAKE A BACKUP OF YOUR ORIGINAL FILE (ON A SEPARATE DISK) BEFORE YOU MAKE ANY SIGNIFICANT CHANGES.

Here's another short lesson on copying. Now you finally have your book back in order. You have been talking to a friend in Chicago about the possibility of turning this book into a screenplay. He is anxious to see the latest revision; therefore, because you are going on vacation for a few days, you give him your disk. Wouldn't you know it—while he is sorting through his disks he spills a cup of coffee. Your disk was on top of the pile. MORAL OF ACT 2: MAKE A COPY OF ALL FILES BEFORE THEY LEAVE YOUR POSSESSION.

I'm sure that you are beginning to get the picture. The thing to remember about disk files, as opposed to paper files, is that unless you make one, there is no copy of anything in the file. You can't hunt through the wastepaper basket for the piece of information you deleted. But you can find it on a copy. Here are some reasons why you should make copies:

❑ For insurance

❑ In case you need a copy of an earlier version of a file

❑ To reorganize files

There are other, less drastic, reasons to make copies. You might also copy files when you want to put them in new groups on a disk or use parts of a file to reorganize its contents.

Earlier in this chapter you saw the advantage of grouping files by using extensions:

letters.bus
letters.sue
letters.tax

Suppose the "letters.bus" file has become too large to be efficient. Here's how you would use a copy to solve that problem. (Of course, you should already have an updated backup of this file before going any further.)

First, you make a copy of the entire "letters.bus" file. You want to make a new file that contains only the letters from the "Live Now, Die Later" company. By deleting all the other correspondence in your newly copied file, you are left with only the relevant letters. You then give this file a new name using RENAME (a command discussed later in this chapter). The result is the file "letters1.bus", which holds only a part of your original file "letters.bus" (see fig. 7-6).

In most cases you will be copying from one disk to another. This means that you have to tell MS-DOS where to find the original and where to put the copy.

Hard Disk Users Need Copies, Too!

If your system has a hard disk, you may be feeling a little smug. After all, you can put all your files on the hard disk and not worry about where to find them. Still, suppose you want to give someone a copy of your file. You can't hand them your hard disk. And while hard disks are quite reliable, they do have breakdowns. MORAL FOR HARD DISK USERS: Don't keep all your eggs in one basket. Always make at least one backup copy of each important file on a floppy disk! In Chapter 10 you'll learn how to use the BACKUP command to make an insurance copy of all the files on your hard disk.

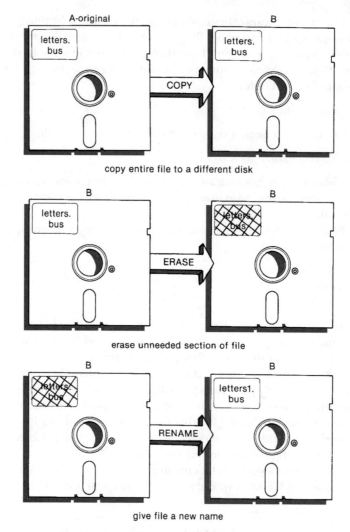

Fig. 7-6. Copying, erasing, and renaming files.

May the Source Be with You

You were introduced to the concept of source and target disks when you used the DISKCOPY command. They are equally important in the use of the command you are about to execute—the COPY command—and deserve a brief review here.

The source disk contains the original file. The target disk is the destination of the copied file. With two drives, the source is usually the disk in drive A, and the target is the disk in drive B. MS-DOS reminds you to keep track of your source and target:

```
Insert source diskette in Drive A
Insert target diskette in Drive B
```

The source and target disks are indicated by drive specifiers (a and b).

If you have a single-drive system, refer to the discussion of DISKCOPY (in Chapter 4) to review how MS-DOS "pretends" you have two drives.

With this theoretical discussion of why and when to make copies behind you, revert to your novelist's role as you learn to use the COPY command.

Being Redundant

The COPY command is very versatile. You will use this command frequently to copy a file from one disk to another, keeping the same name. (This is our old friend the backup.) Let's try this procedure now. To perform these copying exercises, you will need a formatted blank disk and your system disk containing the "novel" file.

The COPY Command

Use: Makes copies of a file or a group of files

Examples: ```
                copy a:novel b:
                copy a:novel b:bestsell
                copy novel bestsell
                ```

---

You want to make an "insurance" copy of your first edition of "EVEN MONEY." Take the disk containing "novel" (in this case, your system disk) and put it in drive A. This is your source disk. (It is just a coincidence that "novel" is on your system disk. Since COPY is an internal command, you do not have to have the system disk in a drive when you execute this command.) Put the disk that will contain the copy in drive B. This is your target disk.

The A:\> prompt shows that drive A is your current drive. Therefore, it is not necessary to include the drive indicator a: when referring to a file on this disk in this drive. Just to keep things clear, however, it's easier to include the drive indicator in these copy commands. As you become more at ease with MS-DOS, you will probably not include the drive indicator when it is unnecessary.

Okay, now copy "novel" to the target disk:

```
A:\>copy a:novel b:<Enter>
```

With this command you tell MS-DOS to copy the file "novel"—now on the disk in drive A—to the disk in drive B. The name of the copied file will also be "novel" (see fig. 7-7).

Here is how MS-DOS responds to this command:

```
1 File(s) copied
```

Short and simple, but to the point. This message says "fine"; your request has been honored. This message is a very convenient part of MS-DOS because it lets you know several things at once. It tells you that the specified file was found on the
```

indicated disk, that there is no problem with the target disk, and that the copying procedure is completed. If anything had gone wrong—for example, an incorrect disk inserted in A or an unformatted disk in B—you would have received an error message.

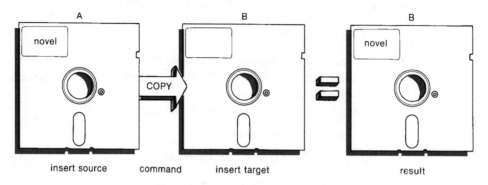

Fig. 7-7. Copying to a different disk.

This seems a little too simple. As a nervous writer, you want to be sure that the copy is on the disk in B. Relieve your skepticism by requesting verification with the DIR command:

```
A:\>dir b:<Enter>
```

MS-DOS responds:

```
Volume in drive B has no label
Directory of B:\

NOVEL              242 08-27-90  11:16a
        1 File(s)        242 bytes
                     361472 bytes free
```

You don't have to use the same name when you copy a file. Suppose you want to copy the file and try changing sections of it. You want a copy of the original and a copy to fool around with. You can copy the file and give it a new name. To do this, include a new filename in the COPY command. Try copying your file, but change the name (see fig. 7-8):

```
A:\>copy a:novel b:bestsell<Enter>
```

Again comes your confirmation:

```
1 File(s) copied
```

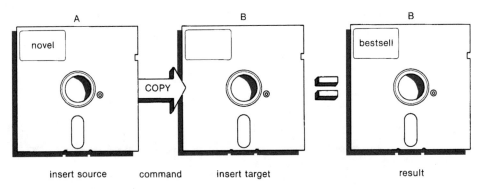

insert source   command   insert target   result

Fig. 7-8. Copying to a different disk, changing name.

If you have done both the preceding exercises, you now have two files copied on the target disk. One is called "novel" and the other is "bestsell." BOTH FILES CONTAIN EXACTLY THE SAME INFORMATION. To make sure that both copies are on the disk, use the DIR command:

```
A:\>dir b:<Enter>

Volume in drive B has no label
Directory of B:\

NOVEL            242 08-27-90  11:16a
BESTSELL         242 08-27-90  11:37a
        2 File(s)        484 bytes
                     361230 bytes free
```

You can also have two copies of a file on the same disk. To copy a file to the same disk, however, you have to give the file a new name, because NO TWO FILES ON THE SAME DISK CAN HAVE THE SAME NAME. Let's make a duplicate copy of "novel" on the disk in drive A. In this case, the disk in drive A is both our source and target disk. This time try leaving out the drive indicators:

```
A:\>copy novel bestsell<Enter>
        1 File(s) copied
```

You now have two copies of the file on the same disk. Only the names are different; the contents are the same (see fig. 7-9).

MS-DOS will not let you copy a file to a disk if that disk already contains a file with an identical filename. This handy reminder comes in the form of an error message:

```
File cannot be copied onto itself
        0 File(s) copied
```

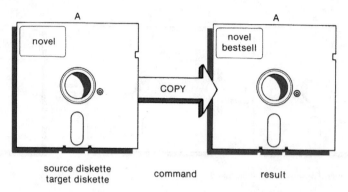

Fig. 7-9. Copying to the same disk, changing name.

One thing to remember, though. It's useful to have two copies of each file on the same disk. This way you can edit one and have the other to go back to if you decide you don't want the editing changes you've made. But remember that your "insurance" copy of a file should be on a different disk. That way if Fido does something nasty to the disk, you don't lose all the copies of your precious file!

If you want to make sure that all your files are, in fact, duplicate copies of the same disk, you can check their contents by using the TYPE command:

```
A:\>type novel<Enter>
A:\>type bestsell<Enter>
A:\>type b:novel<Enter>
A:\>type b:bestsell<Enter>
```

The results of all these commands are the same; you have not altered the contents, just the filenames. The next command also allows you to change the name of a file.

A Rose by Any Other Name

There are several reasons why you might want to rename a file. It could be that you have files with very similar names and there is a danger of confusing them. Or you may, in a flight of fancy, have given your file the very esoteric name "ZST8$E" but now can't remember what's in it. Or you may want to group a set of files together under a new name: for example, when the "Handydandy Company" becomes the "At Your Service Company" and you need to change their name in all your files dealing with them. RENAME is also the command you use to remove the .BAK extension from files so that you can use backup files for editing purposes. See "Safety In Numbers" in Chapter 5.

The RENAME Command

Use: Changes the name of a file

Example: `ren novel opus1`

Abbreviation: ren

As an aspiring writer, you realize that there is another book inside you, dying to get out. The filename "novel" is now too limiting. You want to know which novel. So you decide to give your file the more specific name "opus1." Using the RENAME command, change the filename. You can enter this command with its entire name "RENAME" or you can use the abbreviation "REN". You must include the old and new filenames. To RENAME the file on the current drive, you don't have to include drive indicators:

```
A:\>ren novel opus1<Enter>
```

This is a silent job by MS-DOS. It simply returns you to the `A:\>` prompt after renaming the file. To verify the name change you must use DIR:

```
A:\>dir<Enter>
```

This gives you a listing of the entire disk. Note that the listing no longer contains "novel" but does contain "opus1."

You can also make sure that the change has occurred by using DIR with the new filename:

```
A:\>dir opus1<Enter>
```

MS-DOS confirms that the filename has been changed:

```
Volume in drive A has no label
Directory of A:\

OPUS1                242 08-27-90  11:16a
        1 File(s)          242 bytes
                         29786 bytes free
```

If you want to be absolutely sure that "novel" no longer exists, you can ask for a directory of that file:

```
A:\>dir novel<Enter>
```

Because no file by that name is on the disk, MS-DOS answers:

```
File not found
```

As with the other commands, you can RENAME a file on a drive other than the current drive by including a drive indicator. Now, RENAME the file "novel" that is on the disk in the B drive, by including the drive indicator in the command. Enter this command:

```
A>ren b:novel opus1<Enter>
```

Note that you use the drive indicator only with the first filename, "novel."

"Novel" is no more. Again you will be returned to the system prompt. You still have two copies of the file on each disk, but they are named "opus1" and "bestsell." A listing of the files on the disk in B confirms this change:

```
A:\>dir b:<Enter>

 Volume in drive B has no label
 Directory of B:\

NOVEL               242 08-27-90  11:16a
BESTSELL            242 08-27-90  11:37a
        2 File(s)          484 bytes
                        361230 bytes free
```

You may be confused about how this command is different from using the COPY command with a new filename. Both change the name of the file, but COPY creates a second file.

COPY Versus RENAME	
A:\>copy novel bestsell	Creates a duplicate file with a new name
A:\>ren novel opus1	Changes the name of the existing file

Wiped Out

Files seem to have the reproductive capacity of rabbits. Every time you think you have them under control, files seem to multiply at an alarming rate. Many of the files you use, such as program files, will serve you well for many years. Other files quickly become outdated or irrelevant. Even the worst pack rat cannot save every file forever. Sooner or later you will want to do some housekeeping and clean up your files. You eliminate unneeded files with the ERASE command.

The ERASE Command

Use: Deletes files from a disk

Examples: `erase bestsell`
                 `del b:bestsell`

NOTE: The DEL (Delete) command is identical to the ERASE command.

There is one thing to keep in mind when you use the ERASE command: once you erase a file, you can't recover it with regular MS-DOS commands. (You *may* be able to recover the file with one of the third-party utility programs described in Chapter 13 or a special feature of MS-DOS version 5.0. If you accidentally delete a file, stop! Don't do anything else involving the disk with the erased file. Go directly to Chapter 13, and read the section on "Restoring Erased Files.")

Before using the ERASE command, make sure that the intended victim is a duplicate or useless file. Also, enter the filename with care; if your files have similar names, a simple typing error can cause you great grief.

At this point, you have duplicated copies of your file on both disks. You want to do a little tidying up, so you are going to erase one file on each disk. You decide to stick with the name "opus1" because it most clearly defines the file for you. Before you do any erasing, it's a good idea to make sure exactly which files are on a disk. If you have a directory in front of you, you're less likely to enter a filename by error and find out too late that you made a mistake. A directory also confirms that the file you want to delete actually resides on the disk.

With all the copying and renaming you have done on this file, you may be confused about which names are still valid filenames. Get a directory of each disk:

```
A:\>dir<Enter>

 Volume in drive A is STARTUP
 Volume Serial Number is 1515-83AB
 Directory of A:\

COMMAND   COM     41035 06-07-90    2:24a
FDISK     EXE     54380 06-07-90    2:24a
FORMAT    COM     27131 06-07-90    2:24a
ANSI      SYS      9119 06-07-90    2:24a
COUNTRY   SYS     12820 06-07-90    2:24a
DOSKEY    COM      4518 06-07-90    2:24a
DRIVER    SYS      5286 06-07-90    2:24a
HIMEM     SYS     10560 06-07-90    2:24a
KEYB      COM     10334 06-07-90    2:24a
KEYBOARD  SYS     49282 06-07-90    2:24a
MOUSE     COM     31833 06-07-90    2:24a
PARTDRV   SYS      2112 06-07-90    2:24a
SETVER    EXE      7994 06-07-90    2:24a
```

```
SYS      COM    12064 06-07-90    2:24a
4201     CPI     6404 06-07-90    2:24a
4208     CPI      720 06-07-90    2:24a
5202     CPI      370 06-07-90    2:24a
DISPLAY  SYS    16088 06-07-90    2:24a
EDLIN    EXE    14121 06-07-90    2:24a
EGA      CPI    49068 06-07-90    2:24a
EMM386   EXE    61010 06-07-90    2:24a
FASTOPEN EXE    12307 06-07-90    2:24a
GRAFTABL COM    10033 06-07-90    2:24a
GRAPHICS COM    19230 06-07-90    2:24a
GRAPHICS PRO    21227 06-07-90    2:24a
JOIN     EXE    17991 06-07-90    2:24a
LCD      CPI    10703 06-07-90    2:24a
NLSFUNC  EXE     7344 06-07-90    2:24a
PRINTER  SYS    18978 06-07-90    2:24a
RAMDRIVE SYS     5719 06-07-90    2:24a
REDIR    EXE    27822 06-07-90    2:24a
SHARE    EXE    13388 06-07-90    2:24a
SMARTDRV SYS     6866 06-07-90    2:24a
UNFORMAT EXE    11879 06-07-90    2:24a
AUTOEXEC BAT       24 08-21-90    4:35p
CONFIG   SYS       22 08-21-90    4:35p
OPUS1             242 08-27-90   10:11a
BESTSELL          242 08-27-90   10:11a
       38 File(s)     609894 bytes
                       29786 bytes free
A:\>_
```

Now take a look at the other disk:

```
A:\>dir b:<Enter>
 Volume in drive B has no label
 Directory of B:\

NOVEL            242 08-27-90   11:16a
BESTSELL         242 08-27-90   11:37a
        2 File(s)        484 bytes
                      361230 bytes free
```

First eliminate the "bestsell" file from the disk in drive A (see fig. 7-10):

```
A>erase bestsell<Enter>
```

You don't get any response from MS-DOS when you use the ERASE command. To make sure the file is gone, use the DIR command:

```
A>dir bestsell<Enter>
```

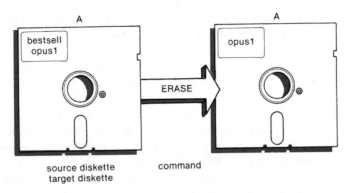

Fig. 7-10. The ERASE command.

If everything has gone according to the script you get the following message:

```
File not found
```

Don't panic! Are you worried that you have eliminated all traces of your book? Just ask for it by name:

```
A:\>dir opus1<Enter>

Volume in drive A has no label
Directory of A:\

OPUS1                242 08-27-90  11:16a
        1 File(s)         242 bytes
                        29786 bytes free
```

Perform the same procedure on the disk in drive B:

```
A:\>erase b:bestsell<Enter>
```

Use the DIR command either way you want to make sure the file is gone:

```
A:\>dir b:<Enter>

Volume in drive B has no label
Directory of B:\

OPUS1                242 08-27-90  11:16a
        1 File(s)         242 bytes
                       360988 bytes free
```

Great! Everything is in tiptop shape. You have two copies of your book: one on the disk in drive A and the backup on the disk in drive B. Now you can get on with writing the History of Civilization.

Now you're right back where you started, two copies of the file, one on each disk. This concludes your performance as the up-and-coming literary sensation of the '90s!

If you still feel a bit confused, it is worth your time to create, copy, type, rename, and erase some more files. These commands are really the "bread and butter" of your everyday work with MS-DOS. COPY especially is essential, because you will be making frequent backups of your files. It may also surprise you how often you use TYPE to see the contents of a file. RENAME and ERASE are commands that become increasingly useful as you accumulate more and more files and want to clarify and keep clean your various directories.

This chapter has set a new pace for your conquest of MS-DOS. First you discovered files and learned the ins and outs of filenaming. You were then introduced to MS-DOS commands in general and the difference in the use of internal and external commands. In the guise of a struggling writer, you used EDLIN or EDIT to create a file. Using this file you put MS-DOS to work by using the TYPE, COPY, RENAME, and ERASE commands. You are now well on your way to effective file management using MS-DOS.

Shifting into High Gear

8

- Let Your Fingers Lead the Way
  - Text and Graphics Screens
  - The Numeric Keypad on the Regular PC Keyboard
  - The Numeric and Cursor Pads on the Enhanced Keyboard
- The Editing Express
- The Functions at the Junctions
- Exercising Control
- Dealing with a Full Deck
- Some Old Friends Revisited
  - Reorganizing the Filenames in Your Directory with MS-DOS 5.0
  - Getting On-line Command Help in MS-DOS 5.0
  - Putting a Label on a Disk
  - Changing the Disk Label
  - Making a Bootable (System) Disk
- Making New Acquaintances

8 Shifting into High Gear

You can cast off your acting cloak for a while. This chapter is going to refine your computing skills so that you'll be ready to use your computer to tackle even loftier roles in the future. In the last two chapters you have been working with files, creating them with EDLIN or EDIT, and managing them with basic MS-DOS commands such as DIR, COPY, and ERASE.

This chapter teaches you how to use your keyboard more effectively, by presenting some special keys and key combinations that make file creation and editing easier. In addition, it expands your knowledge of commands by showing you how to use switches with the DIR and FORMAT commands. Finally, three new commands are discussed: SYS, CHKDSK, and MODE.

Let Your Fingers Lead the Way

Through your experience with MS-DOS you have already become acquainted with some of the special keys on your computer keyboard. By this time you are probably familiar with the location of the standard alphabet, number, and punctuation keys. After all, most of the standard keys are in the same positions as they were on your battered old typewriter.

Two kinds of keyboards are widely available in the MS-DOS world today. First is the "regular" PC keyboard, which is used mainly on older IBM PC and XT systems and their compatibles. Second is the newer 101-key "enhanced" keyboard, which usually comes with IBM PC AT and PS/2 systems and their compatibles. The enhanced keyboard has two additional function keys plus an extra keypad for moving the cursor around. When we discuss each special key in this chapter, we'll let you know if it is located in a different place on the two keyboards. As each special key is discussed, be sure to locate it on your keyboard (see fig. 8-1 for examples).

The first two special keys are already in your repertoire. They are included here as a brief review.

The <Enter> Key

Use: Indicates the end of an entry and tells MS-DOS to process your command

The <Backspace> Key

Use: Moves the cursor to the left along a line

              <Backspace> erases characters as it moves

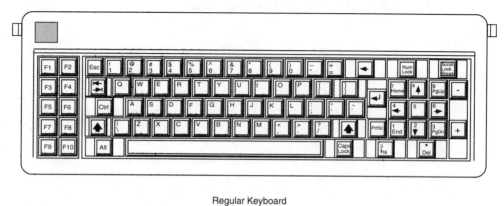

Regular Keyboard

Enhanced Keyboard

Fig. 8-1. Differences between old and new keyboards.

You wouldn't be this far along had you not already mastered the <Enter> key (see fig. 8-2). This important key must be pressed to give the go-ahead signal to MS-DOS. This key may look like this <↵> on your keyboard.

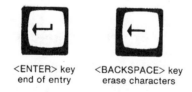

<ENTER> key   <BACKSPACE> key
end of entry   erase characters

Fig. 8-2. The <Enter> and <Backspace> keys.

Unless you are perfect, you've probably had a lot of experience with the <Backspace> key as well (see fig. 8-2). This key is an easy way to erase characters to correct mistakes. You will learn some additional mistake-correcting procedures later in this chapter. This key may be represented as a left arrow <←> on your keyboard.

Now we are going to introduce some other keys that make using MS-DOS, EDLIN, and other programs more convenient. One word of caution—your keyboard may not contain some of these keys. But by reading through the entire section on editing characters, you will find out how to use your keyboard to the best advantage.

Most of these keys are only operational when you are using MS-DOS and/or EDLIN, although there are exceptions. They usually are inoperative or perform different functions in other programs. Word processors, in particular, often assign new meanings to many of the special keys. After a little experience in a variety of computing applications, you will learn the "quirks" of each key and its uses.

The <Caps Lock> Key

Use: Enters all alphabetic keys in uppercase
            <Caps Lock> does not affect number or punctuation keys

            When <Caps Lock> is in effect, pressing <Shift> causes
            all alphabet keys to be entered in lowercase

You have used the <Shift> key to enter uppercase letters, but you may not know that there is another key which also lets you type in uppercase. This is the <Caps Lock> key (see fig. 8-3). When <Caps Lock> is not in use, all letter and number keys are normally entered in lowercase. When you turn on Caps Lock mode by depressing this key, all letters are entered in uppercase. <Caps Lock> affects only the letter keys on your keyboard. <Shift> is still required to enter the punctuation symbols found above the number keys and on the upper section of other keys. Caps Lock mode stays in effect until you depress the key again.

One result of using the <Caps Lock> key may surprise you. When you are in Caps Lock mode, pressing the <Shift> key causes all letters to be entered in lowercase. Try using <Caps Lock> to enter some information, just to get the general idea.

In Normal Mode (<Caps Lock> off)

Pressing	<m>	*results in*	m
Pressing	<Shift><m>	*results in*	M
Pressing	<Shift><2>	*results in*	@

In Caps Lock Mode (<Caps Lock> on)

Pressing	<m>	*results in*	M
Pressing	<Shift><m>	*results in*	m
Pressing	<Shift><2>	*results in*	@

The <Esc> Key

Use: Cancels the current line. <Esc> must be pressed before
            the <Enter> key

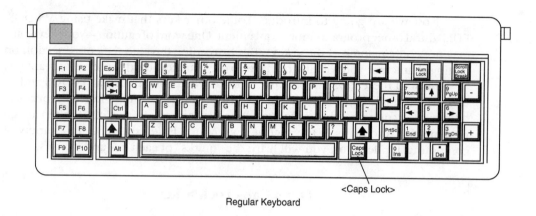

Regular Keyboard

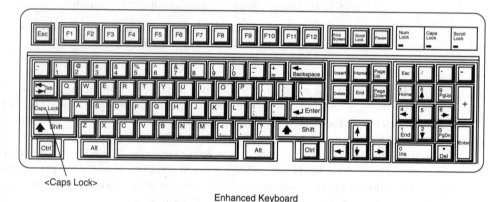

Enhanced Keyboard

Fig. 8-3. The <Caps Lock> key.

Suppose you discover that you have made a mistake on an entry just as you finish typing in the entire line. Of course, the mistake is way back at the front of the line. You just don't feel like sitting there using <Backspace> to erase the whole thing. There is a way to cancel an entire line.

To eliminate a line you use the <Esc> (Escape) key. (See fig. 8-4 for the location of this key.) <Esc> puts a backslash (\) on your command line, to indicate that the command has been canceled. It then moves the cursor down one line so you can enter a new command. When you cancel a line with <Esc> it is not received by the computer. Try this now. Imagine that you are looking for a file in a directory called "fishing.123". As you enter the extension you realize that you have made a mistake:

```
A:\>dir wishing.123<Esc>
```

After you press <Esc> the screen looks like this:

```
A>dir wishing.123\
```

The <Esc> key cancels this command and moves you down to the next line. The cursor appears and waits for a new command.

You can now enter the correct information and continue with your work. Additional editing commands will be explained in "The Editing Express" later in this chapter.

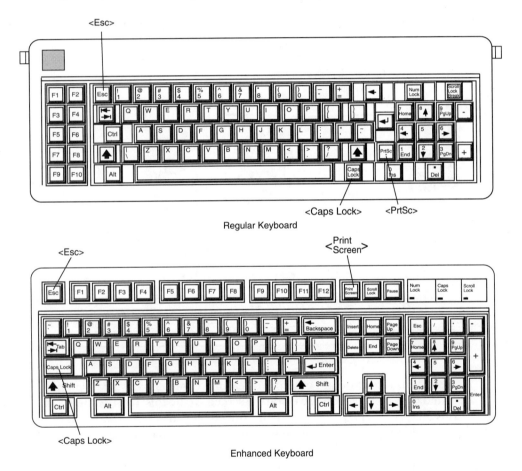

Fig. 8-4. The <Esc> and <PrtSc> keys.

The <PrtSc> Key

Use: <Shift><PrtSc> prints everything currently displayed on
the entire screen

<Ctrl><PrtSc> echoes each line to the screen as it is
entered

Often, when you are entering or editing commands or text, you may want a
printed copy of what is displayed on the screen. To do this, you use the <PrtSc> key.
(This key is labelled "Print Screen" on enhanced keyboards.) A few very old
keyboards do not have this key, but even if you do not have it, you can print out your
display by pressing <Ctrl>P.

To print out everything that is currently displayed on your screen, first make
sure that your printer is turned on and ready. When you print out the contents of a
display it is known as "dumping the screen." To perform this dump, hold down one
of the <Shift> keys and press <PrtSc>.

You can also make a printed copy of everything you enter on the screen, at the
same time as you enter each line. This is called "echoing" the screen to the printer.
To echo each line as it is entered, hold down the <Ctrl> key and press the <PrtSc>
key. All typed-in entries are echoed to the printer until you press <Ctrl><PrtSc>
again.

Text and Graphics Screens

MS-DOS, EDLIN, EDIT, and many other programs display only text (the ASCII characters you learned about in Chapter 5) on the screen. Many new programs, including word processors such as Microsoft Word, use a graphics display. If you see pictures as well as words, or the characters are displayed in a typeface different from your regular display, the program is probably running in *graphics mode*.

You can print a copy of a graphics-mode screen by pressing <Shift><PrtSc>, but first you have to run the GRAPHICS command. This command enables MS-DOS to send the graphics image to the printer. GRAPHICS is an external command, so floppy disk users need to have a system disk in drive A to run it. Here's how:

```
A:\>graphics<Enter>
```

MS-DOS versions earlier than 4.0 can only print graphics screens on a CGA (Color Graphics Adapter) display. Versions 4.0 and later can print graphics from an EGA (Enhanced Graphics Adapter) or VGA (Video Graphics Array) display. If you aren't sure what kind of graphics display your computer has, check your computer's user manual or ask your dealer.

Most dot-matrix or laser printers can print graphics, but first you have to check your MS-DOS manual under the GRAPHICS command to see which printers will print graphics with your particular version of MS-DOS. Generally, MS-DOS versions before 5.0 support only IBM and Epson-compatible dot-matrix printers, but version 5.0 supports a wide variety of printers, including the HP Laserjet. To issue the GRAPHICS command with version 5.0 you enter GRAPHICS LASERJETII if you have a Laserjet.

The <Num Lock> Key on the Regular PC Keyboard

On the regular PC keyboard, the keys on the numeric keypad have a dual purpose. They may be used to enter numbers as input or to control the movement of the cursor. As shown in figure 8-5, these keys comprise a set of arrows and terms such as "Home," "End," "PgUp" (page up), and "PgDn" (page down). The <Num Lock> key controls which function these keys perform.

Normally, <Num Lock> is in the cursor-control mode. Pressing the keys moves the cursor up, down, left, right, or to a certain location on the screen or in a file. These cursor-control keys are not normally used in MS-DOS operations, but they are used in many application programs.

The <Num Lock> Key

Use: Switches the numeric keypad between numbers and cursor control

                <Ctrl><Num Lock> stops the screen from scrolling (on some systems)

Cursor control mode.　　　　　　　Numeric mode.

Fig. 8-5. The numeric keypad.

Pressing <Num Lock> while it is in this cursor-control mode shifts the keyboard to the numeric mode. Now, when you press these keys, the numbers are entered as input. However, when using MS-DOS you will probably use the number keys across the top of the keyboard for numeric input.

When you look at a piece of information more than 23 lines long, the screen scrolls. As new information appears on the bottom of the screen the entries at the top disappear. Remember what happened the first time you used DIR to look at the contents of your system disk? To stop the screen from scrolling, use the <Ctrl><Num Lock> key combination. To "unfreeze" the screen, press the spacebar or <Ctrl><Break>.

If you do not have <Num Lock> on your keyboard or it does not stop the scrolling, you can stop the screen from scrolling by pressing <Ctrl>S.

The Numeric and Cursor Pads on the Enhanced Keyboard

The new enhanced keyboard has a second set of cursor-movement keys to the left of the numeric keypad (see fig. 8-6). This second keypad has the same cursor-movement keys—arrow keys, Page Up, Page Dn, and so on—as the numeric keypad. With this keypad, however, you don't have to use the <Num Lock> key to switch the numeric keypad between numeric and cursor-control functions; you can leave <Num Lock> on so the numeric keypad is always ready for you to enter numbers while keeping the cursor-control pad available for cursor movement. The IBM PS/2 and many modern machines automatically turn on the <Num Lock> key when the system starts up. Most enhanced keyboards also provide little indicator lights to show you when the <Num Lock>, <Caps Lock>, or <Scroll Lock> keys are on.

With the enhanced keyboard you can't press the <Ctrl><Num Lock> key combination to stop scrolling. Instead, use <Ctrl>S to stop scrolling, and press any other key to resume scrolling.

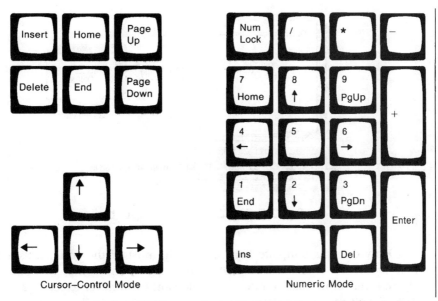

Fig. 8-6. Enhanced keyboard with separate cursor-control and numeric keypads.

The Editing Express

Whether you are writing the great American novel, figuring out how you can make the most of your new tax shelter, or creating your first BASIC program, most of your interactions with the computer take place via the keyboard. And unless you are a typing champion, you will frequently make mistakes while entering your information.

Now, as Mr. Rogers tells us, "Everyone makes mistakes, oh yes they do...." Most computer programs provide some help for you in correcting these mistakes. A word processor, for example, allows for certain keys and key combinations that help you move forward and backward in a line or around in a file to change information or even provide internal spelling checks. BASIC, the programming language that comes with MS-DOS, has a built-in editor to help make error correction easier. MS-DOS also provides some special keys to speed up the editing process when you are entering commands or using the EDLIN program. (As you will see in Chapter 11, MS-DOS version 5.0 provides some additional convenient features that make it easier to use complicated commands.)

Any line you type into the computer is stored in a special place in the computer's memory. This location is called the input buffer. As soon as you press <Enter>, the last line you typed is placed in the input buffer. The line currently stored in the input buffer is called a template. By recalling this template, you can use it as a pattern and make minor changes within a line by using just a few keystrokes (see fig. 8-7).

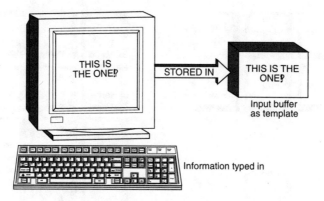

Fig. 8-7. Template in the input buffer.

How can this template help you? Well, most of the commands and other information you enter into MS-DOS consist of very short lines. Commands, after all, are rarely more than 4 letters, and filenames will never exceed 12 characters. MS-DOS editing keys are designed to make correcting mistakes in these short lines easier and faster.

The Functions at the Junctions

Some of the editing keys are already familiar to you. You know about using <Esc> to cancel the line you are typing, and you have used <Backspace> to erase characters on a line. The other editing operations require the use of function keys (see fig. 8-8) or a combination of two keys.

One problem with explaining the editing keys is that they are among the least standardized parts of personal computer systems. That means, unfortunately, that this discussion can tell you how the editing keys work, but it can't identify exactly which keys perform these functions on your computer. Here is another situation where you must check your user's guide to find out the specifics for your machine.

Function keys perform special editing tasks in MS-DOS and certain application programs. Most PC keyboards have either ten or twelve function keys (see fig. 8-8). These keys are numbered starting with F1 and are found either in a block on the left side of the keyboard or across the top of the keyboard. On many laptop computers, the function keys are omitted, to make the keyboard more compact. Many laptop keyboards have a special key marked <Fn> (for "function")—you press this key in combination with a number key to get the equivalent function key. For example, pressing <Fn>3 is the same as pressing F3 on a full-size keyboard.

A reference chart at the end of this section lists the most frequently used key for each function. If the keys your computer uses are different from those listed, write down the keys you use in the blank box before the description of each operation. Note that application programs, particularly word processors, assign their own special functions to the function keys (sometimes in combination with other keys such as <Shift>, <Ctrl>, and <Alt>. Many programs, for example, will give you a "help" display if you press F1. Our discussion here refers to the use of the function keys for editing MS-DOS commands.

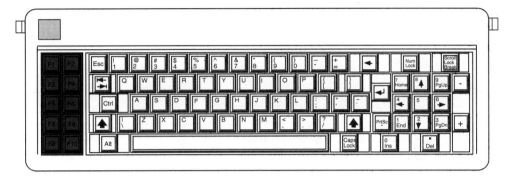

Regular Keyboard

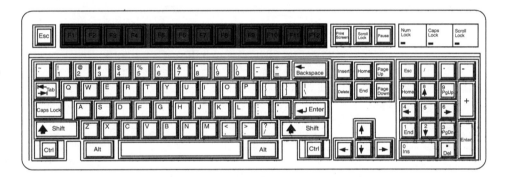

Enhanced Keyboard

Fig. 8-8. Location of function keys.

But how do you actually use the editing keys? Let's look at a hypothetical situation. You have a file in which the last line reads like this:

```
This is the final line. <Enter>
```

Now assume that you want to make some editing changes in that line. (Don't actually type it in. It isn't an MS-DOS command, so if you type it in, MS-DOS will give you an error message.)

The <F3> (Copy All) Function

Use: Copies the entire template

After you press the <Enter> key, this line becomes the template in your input buffer. But suppose that you then decide you want to add more information at the end of the line. First you need to recall the line from the template. To retrieve the entire line you use the `Copy All` function:

`This is the final line.` You press <F3> (copy all).

MS-DOS returns the template:

`This is the final line.` To add more information, first use the <Backspace> key to erase the period, then type in the new text as follows:

`This is the final line`
`This is the final line of this program.` `<Enter>`

Now "This is the final line of this program" is your template.

The <F1> (Copy One Character) Function

Use: Copies one character at a time from the template

You can use the editing keys to copy part of a line. There are several ways to do this. The simplest is to copy one character at a time:

`This is the final line of this program.`   You press <F1> to copy one character.

`T`

`This`   If you press <F1> four times.

The <F2> (Copy Up To) Function

Use: Copies the characters in the template up to the first occurrence of the specified character

---

There is a quicker way to copy part of the template. You can use the Copy Up To function, <F2>. "Copy up to" means retrieve all of the template up to a specified character. The specified character is not included in the new template:

`This is the final line of this program.`   Press <F2> and then "f".

`This is the`

"Copy up to" copies up to the first occurrence of the indicated letter. Suppose the line in the template was:

```
This is often the final line of this program.      You press
                                                   <F2> and
                                                   then "f".
This is o
```

The characters in the template are copied up to the first occurrence of "f" in the word "often." To copy up to the word "final" you would enter <F2> and "f" once more:

```
This is o            You press <F2> and then "f".
This is often the
```

The <Del> (Skip Over One Character) Function

Use: Skips over the next character in the template

You can also use the editing keys to skip over part of the template. You use the <Del> key to skip over one character:

```
This is the final line of this program.      You press <Del>
                                             and then <F3> to
                                             copy the remaining
                                             characters.
his is the final line of this program.
```

If you press <Del> and <F3> again you see the following:

```
is is the final line of this program.
```

The <F4> (Skip Up To) Function

Use: To skip over characters in the template up to the first
                  occurrence of the specified character

Just as you can copy up to, you can also "skip up to." To do this you use the <F4> key and indicate the character you want to skip up to. The specified character is not included in the template:

```
This is the final line of this program.      You press <F4> and
                                             then "n." Press <F3>
                                             to copy the remain-
                                             ing characters.
nal line of this program.
```

163

Just as "copy up to" copies up to the first occurrence of the character, "skip up to" skips all characters up to the first occurrence of the letter given:

```
This is the final line of this program.
```
You press <F4> and then "l". Press <F3> to copy the remaining characters.

```
l line of this program.
```

You may have been intending to skip up to the word "line" but the "l" in final is encountered first. Pressing <F4> and "l" again brings you up to the desired location in the template.

The <Ins> (Insert a New Character) Function

Use: Inserts new characters into the existing template

You can also insert new information into the middle of a template. To do this you use the <Ins> key. This may seem tricky. See if you can follow this example:

```
This is the final line of this program.
```
You press <F2> and then "o".

```
This is the final line
```
Press <Ins>, type "and end", and then press <F3>.

```
This is the final line and end of this program.
```

Did you get all that? If not, just take another look. First you copied the template up to the first occurrence of the letter "o" (in the word "of"). Then you pressed the <Ins> key to indicate that you wanted to add new characters. The characters added are "and end". <F3> then copies all the remaining characters in the template, resulting in the new line. Once you get used to them, these function keys can really cut your editing time when entering MS-DOS commands or using EDLIN.

The <F5> (Create a New Template) Function

Use: Makes the most recently entered line the new template

The <F5> editing key makes your current line the new template. In the previous example, pressing <F5> after you finished editing the line but before you pressed <Enter> would make "This is the final line and end of this program" the template. Note that although this line is now the template, it has not been sent to the computer. If the new line was a command, it would not be executed by the computer. Suppose that the most recent line read:

COPY a: b: You do not press <Enter> at the end of the line, but do press <F5>. Then you press <F3>.

COPY a: b: This is the new template, but the command has not been sent to the computer.

The <Esc> (Escape) Function

Use: Cancels a line (the template is not affected)

Surprise! You already know how to use this function. This is just a reminder that <Esc> is a function as well as a key. When you use <Esc> to cancel a line, the template is not changed (that is, it is not canceled and left blank). The last line entered is still the current template. The backslash on the line indicates that it has been canceled:

```
This is the final line          You press <Esc>.
This is the final line \
```

The line entered just before this one would still be the template.

Using editing keys takes a bit of getting used to, and you may be a little confused until you get the hang of it. But these keys can be very useful when you are entering duplicate or repetitive commands or when you want to correct mistakes without typing in the entire line again. Experiment with these keys and see if they are helpful.

The following is a reference chart of the editing functions and the probable keys used to perform each function. While it is unlikely that your system uses different keys for these functions, we have left a column called "your key" just in case, so that you can fill in your own key combination for each function.

Editing Functions and Keys

Your Key	Key	Function	Explanation
	\<Esc\>	Cancel	Cancel the last line
	\<Backspace\> \<←\>	Back up	Erase the last character
	\<F3\>	Copy all	Copy the entire template
	\<F1\>	Copy one	Copy one character
	\<F2\>	Copy up to	Copy up to a specified character (character is not included in the copied template)
	\<Del\>	Skip one	Skip one character in template
	\<F4\>	Skip up to	Skip up to the specified character (specified character not included in the template)
	\<Ins\>	Enter new	Insert new information in characters in the middle of the template
	\<F5\>	New template	Make this line the new template (if a command, not executed until \<Enter\> is pressed)

Exercising Control

Throughout this book you have been gradually introduced to the \<Ctrl\> key in its various guises. You used \<Ctrl\>\<Alt\>\<Del\> to perform a warm boot, and you used \<Ctrl\>S to stop the screen from scrolling.

Some computer keyboards use specific keys to perform specific actions such as \<PrtSc\> and \<Num Lock\> described previously. But if your machine does not have these special keys or if the specified combinations don't work, you can often use \<Ctrl\> in conjunction with another key to perform these actions. Even if you do have these special keys, you can use the \<Ctrl\> combinations too, because these keys are standard on all computers using MS-DOS. These control functions operate not only in MS-DOS but also in a wide variety of other programs. They are presented in the following chart for quick reference.

Control Functions and Keys

Keys	Explanation
\<Ctrl\>\<Alt\>\<Del\>	Reboots the MS-DOS system
\<Ctrl\>C	Cancels the current line (like the \<Esc\> key) or cancels the currently running program
\<Ctrl\>H	Moves the cursor to the left and erases the last character, just like the \<Backspace\> or \<←\> key
\<Ctrl\>P	Echoes the display to the printer, line by line
\<Ctrl\>N	Turns off the echoing function
\<Ctrl\>S	Stops the scrolling on the screen; to resume scrolling, press any key
\<Ctrl\>Z	End-of-file marker

Dealing with a Full Deck

Special keys, function keys, and control-key combinations help you use MS-DOS and EDLIN with less wasted motion. Not surprisingly, filenames also have a few shortcuts that can increase your standing as an efficiency expert.

You probably haven't thought of your experience in computing as resembling a card game, although you have taken a few chances. But now you are going to learn to use that old favorite of traveling gamblers, wild cards.

Like their playing-card antecedents, wild cards can stand for something else or a lot of something elses. When used in filenames, wild cards replace one or more specific characters in the filename or extension.

As you know, each file's name must be unique, but many of your filenames probably have a lot in common. For example, if you had written Sue three letters you could have called the files "sue1," "sue2," and "sue3." Wild cards allow you to perform an action on a group of similarly named files, using only one command. The wild card replaces one or more characters in the filename. Wild cards are especially useful when you are using the DIR, COPY, ERASE, and RENAME commands, because in these situations you are frequently referring to groups of files.

The wild-card symbols (sometimes called global characters) are the question mark (?) and the asterisk (*).

The question mark is used to match one character in one specific character position in a filename or extension. For example, if you had all your monthly salary records on one disk, the files might look like this:

```
JA-MAR.SUM
JANSAL.
FEBSAL.
MARSAL.
MARTOT.
JA-JUN.SUM
```

You want a directory of all the files that concern monthly salaries. You could look at the whole directory or use DIR to check on the presence of each individual salary file. But you can get this information much more quickly by entering the following command:

```
A:\>dir ???sal<Enter>
```

The following directory would appear:

```
Volume in drive A has no label
Directory of A:\

JANSAL          128      8-28-90      12:24p
FEBSAL          128      8-28-90      12:24p
MARSAL          128      8-28-90      12:24p

        3 File(s)          384 bytes
                        294912 bytes free
```

This command tells MS-DOS to look through the root directory of the disk in drive A and list all files which end in "sal." Any characters may be used in the first three positions. The use of the question mark in the first three positions means that each of these files fulfills the qualifications of the command. This is the key to the question-mark wild card: any character can occupy the position indicated by the ?, but the rest of the name must be exactly the same. If you had entered

```
A:\>dir mar?????<Enter>
```

the following files would be listed:

```
Volume in drive A has no label
Directory of A:\
```

```
MARSAL          128     8-28-90         12:24p
MARTOT          128     8-28-90         12:24p

        2 File(s)       256 bytes
                    294912 bytes free
```

In response to this command, MS-DOS looks for files that have "mar" in the first three positions and any characters in the last five positions.

When you include the ? wild card as the last character in a filename or extension, you must account for all eight characters in the filename proper or all three characters in the extension.

The asterisk wild card is just like using a lot of question marks. When you include an "*" in a filename specification, any character can occupy that position or any of the remaining positions in the filename or extension. An asterisk pretends that there are as many question marks in the filename as there are positions.

Asterisks do not include the extension of a filename unless you specify this with another asterisk after the period. Then it will accept any extension. Suppose that for our sample files you entered this command:

```
A:\>dir ja*.*<Enter>
```

MS-DOS would list the following files:

```
Volume in drive A is has no label
Directory of A:\

JA-MAR      SUM     128     8-28-90     12:24p
JANSAL              128     8-28-90     12:24p
JA-JUN      SUM     128     8-28-90     12:24p
                3 File(s)   384 bytes
                        294912 bytes free
```

Here MS-DOS is looking for any files that contain "JA" in the first two positions. Any characters can occupy the remaining positions in the filename. Since you also included an asterisk in the extension, the filename can contain any extension.

And for a completely wild filename:

```
*.*
```

As you have probably guessed, this means all files! One good use for the *.* wild-card specification is to copy all the files from a disk in one drive to a disk in another; for example,

```
copy a:*.* b:
```

copies all the files on the disk in drive A to the disk in drive B.

Wild cards can be useful because of their power, but they can also be dangerous. When you want to copy all the files on a disk (COPY *.*) or list an entire directory (DIR *.*), they can make your task easier.

Beware the use of wild cards with the ERASE command. As you probably guessed, ERASE *.* would mean goodbye to all the files on your disk. MS-DOS is looking out for your best interests, though. When you use *.* with the ERASE command, MS-DOS gives you a chance to back out. When you enter

```
A:\>erase *.*<Enter>
```

You get the following message:

```
All files in directory will be deleted!
Are you sure (Y/N)?
```

(Earlier versions of MS-DOS just give the "Are you sure (Y/N)" part.) Enter "Y" if you are really sure or "N" if you have any doubts about what you're doing.

This concludes your lesson in "Special MS-DOS Shortcuts." The keys, functions, and tools described in this chapter move you up one notch on the climb through the "discovery mountains" of MS-DOS. Now you're going to go back and visit some familiar spots along the way, but with a few new twists and turns.

Some Old Friends Revisited

As you become better acquainted with MS-DOS, you are able to use it more easily, and also come to appreciate some of its finer points. Up to this point, you have been using commands in their simplest form. Often, indeed, the simple way gets the job done. But there are some options to commands that can make them even more useful.

Commands can contain switches. As the name implies, switches can turn on and off certain operations within a command. When you add a switch to a command you indicate it with a slash (/) and a letter. Switches always follow the command and any drive indicators.

The DIR Command (The Second Time Around)

Use:	Displays a directory of the specified disk or lists the specific attributes of a single file
Switches:	/w Display the directory in several columns across the screen (only the filenames are displayed)
	/p Pauses when the directory fills one screen
	/o Sort-order (MS-DOS 5.0). Sorts the files by specified order; for example, /o:n sorts files alphabetically by name
Examples:	dir /w
	dir /p
	dir /o:n

You are familiar with your first MS-DOS friend, the DIR command. You know this command lists the files on a directory, displaying their names, extensions, sizes, and the time and date they were last accessed. If the directory contains more files than will fit on one screen, the display scrolls until it reaches the end of the listing.

There are two optional switches you can include in the DIR command that alter how the directory is displayed: /w and /p. The /w switch lists the files in columns across the screen.

Assume that the disk listing you want to see is in drive A, which is your current drive. You enter the command like this:

```
A:\>dir /w<Enter>
```

If this disk is a typical system disk, the listing will look something like this:

```
Volume in drive A is STARTUP
Volume Serial Number is 1515-83AB
Directory of A:\

COMMAND.COM    FDISK.EXE      FORMAT.COM     ANSI.SYS       COUNTRY.SYS
DOSKEY.COM     DRIVER.SYS     HIMEM.SYS      KEYB.COM       KEYBOARD.SYS
MOUSE.COM      PARTDRV.SYS    SETVER.EXE     SYS.COM        4201.CPI
4208.CPI       5202.CPI       DISPLAY.SYS    EDLIN.EXE      EGA.CPI
EMM386.EXE     FASTOPEN.EXE   GRAFTABL.COM   GRAPHICS.COM   GRAPHICS.PRO
JOIN.EXE       LCD.CPI        NLSFUNC.EXE    PRINTER.SYS    RAMDRIVE.SYS
REDIR.EXE      SHARE.EXE      SMARTDRV.SYS   UNFORMAT.EXE   AUTOEXEC.BAT
CONFIG.SYS
        36 File(s)      609782 bytes
                         29696 bytes free
```

This horizontal layout of the directory can be useful when the disk holds a lot of files and you want to see only their names (see fig. 8-9). Note that this directory does not give you any information about file size or the date or time the file was last accessed.

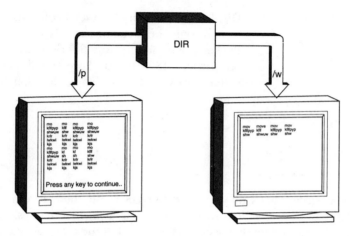

Fig. 8-9. The DIR command.

Another switch used with the DIR command is /p. The /p switch operates like an automatic scroll control. It stops the display of a directory when the screen is filled. This switch is useful when you want to look at the listing of a large directory. You can study the display and then indicate when you are ready to proceed. Again, the switch follows the command:

```
A:\>dir /p<Enter>
```

This is how the output of this command appears on the screen:

```
Volume in drive A is STARTUP
Volume Serial Number is 1515-83AB
Directory of A:\

COMMAND   COM    41035 06-07-90   2:24a
FDISK     EXE    54380 06-07-90   2:24a
FORMAT    COM    27131 06-07-90   2:24a
ANSI      SYS     9119 06-07-90   2:24a
COUNTRY   SYS    12820 06-07-90   2:24a
DOSKEY    COM     4518 06-07-90   2:24a
DRIVER    SYS     5286 06-07-90   2:24a
HIMEM     SYS    10560 06-07-90   2:24a
KEYB      COM    10334 06-07-90   2:24a
KEYBOARD  SYS    49282 06-07-90   2:24a
MOUSE     COM    31833 06-07-90   2:24a
```

```
PARTDRV   SYS       2112  06-07-90    2:24a
SETVER    EXE       7994  06-07-90    2:24a
SYS       COM      12064  06-07-90    2:24a
4201      CPI       6404  06-07-90    2:24a
4208      CPI        720  06-07-90    2:24a
5202      CPI        370  06-07-90    2:24a
DISPLAY   SYS      16088  06-07-90    2:24a
EDLIN     EXE      14121  06-07-90    2:24a
Press any key to continue . . .
```

When the entire screen is filled, MS-DOS gives this message:

```
Press any key to continue
```

(Earlier versions say, "Strike any key when ready," which means the same thing.)
Press any key, and the directory continues:

```
(continuing A:\)
EGA       CPI      49068  06-07-90    2:24a
EMM386    EXE      61010  06-07-90    2:24a
FASTOPEN  EXE      12307  06-07-90    2:24a
GRAFTABL  COM      10033  06-07-90    2:24a
GRAPHICS  COM      19230  06-07-90    2:24a
GRAPHICS  PRO      21227  06-07-90    2:24a
JOIN      EXE      17991  06-07-90    2:24a
LCD       CPI      10703  06-07-90    2:24a
NLSFUNC   EXE       7344  06-07-90    2:24a
PRINTER   SYS      18978  06-07-90    2:24a
RAMDRIVE  SYS       5719  06-07-90    2:24a
REDIR     EXE      27822  06-07-90    2:24a
SHARE     EXE      13388  06-07-90    2:24a
SMARTDRV  SYS       6866  06-07-90    2:24a
UNFORMAT  EXE      11879  06-07-90    2:24a
AUTOEXEC  BAT         24  08-21-90    4:35p
CONFIG    SYS         22  08-21-90    4:35p
        36 File(s)      609782 bytes
                         29696 bytes free
```

(The "continuing A:\" message appears if you are using MS-DOS version 5.0.)
  While the listing from DIR /p takes up more space than DIR /w on your screen,
it has the advantage of allowing information on all files to be displayed in a fashion
that's convenient to read. It also provides complete information on each file.

Reorganizing the Filenames in Your Directory with MS-DOS 5.0

Starting with MS-DOS version 5.0, you can use the /o ("order") option to sort the
filenames in the directory. Sorting means to rearrange, or reorganize, filenames

according to a criterion you choose. For example, MS-DOS lets you reorganize the directory listing by name, extension, time and date, or size. You do this by following the /o with a colon (:) and one of the following: an n (for name), an e (for extension), a d (for time and date), or an s for (size). (There are other options, but we won't discuss them all here.) Consider the following directory listing as provided by the plain old DIR command:

```
A:\>dir b:<Enter>

 Volume in drive B is MISC
 Volume Serial Number is 1515-83AB
 Directory of B:\

 .              <DIR>      08-28-90   12:47p
 ..             <DIR>      08-28-90   12:47p
 NOTES    TXT     6404 06-07-90    2:24a
 FINANCE  BAS      824 08-21-90    4:35p
 DRIVER   SYS     5286 06-07-90    2:24a
 SCANNER  SYS     2112 06-07-90    2:24a
 ADDRESS  TXT      720 06-07-90    2:24a
 ENVELOPE BAS      370 06-07-90    2:24a
         8 File(s)      15716 bytes
                       346780 bytes free
```

Note that the files aren't listed in alphabetical order. It's not hard to find the file you want in this short listing, but suppose the disk had forty or fifty files in it. With MS-DOS 5.0 you can get the listing sorted by filename in alphabetical order:

```
A:\>dir b: /o:n<Enter>

 Volume in drive B is MISC
 Volume Serial Number is 1515-83AB
 Directory of B:

 .              <DIR>      08-28-90   12:47p
 ..             <DIR>      08-28-90   12:47p
 ADDRESS  TXT      720 06-07-90    2:24a
 DRIVER   SYS     5286 06-07-90    2:24a
 ENVELOPE BAS      370 06-07-90    2:24a
 FINANCE  BAS      824 08-21-90    4:35p
 NOTES    TXT     6404 06-07-90    2:24a
 SCANNER  SYS     2112 06-07-90    2:24a
         8 File(s)      15716 bytes
                       346780 bytes free
```

Here we specified /o for the "order" option, followed by a colon and n for "sort by name."

Suppose you have lots of BASIC programs on your disk and also lots of text files. It would be nice for your listing to list each of these very different categories of files in its own group, by extension. Here's how you do it:

```
A:\>dir b: /o:e<Enter>

 Volume in drive B is MISC
 Volume Serial Number is 1515-83AB
 Directory of B:\

 .                <DIR>      08-28-90   12:47p
 ..               <DIR>      08-28-90   12:47p
 FINANCE   BAS       824 08-21-90    4:35p
 ENVELOPE  BAS       370 06-07-90    2:24a
 DRIVER    SYS      5286 06-07-90    2:24a
 SCANNER   SYS      2112 06-07-90    2:24a
 NOTES     TXT      6404 06-07-90    2:24a
 ADDRESS   TXT       720 06-07-90    2:24a
          8 File(s)      15716 bytes
                        346780 bytes free
```

Here's one more example using the versatile MS-DOS 5.0 version of the DIR command—suppose we want to sort the files by the date and time they were created or last modified, starting with the earliest file. Here's how:

```
A:\>dir b: /o:d<Enter>

 Volume in drive B is MISC
 Volume Serial Number is 1515-83AB
 Directory of B:\

 NOTES     TXT      6404 06-07-90    2:24a
 DRIVER    SYS      5286 06-07-90    2:24a
 SCANNER   SYS      2112 06-07-90    2:24a
 ADDRESS   TXT       720 06-07-90    2:24a
 ENVELOPE  BAS       370 06-07-90    2:24a
 FINANCE   BAS       824 08-21-90    4:35p
 .                <DIR>      08-28-90   12:47p
 ..               <DIR>      08-28-90   12:47p
          8 File(s)      15716 bytes
                        346780 bytes free
```

There are many other options with the MS-DOS 5.0 DIR command—why not look up DIR in your MS-DOS manual and try some of the others? For example, you can reverse the order of the sort by putting a minus sign before the sort type:

```
A:\>dir b: /o:-s<Enter>
```

sorts the files by size, but with the largest files first.

Getting On-line Command Help in MS-DOS 5.0

Another new feature of MS-DOS 5.0 is a built-in help display that summarizes the important elements of each command. To get this display, simply give the command and add the /? switch. Instead of executing the command, MS-DOS shows you the syntax, or order in which you specify the various parts of the command. There is also a list of the valid switches for the command and their meanings. Let's try it with DIR:

```
A:\>dir /?<Enter>
Displays a list of files in a directory.

DIR [pathname] [/p] [/w] [/a:attributes] [/o:sortorder] [/s] [/b]
     /p  Pause after each screen page of display.
     /w  List Files in columns with up to five filenames on each line.
     /a:attributes  Displays only files with the attributes you specify.
     /o:sortorder   Displays files sorted in the specified order.
     /s  Displays files in the specified directory and all subdirectories.
     /b  Lists filenames, one per line, without any file information.
```

This summary is similar to the ones you will see in your MS-DOS manual, but it's available instantly, right at your PC. The syntax summary on the third line down tells you to start by typing the word "dir." Then type a pathname, a complete specification including a drive letter, filename, and extension, with some parts being optional depending on circumstances. (You'll learn more about paths in Chapter 10. So far we've used just a drive letter such as b: or a drive letter and a filename such as b:opus1.) After the syntax summary tells you to enter DIR and the pathname, it lists various switches you can use with the DIR command. You've already seen how to use /w, /p, and /o.

Suppose, however, that you know what you want to do, but you don't know how to tell MS-DOS to do it. For example, you want to list the contents of a file, but you don't remember whether the command to use is called "show," "list," or something else. You can use the HELP command with MS-DOS 5.0 to get a list of all DOS commands, with a brief description of the purpose of each one. Just type HELP (followed by <Enter> as usual).

```
C:\>help<Enter>
```

APPEND   Allows applications to open data files in specified directories as if
            they were in the current directory.

ASSIGN   Assigns a different drive letter to an existing drive.

ATTRIB   Displays or changes file attributes.

BACKUP   Backs up one or more files from one disk to another.

BREAK   Turns extra CTRL+C checking on or off.

CALL   Calls one batch file from another.

CD   Displays the name of or changes the current directory.

CHCP   Displays or changes the active code page number.

CHDIR   Displays the name of or changes the current directory.

CHKDSK   Checks a disk and displays a status report.

CLEANUP   Cleans up left-over files after MS-DOS 5.0 installation.

CLS   Clears the screen.

COMMAND   Starts a new MS-DOS command processor.

COMP   Compares the contents of two files or sets of files.

COPY   Copies one or more files.

CTTY   Changes the terminal device used to control your system.

DATE   Displays or sets the date.

DEBUG   Starts Debug, a program testing and editing tool.

DEL   Deletes one or more files.

DIR   Displays a list of files in a directory.

DISKCOMP   Compares the contents of two floppy disks.

DISKCOPY   Copies the contents of one floppy disk to another.

DOSKEY   Edits command lines, recalls MS-DOS commands, and creates macros.

DOSSHELL   Starts the MS-DOS Shell.

ECHO   Echoes messages to the display, or turns command echoing on or off.

EDIT   Starts the MS-DOS Editor.

EDLIN   Simple text editor.

EMM386   Enables or disables EMM386 expanded memory.

ERASE   Deletes one or more files.

EXE2BIN   Converts .EXE (executable) files to memory-image format.

EXIT	Exits the COMMAND interpreter.
FASTOPEN	Decreases the amount of time needed to open frequently used files and directories.
FC	Compares two files or sets of files.
FDISK	Configures a hard disk for use with MS-DOS.
FIND	Searches for a text string in a file or files.
FOR	Executes a command for each of a set of files.
FORMAT	Formats a disk for use with MS-DOS.
GOTO	Directs batch file execution to a labelled line.
GRAFTABL	Loads an extended character set to display in graphics mode.
GRAPHICS	Installs a resident program that can print graphics screens.
HELP	Provides help information for MS-DOS commands.
IF	Executes a command if a condition is true.
JOIN	Joins a disk drive to a directory on another drive.
KEYB	Loads a keyboard program.
LABEL	Creates, changes, or deletes the volume label on a disk.
LH	Loads a program into upper memory.
LOADHIGH	Loads a program into upper memory.
MD	Makes a new directory.
MEM	Displays the amount of used and free memory.
MIRROR	Creates a disk recovery file, and starts delete tracker.
MKDIR	Makes a new directory.
MODE	Configures devices.
MORE	Displays output one screen at a time.
NLSFUNC	Loads country-specific information.
PATH	Displays or defines a list of directories to be searched for commands.
PAUSE	Suspends execution of a batch file.
PRINT	Prints a text file while you are using other MS-DOS commands.
PROMPT	Changes the MS-DOS command prompt.
QBASIC	Starts the QBasic programming environment.
RD	Removes a directory.
RECOVER	Recovers readable information from a bad or defective disk.

```
REM        Records comments (remarks) in batch files.
REN        Renames a file or files.
RENAME     Renames a file or files.
REPLACE    Replaces files.
RESTORE    Restores files that were backed up using the BACKUP command.
RMDIR      Removes a directory.
SET        Displays, assigns, or removes MS-DOS environment variables.
SETUP      Installs MS-DOS 5.0.
SETVER     Sets the version number that MS-DOS reports to a program.
SHARE      Installs file sharing and locking.
SHIFT      Shifts the numbering of replaceable parameters in batch files.
SORT       Sorts input.
SUBST      Substitutes a drive letter for a path.
SYS        Transfers system files from one disk to another.
TIME       Displays or changes the system time.
TREE       Graphically displays the directory structure of a drive or path.
TYPE       Displays the contents of a text file.
UNDELETE   Recovers deleted files.
UNFORMAT   Restores a disk that has been accidentally formatted.
VER        Displays the MS-DOS version.
VERIFY     Turns disk-write verification on or off.
VOL        Displays a disk volume label and serial number.
XCOPY      Copies files and directory trees.
```

It may take a while to browse through this list, but eventually you'll find that the TYPE command displays the contents of a text file. You can also type HELP followed by the name of a command to get instructions on how to use the command:

```
C:\>help type <Enter>
displays the contents of a text file.
TYPE pathname
```

You are told that you follow TYPE with a pathname. This display is the same as you would get by using the /? switch with the command; for example:

```
C:\>type /? <Enter>
displays the contents of a text file.
TYPE pathname
```

As you can see, you can often get the answer to a question about MS-DOS 5.0 without having to look in the manual.

Want to Learn More about MS-DOS Command Options?

Your MS-DOS manual lists all the options for each command and gives some examples of how to use them. Most MS-DOS manual reference sections are written in rather terse language, however, and often don't give enough examples. If you are interested in learning more about the nuances of MS-DOS usage, we recommend that you try *The Waite Group's MS-DOS Bible, 4th Edition* (SAMS, Carmel, IN, 1991). This book includes tutorials for intermediate users and a complete reference section for MS-DOS commands.

Putting a Label on a Disk

As you know, FORMAT sets up your disk to receive information. Up to this point we have only briefly discussed a very important capability of FORMAT: the ability to put a name on a disk.

The FORMAT Command (New and Improved Version)

Use:	Readies a disk to receive data
Switches:	/v Gives the disk a volume label
	/s Puts the operating system on the disk during the formatting procedure
Examples:	`format b: /v`
	`format b: /s`

How many times have you looked at the results of a DIR command and wondered "Why doesn't the volume in drive A have a label?" You keep getting this same message over and over but can't do anything about it. Well, the time has come.

The volume name (which simply means the name of the disk) can be helpful to you in identifying the contents of a disk. One way to put a volume name or volume label (as MS-DOS refers to it) on a disk is to use the /v switch with the FORMAT command. Let's put a volume label on a disk we're going to use for the examples in Chapter 10. Put your system disk in drive A and a new, unformatted disk in drive B. Be sure the disk is empty or contains information you no longer need, because the FORMAT command will erase any existing information on a disk.

Okay, now begin the procedure by entering the FORMAT command and including the /v switch:

```
A:\>format b: /v<Enter>
Insert new disk for drive B:
and press any key to continue
```

Check, you've already put in your new disk, so FORMAT away:

```
Formatting...Format complete
```

So far everything seems exactly normal. But now MS-DOS inserts a new message:

```
Volume label (11 characters, ENTER for none)?
```

Here is your chance to individualize your disk. You can name the disk anything you want up to 11 characters. Name your disk "wine cellar." An intriguing title. Are you peeking at Chapter 10 right now? If you had decided against including a volume label, you would just press <Enter>. Type in the volume label now:

```
Volume label (11 characters, ENTER for none)?wine cellar<Enter>
```

The formatting then continues as usual:

```
362496 bytes total disk space
362496 bytes available on disk

Format another (Y/N)?n<Enter>
```

Again, the messages you see vary with the version of MS-DOS you are using; for example, version 4.0 adds additional technical information about "allocation units," which you don't need to worry about now.

**The FORMAT Command in MS-DOS Version 4.0
and Later Automatically Prompts for a Volume Label**

With the FORMAT command in MS-DOS version 4.0 or later, you can still use the /v switch and a label if you wish. If you do not include the /v switch, however, FORMAT automatically prompts you for a volume label. Press <Enter> if you don't want to use a volume label; otherwise type in the volume label and press <Enter>.

The disk is now ready to receive data. How do you know the volume label of a disk? Enter the DIR command and you'll find out:

```
A:\>dir b:<Enter>

Volume in drive B is WINE CELLAR
Directory of B:\
```

The contents of the disk would then be listed. Since you don't have any files on this disk yet, you will see this message:

```
File not found
```

Changing the Disk Label

Suppose you decide to use a disk for something completely different. For example, suppose you decide that you are not interested in stocking your wine cellar, but in starting your own beer brewery. How can you change the label WINE CELLAR to BREWERY?

You could, of course, run FORMAT /v on the disk. But, as you know, FORMAT takes several minutes to run. Besides, you might want to keep your wine-related files in case you should decide to go back into the wine business someday. FORMAT, of course, wipes out all of the data on the disk. To change the disk label without reformatting the disk, use the LABEL command. (This command is available starting with MS-DOS version 3.0.)

The LABEL command is very easy to use. One way to use it is to just type "label" followed by the letter of the drive containing the disk in question:

```
A:\>label b:<Enter>
```

MS-DOS will reply:

```
Volume in drive B is WINE CELLAR
Volume Serial Number is 3F6A-17CD
Volume label (11 characters, ENTER for none)brewery<Enter>
```

In response to the "Volume label" message, just type the new label and press <Enter>. (In the example we typed "brewery".) Note that case doesn't matter—MS-DOS always changes the label name to all caps. If you decide that you don't want to change the label after all, press <Enter> without typing in the label. (By the way, you can't change the serial number, which is provided starting with MS-DOS version 4.0. It is generated randomly and automatically each time you format or reformat a disk.)

There's a shortcut way to relabel a disk—you can type "label," the drive letter (with a colon), and then the name of the new label:

```
A:\>label a:brewery<Enter>
```

The label is changed automatically without any prompting.

Making a Bootable (System) Disk

The /s switch on the FORMAT command allows you to put a copy of the operating system on a disk. This can be a timesaver because it allows you to boot the system from any disk that has been formatted this way. (Even if you normally run your system from the hard disk, it's important to have a few bootable floppy disks handy to use if your hard disk develops a problem that prevents it from booting.)

As an example of why you would use the /s switch, suppose you have obtained a program that you know you will use quite often. This program requires you to input information from a data disk. If you have the system on your program disk, you can just insert it in drive A, insert the data disk in drive B, turn on the machine, and away you go. No more inserting the system disk in drive A, then removing this disk to put in your program disk, and then beginning to run the program.

When you include the /s switch in the FORMAT command to set up a system disk, it transfers three files to the new disk. Two of these files are hidden. (Hidden files contain program code that is used by MS-DOS for its internal operations, such as keeping track of files and communicating with various devices.) Being hidden doesn't mean DOS can't find them. It means you won't see them listed among the files on a disk when using the DIR command. The CHKDSK command, coming up soon, will tell you if a disk contains any hidden files. These files cannot usually be accessed by you; that way, you can't change them or do anything to make the system act crazy.

The third file (not hidden) transferred by the /s switch is COMMAND.COM. This file does appear as part of a disk's contents when you use DIR to look at the disk. These three files make up the system.

Putting the system on the disk does take up some space. Not every disk needs to have the system on it. However, if you think you are likely to be booting from a disk, or you know you will need the internal commands handy when you are using the disk, put the system on it. You can take the COMMAND.COM file off (using ERASE) if you find you need more space on the disk.

Important Notice!

Hear ye! Hear ye! To put the system on a blank disk, you must include the /s switch at the time you format the disk.

To format the disk in drive B and make this disk a system disk, enter the command and the switch:

```
A:\>format b: /s<Enter>
```

MS-DOS follows the usual steps in the formatting sequence:

```
Insert new disk for drive B:
and press ENTER when ready

Formatting...Format complete
```

Here's the new twist, another message:

```
System transferred
```

The space occupied by the system is included in the message at the completion of the formatting operation:

```
362496 bytes total disk space
 40960 bytes used by system
321536 bytes available on disk

Format another (Y/N)?n<Enter>
```

And that's all there is to it! You now have a self-booting disk ready for your data or programs (see fig. 8-10).

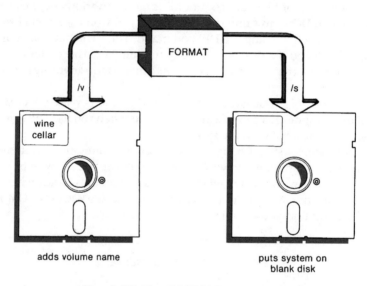

Fig. 8-10. The FORMAT command.

You can put a volume label and the system on the same disk. Simply enter both switches when you format the disk:

```
A:\>format b: /v /s<Enter>
```

With most versions of MS-DOS, the order of the switches does not matter. A few require the /s to come last. You can never go wrong by putting the /v first and the /s second.

You will see the "system transferred" message and be asked for a "volume label" during the formatting procedure.

Remember, the /s switch is only for transferring the system onto a new, blank disk. Since you will quickly find how convenient it is to have the system on a disk, your next logical question is "How can I put the system on disks that already contain information?" Read on.

Making New Acquaintances

The SYS command performs the same function as the /s switch in the FORMAT command. That is, it transfers the operating system onto a designated disk. Since the use of FORMAT erases all previous information on a disk, you cannot use FORMAT /s to put the system on a disk that already contains important programs or data. But, by using SYS, you can have the system on most such disks.

The SYS Command

Use: Transfers the hidden files of MS-DOS to a disk

Example: sys b:

Just like the /s switch in FORMAT, SYS transfers two hidden files to the specified disk. You can't see these files, but don't worry, MS-DOS knows they are there. System files occupy a unique position on the disk; they are always located in the first track, at the very beginning of the disk. Even if the files are not on the disk, MS-DOS allocates this space to them when you format the disk. When you use the SYS command, you put the system in this already available location. Most preprogrammed or application disks are produced with this predefined location for the system files. If you save data to a formatted disk, this reserved area will be written over and you will not be able to transfer the system files successfully. However, the SYS command in MS-DOS versions 4.0 and later is more versatile. In these versions, MS-DOS can move existing files around on the disk if necessary to free the reserved area for the system files. There just has to be enough empty space on the disk to hold the system files and room in the disk directory for directory entries for the files. (The latter is usually not a problem.)

SYS transfers the hidden files but, unlike the /s switch, it does not transfer MS-DOS's COMMAND.COM file. To have a disk that is self-booting, you must also transfer the COMMAND.COM portion of the operating system. First use SYS to put the system on the disk and then use COPY to transfer the COMMAND.COM file. You may also use COPY to transfer other files that you use a great deal, such as FORMAT.COM or DISKCOPY.COM.

Putting the System on a Disk

Using FORMAT /s
On a blank disk, FORMAT /s transfers the COMMAND.COM file and two "hidden files."

Using SYS
On a blank disk, SYS transfers two "hidden files." Use the COPY command to transfer the COMMAND.COM file.

Since SYS is an external command, you must have your system disk in drive A (if you are running MS-DOS from a floppy disk) before issuing the command. Don't forget to put your target disk in drive B.

```
A:\>sys b:<Enter>
```

MS-DOS tells you when the transfer has been completed.

```
System transferred
A:\>
```

When you look at the directory of this disk, you see that COMMAND.COM is now one of its files. But how can you be sure that the hidden files were also transferred? The next command gives you that information.

The CHKDSK Command

Use:	Checks the condition of the file allocation table and directories on a disk
Switches:	/f Fixes the file allocation table if there are errors
	/v Gives more explanation of error (verbose)
Examples:	chkdsk
	chkdsk b: /f
	chkdsk b: /v

This command is used to check the status or condition of any specific disk. CHKDSK is useful for finding out exactly how much room is taken up on a disk, how much room is still available, and what types of files are currently on the disk. As a nice extra, CHKDSK also reports on how much memory is taken up and how much is still free, but this has nothing to do with the disk itself.

As the name implies, you use CHKDSK ("check disk") to find out whether everything is okay on a disk. This is especially useful if you are having trouble using a disk and want to try to locate the problem and save the information.

The first thing CHKDSK examines is the file allocation table (FAT). MS-DOS uses the FAT to keep track of the available space on a disk. The FAT records where a file is on the disk; it's rather like a table of contents. It also records unused space on the disk. MS-DOS tries to make the most out of each disk, so it does not like to have wasted space, or noncontiguous files. CHKDSK checks on space allocation and reports any problems to you.

Since CHKDSK is an external command, you must have your system disk in a drive to use it. To check on the status of a disk, just enter the command and the drive indicator. Let's run a CHKDSK on the system disk:

```
A:\>chkdsk a:<Enter>
```

Here is the resulting display of a "typical" system disk:

```
Volume STARTUP    created 08-21-1990 4:29p
Volume Serial Number is 1515-83AB

  730112 bytes total disk space
   69632 bytes in 2 hidden files
    1024 bytes in 1 directories
  650240 bytes in 42 user files
    9216 bytes available on disk

    1024 bytes in each allocation unit
     713 total allocation units on disk
       9 available allocation units on disk

  655360 total bytes memory
  545760 bytes free
```

This disk seems to be in good shape. CHKDSK gives us lots of information on the status of the disk. We know how much total disk space is taken up, how many files are on the disk, and how much space is still available. This is followed by the information on memory. Of course, all these numbers depend on the specifics of your computer system, including the size and capacity of your disk.

The second line of the display gives the information on hidden files. Since this disk has two hidden files, it is reasonable to assume that the system is on this disk. Remember that FORMAT /s and SYS transfer two hidden files when the system is placed on a disk.

Well, so far, our disks have been in good shape. Here is an example of a status report that indicates a problem:

```
A:\>chkdsk b:<Enter>
```

The screen reports this condition:

```
Disk error reading FAT 1

  362496 bytes total disk space
   38912 bytes in 6 user files
  323584 bytes available on disk

  262144 bytes total memory
  237568 bytes free
```

CHKDSK encountered a problem as soon as it began reading the disk.

Here is another status report which you might receive:

```
362496 bytes total disk space
     0 bytes in 1 hidden file
   124 bytes in bad sectors
352256 bytes available on disk

262144 bytes total memory
237568 bytes free
```

In this example, the problem is not in the FAT, but in the disk sectors.

CHKDSK does have the capability to attempt to correct some errors. If you want MS-DOS to check for errors and attempt to repair the problem, you issue the CHKDSK command with the /f switch (see fig. 8-11). The /f switch means fix if possible:

```
A:\>chkdsk b: /f<Enter>
```

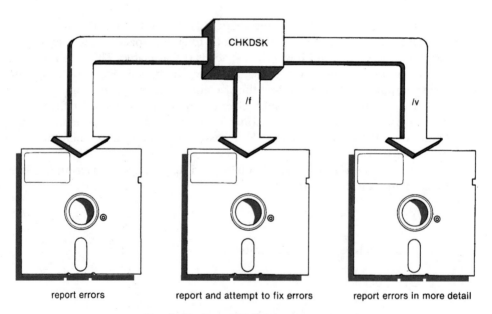

report errors   report and attempt to fix errors   report errors in more detail

Fig. 8-11. The CHKDSK command.

If an error is found, MS-DOS asks permission to fix it. There are many types of errors and consequently many types of error messages. Here are two more error messages that might result from CHKDSK:

```
xxx lost clusters found in xxx chains
Convert lost chains to files(Y/N)?
```

or:

```
Allocation error for file, size adjusted
```

When you use CHKDSK with the /f switch you will have to refer to your MS-DOS manual to understand the error message. Your manual will also advise you about what action is appropriate for each error condition. (Some third-party programs offer more extensive help in fixing common disk problems. You will learn about them in Chapter 13.)

A Tip: Save the Good Files!

If you run CHKDSK on a disk and get any messages about problems, take an extra precaution: use COPY to copy as many important files as possible to another disk. (You may not be able to copy certain files, however, because the disk problem involves the sectors used by the file.) After you have tried to make backup copies of the important files, try CHKDSK with the /f switch and see if MS-DOS can fix the disk for you.

You may also use another switch with the CHKDSK command. The /v switch gives you more information about the error it has found. When you use this switch, CHKDSK lists each directory and the files in that directory as part of the status report. For example:

```
A:\>chkdsk b: /v<Enter>
```

```
Disk error reading FAT 1
Directory B:
    B:\SAMPLE.BAK
    B:\LETTERS.BAK        These are sample filenames within the directory.
    B:\SAMPLE
    B:\LETTERS

    362496 bytes total disk space
     38912 bytes in 4 user files
    323584 bytes available on disk

    262144 bytes total memory
    237584 bytes free
```

You can combine both CHKDSK switches in one command:

```
A:\>chkdsk /f /v<Enter>
```

This command not only lists the contents of the disk, it also attempts to fix any problems noted.

It's a good idea to use CHKDSK often. Not only can it prevent minor problems from growing into major ones, but it brings you peace of mind just knowing that everything on your disks is "all right with the world."

The MODE Command

Use: Controls input/output devices

Examples: `mode LPT1:80,6`
                     `mode com1:12,n,8,1,p`
                     `mode ,r,t`

The MODE command is a bit unusual in MS-DOS, in that it has nothing to do with disks. Instead, MODE is used to control the way your input/output devices operate. For instance, some computer systems allow you to use a printer in a variety of different ways. You use the MODE command to tell your system how to operate the printer. (MODE is an external command, so floppy disk users should make sure it is on the disk in drive A.) For example:

```
A:\>mode LPT1:80,6<Enter>
```

This may seem like gibberish to you, but MS-DOS understands it.

Broken down, this command tells MS-DOS to set the printer (LPT is the system's designation for printer) that is number 1 (some systems can have more than one printer attached at one time) so that it outputs 80-character lines, at the vertical spacing of 6 lines per inch. Don't worry about using MODE like this right now. Your operations guide and MS-DOS manual describe your system's use of MODE in dealing with printers and other input/output ports.

There is a more usual use of MODE, however. This is to adjust your display screen. You are probably saying, "There's nothing wrong with my display—or have I been missing something?" Well, chances are you are right. In most situations, your display is perfectly all right. If, however, you use a Color Graphics Monitor Adapter (CGA) you may need the MODE command.

On a television set or color monitor, you may occasionally notice that the first few characters of the display line are somewhere off in the hinterland beyond the left edge of the screen. Even the prompt may be out of sight. You use the MODE command to correct this alignment problem. Assume that the prompt is there even if you can't see it:

```
A:\>mode ,r,t<Enter>
```

Be especially careful when entering this command; you must leave a space after mode and put a comma in front of the letter r as well as a comma separating the two letters. This command tells MS-DOS to move the display to the right. Here is how MS-DOS responds:

```
Resident portion of MODE loaded
012345678901234567890123456789012345678901234567890123456789

Do you see the leftmost 0? (Y/N)
```

If you still need to move the display to the right, enter "N." If you can see the 0 at the far left, enter "Y." It would be nice if all problems could be solved so easily.

If you can't see the characters to the far right of your screen, use MODE to move them to the left. Issue the same command, but substitute an "L" for the "R":

```
A:\>mode ,l,t <Enter>

012345678901234567890123456789012345678901234567890123456789

Do you see the rightmost 9? (Y/N)
```

Respond yes if you can see the 9, or no to move the display farther to the left. After you have adjusted the display and answered yes, MS-DOS returns you to the operating system.

In addition to setting up your printer and aligning your display, MODE can also be used for setting up additional advanced applications, such as communications. You can find this additional information in your user's manual or in the *MS-DOS Bible* (SAMS P/C #22408).

Well, you have expanded your knowledge of MS-DOS rather significantly in this chapter. Not only can you now use the keyboard and special keys to edit, but you can list your files to your specification (DIR /w and DIR /p), you can FORMAT with new options (/v and /s), and you can put the system on preprogrammed disks (SYS). Users of later versions of MS-DOS have also learned about some nice features available with those versions. To verify that your disks are holding up, you can use CHKDSK and, if your display is askew, you can fix that too. In the next chapter we will present a whole new idea about how to use MS-DOS files: batch processing!

Mixing up a Fresh Batch

- What Are Batch Files?
- Creating a Batch File from Scratch
    - A Choice of Cooking Methods
- How Do You Use a Batch File?
    - Starting a Batch File
    - Solving a Problem with a Batch File: FORMAT Revisited
    - Stopping a Batch File
- Adding More Ingredients
- Commands in Batch Processing
    - You Can CALL On Me (Chaining Batch Files)
- Putting It on Automatic

9 Mixing up a Fresh Batch

As you've become more familiar with MS-DOS commands, you've gained an understanding of how, when, and why to use specific commands. What you may have found difficult at first has become increasingly routine as you've employed the same combinations of commands over and over.

By now you've seen that many of the operations you perform with the computer are repetitive. You've probably found yourself using certain sequences of commands, in the same pattern, over and over again (for example, formatting a new disk and then running CHKDSK to make sure everything was all right). Just as the editing keys gave you one shortcut to avoid useless repetitiveness, MS-DOS has another helpmate to save you time and frustration. This new tool is called a *batch file*, and in this chapter we are going to see how batch files can make your computing more efficient.

What Are Batch Files?

Batch files are something like a cookbook for commands. They contain lists of "steps" in the form of MS-DOS commands that combine to produce one result. After this "recipe" is established, the batch file gives you the same result every time you run it. The "ingredients" in a batch file are data files. These may change from time to time, but the product of the batch file still takes the same form. A real-life example may explain this concept further.

There is a standard commodity in everyone's life, called "bread." But bread does not just spring full-grown from the earth. What is called bread is really a combination of wheat, liquid, and flavoring that, mixed together and baked, is recognized as bread. When you make bread, the ingredients may vary. You can use whole wheat or white flour; you may include water or milk; you may add raisins or caraway seeds. The steps, however, in making bread always follow a specific pattern. First you measure, then you combine, then you knead, and finally you bake. The result is bread: white, wheat, rye, or whatever.

A recipe for bread is a shortcut most cooks use, because it defines what and how much and in what order. Not only does this reduce mistakes, it makes the process go faster, because the procedure is already laid out; you just follow the instructions. When you want to make some bread, you simply reach for the recipe and the ingredients. You don't have to stop and think, "How much of this? How long do I do that?" Indeed, you can buy bread-making machines that automatically follow the recipe; you just put the ingredients in the hopper, and a few hours later the bread is ready.

Batch files perform for MS-DOS users a service similar to the bread-making machine. You provide a series of commands—the "recipe" that, when executed in order, provides specific results. The product is always the same because you follow the same steps each time. The "ingredients" may change, however. Even if you enter different file names, the commands still perform in the same order. And since all these commands are stored in one file (identified by a "batch file name"), you can use this formula over and over again simply by entering the batch file name. Not only is this faster than entering each command separately, it also eliminates mistakes, because the commands are already correctly entered in the batch file. The batch file is already "made up."

sequence of instructions + ingredients	= bread
series of commands + data-file names	= batch file

The bottom line is that assembling a "cookbook" full of well-chosen batch files will save you time and effort. You save time because, once you've created the batch file, you don't have to stop and think about all of the steps involved in a particular procedure. And you save effort, because you don't have to memorize arcane MS-DOS commands with many switches and file names attached to them. Furthermore, batch files never forget part of a command or make typing errors! Indeed, batch files are so popular that magazines for PC users run regular columns in which users share their favorite batch discoveries.

Batch files are ordinary ASCII text files, just like the files you use when you work with typical MS-DOS commands such as DIR, COPY, and TYPE. Batch files contain MS-DOS commands, plus some explanatory statements. How much a batch file can do is dependent on how many and what kinds of commands you enter. Batch files are most useful when they perform a lengthy sequence of commands that you use very frequently or an obscure, complex command that you use only once in a while. In the first case you save time by avoiding repetitive typing; in the second case you save the effort of looking up or memorizing a complex command.

Creating a Batch File from Scratch

Before you can follow a recipe, it has to be written down. Putting a series of commands in a batch file is simple. The rules for a batch file's name are the same as for other file names, but in a batch file you must include the extension ".BAT."

To run through this exercise on batch files, take on the role of a computer "baker." The goodie you are going to whip up is a practice file called "datafile." For brevity's sake, this file will contain only one line: "This is test data for a batch file." This is an ASCII file, so you can use EDLIN or EDIT to create this data file. Here we'll show you how to do it using EDLIN.

EDLIN is on your system disk as the file "EDLIN.COM" ("EDLIN.EXE" for MS-DOS version 5.0). Your "datafile" will also be placed on the system disk. Put this disk in drive A and call up EDLIN.

A Note to Hard Disk Users

Hard disk users don't need a system disk in drive A to run EDLIN or other commands. However, it is safest to make a floppy drive such as A the current drive while developing batch files, and to put your test data files on the floppy disk. That way, if you make a mistake you won't hurt anything on your hard disk.

```
A:\>edlin datafile<Enter>
New file
*i<Enter>
     1:*This is test data for a batch file.<Enter>
     2:*^C

*e<Enter>
```

This file is going to be the "generic" data file for testing batch files. It stands for any files you might want to use in the batch file.

A Choice of Cooking Methods

Up until now, using EDLIN or EDIT was the only method you knew for creating a file. But there is an alternative way to create files: the COPY command. You are going to use both methods to create your batch file. Let's start with EDLIN.

As is true whenever you use EDLIN, you must be sure the system disk you are using contains the EDLIN.COM (or EDLIN.EXE) file. This disk is probably still in drive A from the creation of "datafile" in the previous example. Use it now to combine the ingredients in your batch file "typedata.bat":

MS-DOS Version 5.0 Users Can Use EDIT

Users of MS-DOS version 5.0 may prefer to create batch files with EDIT, not EDLIN. Like EDLIN, EDIT creates ASCII text files, but EDIT is easier to use, particularly with longer files. See chapter 6 for details about EDIT.

```
A:\>edlin typedata.bat<Enter>    The file name must contain the .bat extension.
New file
*i<Enter>                        Enter one command per line:
    1:*cls
    2:*echo Now typing the data file!
    3:*type datafile<Enter>
    4:*^C

*e<Enter>
```

Each command is entered on a separate line. This is the standard EDLIN procedure. The only difference is that your file name contains the "BAT" extension. What commands does this batch-file recipe perform for you? The first one, CLS, you will recognize. This command clears the screen so that it won't be cluttered with old information. The second line introduces a new command, ECHO. We'll look at ECHO in more detail later. For now, you've probably guessed that ECHO displays whatever text is put on the rest of the line. Finally, you know that TYPE displays the lines in a file on the screen—in this case the "datafile" you created earlier.

Another way to create a file is to use the COPY command to enter the information directly into a file. To do so you use COPY with the CON device name. You know that COPY copies from one file to another. CON is one of those reserved device names that MS-DOS uses to recognize parts of the computer system. CON stands for console (your keyboard). As you will see in chapter 11, MS-DOS actually treats these reserved, built-in device names just like files, which makes it easy to use familiar commands with them. Here, when you use COPY CON, you tell MS-DOS to COPY all the information you are typing in on your keyboard (which acts as the source file) and put it directly into a *destination file* on disk. The advantage of using COPY CON is that you do not have to have EDLIN on the disk to create the file. The disadvantage is that you cannot edit a line in a COPY CON file after you have pressed <Enter>.

To create "typedata.bat" using COPY CON, enter the commands in sequence. There are no line numbers when using COPY CON. Again, enter one command per line:

```
A:\>copy con: typedata.bat<Enter>
cls<Enter>
echo Now typing the data file!<Enter>
type datafile<Enter>

^Z<Enter>
```

^Z (Ctrl Z) is the end-of-file marker. It tells MS-DOS that it has reached the end of the keyboard "file."

After you enter the end-of-file marker, MS-DOS responds:

```
1 File(s) copied
```

The file has been copied onto the disk in drive A, as indicated by the fact that A:\> is shown as the current drive. Creating a batch file using COPY does not cause any of the commands within the file to be executed. As far as the COPY command is concerned, they are just like any other text. The "1 File(s) copied" message means that this newly created file is now stored on the disk in drive A.

Two Ways To Create a Batch File	
Using EDLIN	**Using COPY CON:**
External command (floppy users need the system disk)	Internal command (you don't need the system disk)
You can edit lines within the file	You can't edit a line in the file if you've already pressed <Enter>

How Do You Use a Batch File?

Starting a Batch File

Now that you have created the batch file, what do you do with it? Well, you simply enter the name of the batch file in response to the MS-DOS prompt. All the commands in the file will be executed exactly as though you had typed them in one-by-one. Of course, you must have in the correct drive the disk containing the batch file and any files to be copied. The sequence of commands is executed automatically. MS-DOS shows you each command as it is processed. The appearance is the same as if you were entering each command separately:

```
A:\>typedata<Enter>
```
Enter the batch file's name. You do not need to include the extension.

The batch file begins executing:

```
A:\>echo Now typing data file!
Now typing data file!

A:\>type datafile
This is test data for a batch file.

A:\>
```

First the batch file displayed the first command:

```
A:\>cls
```

but you didn't see it unless you have very fast eyes, because CLS took effect and erased the screen. Next, the batch file displayed the command:

```
A:\>echo Now typing data file!
```

and then executed it:

```
Now typing data file!
```

Finally, it displayed the last command

```
type data file
```

and executed it, displaying the one line in "datafile":

```
This is test data for a batch file.
```

When it was finished, MS-DOS gave us a new A:\> prompt.

Running a Batch File

1. Create a batch file with EDLIN, EDIT, or COPY.CON.

2. Name the file with a .BAT extension.

3. To run the file, enter the file name (.BAT is not necessary).

When you run your first batch file you will be amazed at how quickly the commands happen. You may even feel a lack of control as you watch messages and commands appear on the screen. But MS-DOS keeps you informed of what it is doing each step of the way. Each command is displayed as the batch file reaches it, and all messages and queries associated with the command are displayed during processing. The difference is that you can just sit back and observe!

Solving a Problem with a Batch File: FORMAT Revisited

Here is a more practical example of the convenience of batch files. It involves our old friend the FORMAT command. We haven't yet looked at how to format disks with a lower capacity than the disk drive in which they are formatted. To understand the problem, consider a 3 1/2" disk drive designed to format high-density disks to a capacity of 1.44 MB (almost 1.5 megabytes). Besides high-density disks, these 3 1/2" drives can also accommodate lower-density disks with a capacity of 720K, the disks frequently used in laptop computers. If you wanted to give some files to someone with a 3 1/2" disk drive, the safest thing to do would be to format a 720K disk. That's because all PC 3 1/2" drives can handle 720K disks, but not all can deal with 1.44 MB disks.

Your first impulse might be to stick a blank 720K 3 1/2" disk in your 3 1/2" drive, say drive B, and enter the following command:

```
A:\>format b:
```

The problem is that by default MS-DOS always formats to the full drive capacity. If drive B is a 1.44MB drive, the 720K disk will be formatted to 1.44 MB. Someone with a 720K drive won't be able to read the disk. Indeed, since the disk isn't designed to hold 1.44 MB, anyone who uses the disk at all is likely to get errors.

As you might expect, MS-DOS provides a number of switches to tell the FORMAT command the capacity at which to format the disk. For example, in MS-DOS version 3.3 you can format a 720K disk in a 1.44 MB drive with the /n:9 switch. The n stands for "number of sectors," which happens to be 9 for a 720K 3 1/2" disk. Fortunately, you don't *have* to remember this switch because you can create your own formatting command that runs it automatically. In other words, you can put this obscure command in a batch file "recipe" that formats 720K disks. But before you can do this, you need to know more about disk formats.

Dealing with four different MS-DOS disk formats can be a bit confusing, but a few simple rules can help you keep things straight. First, don't confuse the drive capacity and the disk capacity. Each drive is designed for a maximum capacity (360K, 720K, 1.2MB, or 1.44MB).

Each *disk* is designed for a specific capacity and should always be formatted to that capacity. This means that you can format a lower-capacity disk in a higher-capacity drive, but you should format it to its designed capacity. (For example, you can format a lower-density disk to 720K in a high-density 1.44MB drive.) However, you can't safely format a lower capacity disk to a higher capacity *or a higher capacity one to a lower capacity*. (In other words, you shouldn't format a double-density 360K disk to 1.2MB, even if you are using a 1.2MB drive. You should format it to 360K. Similarly, you shouldn't try to format a 1.2MB disk to 360K capacity.)

By the way, starting with MS-DOS version 2.0, you can format a 360K 5 1/4" disk in a 1.2MB drive by adding the /4 switch (that's right, the number four) to the FORMAT command. However, unlike the case with the 3 1/2" drives, some 360K drives can't reliably read 360K disks that were formatted in a 1.2MB drive. If possible, format 360K disks in a 360K drive (though you can safely copy files to an already-formatted 360K disk in a 1.2MB drive).

Starting with version 4.0, MS-DOS provides a new switch, /f, that allows you to simply specify the capacity to be used. For example, /f:720 specifies a 720K disk, and /f:360 specifies a 360K one.

Now that you know how to create and run a batch file, you can come up with one recipe to perform the obscure commands for formatting low-density disks. All you have to do is put the appropriate version of the FORMAT command in a batch file. Here's how you can do it with the COPY CON technique:

```
A:\>copy con make720.bat
format b: /n:9<Enter>
^Z
1 file(s) copied.
A:\>
```

That's it! Run the batch file "make720.bat" whenever you need to format a 720K disk. Do you need to format 360K disks in a 1.2MB drive? Just make another batch file:

```
A:\>copy con make360.bat
format a: /4<Enter>
^Z
A:\>
```

In the two preceding batch files, we assumed that your system has a 1.44MB drive B and a 1.2MB drive A, but perhaps your drives are different. If so, just change the drive letters in the FORMAT commands as appropriate. (Remember that you can use EDLIN or EDIT to create or revise batch files, though COPY CON is a bit faster for "one liners" like these.)

Now let's see how to format a 360K disk in your 1.2MB drive A. First copy "make360.bat" to your system disk (if you're not using a hard disk to run MS-DOS) and put the system disk in drive A. Next, get a blank, unformatted 360K disk (or a disk that has data that you no longer need). At the A:\> prompt, enter:

```
A:\>make360
```

Remember that you don't have to enter the ".bat" file name extension. As the batch file starts to run, MS-DOS displays the command it is processing:

```
A:\>format a: /4
```

The next thing you see is the familiar message from the FORMAT command:

```
Insert new diskette for drive A: and press ENTER
when ready...
```

Replace the system disk with your blank disk and press <Enter>. Now the formatting begins. Eventually you see the message

```
Format complete
```

And, if you are using MS-DOS 3.0 or later, you are asked

```
Volume label (11 characters, ENTER for none)?
```

Enter the volume label (if you want to use one), and press <Enter>.

That's it. You'll see the usual statistics showing the capacity of your new disk. Then, as usual, FORMAT will ask you if you want to format additional disks.

The important thing is that you didn't have to remember how to format a 360K (or 720K) disk. All you had to do was remember to run "make360.bat" or "make720.bat" as appropriate. In effect, you have added your own custom commands to MS-DOS!

Our FORMAT example is a simple illustration of how useful batch files can be. Let's look at some of the other commands you use regularly that involve a series of switches and then create custom batch files to simplify their use. For example, you know from Chapter 8 that with MS-DOS version 5.0 you can tell the DIR command to sort the file listing alphabetically. What was that switch again? Oh, yes, it was "/o:n." That's really intuitive, isn't it? Therefore, if you are using MS-DOS version 5.0, just create a batch file with the command

```
dir /o:n
```

and call it, say, "sdir.bat" (for "sorted directory"). Now just enter

```
A:\>sdir
```

when you want a sorted directory of the current disk. (By the way, if you don't have the latest, greatest version of MS-DOS, don't despair. In Chapter 11 we'll show you how you, too, can sort your directories alphabetically.)

As you can see, batch files are a wonderful way to "personalize" MS-DOS to your needs. By all means, start experimenting with your own batch files. Be sure to place in drive A a disk that doesn't have anything valuable on it. As you learn more batch-file commands throughout this chapter, you will soon be able to add powerful new capabilities to your batch files.

Stopping a Batch File

Occasionally you may find yourself in the middle of a batch file and want to stop the processing. Perhaps you realize that you don't have time to complete the batch file, or you don't have the correct capacity disk for a formatting operation. MS-DOS allows you the option of stopping batch files in the middle of an operation. Another name for "executing batch files" is "batch processing." You stop batch processing just like you interrupt any ongoing operation on the computer, you press <Ctrl>C or <Ctrl><Break>. When a batch file is processing and you press <Ctrl>C, MS-DOS displays this message:

```
Terminate batch job (Y/N)?
```

A "Y" answer tells DOS to ignore the rest of the commands in the batch file and return you to the DOS prompt. An "N" answer tells DOS to terminate processing of the current command but continue processing with the next command in the batch file. For example, suppose that you had a batch file with these three commands in it:

```
type datafile
print datafile
copy datafile b:datafile.bak
```

You decide, after viewing the output of the TYPE command, that you don't need a "hard copy" of the datafile after all. Press <Ctrl>C or <Ctrl><Break>, and when MS-DOS asks the "terminate" question, press *n* for "no" (see fig. 9-1). Now MS-DOS will skip over the PRINT command, but the COPY command will still make your backup copy on the disk in drive B.

Adding More Ingredients

Often you may want to perform the same sequence of commands on different sets of files. In the initial version of "typedata," you were only able to copy one particular file, "datafile." But this situation is very limiting. It means that, whenever you want to copy some other file besides "datafile," you need to create a new batch file containing the new file name. Obviously this limits the timesaving capabilities of batch files. But MS-DOS has provided for this situation by allowing you to use replaceable parameters in batch files.

A parameter is the part of a command that indicates what the command is to be performed "on." Usually this is the name of the file that will be affected by the command. The command "type a:datafile" consists of the actual command name "type" and the parameter that identifies on what it is to operate, that is, on the file in drive A called "datafile." "Datafile" is thus a parameter of this command.

Replaceable parameters are "dummies." That doesn't mean that they sit in the corner and wear funny hats. They are symbols that stand for the actual names of real files. In batch files, replaceable parameters are indicated by the percent sign (%) followed by a number; for example, %1, %2. The actual files that replace these symbols are specified when you call the batch file. The name of the file to replace %1 follows the batch file's name; the file to replace %2 comes next on the command line. This probably sounds a bit confusing right now, so let's see an example of how parameters work.

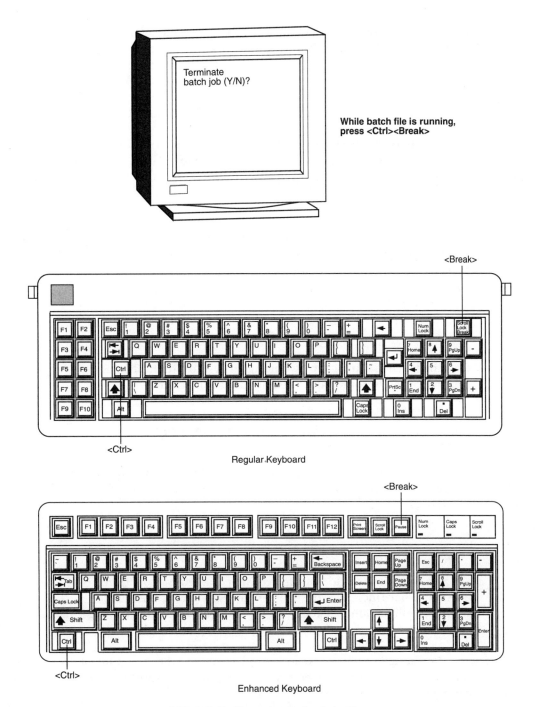

Fig. 9-1. Stopping a batch file.

Imagine that you have created a batch file to display the contents of several files. You want to use this file over and over again, but you will type out different files each time, so you create the batch file using replaceable parameters. The name of this file is "typeit.bat." Within the file are these three commands:

```
type %1
type %2
type %3
```

When you call the file you indicate the files to be substituted for the %1, %2, and %3 parameters by listing them, in order, on the command line. Leave a space between parameters.

```
typeit chap1 chap2 chap3
```

When MS-DOS encounters the first dummy parameter, %1, it substitutes "chap1" for this parameter. The file name "chap2" is then substituted for %2, and "chap3" for %3. If the file also contained another command using these parameters, for example:

```
copy %1
copy %2
copy %3
```

then chap1, chap2, and chap3 would again be substituted. The replaceable parameters will have the same values throughout the batch file.

Replaceable Parameters

```
type %1
type %2     The parameters listed after the file name are substituted
type %3     whenever %1, %2, or %3 is called for in the batch file.
copy %1
copy %2
copy %3
```

You can have up to ten replaceable parameters (%0-%9) in a batch file. It is possible to have more; see the SHIFT command later in this chapter for ways to get around this limitation. The replaceable parameter %0 is reserved for the name of the batch file itself. Thus, typing %0 in the preceding file would cause MS-DOS to type the "typeit" file itself.

Replaceable parameters can be used in any batch file. Just remember that when you call the file you must specify which files are to be substituted for the dummy parameters.

Now that you know about replaceable parameters, you can write an improved version of "typedat.bat" that includes these commands:

```
cls
echo Now displaying %1%!
type %1
```

Now you can use "typedata.bat" with any file, not just "datafile." Note that the second line has a special format: the replaceable parameter (%1%) is enclosed by percent signs. This tells MS-DOS to display the name represented by that parameter. The last line, of course, uses the TYPE command, which lists the file specified in parameter %1. Thus if you enter:

```
typedat mydata                    Run batch file with "mydata" as parameter
A:\>echo Now typing mydata!
Now typing mydata!                Displays contents of "mydata" file
```

you can see that MS-DOS substitutes "mydata" for %1% in the batch file, and the contents of "mydata" will be displayed on the screen.

Do you remember "sdir.bat," which prints a sorted directory of the current drive? Well, the DIR command can display the directory of any drive you specify, not just the current drive. How would you give this same flexibility to "sdir.bat"? Right—have the DIR command inside "sdir.bat" refer to a dummy parameter:

```
dir /o:n %1
```

When the new "sdir.bat" runs, whatever drive letter you give will be "plugged into" the DIR command in place of the dummy parameter %1. For example, you can enter:

```
a:\>sdir b:
```

to get a sorted listing of the files on drive B.

Here's another useful batch file. Suppose that you want to remove a file from your current working disk but keep an "archive" copy on another disk. Normally, with MS-DOS you will have to copy the file to the other disk (with the COPY command), and then erase it from the original disk with the ERASE (or DEL) command. With a batch file, however, you can combine these two steps into "move.bat." Here's how:

```
copy %1 %2
del %1
```

How does this work? You call the batch file by giving it the name of the file you want to move and the name of the drive to which you want to move it. For example:

```
A:\>move oldstuff b:    "Oldstuff" is parameter 1, "b:" is parameter 2
A:\>copy oldstuff b:    MS-DOS fills in parameters for COPY command
A:\>del oldstuff        File in %1 is deleted
```

moves the file "oldstuff" to the disk in drive B and erases the original copy on drive A. (Be careful with this batch file, however. If a problem occurs with the COPY command and the file is not copied, the original file may still be deleted. We'll show you how to fix this problem later.)

All MS-DOS commands can be used in batch files. But, in addition, there are specific batch commands (or subcommands) that are usually used only in batch files. Let's look at some of the important ones now.

Commands in Batch Processing

The ECHO Command

Use: Turns on or off the echoing of commands to the screen, or displays messages when ECHO is off

Examples:
```
echo on
echo off
echo Here are the contents of datafile
```

You have already seen an example of how the ECHO command works in "typedata.bat." The concept of echoing is not new to you. We discussed echoing in a different context earlier, when we used the editing keys ^P and ^N to control the echoing of the screen to the printer. Here we mean the same type of echoing, but we are talking about echoing to the screen the commands in a batch file.

Normally, the ECHO command is in the ON mode. In the ON mode, each command is echoed (displayed) on the screen as that command is processing.

The batch file examples you have seen thus far have echoed each command before executing it. This display of each command can be useful when you want to keep close track of what is happening inside a batch file—especially when you are developing and testing a new one. But this echoing feature can also be bothersome when you don't need it, cluttering up the screen with useless information.

If you don't want to see each command displayed on the screen, you can set ECHO to the OFF mode. When ECHO is OFF, the commands themselves do not appear on the screen, but all messages associated with the commands are still displayed. To eliminate echoing, enter this command prior to any commands you don't want to see. For example, if we wanted to include ECHO OFF in our new, improved "typedata.bat" file, we would enter it first:

```
A:\>copy con: copydata.bat<Enter>
echo off<Enter>
cls
echo Now typing %1%!<Enter>
type %1<Enter>
^Z<Enter>

        1 File(s) copied
```

When you run this version of "typedata," you will not see any command lines on the screen after the initial ECHO OFF command. Even with ECHO OFF, however, the ECHO command still displays the message: "Now typing" along with the name of the specified file. In effect, ECHO serves two different purposes: it turns ON or OFF the automatic echoing of commands and it displays a specific line of text.

Getting back to the new improved "typedata.bat", suppose that you enter:

```
A:\>typedata datafile
```

You will see the following:

```
A:\>echo off
A:\>Now typing datafile!
This is test data for a batch file.
A:\>
```

A much neater and easier-to-follow display!

Additional Control over Echoing
with MS-DOS Version 3.3 and Later Versions

If you are using MS-DOS version 3.3 or a later version , you can turn off the echoing of some commands and still allow the display of others. Simply precede the command with an at sign (@), for example:

```
@type %1
```

ensures that this command won't be echoed, although it will be executed. This feature also lets you prevent the line ECHO OFF from being echoed before it takes effect. Simply start the batch file with:

```
@echo off
```

If, at some point in the batch file, you again want to see the echoing of each command as it is processed, enter a new ECHO command, ECHO ON. All subsequent commands will appear on the screen.

Finally, if you enter ECHO with no parameters, MS-DOS displays the current status of ECHO (ON or OFF). Use ECHO to decide which commands you want to see during batch-file processing and to give yourself helpful messages regardless of the status of the ECHO command.

The REM Command

Use:	Puts comments in a batch file
Example:	`rem This file checks disks`

The REM (REMark) command is used, like the ECHO command, to put comments in a batch file. These can be statements to you (or any user of the batch file) that explain what the file does or what is happening at a specific moment. REM statements are affected by the status of ECHO. When ECHO is in the OFF mode, REM statements are not displayed, just as commands are not displayed.

REM commands can contain any information you think will help you understand the batch file better. You can also use REM to insert blank lines in a file. The following batch file, "newdisk," formats and puts the system (including the file COMMAND.COM, so the disk will be usable as a start-up disk) on a new disk. It then checks the condition of the disk:

```
copy con: newdisk.bat<Enter>
rem This file formats and checks new disks.<Enter>
rem The system will be put on the disk.<Enter>
format b:/s<Enter>
copy command.com b:
dir b:<Enter>
rem Here is the condition of this disk.<Enter>
chkdsk b:<Enter>
rem This disk is ready to use; don't forget to label it!<Enter>
^Z<Enter>

       1 File(s) copied
```

To run "newdisk", enter the file name

```
A:\>newdisk<Enter>
```

This is what you will see on the screen:

```
A:\>rem This file formats and checks new disks.

A:\>rem The system will be put on the disk.

A:\>format b:/s
Insert new diskette for drive B:
and press Enter when ready

Formatting...Format complete
System transferred

   362496 bytes total disk space
    68608 bytes used by system
   293888 bytes available on disk

Format another (Y/N)?n    You answer n.
A:\>copy command.com b:
1 file(s) copied.
```

```
A:\>dir b:

Volume in drive B has no label
Directory of B:/


COMMAND  COM     41035 06-07-90   2:24a
        1 File(s)      41035 bytes
                      252853 bytes free
A:\>rem Here is the condition of this disk.

A:\>chkdsk b:

   362496 bytes total disk space
    68608 bytes in 2 hidden files
    41035 bytes in 1 user files
   252853 bytes available on disk

   655360 bytes total memory
   545760 bytes free


A:\>rem This disk is ready to use; don't forget to label it!

A:\>
```

From this example you can see how the addition of REM statements can help clarify the contents and operations of a batch file. If you want, you can use the ECHO OFF mode to eliminate the display of all command lines, but remember that this will also eliminate the display of all REM statements. (You may want to eliminate command-line displays anyway, once you're sure your batch file works correctly. This way you'll avoid confusing less-experienced users, and you can still use ECHO commands to give the user important information. Remember that the display of text by an ECHO command isn't affected when ECHO is OFF.)

Comparison of ECHO and REMark

ECHO		REMark	
ON	Commands are displayed	**ECHO ON**	REM statements are displayed
OFF	Commands are not displayed, but messages still appear	**ECHO OFF**	REM statements are not displayed

```
                        The PAUSE Command

Use:              Temporarily halts the processing of a batch file

Example:          pause Remove the disk currently in drive B.
```

The PAUSE command puts a built-in stop in a batch file. You use this command when you need to do something before the next command is executed, for example, to change a disk or turn on the printer. You might also use PAUSE to allow a full screen to be read before proceeding to the next screen.

After processing stops with the PAUSE command, you must press a key to continue the batch file. As part of the PAUSE command, MS-DOS has an automatic message which appears after the PAUSE command: "Strike any key when ready." (Later versions of MS-DOS use the message "Press any key to continue.") You don't need to add this message—it always appears after every PAUSE command. Here is how PAUSE might be incorporated into our "newdisk" batch file:

```
A:\>copy con: newdisk.bat<Enter>
rem This file formats and checks new disks.<Enter>
pause Remove the disk currently in drive B.<Enter>
rem The system will be put on the disk.<Enter>
format b: /s<Enter>
copy command.com b:
dir b:<Enter>
rem Here is the condition of this disk.<Enter>
chkdsk b:<Enter>
rem This disk is ready to use; don't forget to label it!<Enter>
^Z<Enter>

        1 File(s) copied
```

Here is how you see this version of "newdisk":

```
A:\>rem This file formats and checks new disks.

A:\>pause Remove the disk currently in drive B.
Strike a key when ready . . .                      You press a key.

A:\>rem The system will be put on the disk.

A:\>format b: /s
Insert new diskette for drive B:
and press Enter when ready

Formatting...Format complete
System transferred
```

```
  362496 bytes total disk space
   41035 bytes used by system
  293888 bytes available on disk

Format another (Y/N)?n                                You answer n.
A:\>copy command.com b:
1 file(s) copied.
A:\>dir b:

Volume in drive B has no label
Directory of B:\


COMMAND  COM      41035 06-07-90    2:24a
         1 File(s)        41035 bytes
                        252853 bytes free
A:\>rem Here is the condition of this disk.

A:\>chkdsk b:

  362496 bytes total disk space
   68608 bytes in 2 hidden files
   41035 bytes in 1 user files
  252853 bytes available on disk

  655360 bytes total memory
  545760 bytes free

A:\>rem This disk is ready to use; don't forget to label it!

A:\>
```

PAUSE is useful as a safety device within a batch file. In the preceding example you used it as a warning so that you will be sure not to format a disk that contains data. This warning can be very effective in helping you avoid those heartrending errors that we all make at one time or another. For example, you might have included in a batch file the command to erase all old files. Inserting a pause command could save you from a frustrating mistake:

```
dir b:
pause Make sure all desired files have been copied, or BREAK.
del oldfiles
```

Unfortunately, however, PAUSE will not display your message when ECHO is off—you'll see only the "Press any key to continue" message.

The IF Command

Use:	Executes a command depending on a condition
Example:	IF *condition command*

There are three conditions:
```
IF exist
IF string 1 = = string 2
IF errorlevel#
```

Thus far all of our batch files have been executed straight through, one command after the other. Sometimes, however, you may want to execute a particular command only if some particular condition is true—or only if it is false. For example, you might want to copy a file to a destination only if there isn't a copy of that file already there. You use the IF command to specify conditions for batch processing.

The IF command tells the batch file to execute the specified command if a certain condition is true. The condition can be one of three options. The first is IF EXIST. IF EXIST uses a file specification as the test. If the file exists (the condition is true), then the specified command is executed. If the file does not exist (the condition is false), then the specified command is not executed and batch processing continues with the next command.

For our "IF EXIST" example, let's modify "f720.bat" so that it won't format a disk that already is bootable (that is, it has the hidden system files and COMMAND.COM on it).

You may recall that "f720.bat" consists of the command

```
format /n:9 b:
```

Suppose, however, that you use EDLIN or another text editor to change this batch file so that it reads as follows:

```
if exist b:command.com exit
format /n:9 b:
```

Now, if drive B: has the file "command.com" on it, the EXIT command immediately terminates the batch file without running the FORMAT command (see fig. 9-2). On the other hand, if "command.com" isn't on the disk in drive B, then the FORMAT command is executed.

The second IF option uses a string as a test. The term "string" is simply computerese for a group of characters. In this IF command you tell DOS to perform a certain operation when the strings match (the condition is true). When you enter the strings into the command, they are separated by two equal signs (==).

To see how IF conditions work with strings, consider the following example. Suppose that you have a utility program called "printer." This program prints files using various switches such as the number of spaces between lines (/s) and the number of characters per line (/c). Let's assume that you commonly use three different kinds of printout: single-spaced, 80 characters per line; single-spaced, 60 characters per line; and double-spaced, 80 characters per line. Rather than having to remember (and type in) the various combination of switches for each setting, you create a batch file called "myprint.bat" that does the work for you:

```
if %1==wide printer /s:1 /c:80 %2
if %1==narrow printer /s:1 /c:60 %2
if %1==double printer /s:2 /c:80 %2
```

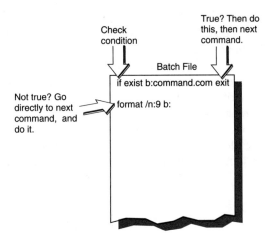

Fig. 9-2. The IF command.

When the batch file runs, MS-DOS checks parameter %1 against each of the IF statements, and the appropriate command is executed. For example, suppose you enter:

```
A:\>myprint wide datafile
```

Since the condition "if %1==wide" is true, its corresponding command, "printer /s:1 /c:80 datafile", is executed. (In this case "datafile" is used because it is parameter %2). Again, once you put the appropriate commands in the batch file, you don't have to remember command switches any more. This example also shows that batch files aren't limited to executing MS-DOS commands such as FORMAT or PRINT. They can just as easily execute any other program, such as a word processor or a disk-checking utility.

The third IF option uses ERRORLEVEL as the test. ERRORLEVEL is an indicator (sometimes called a flag) that signals the status of a certain condition. ERRORLEVEL is internally set as a part of certain MS-DOS commands. (The commands that provide ERRORLEVEL flags, and the flags provided, vary considerably from version to version of MS-DOS. Later versions define more ERRORLEVEL values.) ERRORLEVEL provides a value for the IF statement, and that value indicates whether an operation was successfully performed. ERRORLEVEL 1 indicates failure of the operation; ERRORLEVEL 0 indicates successful completion of the command. Some commands have additional ERRORLEVEL values that indicate whether a problem occurred and what the problem was—see the reference section of your MS-DOS manual (or *The Waite Group's MS-DOS Bible, 3rd ed.*) for details.

Imagine that you had a program that copied all files from one disk to another. This "copyall" file includes these commands:

```
copy a:*.* b:
if errorlevel 1 echo copyall failure
dir b:
```

The message "copyall failure" appears on the screen whenever all the files are not successfully copied. Failure to complete the operation in this case makes the condition true because the value 1 meant that the COPY command failed at some point. The message does not appear when all the files are copied, because this results in an ERRORLEVEL of 0 and the IF condition is false.

These IF commands may seem a bit complicated at first. As you begin to use this command, take your time and go slowly. A few practice sessions will increase your confidence tremendously. You will discover very quickly just how useful the IF command can be in making your batch commands do exactly what you need them to do.

The GOTO Command

Use:	Transfers processing to a specified location defined by a label
Example:	`GOTO :repeat`

As you can see, the IF command can make your batch files more versatile and make their behavior more appropriate to the circumstances in which they are run. But by itself, IF can only control the execution of a single command. What if you want several things to happen if a condition is true, and several other things to happen instead if it is false? You need a way to let the IF statement determine which part of the batch file (and thus what group of commands) to execute next. The GOTO command serves this purpose.

The GOTO command works in conjunction with a label. A label is a name you choose to identify a location in a batch file. Labels are similar to the line numbers in EDLIN that indicate a location in a text file. The label is preceded by a colon (:). GOTO transfers control of processing to the line after the label, as shown in figure 9-3.

For example, our latest version of "f720.bat" includes an IF statement that checks whether there is a copy of COMMAND.COM on the disk in drive B. If there is one, "f720.bat" refuses to format the disk. It just exits abruptly, without explanation. This may be all right with you, since you know how the batch file works, but it might puzzle another user, who might think that something is wrong with the computer or the disk. Let's use a GOTO to improve the processing:

```
if exist b:command.com goto :exists
format b: /n:9
goto :end
:exists
echo The disk in B: is a system disk!
echo Please use a blank disk instead, and try again.
:end
```

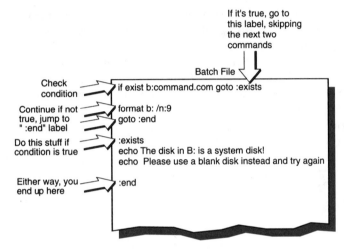

Fig. 9-3. The GOTO command.

To see how this works, go through the batch file step by step. First, assume that the file "command.com" is on drive B. If it is, the IF EXISTS command is true, and the part that says "goto :exists" is executed. Execution now continues following the ":exists" label, and the two ECHO commands tell the user of the batch file what the problem is.

On the other hand, if "command.com" isn't found on drive B, then the IF EXISTS statement is false, and execution continues with the next line, the FORMAT command. After that command is finished, the next line in the batch file—"goto :end"—is executed; Execution then jumps to the very end of the batch file—to the label ":end:"—and the batch file terminates.

You may wonder why we need both the "goto :end" command and the ":end" label. What happens if you take them out? In that case, if "command.com" is not found, the FORMAT command is executed, and execution continues at the ":exists" label, displaying the messages. But we don't want these messages displayed if the disk in B is not a system disk. The rule is this: MS-DOS always executes batch-file lines in sequence *unless* you tell it to go somewhere else with the GOTO command. Thus we need the second GOTO to skip over the ":exists" section when it is not needed.

Earlier we showed you a simple batch file, MOVE.BAT, which makes a copy of a file and then deletes the original file. We noted that this batch file could cause a problem if the COPY command was unsuccessful (perhaps there was no disk in the drive to be copied to). The problem is that the original file will be deleted even if the copy was not successfully made.

We can use the "IF EXIST" condition to have the batch file check to make sure the copy exists before deleting the original file. Here's a new version of MOVE.BAT that includes this safety feature:

```
copy %1 %2
if exist %2 del %1
```

Now the file specified in %1 will be deleted only if the copy specified in %2 exists.

Another useful way to combine IF and GOTO is to have your batch file make sure that whoever is running it has provided all the necessary information. You do this by checking whether a particular parameter was supplied on the command line. If it wasn't, you have the batch file tell the user what is missing. For example, consider our old friend "typedata.bat," which we have made more flexible by using the dummy parameter %1. For this batch file to work, a file name must be specified at the time the batch file is run. If no file is specified, %1 will have no value. To test whether a parameter has no value because none was supplied, use the following version of the IF command:

```
if "%1"=="" goto :error
cls
type %1
goto :end
:error
echo "You need to specify a filename"
:end
```

Here's how it works: if you don't specify a file name when running this version of "typedata.bat," the parameter %1 is filled in with "nothing" when the IF command is run. In other words, the command becomes:

```
if ""==""
```

Which is true, of course, and thus the ":error" section of the batch file is executed. On the other hand, if a file name, say "datafile", had been supplied, the IF command becomes:

```
if "datafile"=""
```

which is not true, and so the TYPE command is executed.

The SHIFT Command

Use:	Allows more than ten replaceable parameters in a batch file
Example:	`shift`

After you have developed some of your own batch files and have seen just how much time they can save, you may eventually run into the problem of wanting to use more than ten replaceable parameters. You may want to type out twelve files or copy fifteen files. The SHIFT command solves this dilemma by allowing you to exceed ten replaceable parameters. You can't just add %11, %12, and so on. Instead, after you have substituted the first ten parameters, your %1 parameter drops off the list and all the remaining parameters shift one position to the left.

Suppose you want to create a batch file to display the letters of the alphabet up to and including the letter "L". This means that there are twelve parameters you want substituted into the file. This is how the contents of "alphabet" appear:

```
echo off
echo %0 %1 %2 %3 %4 %5 %6 %7 %8 %9
SHIFT
echo %0 %1 %2 %3 %4 %5 %6 %7 %8 %9
SHIFT
echo %0 %1 %2 %3 %4 %5 %6 %7 %8 %9
SHIFT
echo %0 %1 %2 %3 %4 %5 %6 %7 %8 %9
SHIFT
```

You execute this file by calling the batch file:

```
A:\>alphabet A B C D E F G H I J K L<Enter>
```

The first time you use parameters in your batch file, the first ten parameters are substituted just as they were entered. But after the SHIFT command, all the parameters move over one space to the left. The leftmost parameter is dropped and the new parameter (number 10 in the list) is moved into the %9 position. This move to the left continues each time you issue the SHIFT command.

The output of "alphabet" looks like this:

```
A:\>echo off
alphabet A B C D E G F G H I
A B C D E F G H I J
B C D E F G H I J K
C D E F G H I J K L
```

You can easily see how you could continue substituting parameters until all that you included have been displayed. When less than ten parameters remain, the spaces to the right are left blank.

The FOR Command

Use: Allows repetition of the same command on a series of files

Example:
```
for %%A in (chap1.txt chap2.txt
chap3.txt) do dir %%A
```

You have already learned how "wild cards" can help you work with more than one file at a time. With the FOR command, you can design a batch file that works with groups of files that share particular specifications. This batch command uses a few new concepts. The first is *set*. A set is a group of files that follow the "in" portion of the FOR command—they specify what the command will work with. Thus, the set in our example above is "chap1.txt," "chap2.txt," and "chap3.txt." Immediately following the FOR command is a variable designated with two percent signs (%%) and a name. This variable also follows the "do" section of the command. The FOR command allows you to repeat an action or operation for each of the files contained in the set, as shown in fig. 9-4.

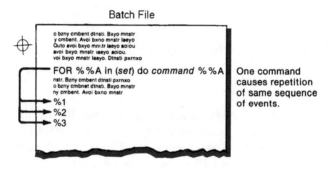

Fig. 9-4. The FOR Command.

Suppose you want to create a batch file to check for the existence of files on a disk, in this case, three files named "chap1", "chap2", and "chap3". Here is how the FOR command can accomplish this:

```
for %%A in (chap1.txt chap2.txt chap3.txt) do dir %%A
```

If the files are found, these three commands are executed:

```
dir chap1.txt
dir chap2.txt
dir chap3.txt
```

Thus you see a directory listing for each of the files.

Another nice feature of the FOR command is that it automatically matches any wild-card characters given in the file specification. To see how this works, consider the TYPE command. By itself, TYPE doesn't know how to deal with wild cards. Whereas "copy *.txt" will copy all files with the extension ".txt", "type *.txt" will return an error message.

By using a FOR command, however, you can get TYPE to work with wild cards. Here is an improved version of "typedata":

```
cls
for %%F in (%1 %2 %3) do type %%F
```

Now you can use "typedata" with up to three separate file specifications, and any specification can include wild cards. For example:

```
A:\>typedata letter *.txt *.bas
```

lists the file "letter", all files with the extension ".txt", and all files with the extension ".bas". And with this approach, there is no problem if you don't specify three different file specifications—the additional parameters will simply be ignored.

You Can CALL On Me (Chaining Batch Files)

You can "chain" batch files together so that they run one after another. For example, suppose you have been using our earlier version of "typedata.bat," the one with just the following commands:

```
cls
echo Now listing %1%!
type %1
```

and you decide that you want to use "myprint.bat" (which we showed you earlier) to print the file, double-spaced, after it is shown on the screen. To run a second batch file at the end of the first one, just put the name of the second batch file at the end:

```
cls
echo Now listing %1%!
type %1
myprint double %1
```

There's one catch about chaining batch files in this way: once the second batch file runs, there is no way to get back to the first one.

The CALL command, which is available starting with MS-DOS version 3.3, runs the specified batch file and then returns to execute the next statement in the original batch file.

The CALL Command

Use:　　　　　　**Runs a second batch file and then returns**

Example:　　　　`call printer`

To see how CALL works, suppose that you want to set up "typedata.bat" so that it can perform in two different ways (see fig. 9-5). With the first approach, it prints out the file (and displays it on the screen); the second way it only displays the file. The first version, which performs both tasks, is run as follows:

```
A:\>typedata print datafile
```

To use the second approach, enter the following:

```
A:\>typedata datafile
```

In other words, "typedata.bat" should run "printer.bat" if the first parameter is "print"; otherwise, it should just display the file on the screen. Here's one way you can do it:

```
cls
if %1==print goto :print
type %1
goto :end
:print
call myprint double %2
type %1
:end
```

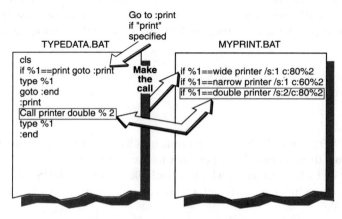

Fig. 9-5. The CALL command.

The CALL command runs "printer.bat" and gives it two parameters: the word "double," which tells it to print double-spaced, and the name of the file to print, which is in %2. After "printer.bat" has finished, execution continues with the statement, "type %1."

By the way, if you have a version of MS-DOS earlier than 3.3, you can still run another batch file and return. In place of a CALL command in your original batch file, use the command:

```
command /c batfile
```

where "batfile" is the actual name of the batch file you want to run. In the previous example you would use:

```
command /c printer double %2
```

(What this actually does is run COMMAND.COM, the MS-DOS command processor, which in turn runs the batch file.)

Putting It on Automatic

Up to now, when you created batch files each was given its own unique name. There is, however, one type of batch file that comes prenamed, and it performs one very specific and very useful function. This is the AUTOEXEC.BAT file.

AUTOEXEC.BAT is designed to make starting up the computer more efficient. When you boot the system, MS-DOS automatically examines the contents of the boot disk. If it finds an AUTOEXEC.BAT file on the disk, it immediately executes this batch file first. Thus, by putting an AUTOEXEC.BAT file on your boot disk, you can make various system settings (discussed in Chapter 13) and, if you wish, go directly to the program you want. For instance, most of the time when I use my computer, I want to use the word-processing program. If I booted normally, I would take the following steps to arrive at the opening menu of my word-processing program, called with the letters "wp."

First I turn on the computer (or press <Ctrl><Alt><Del> if it is a warm boot) and let the computer start up. My first message after the boot is the "time and date" request:

```
Current date is Tue 01-01-1980
Enter new date:
Current time is 0:00:00
Enter new time:
```

After responding to these requests, the opening screen is shown:

```
The XYZ Personal Computer DOS
Version 3.3 (C) Copyright XYZ Company, 1989,1990

A:\>
```

Now I remove the system disk, insert my word-processing disk, and call the file I want: wp (WordPerfect).

But by using AUTOEXEC.BAT I can arrive at this same point with only one entry. My AUTOEXEC.BAT contains only two lines, the ECHO OFF command and the name of the file I want to go to:

```
A:\>copy con: autoexec.bat<Enter>
echo off<Enter>
wp<Enter>
^Z<Enter>
```

As a bonus feature, when you have an AUTOEXEC.BAT file, MS-DOS automatically sets the time and date from the internal clock, so that you don't have to enter the time and date at the start of each session. This in itself is a good reason to have an AUTOEXEC.BAT file!

Of course, to make this work, I first have to put the system on my word processing disk so that I can boot using this disk. The AUTOEXEC.BAT file must also be on this disk.

Hard Disk Users and AUTOEXEC.BAT

Hard disk users should always have an AUTOEXEC.BAT file, because there are a number of special system-configuration commands (discussed in detail in Chapters 10 and 13) that hard disk users usually need to run at start-up. In fact, if you installed MS-DOS version 4.0 or later, MS-DOS creates a "starter" AUTOEXEC.BAT file for you on the hard disk. Later, as you learn more, you can add additional commands. Make sure to make a backup copy of your hard disk's AUTOEXEC.BAT before making any changes in this file.

Now, to get to my word processing program I simply start the system. Like magic, the opening menu of my program appears, with no input from me.

Here is how AUTOEXEC.BAT could be used to move you right into a BASIC program:

```
copy con: autoexec.bat<Enter>
echo off<Enter>
basica b:begin<Enter>
^Z<Enter>
```

When you boot, the BASICA interpreter on drive A is loaded into the computer, followed by the "begin.bas" program on drive B, which then begins to run. All you have to do is make sure that the correct disks are in the correct drives.

One note of caution: you can only have one AUTOEXEC.BAT file on each disk. Since each file must have a unique name, you are limited to one AUTOEXEC.BAT. If you try to create more than one AUTOEXEC.BAT file, the previous AUTOEXEC.BAT will be erased as you enter the new data.

This chapter on batch files and batch processing marks your entry into the world of the "How did I live without this?" computer user. Up until now you have been easing your way into MS-DOS knowledge. From this point on you will begin using that knowledge to make the computer work for you.

In this chapter you were introduced to batch files and batch processing. You learned that you can create files using both the EDLIN program and the COPY CON command. Each of the batch commands—ECHO, REM, PAUSE, IF, GOTO, SHIFT, FOR, and CALL—was explained. The creation of an AUTOEXEC.BAT file and some common uses of this type of file were explored. Batch processing is an area in which you will continue to develop as you find your own uses for this special feature of MS-DOS.

In fact, you have now learned how to create sets of instructions your computer will automatically execute. Another name for such a set of instructions is a "program"—and that makes you "a programmer." Take a deep breath. That wasn't so bad, was it? As you read the following chapters, we will show you some additional ways that batch files can help you run your computer effortlessly.

Of course, the more you work with your computer, the more files you create and need to store and retrieve. Some of your disks may be pretty confusing by now, and your directories are probably becoming a maze of names. Well, take heart. In the next chapter you are going to learn how to organize those directories so that you can find what you want, when you want it.

And you'll find that batch files and AUTOEXEC.BAT can help you there as well.

10

You Can See the Forest for the Trees

• Directly on the Path in Front of You
• Getting to the Root of the Matter
• Subdirectories and Pathnames
• Special Path Markers
• Getting Back to Your Roots
• Keeping Current
• Finding the Right Home for a File
• Blazing New Trails
• The Path of Least Resistance
• Taking a Shortcut
• Climbing Around in the Tree
• Watching Out for the Wildlife
    • A SUBSTitute for Lengthy Pathnames
    • Better Forest Managment: Pruning and Grafting with XCOPY
    • Jogging Along the PATH
    • Supplementing PATH with APPEND
• Organizing Your Hard Disk
• Hard-Disk Insurance with the BACKUP Command
• Using Batch Files to Simplify Backup
• The RESTORE Command

10 You Can See the Forest for the Trees

By now you are well-acquainted with the use of directories. As you have seen, directories serve as a quick reference index to the contents of each floppy disk. When listed with the DIR command, directories give the names and sizes of files and a date-time reference indicating when they were created or last modified.

Directories, of course, are not unique to the computer world. The most frequently used directory in the world is the phone book. The phone book is a simple directory. The listings are alphabetized by last name. An entry is listed in one location only, according to surname. When you know exactly the name you are looking for, the correct spelling, the first name initial or name and the address, you can find a number quickly.

But the phone directory also illustrates a problem with simple directories. When they have too much information, like when there are pages and pages of the same last name and that's all the information they have, directories lose their effectiveness. Instead of being a helpful shortcut to information, they become a cumbersome burden.

This same situation can occur in your PC's information retrieval system. When you accumulate too many files on a disk, you may actually dread the output of the DIR command. Today's high-capacity floppy disks can hold several hundred files, and listing the directory of a full disk can involve several screens. As you have seen, you can use the DIR /p command to pause the display automatically after each screen. Users of MS-DOS version 5.0 can use the DIR /o:n command to get an alphabetical listing. Such a listing helps, but long listings of many files are still cumbersome. They are like a shoe box full of sales receipts that seemed to be such a simple and easy record system: come April and tax time, its shortcomings become painfully apparent.

Directly on the Path in Front of You

The difficulty of accessing and storing many files demanded a solution in two different areas. First, a new physical tool was needed that could store more files in less space. Actually, this tool, the hard or fixed disk, was borrowed from larger mainframe computer systems, which have always had a great deal of information to process. Now, hard disks that can hold 20, 30, 40 or more megabytes of data are available for personal computers at quite reasonable prices. Indeed, today's hard disk drives cost less than the floppy disk drives in the first PCs. Most new machines sold today come with a hard disk, and you can buy an add-on hard disk for an older machine for only a few hundred dollars. A 20-megabyte hard disk stores approximately 20 million characters. As you can imagine, that could be either one incredibly long super-file, which might be impossible to use, or hundreds of smaller files. A typical number of files on a 20-megabyte hard disk might be anywhere from 500 to 800. Can you imagine using a DIR command and sitting through the listing? To say nothing of thinking up 798 unique filenames. And if you have a larger hard disk with 60 or 80 megabytes, you're talking about not several hundred but several *thousand* files!

The hard disk necessitated a solution in a second area: a logical tool to organize directories. MS-DOS, again borrowing from mainframe computers and minicomputers, has provided the answer with the use of tree-structured directories.

In this type of structure, a main or root directory branches into several subdirectories, which in turn can contain other subdirectories. To move around from root to subdirectory or from subdirectory to subdirectory, you use a *pathname* that describes how to get from "here" to "there."

The tree-structured directories are designed to help you create order out of the confusion of many, many files. But their use is not limited to the larger capacity of hard disk systems. You can use this structure on floppy disks as well.

Ultimately, however, tree-structured directories are most important to users with hard disks. Even if you don't have a hard disk yet, you are likely to be shopping for one soon, since many of today's sophisticated application programs are so large and complex it isn't practical to run them on floppy-only systems. Therefore, the material in this chapter is important and helpful for everyone.

We will start this chapter by having you create and work with files and directories on a floppy disk. This way, floppy disk users won't be left out and those of you with hard disks won't risk accidentally deleting or changing the complex directory structure that may already exist on your hard disk. Toward the end of the chapter we'll look specifically at ways to help you check the status of your hard disk and keep track of its contents.

To illustrate the use of directories, you are again going to take on a challenging role. In this chapter you are going to assume the identity of an agriculturalist who is using a new computer to organize the files in a "growing" business. To travel along your soon-to-be-created path, you will need an example disk.

Preparing this disk is going to do two useful things for you. First, it will show you just how much you have learned. These instructions, which would have seemed like Greek to you just a few short chapters ago, will now seem very easy to follow. Second, it will provide you with the necessary provisions to venture down the path to greater directory control.

If you are running MS-DOS from a floppy disk, you will need your system disk to format a new disk for use with these examples. In addition, you will be copying an external command, TREE.COM, from the system disk to your practice disk. Be sure your system disk contains this file. For the purposes of this discussion, assume that your system disk is in drive A and the disk you are making is in drive B, but if you have only one floppy drive, MS-DOS will "pretend" that you have two, and prompt you when it's necessary to change disks.

For Hard Disk Users

Hard disk users can just put a disk in a floppy drive and run FORMAT, TREE, and other commands from the hard disk. You can ignore references to a "system disk" in these exercises. When you format your "practice" floppy disk, you don't need to include the system on it. Remember, though, that you will be creating all files and directories on the floppy disk, not the hard disk.

To create the files on your example disk, use the COPY CON method described in Chapter 9. Enter the commands listed on the left. Instructions and explanations are in the right-hand column.

```
A:\>copy tree.com b:<Enter>
```
Put your system disk in drive A and a new disk in drive B.

```
A:\>format b: /s<Enter>
```
Format the disk (include the system). When "Format another (Y/N)?" appears, press n.

```
A:\>copy command.com b:<Enter>
1 File(s) copied
```
This is a command file you'll need on the disk.

```
A:\>copy tree.com b:<Enter>
```
This is a utility command you'll need later.

```
A:\>b:<Enter>
```
Change the current drive to B.

```
B:\>copy con: weather<Enter>
```
Now we are going to create some "dummy" files. You can use EDLIN or EDIT instead of COPY CON if you prefer.

```
File contains weather information.<Enter>
^Z<Enter>
1 File(s) copied
```
The contents of the files do not matter. We are making them short and to the point.

```
B:\>copy con: soil<Enter>
File contains soil information.<Enter>
^Z<Enter>
1 File(s) copied
```

```
B:\>copy con: yields<Enter>
Record of last year's yields.<Enter>
^Z<Enter>
1 File(s) copied

B:\>copy con: texture<Enter>
Notes on fruit texture.<Enter>
^Z<Enter>
1 File(s) copied

B:\>copy con: color<Enter>
Notes on fruit color.<Enter>
^Z<Enter>
1 File(s) copied
```

That's all there is to it. Five files created, just like that. You can take a look at your example disk with DIR:

```
B:\>dir<Enter>

Volume in drive B has no label
Directory of B:\


COMMAND   COM    41765   8-15-90   12:00p
TREE      COM     6719   8-15-90   12:00p
WEATHER             36  12-17-90    1:04p
SOIL                33  12-17-90    1:04p
YIELDS              31  12-17-90    1:05p
TEXTURE             25  12-17-90    1:05p
COLOR               23  12-17-90    1:06p
        7 File(s)        148 bytes
                      243564 bytes free
```

You've now created a bootable practice disk with the system files, commands, and data files you will need for the next examples. Any time you want to experiment with directory-related commands, you can start the system from this disk and not have to worry about damaging important data.

Everything all set? Let's begin blazing a path.

Getting to the Root of the Matter

Creating a root directory is easy. You have done it many times already. You see, FORMAT automatically creates a root directory every time it formats a disk. The directory, which can hold up to 112 files (more on a hard disk), is the root directory of the tree-structured system. In MS-DOS version 2.0 and all later versions, this root directory can also hold subdirectories.

Subdirectories can hold files as well as other subdirectories. A subdirectory, in fact, is simply a file that contains information about other files and how to get to them. MS-DOS treats all files the same. The only difference is that you can use subdirectories to get to other subdirectories. Once you are in a regular data or program file, however, all you can do is go back to a directory. Sound a bit confusing?

Think about the maps you use when you go into the forest. These maps contain a maze of trails. Suppose a group of hikers starts out from the same point. This starting point, the "straight and narrow" trail, is like the root directory. It is the source of all other paths.

Some hikers follow the "straight and narrow" to "dead end" or "direct" (see map in fig. 10-1). These are their final destinations. Like a root directory, "straight and narrow" contains final destinations (locations where files are stored).

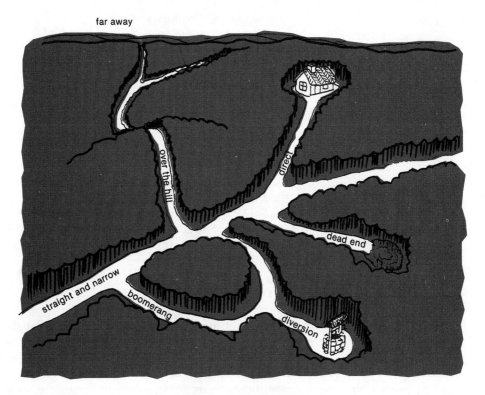

far away

Fig. 10-1. The map.

For other hikers, the "straight and narrow" is just the first step on a journey to "boomerang" or "over the hill." In this case, the root is the path to other subdirectories. The subdirectories "boomerang" and "over the hill" may contain final destinations of their own, where files are stored, or they may be links to other subdirectories such as "far away" and "diversion." In other words, files are final destinations, but directories and subdirectories are only signposts.

The important thing to realize about directories and subdirectories is that they contain files. Any of these files (locations) can also be subdirectories (paths to other files).

Subdirectories and Pathnames

The only function of a subdirectory is to group files. Like filenames, subdirectories may contain up to eight characters plus an optional three character extension. Each subdirectory must have a unique name and it cannot be a name of a file already contained in the root directory. Subdirectory names follow all the other rules for filenames.

Naming Subdirectories

Filenames can consist of up to eight characters plus an optional three character extension.

Each subdirectory must have a unique name.

Subdirectories cannot have the same name as another file in the same directory.

Names must be valid characters for filenames and follow all other filenaming rules.

You find your way around in the directory by specifying a pathname. This is simply a list of names that tells MS-DOS where to start and which subdirectories to use to get to a final destination. Each subdirectory is separated from the next with a backslash (\). In your hiking adventure with the illustrated map, the following would be the path to the "edge of the forest":

```
\boomerang\diversion\edge of the forest
```

You will notice that we did not mention the root directory, "straight and narrow," in this pathname. That is because the root directory is indicated by the initial backslash in the pathname. You never actually enter the name of the root directory; instead you use an initial backslash as a shorthand for this directory.

As a budding young agriculturist you are anxious to begin organizing your files. Your files are now on a disk (the one you created earlier) and they are stored in the root directory. Files are always stored in the root directory until you tell MS-DOS to put them somewhere else. First, you are going to create a subdirectory called FRUITS. Within FRUITS you are going to have a subdirectory called CHERRIES. The CHERRIES subdirectory will contain a file named "yields." How do you clear a path to this file? First you tell MS-DOS where to start and then you give clear directions:

```
ROOT → FRUITS → CHERRIES → YIELDS
```

which, in MS-DOS terminology, is represented as follows:

```
\fruits\cherries\yields
```

This path translates into: starting from the root (indicated by the initial backslash), go to the file FRUITS (which is a subdirectory); inside this subdirectory go to the file CHERRIES (which is another subdirectory), and then find the file "yields" in the CHERRIES subdirectory. Don't worry how MS-DOS knows which files are really subdirectories; you'll find that out later in this chapter.

Almost all the commands in MS-DOS can be performed on specific files in different subdirectories. All you need to do is tell MS-DOS which path to take to get to the file.

Pathnames are the secret to sophisticated use of your disks. Subdirectories can save you lots of time and help you keep your files better organized. Pathnames are a quick way to create, copy, delete, and reorganize files. But don't get carried away. The best tree-structured directory is one that is simple.

If you make your structure too complicated, not only will you get lost on the path, MS-DOS will spend a lot of time simply arriving at the specified destination. One good idea, until you are more familiar with subdirectories and pathnames, is to limit your subdirectories to the root directory. This way, you will have only two levels of directories, and you won't be able to stray too far from the beaten path.

Special Path Markers

There are some special commands MS-DOS reserves for creating and maintaining tree-structured directories: MKDIR, CHDIR, RMDIR, TREE, and PATH. Let's look at each of these commands in turn.

Be sure the disk you have created for use with these examples is in drive A. For safety's sake, remove any disk in drive B. Don't use the hard disk (drive C) if you have one.

The MKDIR Command

Use:	Creates a subdirectory
Example:	`mkdir \fruits`
Abbreviation:	`md`

When you FORMAT a disk it contains one directory, the root directory. To create subdirectories on the disk, use the MKDIR (MaKe DIRectory) command. Let's use MKDIR to create the subdirectory FRUITS. When using this command you may enter MKDIR or the shorter abbreviation MD. Put your example disk in drive A.

MKDIR is an internal command. This means you can create a new directory without worrying about where the MS-DOS system files are. This directory is being created from the root directory. Type in the command, followed by the symbol for the root (\) and then the subdirectory name:

```
A:\>mkdir \fruits<Enter>
```

The computer makes those whirring sounds familiar to you from using the FORMAT and COPY commands. Then the MS-DOS prompt reappears. That's it, your new subdirectory now exists in the root directory on the disk (see fig. 10-2) in the current drive.

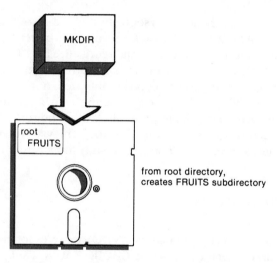

Fig. 10-2. The MKDIR command.

Seems a bit too simple? Well, for you skeptics there is an easy way to verify the creation of FRUITS; use DIR to list the contents of the root directory. Nothing special is needed to do this; it is the same old DIR command you have come to know and love:

```
A:\>dir<Enter>

Volume in drive A has no label
Directory of A:\

COMMAND   COM   41765   8-15-90   12:00p
TREE      COM    6719   8-15-90   12:00p
WEATHER            36  12-17-90    1:04p
SOIL               33  12-17-90    1:04p
YIELDS             31  12-17-90    1:05p
TEXTURE            25  12-17-90    1:05p
```

```
COLOR                 23 12-17-90    1:06p
FRUITS        <DIR>      12-17-90    1:45p
        8 File(s)       148 bytes
                     243564 bytes free
```

Right there at the bottom of the list is FRUITS. MS-DOS nicely reminds you that this is a subdirectory by including the <DIR> descriptor. You are also given the date and time of "germination." The second line of this listing (Directory of A:\) tells you by means of the backslash, which is the root symbol, that you are looking at the root directory of A.

Since you created this subdirectory from the root directory, you could have eliminated the first backslash. MS-DOS will always begin a directory operation from the directory you are in. In this case you are in root, so you don't need to include the initial \. The command could also look like this:

```
A:\>mkdir fruits<Enter>
```

Suppose you wanted to do a lot of work with the FRUITS subdirectory. You were going to copy many files and perhaps create a few new subdirectories. You can always get to a subdirectory by starting at the root and moving down one level with the pathname \FRUITS. But, just as you often change your current drive when you want to use drive B extensively, you can also change your current directory. This makes it easier to issue commands that refer only to files in a specified subdirectory.

The CHDIR Command

Use:	Changes directories or identifies current directory

Examples:	`chdir fruits`
	`chdir \`
	`chdir`

Abbreviation:	`cd`

Changing directories is as easy as making them; simply give the CHDIR (CHange DIRectory) command. The command is followed by the name of the directory that you want as your base of operations. You may use the abbreviation CD if you wish. Since you are currently in the root directory, you don't need to include the opening \ in this command:

```
A:\>chdir fruits<Enter>
```

This command instructs MS-DOS to change from the current directory to the subdirectory FRUITS. You can check which directory you are in by using DIR. No beginning backslash is necessary since you are currently in the root subdirectory:

```
A:\FRUITS>dir<Enter>
```

What you are requesting is a directory listing of the current directory. Here is how MS-DOS responds:

```
Volume in drive A has no label
Directory of A:\fruits

.          <DIR>      12-17-84     1:29p
..         <DIR>      12-17-84     1:29p
       2 File(s)           0 bytes
                      243564 bytes free
```
Your numbers may be different.

The second line of the directory message tells you what you want to know. It indicates this is a directory of the disk in drive A:\ fruits (see fig. 10-3). Since the directory name is preceded by one backslash, indicating the root directory, you know that this directory is a "first-level" subdirectory. That is, it's at the first level "below" the root directory. (The trees in our tree-structured directories are a bit peculiar from the botanical point of view, since the root is on top and the branches extend downward.)

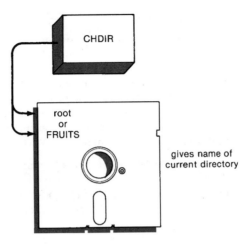

CHDIR

root
or
FRUITS

gives name of
current directory

Fig. 10-3. The CHDIR command.

The next two lines of the directory listing are something you have not seen before. The single period and the double period stand for the directory itself and its "parent" directory. You'll explore these mysterious directory symbols a bit later.

The final line of the directory listing puts you back on familiar turf. It says there are two files in this directory and gives the amount of bytes still free (available) on the disk. Starting with version 5.0, as shown here, MS-DOS also tells you how many bytes are being used by the files listed. Directories are not stored like data files, so they take up "zero" bytes. What, you may ask, are these two files? Well, if you remember, we said that MS-DOS considers subdirectories to be a type of file, so the entries "." and ".." are considered to be two files. This means that any subdirectory will have at least two "files" in it.

While you are in this directory, you can do all the normal file operations as long as the files exist in this directory. If you try to do something with files in the root directory or in another subdirectory, you will be out on a limb. MS-DOS reminds you of your predicament with a "File not found" error message. Remember that MS-DOS looks only in the current directory for a file unless you tell it to look elsewhere.

You are currently stuck in the FRUITS subdirectory. You must issue another CHDIR command to get out of the subdirectory.

Getting Back to Your Roots

There is a quick and easy way to get back to the root directory no matter where you are within the subdirectory structure. You simply issue the CHDIR command with the root symbol, the single backslash (\):

```
A:\>chdir \<Enter>
```

The MS-DOS Prompt and the Current Directory

You already know that an MS-DOS prompt, such as A:\> or C:\>, tells you which disk drive you are working with. In addition, the "install" program for MS-DOS versions 4.0 and later sets the prompt so that it also displays the current directory. You now know that when you see the prompt A:\> you are in the root directory (backslash) of drive A. Now that you are in the FRUITS subdirectory on drive A, your prompt may show A:\FRUITS>.

If you have a version of MS-DOS earlier than 4.0, your prompt may show only the current drive, such as A> or C>. In this case, we recommend that you enter the PROMPT command to change your prompt to show the current directory. For example, let's suppose you are in the FRUITS subdirectory and the prompt is currently A>:

```
A>prompt $p$g<Enter>
A:\FRUITS>
```

The special symbols pg tell the PROMPT command to include both the drive letter and the pathname of the current directory in the prompt. As you can see, the prompt has now changed from A> to A:\FRUITS>. It is a good idea to add the command prompt pg to your AUTOEXEC.BAT. This will set up the current directory prompt for you automatically each time you start your computer. Having the prompt show the current directory makes it much easier to keep track of where you are in the file tree. Our examples will assume that you have set up the prompt in this way.

Quicker than a summer downpour, you are home again. Use DIR to verify this:

```
A:\>dir<Enter>
Volume in drive A has no label
Directory of A:\

COMMAND  COM    41765  8-15-90   12:00p
TREE     COM     6719  8-15-90   12:00p
WEATHER            36 12-17-90    1:04p
SOIL               33 12-17-90    1:04p
YIELDS             31 12-17-90    1:05p
TEXTURE            25 12-17-90    1:05p
COLOR              23 12-17-90    1:06p
FRUITS        <DIR>    12-17-90    1:45p
        8 File(s)         148 bytes
                       243564 bytes free
A:\>
```

You can tell you are in the root directory because A:\, rather than A:\FRUITS, appears in the second line of the display, and the MS-DOS prompt has changed. Of course, you probably know that you are in the root because of the files listed. But when you have lots of files and lots of disks, this second line will become very handy in identifying your current directory.

Keeping Current

There is another factor to keep in mind about current directories. Each drive you are using has its own separate current directory. For instance, you may have the example disk in drive A. In drive B you have other data and program files, and, if you have a hard disk, it contains many more files and programs. MS-DOS keeps track of a separate current directory for each drive. This can cause some confusion when you want to perform operations from one drive to another.

Suppose you want to copy the file "yields" into the root directory on the disk in drive B. When you last worked on drive B you were using a word processing program, which is contained under its own subdirectory, WP.

This is how MS-DOS views the current directories:

In drive A   The root directory of the example disk
In drive B   The WP subdirectory

If you issue the following copy command:

```
A:\>copy yields b:<Enter>
```

MS-DOS complies with your wishes. However, since the current directory on drive B is WP, that is the directory to which it would copy the file. You can see how this might confuse you when you went searching for "yields" in the root on B. For safety's sake, it is always a good idea to check on your current directories before you perform any operation. See figure 10-4.

To find out the current directory, just enter CHDIR by itself:

```
A:\>chdir<Enter>
```

In this case, the change directory command really becomes the check (or identify) the current directory command. If you were in the root directory, you would see this listing:

```
A:\
```

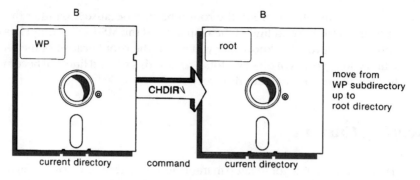

Fig. 10-4. Current directory.

If you were in a subdirectory, the current directory would look like this:

```
A:\fruits
```

Of course if your prompt is set to show the current directory, you don't need the CD command to find out where you are on the current drive. However, it is still useful for finding out what the current directory is on a different drive. For example, suppose you are working with drive B and you want to know what the current directory on drive A is. You would type:

```
B:\>cd a:<Enter>
A:\FRUITS
B:\>
```

As you can see, when you include a drive letter with the CD command, MS-DOS tells you what the current directory is on that drive. Here you see that the current directory on drive A is FRUITS.

You can see that CHDIR is a versatile command and also one that you will use a great deal. It allows you to change directories easily and quickly return to the root directory, and it provides quick identification of the current directory.

Finding the Right Home for a File

When you listed the contents of the FRUITS subdirectory, you noticed that the directory listed only the mysterious "." and ".." files; the rest of the subdirectory was empty. How do you get files into a subdirectory? The same way you always move files, with the COPY command.

On the disk in drive A you have two files, "weather" and "soil," along with some other files. Since the "weather" file contains weather data on all fruit crops and the "soil" file contains soil data on all fruit crops, we would like to have these files in the FRUITS subdirectory.

Make sure that root is your current directory. Enter CHDIR to check the current directory status; if necessary, enter CHDIR \ to get to the root directory. "Weather" and "soil" are now part of the root directory. To be sure that everything is according to plan, use DIR to check the directory:

```
A:\>dir<Enter>

Volume in drive A has no label
Directory of A:\

COMMAND  COM   41765  8-15-90   12:00p
TREE     COM    6719  8-15-90   12:00p
WEATHER           36 12-17-90    1:04p
SOIL              33 12-17-90    1:04p
YIELDS            31 12-17-90    1:05p
TEXTURE           25 12-17-90    1:05p
COLOR             23 12-17-90    1:06p
FRUITS       <DIR>     12-17-90   1:45p
        8 File(s)       148 bytes
                     243564 bytes free
```

Since copying files from one directory to another is very similar to copying from one disk to another, think of the transfer in terms of source and target (see fig. 10-5). The directory which currently holds the files is the source directory. The subdirectory to which the files will be copied is the target directory. To MS-DOS, FRUITS is just like any other file. As long as you specify a source and a target, it will copy the files, even if one of those files happens to be a subdirectory:

```
A:\>copy weather fruits<Enter>
        1 File(s) copied

A:\>copy soil fruits<Enter>
        1 File(s) copied
```

That's all. As easy as that you have two new files in your FRUITS subdirectory. The files have not been deleted from the root directory; they have simply been duplicated in the FRUITS subdirectory. You can check this by using DIR. First make sure the files are still in the root directory. Since this is your current directory, just enter DIR:

```
A:\>dir<Enter>

Volume in drive A has no label
Directory of A:\
```

```
COMMAND   COM    41765   8-15-90   12:00p
TREE      COM     6719   8-15-90   12:00p
WEATHER             36  12-17-90    1:04p
SOIL                33  12-17-90    1:04p
YIELDS              31  12-17-90    1:05p
TEXTURE             25  12-17-90    1:05p
COLOR               23  12-17-90    1:06p
FRUITS         <DIR>       12-17-90  1:45p
          8 File(s)       148 bytes
                       241516 bytes free
```

You can see that both "weather" and "soil" are still in this directory.

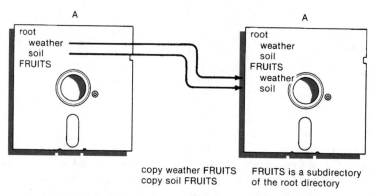

copy weather FRUITS   FRUITS is a subdirectory
copy soil FRUITS   of the root directory

Fig. 10-5. Copying files to a subdirectory.

One way to verify that "weather" and "soil" are also part of the FRUITS subdirectory is to change the current directory to FRUITS and then use the DIR command:

```
A:\>chdir fruits<Enter>
A:\>dir<Enter>
```

But you can also check on FRUITS without leaving the root directory, that is, without changing the current directory. Just ask for a directory listing with a pathname that specifies the directory you want to see:

```
A:\>dir \fruits<Enter>

Volume in drive A has no label
Directory of A:\fruits
```

```
.          <DIR>      12-17-90    1:29p
..         <DIR>      12-17-90    1:29p
WEATHER        36     12-17-90    1:04p
SOIL           33     12-17-90    1:04p
       4 File(s)          69 bytes
                     241516 bytes free
```

You can see that the two files have now been added to the directory of the FRUITS subdirectory. A comparison of the amount of bytes still free will show you that the space on the disk has been reduced by the number of bytes in these two files. (Actually, MS-DOS sets a minimum space allocation for any file. With the particular disk format we are using here, even a tiny file like "weather" is allocated 1024 bytes rather than just 36.)

Both root and FRUITS exist on the same disk. More importantly, two copies of "weather" and "soil" exist on the same disk and they both have the same name. This violates one of our cardinal rules of filenaming: every file on a disk must have a unique name.

Don't let this shake you. It just means we have to make a slight modification of the rule. From now on:

Every file in a directory must have a unique name.

While this capability of having duplicate files may seem confusing at first, it also has many advantages. For one thing, you can use the same name in different situations. For example, the directory for a spreadsheet program might include a file called "readme" with instructions for using the program. Meanwhile, a word processing subdirectory might also have a file called "readme" with other instructions. MS-DOS, however, will never get the two files confused because they are in different directories.

You are now ready to create a new subdirectory on this disk. Not only do you grow fruits, but you also have extensive lumber holdings. So your new subdirectory is named LUMBER. It so happens that your "weather" and "soil" files also contain information on conditions related to effective forest management. So you want these files in this new subdirectory also. If you are still in the \FRUITS directory, change back to root with CHDIR \. Starting in the root directory, you can perform this operation with three simple commands:

```
A:\>mkdir lumber<Enter>

A:\>copy weather lumber<Enter>
        1 File(s) copied

A:\>copy soil lumber<Enter>
        1 File(s) copied
```

To check on the creation of this subdirectory, first ask for a directory of root, your current directory:

```
A:\>dir<Enter>

Volume in drive A has no label
Directory of A:\

Volume in drive A has no label
Directory of A:\

COMMAND   COM    41765  8-15-90   12:00p
TREE      COM     6719  8-15-90   12:00p
WEATHER             36 12-17-90    1:04p
SOIL                33 12-17-90    1:04p
YIELDS              31 12-17-90    1:05p
TEXTURE             25 12-17-90    1:05p
COLOR               23 12-17-90    1:06p
FRUITS      <DIR>      12-17-90    1:45p
LUMBER      <DIR>      12-17-90    1:53p
        9 File(s)          148 bytes
                        239468 bytes free
```

Yes, the new subdirectory LUMBER is part of your root directory.
Now let's make sure that our two files have been copied to the new subdirectory:

```
A:\>dir \lumber<Enter>

Volume in drive A has no label
Directory of A:\lumber

.           <DIR>      12-17-90    1:42p
..          <DIR>      12-17-90    1:42p
WEATHER             36 12-17-90    1:04p
SOIL                33 12-17-90    1:04p
        4 File(s)           69 bytes
                        239468 bytes free
```

And that's it. Now you are proficient not only at creating new directories, but also at modifying their contents to fit your needs.

Blazing New Trails

Your tree-structured directory now has two levels. The home base is the parent or root directory. This is level 0 or the starting point. Beneath this level there are two first-level subdirectories, FRUIT and LUMBER. But what about the files contained in these directories? How do we get to a specific file within a specific subdirectory?

To find a file, MS-DOS must have two pieces of information, the name of the file and the name of the directory that contains that file. And since subdirectories can contain other subdirectories, you need to specify the exact path that leads to the file you want.

You can get to a file in two different ways. The first is to start in the root directory and then list all of the subdirectories that intervene between the root and the directory holding the file. The second is to change to the desired subdirectory with CHDIR and then refer to the file by name.

Alternative Paths

To find and list a file in a subdirectory from the root directory:

- Ask for it by name **TYPE fruits \weather**

- Change the directory **chdir \fruits**
  and ask for the file **TYPE weather**

Suppose you want a listing of a file in the FRUITS directory called "weather." You are now in the root directory. Ask for the listing using the correct pathname:

```
A:\>type fruits\weather<Enter>
```

or use CHDIR to change the current directory:

```
A:\>chdir fruits<Enter>
```

Then use the TYPE command:

```
A:\>type weather<Enter>
```

Your FRUITS subdirectory contains files that pertain to all your fruit crops. But now you want to create another subdirectory within FRUITS to be named CHERRIES. CHERRIES will be a second-level subdirectory; that is, two levels down from the root directory. Get back to the root directory by using CHDIR \ (you might still be in LUMBER). To create subdirectories in subdirectories you use the MKDIR (or simply MD) command:

```
A:\>md \fruits\cherries<Enter>
```

In this pathname you specified two directory names, the subdirectory which already exists and the new subdirectory you are creating within the existing subdirectory. All directories must be separated by backslashes. The actual message received by MS-DOS from this command translates like this: "Starting from the root directory (indicated by the initial backslash), go down to the first-level subdirectory FRUITS, and create a new second-level subdirectory named CHERRIES."

As usual, MS-DOS does not inform you that the directory was created; it simply returns to the prompt. You can confirm that this subdirectory now exists directly from your current position in the root directory:

```
A:\>dir fruits<Enter>
```

Here is how the display looks:

```
Volume in drive A has no label
Directory of A:\fruits

.            <DIR>      12-17-90     1:29p
..           <DIR>      12-17-90     1:29p
WEATHER         36      12-17-90     1:40p
SOIL            33      12-17-90     1:40p
CHERRIES   <DIR>        12-17-90     2:01p
        5 File(s)          69 bytes
                      238444 bytes free
```

You can see that the CHERRIES subdirectory is now part of FRUITS.

If you want to check on the contents of CHERRIES, you must give the correct path:

```
A:\>dir \fruits\cherries<Enter>
```

The first backslash tells MS-DOS that FRUITS is a subdirectory of root; the next backslash indicates that CHERRIES is a subdirectory of FRUITS. If you wish, you can eliminate the first backslash because root is your current directory and MS-DOS always begins its search with the current directory.

Here is the listing for the previous command:

```
Volume in drive A has no label
Directory of A:\fruits\cherries

.            <DIR>      12-17-90     2:01p
..           <DIR>      12-17-90     2:01p
        2 File(s)           0 bytes
                      238444 bytes free
```

The second line in the listing confirms that this is a second-level directory, a subdirectory of a subdirectory, so our entire directory structure now resembles figure 10-6.

Of course, the subdirectories can contain many other files, but for simplicity we will mention only the ones we are using in our examples.

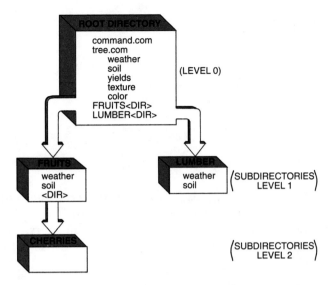

Fig. 10-6. The directory structure.

The Path of Least Resistance

Almost any MS-DOS command can be used on any file in a subdirectory. The only secret is to establish the correct path to the file.

The CHERRIES subdirectory in our FRUITS subdirectory is currently empty. Let's copy the "yields" file, currently in the root directory, into this new subdirectory. Make sure root is your current directory before attempting this. (If you've set your prompt to show the current directory, you should see a prompt such as A:\>.)

```
A:\>copy yields fruits\cherries<Enter>
```

If you want, check the contents of this subdirectory with DIR:

```
A:\>dir fruits\cherries<Enter>

Volume in drive A has no label
Directory of A:\fruits\cherries

.            <DIR>       12-17-90    2:01p
..           <DIR>       12-17-90    2:01p
YIELDS           31      12-17-90    2:07p
        3 File(s)           31 bytes
                       237420 bytes free
```

Or you can specify just the file itself:

```
A:\>dir fruits\cherries\yields<Enter>

Volume in drive A has no label
Directory of A:\fruits\cherries

YIELDS              31   12-17-90   2:07p
        1 File(s           31 bytes
                    237420 bytes free
```

When you are tracing a path to a file, first list the intervening subdirectories (separated by backslashes). The filename comes last.

This illustrates how you move down through a directory. But you can also move up in the tree structure. To move up one level, just change the directory to the "parent" directory:

```
A:\>cd fruits\cherries<Enter>
```

Your current directory is now the subdirectory CHERRIES. Use DIR to be sure you are in the correct subdirectory.

```
A:\FRUITS\CHERRIES>dir<Enter>

Volume in drive A has no label
Directory of A:\fruits\cherries

.           <DIR>      12-17-90   2:01p
..          <DIR>      12-17-90   2:01p
YIELDS          31    12-17-90   2:07p
        3 File(s         31 bytes
                   237420 bytes free
```

Taking a Shortcut

Now you are finally going to find out the meaning of those curious directory entries "." (period) and ".." (double period).

In the previous example, you moved up in the directory structure by using the CHDIR command and listing the name of the "parent" directory. This is a valid way to move up in a directory. But MS-DOS has given us a shortcut to move up one level without changing the current directory.

Be sure your current directory is still CHERRIES. Now enter this command:

```
A:\FRUITS\CHERRIES>dir ..<Enter>
```
Leave a space between "dir" and the periods.

You will see this display:

```
Volume in drive A has no label
Directory of A:\fruits

.              <DIR>      12-17-90    1:29p
..             <DIR>      12-17-90    1:29p
WEATHER            36     12-17-90    1:40p
SOIL              33     12-17-90    1:40p
CHERRIES       <DIR>      12-17-90    2:01p
        5 File(s)           69 bytes
                        237420 bytes free
```

How did you get back to FRUITS? What happened is that you have moved up one level.

This double period symbol tells MS-DOS: "Move me to the current directory's parent directory." (A directory's parent directory is the directory of which it is a subdirectory.) As long as you are not in the root directory, you can use this ".." convention to move one level up without specifying the directory's name. This does not affect the status of your current directory.

Now issue the DIR command with a single period:

```
A:\FRUITS\CHERRIES>dir .<Enter>
```
Leave a space between "dir" and the period.

```
Volume in drive A has no label
Directory of A:\fruits\cherries

.              <DIR>      12-17-90    2:01p
..             <DIR>      12-17-90    2:01p
YIELDS            31     12-17-90    2:07p
        3 File(s)           31 bytes
                        237420 bytes free
```

The CHERRIES subdirectory is listed. The single period tells MS-DOS: "Apply this command to me, the current directory." Notice that using the period conventions does not change the current directory.

(sd)"." and ".."

This symbol	*Tells MS-DOS to apply this command to*
..	My parent directory
.	Me, the current directory

The single and double period conventions are only used in subdirectories. They do not appear in root directories.

You don't have to use these symbols; don't do so at first if they confuse you. But gradually, as you become more familiar with tree-structured directories, try experimenting with their use again. They may save you a lot of time.

Climbing Around in the Tree

To really understand the usefulness of the tree-structured directory system, you need to practice a bit with moving around in the structure. To do this we are going to use the COPY command.

First, let's add a little complexity to our tree. You now want to enter your records on a second crop, peaches. The logical place for this new data seems to be a subdirectory under FRUITS. Move back to the root directory using CHDIR \ (assuming you are still in the FRUITS\CHERRIES subdirectory):

```
A:\>mkdir \fruits\peaches<Enter>
```

The information that you want to store in this subdirectory is in the file "color":

```
A:\>copy color fruits\peaches<Enter>
```

The system replies:

```
1 File(s) copied
```

But to illustrate a point, let's assume that the file you want to include in this directory is on another disk. Then the command would look like this:

```
A:\>copy b:color fruits\peaches<Enter>
```

MS-DOS allows you to copy information from a file on one disk to a directory or subdirectory on a disk in another drive. All you need to do is include the drive indicator when referring to a drive other than the current one.

There is one more file in the root directory that you want to include in this PEACHES subdirectory. It is called "texture."

```
A:\>copy texture fruits\peaches<Enter>
```

If you want to, use the DIR command now to verify the new subdirectory and its contents:

```
A:\>dir fruits\peaches<Enter>

Volume in drive A has no label
Directory of A:\fruits\peaches
```

```
.                <DIR>        12-17-900   2:01p
..               <DIR>        12-17-90    2:01p
COLOR                    23   12-17-90    1:06p
TEXTURE                  25   12-17-90    1:05p
        4 File(s)              48 bytes
                         235372 bytes free
```

As a final step, we are going to create a new subdirectory in LUMBER. This is called REDWOOD:

```
A:\>mkdir lumber\redwood<Enter>
```

As can happen with tree-structured directories, you may be feeling a bit lost right now. So, for your convenience, figure 10-7 shows a map of our current, complete, tree-structured directory.

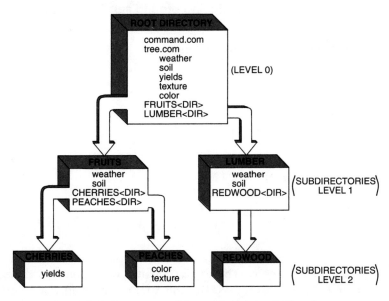

Fig. 10-7. The current tree-structured directory.

The purpose of all this intrigue is to show you how to get information from one subdirectory to another.

Within the CHERRIES subdirectory is a file called "yields." You have spent a lot of time setting up this file and now want to use the same general contents in your REDWOOD subdirectory. Here are the steps you take to transfer "yields" from one subdirectory to another.

First, make sure you are in the root directory. Because you are dealing with second-level directories, you must go up to the root and then down into the subdirectories. You can't go across to level one or level two subdirectories; the path must go through the common link, the root:

```
A:\>copy fruits\cherries\yields lumber\redwood<Enter>
        1 File(s) copied
```

(Figure 10-8 shows how to move from a subdirectory to one in another directory.)

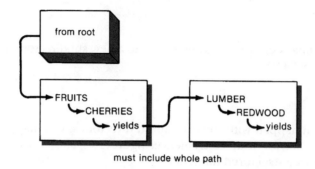

must include whole path

Fig. 10-8. Moving around subdirectories.

A DIR command confirms the copy:

```
A:\>dir lumber\redwood<Enter>

Volume in drive A has no label
Directory of A:\lumber\redwood

.            <DIR>        12-17-90     2:12p
..           <DIR>        12-17-84     2:12p
YIELDS            31      12-17-84     1:05p
        3 File(s)            31 bytes
                        234348 bytes free
```

So here is the advantage of tree-structured directories. You can move quickly within a complex structure. This can be essential when you are dealing with a large number of files on a fixed disk. But this COPY command also demonstrates the importance of clear, easily defined paths. You can see that if you create too many subdirectories within subdirectories, you can easily get lost in the resulting forest. A friendly reminder once again—keep the paths simple.

Watching Out for the Wildlife

All of the normal rules associated with the COPY command are in effect when you are working with subdirectories. Suppose, for instance, that you want to copy the contents of the subdirectory PEACHES into REDWOOD. You want to copy all the files in the subdirectory, so the easiest method is to use a wild card with the COPY command. PEACHES contains two files, "color" and "texture." (Why you would want these files in LUMBER/REDWOOD is a discussion best left to the farmer and his forest supervisor!) Using the wild card you would issue this command:

```
A:\>copy \fruits\peaches\*.* \lumber\redwood<Enter>
```

MS-DOS will tell you what is going on:

```
A:\FRUITS\PEACHES\COLOR
A:\FRUITS\PEACHES\TEXTURE
        2 Files(s) copied
```

Both files in PEACHES are now also in REDWOOD.

The usual caution when using wild cards applies: make sure you want all the files, or a number of files that are similar, to be copied before you use wild cards. Now check the contents of LUMBER\REDWOOD with the DIR command:

```
A:\>dir \lumber\redwood<Enter>

Volume in drive A has no label
Directory of A:\lumber\redwood

.              <DIR>      12-17-90    2:12p
..             <DIR>      12-17-90    2:12p
YIELDS            31      12-17-90    1:05p
COLOR             23      12-17-90    1:06p
TEXTURE           25      12-17-90    1:05p
        5 File(s)             79 bytes
                         232300 bytes free
```

Copying to the Same Disk Isn't Good Insurance

While it may be convenient to have two or more copies of the same file on the same disk, these extra copies aren't good insurance against damage to the disk. After all, if all the copies are on the same disk, one accident or mistake may render all the copies unusable. Make a backup copy of all important files to a *different* disk. Later in this chapter you will learn how to copy large numbers of directories and files to separate backup disks.

After you have worked hard and long to build a beautiful, well-designed, tree-structured directory, you have reason to be proud. But like all things, this structure cannot last forever. As your computing needs expand and change, you will need to keep your directories up-to-date. And eventually you will find that some of them are, sadly, obsolete or pretty useless. If you just go on building bigger and better directories without rearranging or removing existing ones, you will make path finding both confusing and time-consuming.

Well, just as MS-DOS provides DEL (or ERASE) to eliminate unneeded files, it also presents a command to rid you of unnecessary directories.

The RMDIR Command

Use:	Removes directories
Example:	`rmdir peaches`
Abbreviation:	`rd`

The RMDIR (ReMove DIRectory) command helps you with the housekeeping chores in your directory structure. But before you can eliminate a directory you must first provide for the files inside it. This is a safety feature that MS-DOS builds into the directory structure. It can save you from accidentally erasing a file you want while eliminating a directory.

For example, suppose that halfway through the growing season there is a terrible infestation of Tasmanian peach flies. Your entire peach crop is down the drain, and you destroy all your peach trees. Well, you certainly don't need your PEACHES subdirectory cluttering up your directory structure. In fact, even the sight of the name reduces you to tears. To remove this directory you must first get to the correct subdirectory:

```
A:\>chdir fruits\peaches<Enter>
A:\FRUITS\PEACHES>dir<Enter>
```
As with all erase functions, be careful! Make sure that you are in the correct subdirectory.

```
Volume in drive A had no label
Directory of A:\fruits\peaches

.            <DIR>      12-17-900   2:01p
..           <DIR>      12-17-90    2:01p
COLOR             23    12-17-90    1:06p
TEXTURE           25    12-17-90    1:05p
       4 File(s)          48 bytes
                      232300 bytes free
```

Now erase the files in the subdirectory:

```
A:\FRUITS\PEACHES>erase *.*<Enter>
```
Before you erase, make sure that you don't need any of the files!

```
Are you sure (Y/N)? y<Enter>
```
You answer yes.

With the files gone, you can erase the subdirectory. Since you can't erase the directory while it is still the current directory, you must do this from "outside." The easiest way to move outside is to go "one level up" from the subdirectory you want to erase.

`A:\FRUITS PEACHES>cd ..<Enter>` **Move up to the FRUITS subdirectory.**
`A:\FRUITS>rmdir peaches<Enter>` **Now remove the subdirectory.**

Using RMDIR

First, eliminate all files in the subdirectory: erase *.*

Second, go up to the parent directory: chdir ..

Third, use rmdir to remove the directory: rmdir (directory name)

It is a good idea to use DIR to make sure that the directory is gone:

```
Volume in drive A has no label
Directory of A:\fruits


.              <DIR>      12-17-90    1:29p
..             <DIR>      12-17-90    1:29p
WEATHER           36      12-17-90    1:40p
SOIL              33      12-17-90    1:40p
CHERRIES       <DIR>      12-17-90    2:01p
        5 File(s)             69 bytes
                         235372 bytes free
```

Goodbye peaches, better luck next year!

When you modify your tree structure frequently, it is often difficult to keep track of exactly which files and subdirectories belong where. How can you quickly get an overview of the tree structure on any given disk?

Well, one way is to use DIR and note all the files with the <DIR> extension. Then you can use CHDIR to reach each of these subdirectories, and DIR again, while noting which files are <DIR> files here and so on. This is time-consuming and rather frustrating. (With DOS 5.0, you can add the /s switch to your DIR command and get a listing of a directory *and* the contents of any subdirectories.) Once again, MS-DOS has anticipated this need and provides a command to give you a handy pocket guide to your overall directory.

The TREE Command

Use: Displays every pathname on a given drive

Switches: / f Lists the files in each subdirectory

Example: `tree a:`

TREE is an external command. To use it, floppy disk users must have their system disk in drive A or a copy of TREE.COM on the disk they want to examine. And, of course, they must be in the directory that holds that command. Make sure you are in the root directory and issue this command:

```
A:\>tree /f<Enter>
```

Include the /f switch to get a listing of files in each subdiretory, as illustrated in figure 10-9.

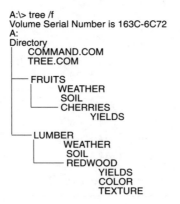

Fig. 10-9. Graphic TREE (MS-DOS 4.0 and later).

The way the TREE display looks varies somewhat with the MS-DOS version you have. Figure 10-9, which shows the TREE display for MS-DOS 4.0 or later, resembles the outlines you probably made in school. Just as each subtopic in an outline is indented under the main topic, subdirectories in the TREE display are indented to the right of their parent directories. Notice the line running from the parent directory to each subdirectory. The line running from the left side of the diagram to FRUITS indicates that FRUITS is a subdirectory of the root directory. Similarly, the line from FRUITS to CHERRIES indicates that CHERRIES is a subdirectory of FRUITS. (Remember that another way to express this relationship is to say that FRUITS is the parent directory of CHERRIES.) Notice that ordinary files, as opposed to directories, are indented without any line connecting them to their directory.

Since this display has horizontal and vertical lines, you may not be able to print it properly by pressing <Shift>-<Print Screen>. Try it anyway, and if the printed version comes out garbled, add the /a switch to your TREE command. This switch tells MS-DOS to use only printable ASCII characters, producing a display that looks like this:

```
A:\>tree /f /a<Enter>
Volume Serial Number is 163C-6C72
A:.
Directory PATH listing
|   COMMAND.COM
|   TREE.COM
|
+---FRUITS
|   |   WEATHER
|   |   SOIL
|   |
|   +---CHERRIES
|           YIELDS
|
+---LUMBER
    |   WEATHER
    |   SOIL
    |
    +---REDWOOD
            YIELDS
            COLOR
            TEXTURE
```

In this version of the TREE diagram, a plus sign distinguishes directories from ordinary files.

Versions of MS-DOS prior to 4.0 produce a display that doesn't look as much like an outline, but the same information is there:

```
DIRECTORY PATH LISTING FOR VOLUME ??????????


Path: \FRUITS

Sub-directories:  CHERRIES

Files:            WEATHER
                  SOIL


Path: \FRUITS\CHERRIES

Sub-directories:  None

Files:            YIELDS
```

```
Path: \LUMBER

Sub-directories:   REDWOOD

Files:             WEATHER
                   SOIL


Path: \LUMBER\REDWOOD

Sub-directories:   None

Files:             YIELDS
                   COLOR
                   TEXTURE
```

Regardless of the MS-DOS version you are using, you can now tell at a glance that, for example, the files WEATHER and SOIL are found in the FRUITS directory, as is the subdirectory CHERRIES. The subdirectory CHERRIES, in turn, contains the file YIELDS. (Since this tree display is such a handy way to represent directory structure, MS-DOS starting with version 4.0 lets you select the directories and files you want to work with directly from a tree diagram. You will learn how to do this in Chapter 12.)

Another advantage of MS-DOS versions 4.0 and later is that you can start the TREE display at any "branch" you wish—you don't have to start at the root. For example, here's how to start the TREE display at the LUMBER subdirectory (which seems an appropriate place to start):

```
A:\>tree lumber /f<Enter>
Volume Serial Number is 163C-6C72
A:LUMBER
Directory PATH listing
¦    WEATHER
¦    SOIL
¦
+---REDWOOD
        YIELDS
        COLOR
        TEXTURE
```

On a large hard disk you might want to see just the directory structure, not the individual files in each directory. To see the forest without seeing the individual trees, just issue the tree command without the /f switch, like this:

```
A:\>tree<Enter>
Volume Serial Number is 163C-6C72
A:.
```

```
Directory PATH listing
+---FRUITS
|   +---CHERRIES
+---LUMBER
    +---REDWOOD
```

Here the relationships between the directories and their subdirectories are shown, but the ordinary files are left out.

A SUBSTitute for Lengthy Pathnames

As you've seen, when you have more than two levels of subdirectories, pathnames can be lengthy and hard to type. Fortunately, MS-DOS version 3.1 and later offer a command called SUBST ("substitute"). This lets you use a kind of shorthand to refer to specific pathnames by letter. Once you have specified a letter to be substituted for the pathname, you can use just the letter to refer to that pathname and save yourself a lot of typing. (SUBST is an external command, so floppy disk users must have a copy of the file SUBST.EXE on their current disk in order to use the command.)

The SUBST Command

Use: Substitutes a letter for a pathname (MS-DOS 3.1 and later)

Examples:
```
subst e: a:\fruits\cherries
subst 1: c:\corres\business\1990
```

To create a shortcut for a path, type SUBST, the letter to be used as a substitute for the pathname, a colon (:), and the full pathname that you want the letter to substitute for. For your substitute letter, don't use a letter that is already assigned to a drive, such as *a*, *b*, or (on hard disk systems), *c*. In the first example in the SUBST command box, the letter *e* will be substituted for the path a:\fruits\cherries).

Once you have created the substitution, you can use the letter in place of the pathname in most MS-DOS commands, including DIR, COPY, and TYPE. For example, if your current drive is B and you want to copy a file called "prices" to the directory A:\FRUITS\CHERRIES, you can either do it this way:

```
B:\>copy prices a:\fruits\cherries<Enter>
```

or you can use this much shorter, easier way:

```
B:\>copy prices f:<Enter>
```

If you will be using certain pathnames frequently, add the appropriate SUBST commands to your AUTOEXEC.BAT file so they will be set up automatically for you.

If you have several substitutions in effect, you might lose track of which letter stands for which path. To get a list of substitutions currently in effect, simply type SUBST and press <Enter>:

```
B:\>subst<Enter>
e: -> a:\fruits\cherries
l: -> a:\lumber\redwood
```

The TRUENAME Command (MS-DOS 4.0 and Later)

Use: Gives the actual path for a substituted name

Examples: `truename e:`

Alternatively, you can use the TRUENAME command in MS-DOS 4.0 or later. In our present example, to find out what the letter *e* stands for, type:

```
B:\>truename e:<Enter>
A:\fruits\cherries
```

If you want to cancel a particular substitution, simply reissue the SUBST command, but this time add the /d switch after the substitute letter:

```
B:\>subst e: /d<Enter>
```

Finally, if you are going to use substitute letters farther along in the alphabet than *e*, you will have to tell MS-DOS to make room for more letters. You do this by using the command "lastdrive=" followed by the last letter you will use. You put this command in a file called CONFIG.SYS ("configure system") which is located in the root directory of your system disk. (If you have a hard disk or have installed MS-DOS 3.3 or later, the CONFIG.SYS file is probably already there. If it isn't, you can create it with EDLIN or EDIT.) Look at the following command:

```
lastdrive=p
```

This command lets you use drive letters *a* through *p*. Of course *a* and *b* are probably already being used to refer to your floppy-disk drives, and if you have a hard disk, it is normally referred to as *c*.

You don't have to use SUBST if you don't want to, but it can be a handy shortcut if you have several levels of directories. Also, a few old programs (such as the original version of WordStar) don't recognize pathnames with backslashes. If you wanted to edit the file "b:\corres\letter" with the old WordStar, for example, you would have to change to the CORRES directory first. But by issuing the SUBST command you can substitute, for example, the letter *l* for this path, and then you can tell WordStar that you want "l:letter" rather than "b:\corres\letter".

Better Forest Management: Pruning and Grafting with XCOPY

Starting with MS-DOS 3.2, you have available a powerful new version of the COPY command called XCOPY (for "extended COPY"). XCOPY makes it easy to copy the contents of whole directories (including their subdirectories) with a single command. This capability is especially useful when you are dealing with the extensive file tree on a hard disk. If you have a hard disk, try the following examples yourself. (XCOPY also works fine on floppies, though, so floppy disk users can use it to copy directories from one floppy drive to another.)

Thus far you have only been copying one (or a few) files at a time. You have learned that you can copy a whole directory to another directory using wild cards. For example,

```
B:\>copy fruits\*.* lumber<Enter>
```

copies everything in the FRUITS directory to the LUMBER directory. (Perhaps the fruit wasn't doing well, and you've decided to sell the trees for lumber.)

But suppose you just bought a nice new hard disk and you want to move your agricultural data to a set of directories there. With COPY, you would first have to issue the MKDIR command to make each of the directories on the destination disk. Then you would have to copy each directory to the corresponding directory on the other disk. For example, suppose that you want to copy the whole directory structure that you've created on drive B to your hard disk and place it in the directory called FARMING. First you would have to change to your hard disk and make the directories and subdirectories:

```
B:\>c:<Enter>
C:\>mkdir farming<Enter>
C:\>mkdir farming\fruits<Enter>
C:\>mkdir farming\fruits\cherries<Enter>
C:\>mkdir farming\fruits\peaches<Enter>
C:\>mkdir farming\lumber\redwood<Enter>
```

That's a lot of typing! Now you would have to copy all of the contents of these directories from drive B to drive C. You might try to do it this way:

```
C:\>copy b:\*.* farming<Enter>
```

Here, the wild card tells MS-DOS to copy all of the files in the root directory of B to the FARMING directory on drive C. But look at the following listing. Where are the subdirectories FRUITS and LUMBER, and their subdirectories and files?

```
C:\>dir farming<Enter>

Volume in drive C has no label
Directory of  C:\FARMING

.            <DIR>      12-17-90    4:13p
..           <DIR>      12-17-90    4:13p
WEATHER        36       12-17-90    1:29p
SOIL           31       12-17-90    1:04p
      4 File(s)            67 bytes
                   21456128 bytes free
```

Unfortunately, COPY copies only *files* in the specified directory, not subdirectories, or the files in subdirectories.

The XCOPY Command (MS-DOS 3.2 and Later)

Use:	Copies directories and subdirectories according to various specifications

Switches:

/s	Copies all subdirectories of the directory specified
/e	Copies empty subdirectories, too
/p	Prompts before copying each file
/d:mm-dd-yy	Copies only files that have been created or modified after the date specified

Examples:
```
xcopy c:\corres a: /s
xcopy b:\letters c:\corres\new
/d:09-15-90
```

Note: there are additional switches—see your MS-DOS manual or a reference book such as *The Waite Group's MS-DOS Bible.*

Now try doing the job with XCOPY. First, if you tried the previous example, make a clean slate by removing the directories you created on drive C:

```
C:\>rmdir farming<Enter>
C:\>rmdir farming\fruits<Enter>
C:\>rmdir farming\fruits\cherries<Enter>
C:\>rmdir farming\fruits\peaches<Enter>
C:\>rmdir farming\lumber\redwood<Enter>
```

Now, copy the whole directory structure from drive B to the FARMING directory on drive C with just one command:

```
C:\>xcopy b: \farming /s<Enter>
Does FARMING specify a file name
or directory name on the target disk d        Type 'd'
Reading source file(s)                        Path for each file
                                              copied is listed
```

Your command tells XCOPY to copy everything on drive B—files, subdirectories, and files in subdirectories—to the FARMING directory on drive C. The /s switch is necessary because it tells MS-DOS to copy subdirectories as well as the root directory. It doesn't matter that you haven't created any of the subdirectories for FARMING on drive C yet. XCOPY creates any subdirectories that have files on the source disk. (If you want it to create empty subdirectories on the destination as well, add the /e switch.)

MS-DOS asks you whether the destination is a directory or a file, because the distinction is important. Suppose FARMING was a destination *file*, not a destination directory. Then everything on drive B would be copied to this file, and each copy would overwrite the previous one. You would end up with a file called "farming" that would contain the last file found on, and copied from, drive B! Therefore, it is very important to type a *d* to tell XCOPY that the destination is a directory. Don't forget that when the destination of a copy operation is a directory, the source files are copied into the directory—they don't replace the directory.

To be on the safe side, you can create the destination directory with the MKDIR command before you give the XCOPY command. (You don't have to create the subdirectories, just the main directory.)

It is a good idea to check the results of any COPY or XCOPY command with the DIR command. When you get a directory listing of \FARMING, you will find that all of the subdirectories, as well as the files, from drive B have been copied there:

```
C:\>dir farming<Enter>
Volume in drive C has no label
Directory of  C:\FARMING

.               <DIR>       12-17-90    4:13p
..              <DIR>       12-17-90    4:13p
WEATHER                 36  12-17-90    1:29p
SOIL                    31  12-17-90    1:04p
FRUIT           <DIR>       07-09-90    4:13p
LUMBER          <DIR>       07-09-90    4:13p
        4 File(s)              67 bytes
                       21357824 bytes free
```

And if you look at the directories of FRUIT and LUMBER, you will find that all of *their* files have also been copied!

You can see that XCOPY can be very useful. Besides copying the directory structure from a floppy disk to your hard disk, you can also copy a set of directories from your hard disk to a floppy for backup or exchange with another user.

XCOPY has a variety of other switches, many of which work in a way similar to that of the BACKUP command. This command is discussed later in this chapter. After you have read about BACKUP, check the entries for XCOPY and BACKUP in your MS-DOS manual, and do some experimenting.

Jogging Along the PATH

Remember that when you call for a file with just the filename, MS-DOS looks for it only in the current directory. If you specify a pathname, then MS-DOS looks there. It looks for the file in only one location. This is true whether you are using an MS-DOS command, such as COPY, or executing a program that needs a data file. Only one directory is searched, either the current one or the one specified in a path. This is also true of your program files. When you call for a program, MS-DOS immediately searches for it in the current directory. If it is not found, it won't be executed.

But programs have an extra advantage over other files in tree-structured directories. You can extend the search for programs to other directories by using a special command.

The PATH Command

Use: Defines a path to search for DOS commands, program files, or batch files not found in the current directory

Example: `path ACCTING;\PROGS\MISC;\`

The PATH command does not have anything to do with the use of pathnames in general. It is only used to search for DOS commands, program files, and batch files. The names in a PATH command must be separated by semicolons.

Since you don't have any program files or batch files in your directory, you will have to abandon the orchards for a moment and dwell in the land of pure fantasy. Imagine that you are in a subdirectory on drive A that is called \NEWPROGS. You are looking for a program called RUNSUM.EXE. Here is how you tell MS-DOS where to look for the program:

         `A:\>path \ACCTING;\PROGS\MISC;\<Enter>`

Then, when you enter the program name "RUNSUM.EXE" (or just "RUNSUM"), MS-DOS searches for the program in four places:

❑ The current directory (this is automatic)

❑ The ACCTING directory under the root

❑ The MISC directory under the PROGS directory under the root

❑ And, finally, the root itself (indicated by \)

The PATH command can also search in directories on other drives. Just include the drive designator in the PATH command:

         `A:\>path \ACCTING;\PROGS\MISC;B:\OLDPROGS<Enter>`

If you enter PATH without any other information, MS-DOS will search the last path it was given. To discontinue this extensive searching feature, enter PATH with a single semicolon:

         `A:\>path ;<Enter>`

After this command, the search reverts to the current directory only.

It would be cumbersome to have to specify your PATH each time you start a session at the computer. Do you remember our brief discussion of the AUTOEXEC.BAT file in Chapter 9? You may recall that commands included in this file are run automatically when the system starts. So if there's a PATH specification that you use regularly, just put the PATH command in AUTOEXEC.BAT, and everything will be set up for you automatically!

Supplementing PATH with APPEND

As mentioned before, PATH finds programs (executable files) only. This can be limiting, however, since some programs have *overlay files* that contain additional program instructions that are loaded from disk as needed. While a correct PATH command enables MS-DOS to run the program from another directory, the program may not be able to find its overlay files. You can solve this problem with the APPEND command, which is available starting with MS-DOS version 3.3. APPEND works in the same way as PATH, except that instead of specifying directories containing programs, APPEND specifies directories containing overlay files.

The APPEND Command

Use:	Tells MS-DOS where to find program overlay files
Example:	`append c:\wp;c:\dbase`

For example, let's say you have a word processing program "wp.exe" in the directory C:\WP on your hard disk, and this program uses an overlay file called "wp.ovl." (An overlay file often has the extension .OVL. If you're not sure whether a program uses overlay files, check its documentation.) To help MS-DOS find "wp.exe," add the directory "c:\wp" to your PATH command. To deal with the overlay file, add an APPEND command as follows:

```
c:\>append c:\wp<Enter>
```

If the program still can't find its overlay file, try adding the /e switch to the APPEND command. This switch puts information in memory that the program may be able to use to find the overlay file. You can add several directories to the APPEND command if necessary.

Organizing Your Hard Disk

If you're only using floppy disks, the PATH command isn't too important—after all, a floppy disk can't hold more than one large application program or a few smaller ones. If you have a floppy-only system, the command

```
A:\>path a:\;b:\<Enter>
```

will probably cover all the bases, unless you have programs stored in subdirectories. Even if your current drive is B, with this path statement in effect, MS-DOS will be able to find MS-DOS commands such as FORMAT and XCOPY on the system disk in drive A.

With a hard disk, however, you probably have several major application programs and maybe dozens of utility programs, games, and so on. Just as every cook's kitchen is arranged to his or her tastes, the organization of your hard disk will eventually reflect your personal preferences and way of working. To start out, though, we recommend that you organize your hard disk so that all of the DOS command files are in one directory, each application program is in its own directory, and each major project or kind of work that you do also has its own directory. One possible setup is shown in the tree structure illustrated in figure 10-10.

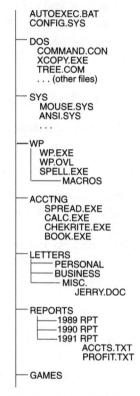

Fig. 10-10. Graphic TREE for hard disk.

In our example directory tree, the root directory has only two files, AUTOEXEC.BAT and CONFIG.SYS. MS-DOS requires that these files be in the root directory. If you want to remove COMMAND.COM from the root directory and put it in the DOS subdirectory, as was done in our example here, you must add the command

```
COMSPEC=C:\DOS\COMMAND.COM
```

to your CONFIG.SYS file so MS-DOS will know where to find COMMAND.COM when it needs it.

Many beginning hard disk users make the mistake of cluttering up their root directory with other files. This makes it hard to find the files you need. As figure 10-10 shows, our hard disk is neatly arranged into separate directories for DOS commands (DOS), other system files (SYS), the word processor (WP), accounting programs (ACCTNG), a LETTER directory with subdirectories for each kind of letter, a REPORTS directory with subdirectories for each year, a GAMES directory, and so on.

Some beginning users simply put all text files in the same directory with their word processor, all data files in the directory that contains database programs, and so on. While this makes it easy for the programs to find their files, it doesn't really provide good organization. After all, we are people, not machines; we think of "business letters" or "1990 reports," not "the word processor" or "the accounting program." Thus, it is better to organize your text files, data files, spreadsheets, and so on according to their subject matter. You then simply use CD to go to the directory containing the files that you want to work with, and run the appropriate programs from there. How can MS-DOS find the programs? Because you've put them in a PATH and possibly included an APPEND command, as shown earlier!

Hard Disk Insurance with the BACKUP Command

The more you develop your directory tree, the more important it becomes to safeguard it. Fortunately, MS-DOS makes protecting your files easier with two commands, BACKUP and RESTORE. BACKUP is used to copy files from the hard disk to floppies. RESTORE is used to put the files back on the hard disk.

The BACKUP Command

Use: Copying files from a hard disk to floppy disks

Switches: /s   Backup all files and subdirectories
               /m   Backup all files modified since last backup
               /d   Backup all files modified since a specific date
               /a   Add the backup files to files already on floppy disk
               /f   Format each floppy disk before use

Examples:
```
backup fruits\cherries a:
backup fruits\cherries a: /s
backup c: a: /s
backup c: a: /d:8-01-90
backup fruits\cherries a:d:8-1-90 /s
backup fruits\cherries a: /a
```

The BACKUP program works a lot like the COPY command. That is, it copies the files from one device to the other, in this case, from the hard disk to a floppy. BACKUP has several useful switches that allow you to precisely define the files to be backed up.

Using BACKUP follows the same pattern as the COPY command. In response to the DOS prompt A:\>, you first indicate the name of the file (with appropriate backslashes if it is not part of the root directory) and then give the letter of the target disk. If you are using unformatted disks and an MS-DOS version earlier than 4.0, you must use FORMAT to prepare the target disk before issuing the command, or add the /f switch to your BACKUP command. To copy all the files in FRUITS but not its subdirectories, you enter

```
A:\>backup fruits a:<Enter>
```

You do not need to include the initial backslash because FRUITS is part of the root directory. All the files in FRUITS are now copied to the floppy disk in drive A.

If you want to copy all the files in FRUITS and include its subdirectories, you must use the /s switch.

```
A:\>backup fruits a: /s<Enter>
```

This command copies the files in FRUITS ("weather" and "soil") and the contents of the subdirectory CHERRIES (the "yields" file), which is the only subdirectory in FRUITS.

You can also use BACKUP to copy only the files in a subdirectory. To copy only the contents of FRUITS\CHERRIES, you issue this command:

```
A:\>backup fruits\cherries a:<Enter>
```

This copies all of the files in the CHERRIES subdirectory.

Remember, if there are subdirectories in the specified directory and you want them included, you must indicate this by including the /s switch. (To see how this works, review the XCOPY command, which was discussed earlier; also see fig. 10-11.) This may sound confusing at first. But if you have a copy of the TREE output for your hard disk, it will quickly tell you what files and subdirectories are included in each section of your overall directory.

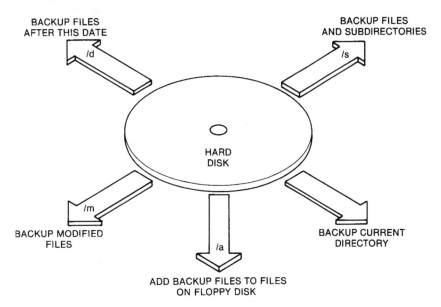

BACKUP FILES
AFTER THIS DATE
/d

BACKUP FILES
AND SUBDIRECTORIES
/s

HARD
DISK

BACKUP MODIFIED
FILES
/m

BACKUP CURRENT
DIRECTORY

ADD BACKUP FILES TO FILES
ON FLOPPY DISK
/a

Fig. 10-11. The BACKUP command.

You may also use the BACKUP command to copy the entire contents of the hard disk (like using *.* to copy all the files on a disk). When you want to copy all the files and their associated subdirectories on a hard disk, you enter this command:

```
A:\>backup c: a: /s<Enter>
```

With this command you are instructing MS-DOS to copy everything on the hard disk (indicated by the c: drive designator) to the floppy in drive A. Of course, if you have lots of files, you will have to keep inserting new floppies until the entire copying procedure is completed. DOS will prompt you when a new disk is needed.

To figure out how many formatted disks you need to have ready in order to copy the entire disk, you can use CHKDSK (yes, this works on a hard disk too!) to find the total number of bytes that you have used. You must then divide the number of bytes by the number of bytes that a floppy can hold (360K, 720K, 1200K, or 1440K depending on disk format) to find out how many floppies are needed. As mentioned earlier, backing up an entire hard disk can be very time-consuming. If you make periodic backups, it is only necessary to back up files you have created or used since the last backup. This is where the /m and /d switches come in handy.

The /m option lets you back up only those files that you have modified since the last BACKUP session. This can save you lots of time. Luckily for nonmethodical users, you don't have to remember the last time you used a file (although you could get this information from the DIR command, but that could take a long time). No, built right into the BACKUP program is an internal "marker" that tells DOS if you have modified a file since your last BACKUP.

This command copies only those files in the \CHERRIES directory and its subdirectories that have been changed since the last BACKUP:

```
A:\>backup \cherries a: /s /m<Enter>
```

Another way to back up new and modified files is to use the /d switch. This copies only files that were modified after a certain date. For example, you last backed up your files on August 1, 1991. It is now August 15, 1991. You want to back up any files in the FRUITS directory that were created or modified since that date:

```
A:\>backup fruits a: /d:8-1-91<Enter>
```

If you wanted to back up files created after a specific date and any files that have been modified in any way (not necessarily related to any particular time), you would add the /s switch:

```
A:\>backup fruits a: /d:8-1-91 /s<Enter>
```

Of course, you can use these switches to copy all modified files on the entire hard disk by using the C: drive designator. But in practice it is probably a better idea to copy modified files in smaller increments, such as subdirectories, so you can assign certain subdirectories to specific floppies. If you just back up all your files in one huge move, it may be difficult to find specific files when you want to use the backup for some operation.

The /a switch tells MS-DOS to add the backup files to any files already on the disk in the designated drive.

```
A:\>backup fruits\cherries a: /a<Enter>
```

If you issue this command, all the files in FRUITS\CHERRIES will be added to the files on the disk in drive A. Of course, you only need to include this switch if you want to save the files that are already on the disk.

If you do not specify this /a switch in the command, MS-DOS will prompt you to insert a formatted disk. When you do not include /a in the command, all the files on the disk in the designated drive are erased before any new files are written.

BACKUP conveniently displays the name of the files it is copying. To get a printout of the files you are backing up, use the control-key combination ^ P. This is a handy way to document the backup session and, if you write on the printout the number of the floppy which contains the files, it can provide a quick reference to the location of your backup files.

Using Batch Files to Simplify Backup

Batch files, which were discussed in Chapter 9, can make the backup procedure easier for you. You will remember that batch files contain MS-DOS commands, and these include the commands used with the hard disk. One of the features of BACKUP is that it sets up an exit code value (a numerical marker which is MS-DOS's version of tying a string to its finger) when it is finished copying. This code ranges from 0 to 4:

0 indicates that everything was completed normally

1 indicates that DOS found no files to back up

2 indicates that some files were in use and could not be backed up at this time

3 indicates that the user terminated the backup procedure

4 indicates that the backup was terminated by an error

Glance back to the IF command that was discussed in Chapter 9. You will see that IF can be used with ERRORLEVEL to cause a certain action to occur. By using IF in a batch file, you can automate the backup procedure and reduce the chance of making errors when performing backups. Using IF with BACKUP in a batch file is a good example of how useful and rewarding batch files can be. Here is how using ERRORLEVEL might clarify the operations going on in a batch file:

```
C:\BATCH>copy con: backall.bat<Enter>
backup c: a: /s<Enter>
if errorlevel echo backall completed<Enter>
if errorlevel 1 echo backall failure<Enter>
if errorlevel 2 echo some files were in use<Enter>
if errorlevel 3 echo you've terminated backall<Enter>
if errorlevel 4 echo an error has terminated backall<Enter>
^Z<Enter>
1 file(s) copied.
```

This discussion on backing up your hard disk has accomplished two things: it has impressed upon you the importance of backing up your hard disk files frequently, and it has demonstrated the ins and outs of the BACKUP command.

Sometimes, when you first read about a command that is unfamiliar to you and has several switches, it may seem like just too much work. But BACKUP is really nothing more than COPY with a few added flourishes.

The RESTORE Command

The entire rationale behind backing up files is, of course, to prepare for the worst, the loss of a file. After you have all your files safely stored away, the next question is "How do I get them back on the hard disk from the floppies?" The answer is the RESTORE command.

The RESTORE Command

Use: Copies one or more files from floppy disks to a hard disk

Switches: /s   Include all subdirectories in the restoration
              /p   Check whether the files being restored have been
                    modified since they were last backed up

Examples: `restore a: c:fruits\cherries`
              `restore a: c:fruits /s`

When you "restore" something you return it to its original condition, such as restoring furniture (or attempting to restore hair). But "restore" might also mean "store again." Both of these meanings tell you what this command does; it copies back your files from the floppy disk to the hard disk in the same form as they were when you last backed them up. For clarification, see figure 10-12.

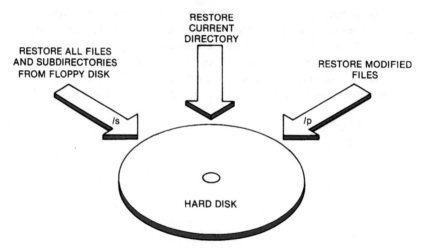

Fig. 10-12. The RESTORE command.

You can only use RESTORE with files that have been copied with the BACKUP command. Files that were copied using COPY won't work with this command. You provide the same information in the RESTORE command as you do in BACKUP: the source disk, the target disk, and the name of the files to be copied. To restore all of the files in the FRUITS directory, you enter this command:

```
A:\>restore a: c:fruits<Enter>
```

Once again, if you want to copy all the files and any subdirectories in the directory, you must include the /s switch:

```
A:\>restore a: c:fruits /s<Enter>
```

RESTORE also has another switch, /p. You include /p when you want to see whether the files you are restoring have changed since they were last backed up. This prevents you from restoring a copy of a file that does not include recent modifications. (Of course, if you have not made a backup since modifying the file, you are out of luck. This is another good reason to make frequent backups.) Including /p verifies the files to be sure they are the latest version:

```
A:\>restore a: c:fruits\cherries /p<Enter>
```

RESTORE can also be used with the IF command and the ERRORLEVEL option when the command is to be included in a batch file.

And really that's all there is to using your hard disk. BACKUP and RESTORE are the only two commands in MS-DOS that are reserved for hard disk use. You can use all the other MS-DOS commands with your hard disk.

Comparing COPY, DISKCOPY, XCOPY, and BACKUP

You may be confused about the differences between the COPY, DISKCOPY, XCOPY, and BACKUP commands. All of these commands copy files, but they do it differently and are designed for different purposes.

COPY simply copies all of the specified files from the source to the destination.

DISKCOPY makes an exact copy of an entire disk. Because it makes an exact copy, you can only use it when the source and destination disks have the same format. (That is, you can't copy a 360K disk to a 1.2M disk, even though there would be plenty of room to spare.)

XCOPY works like COPY, but it can copy all of the subdirectories and their contents. XCOPY is a good way to copy all of the files on a disk to a disk with a different format. Just specify the root directory of the source disk and add the /s switch to copy all the subdirectories.

BACKUP is like XCOPY in that it can copy subdirectories and can select files according to various criteria, such as date. BACKUP, however, copies all of the files into a single large file on each backup disk, and you must use RESTORE to extract the backup files for later use. BACKUP is thus most useful for making "archival" or insurance copies for use only if some problem occurred with the working disks.

This concludes your entry into the complex, exciting world of tree-structured directories. Using this tool, with restraint, on floppy disk systems is a convenience. But using this tool on hard disks is a necessity. In this chapter you have learned about root directories and subdirectories. You have traveled along the path to finding better file organization. In addition to learning how to put files in a subdirectory, you moved around inside the tree-structured directory to create pathnames to find and store files. Finally, you have become familiar with the directory commands: MKDIR,

CHDIR, RMDIR, TREE, XCOPY, SUBST, TRUENAME, PATH, and APPEND. You have also learned how to ensure the safety of your precious data by using BACKUP and RESTORE with your hard disk.

11

Plumbing Techniques

- Diverting the Flow
- Redirecting Standard Output
- Redirecting Standard Input
  - The Trans-DOS Pipeline
- Filtering the Flow
  - To FIND and SORT Still MORE
- The DOSKEY to Command Performance
  - Recalling Previous Commands
  - Editing Commands
  - Using More Than One Command at a Time
  - Holy Macro, DOS Man!

11 Plumbing Techniques

The title of this chapter may sound to you like a text for a beginning plumbing class. You're probably wondering what it is doing as a chapter in a book on operating systems.

But hold on. The plumbing techniques we will discuss—pipes, filters, and redirection—are actually sophisticated data-management commands. These commands give you choices in determining where your information comes from (input) and where it goes after you're finished with it (output). They are the frosting on the cake in allowing you to make the most of your MS-DOS operating system.

In addition to showing you how to hook up MS-DOS commands with the plumbing that gets your data flowing in the right direction, we'll also show you how MS-DOS version 5.0 users can enhance their control of the command line. With the new DOSKEY command, you can keep a list of handy, reusable commands, put more than one command on a line, and define your own command combinations.

Diverting the Flow

You know from your own computer use that you normally enter information from your keyboard. The keyboard is the standard input device in personal computer systems.

When you want to look at your input or see the results of programs, you use your screen. The monitor or display screen is the standard output device in personal computer systems (see fig. 11-1).

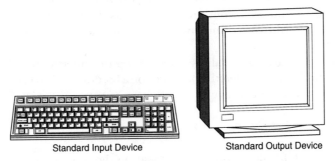

Standard Input Device   Standard Output Device

Fig. 11-1. Keyboard and display.

However, it is possible for MS-DOS to use other devices for input and output. For example, one file can be the source of input and a second file can be the location of the output.

MS-DOS sees things in black and white. There is a standard input device and a standard output device. By default these are the keyboard and display screen. But MS-DOS doesn't really care what provides the input and output as long as you label them as the standard input and output devices when issuing commands. When you designate files, programs, or other devices as the means of input and/or output, you are using the concept of redirection.

Redirecting Standard Output

The reasons to redirect output are numerous. Perhaps a specific program or command results in a new version of your data; you would like to keep this information in a separate file. Or you may want to have data automatically output to the printer. Perhaps you want to add output information to an already-existing file.

No doubt you recognize the ">" symbol from your high school math classes. It means greater than. But in MS-DOS this symbol indicates the redirection of output. Think of it as standing for "send to this place," with the arrow pointing the way to the file or device to receive the information. Here is how you might redirect the output of a DIR command:

```
A:\>dir >listing<Enter>
```

As a result of this command, the directory of the disk in the current drive is sent to a newly created disk file called "listing." The > character before the filename reassigns this file as the standard output device. Since the disk file is now the standard output device, you will not see the information on the screen (it hasn't been sent there).

When you execute the command, the screen will show nothing, but the drives will whirr and the indicator lights will come on. After the information is transferred to the file, the standard output reverts to the display screen. If you want to change the destination of the next command, you must include the redirection symbol again in the command.

Since you haven't actually seen anything on the screen to tell you that the operation has been completed, you might be a bit doubtful. You can check the new file by using the TYPE command:

```
A:\>type listing<Enter>
```

The contents of the file "listing" will appear on the screen.

You can use directories and subdirectories in redirecting output. For example:

```
A:\>dir \fruits\cherries >fruitdir<Enter>
```

This puts the directory of the \FRUITS\CHERRIES subdirectory into a file called "fruitdir."

There's one thing to keep in mind as you redirect output to files. If you redirect to an already existing file, the contents of the file are wiped out. But there is a simple solution to this problem: when you want to append the new output to the end of an already existing file, use >> instead of > in the command:

```
A:\>dir >>fruitdir<Enter>
```

With this command, the directory listing of the current directory is put into the "fruitdir" file, at the end of the contents of the file as it currently exists (see fig. 11-2).

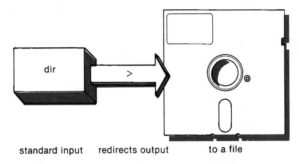

standard input   redirects output   to a file

Fig. 11-2. Redirection of output.

Redirection using >> is a handy way of keeping updated listings of your directories all in one file or for updating any information in a file (e.g., a mailing list). You're going to find this feature very "user-friendly."

Redirecting Standard Input

As you might expect, the opposite of output redirection is input redirection. This operation is symbolized by the less-than symbol, "<". Think of this symbol as an arrow pointing toward the command or program that is receiving the input. It is saying, "Take the contents from the file given after the < and use it as input for the program." Using this option you can make the standard input device a file instead of the keyboard. The uses for input redirection are a bit more obscure than for output redirection. One very common use is to relieve yourself of the repetitious entries needed to start up a program. Simply include the responses necessary in a file named, for instance, "answers." Then redirect the input using this file.

But by far the most frequent use of redirected input is with the use of filters in piping information. Let's look at this piping feature.

The Trans-DOS Pipeline

Although there are no real pipes involved, the analogy of a pipeline will help you understand the flow of information from input to output devices.

When a water department constructs a pipeline, they lay sections of pipe in a line to form one long conduit. The pipeline takes water from its source and pipes it to a water-storage area. Along the way, there are reservoirs which store the water temporarily. The water is then sent to a purification plant, where it is filtered before it is piped to its final destination, your home.

When you construct an MS-DOS pipeline, you do much the same thing. The data you are going to put into the pipeline is stored in a source file or program. You want to use the output of this program or file as the input to the next program or command. In this way you can "hook" commands, programs, and files together, like sections of pipe, in a long chain.

The data, however, does not go directly from the input file to the output file. If it did, you could accomplish the same goal by simply copying the file. Instead, in piping, the data is fed in from the input file, goes through a "filtering" process where it is modified, and then goes to its destination in the output file (see fig. 11-3).

When you use piping, it appears to MS-DOS that the input is the same as if it were typed in from the keyboard. But in reality, MS-DOS creates internal "temporary" files, like reservoirs, to hold the data as it is being piped. You will encounter some of these temporary files as you work your way through the examples in this chapter. Just so that you will have fair warning, note that they appear in your directory like this:

```
%PIPEx.$$$
```

where x is a number to distinguish different PIPE files.

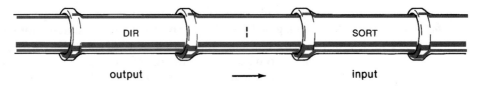

Fig. 11-3. Piping.

Does this still sound like an introductory class in plumbing? Let's see if we can make this concept as clear as a sparkling stream by diving further into filters.

Filtering the Flow

Filters are DOS commands or programs that read data from the designated standard input device, modify the data in some way, and then output the modified data to the designated standard output device. Thus, by its position in the middle of the process, this command works to "filter" the data, as shown in figure 11-4.

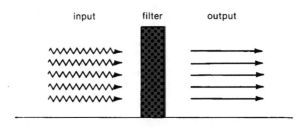

Fig. 11-4. Filtering.

Filters allow us to use a program, command, or file as the standard input device. Filters output to files. MS-DOS contains three filters: SORT, FIND, and MORE. Many other utility programs can also serve as filters.

The SORT Filter

Use:	Sorts file contents either alphabetically or by column number
Switches:	/r Sort in reverse alphabetical order
	/+n Sort on the column indicated by n
Examples:	sort <b:wines
	sort /r <b:wines
	sort /+28 <b:wines
	sort /+50 <b:wines >country
	dir | sort

Learning to use SORT is like learning how to drive. You know you existed without it, but it's hard to imagine how. That is a pretty strong statement, but I think you'll be enthusiastic too. To experience the real pleasure of using SORT, you have to try it on some actual data. So we are going to create a file to play SORT with.

For our SORT adventure you will need a formatted disk; if you can find it, use the disk you formatted with the volume label "wine cellar" in the exercise in Chapter 8. If you can't find it, maybe you should review "The Ten Commandments of Disk Handling and Usage" in Chapter 4. In any case, if you don't have this disk handy, just format another one:

```
A:\>format b:/v<Enter>
```

When the volume name is requested, enter:

```
wine cellar<Enter>
```

Put your system disk, which contains the filters in the SORT.EXE, FIND.EXE, and MORE.COM files, in drive A and your formatted disk in drive B. (If you are running MS-DOS from a hard disk, you don't need to put a system disk in drive A.)

Now here are the rules for the SORT script. You are a connoisseur of fine wines and have a "respectable" wine cellar. But the only way to keep up with its contents is to catalog all new purchases immediately, before you taste any of them.

The first thing you need is a list of your new bottles of wine. Create a file called "wines" on the disk in drive B. The name starts in column 1, the year in column 23, the appellation in column 28, and the country in column 50.

You must create this file as an ASCII text file (see Chapter 5 or 6). That means you should use EDLIN, EDIT, or COPY CON to enter the text. Also, do not use the <Tab> key to space between columns, because SORT cannot handle this character. Okay, here are your latest finds:

```
A:\>copy con: b:wines<Enter>

Lafite                  45    Bordeaux              France
Phelps Insignia         74    Cabernet Sauvignon    U.S.A.
Ridge Gyserville        73    Zinfandel             U.S.A.
La Mission Haut Brion   64    Bordeaux              France
Y'Quem                  58    Sauterne              France
^Z <Enter>
```

You can use the TYPE command to check the contents of your list:

```
A:\>type b:wines<Enter>

Lafite                  45    Bordeaux              France
Phelps Insignia         74    Cabernet Sauvignon    U.S.A.
Ridge Gyserville        73    Zinfandel             U.S.A.
```

```
La Mission Haut Brion    64   Bordeaux               France
Y'Quem                   58   Sauterne               France
```

Is your mouth watering? Wait till you see what SORT can do with this list.

Now, on your mark, get set, go.

The first thing you want is an alphabetical listing of the names of the new bottles to make it easier to enter them into your master file. This means that you want to SORT on the first column. Unless told to do otherwise, SORT automatically sorts alphabetically on the first column of the data.

SORT accepts input from another program, command, or file. But you must include the reassignment character as part of the statement:

```
A:\>sort <b:wines<Enter>
```

With this command you have told MS-DOS to sort the contents of the file "wines." Now watch the screen:

```
La Mission Haut Brion    64   Bordeaux               France
Lafite                   45   Bordeaux               France
Phelps Insignia          74   Cabernet Sauvignon     U.S.A.
Ridge Gyserville         73   Zinfandel              U.S.A.
Y'Quem                   58   Sauterne               France
```

Pretty fast and easy, huh?

SORT will also sort by reverse alphabetical order. I'm not sure why you would want to in this particular case, but it's best to know all your options.

To perform a sort so that the end of the alphabet tops the list, you use the /r option:

```
A:\>sort /r <b:wines<Enter>
```

And here it is!

```
Y'Quem                   58   Sauterne               France
Ridge Gyserville         73   Zinfandel              U.S.A.
Phelps Insignia          74   Cabernet Sauvignon     U.S.A.
Lafite                   45   Bordeaux               France
La Mission Haut Brion    64   Bordeaux               France
```

But SORT has even more surprises in store. Suppose you want to list your acquisitions by year, from the oldest to the newest. This helps in planning storage. To do this you use the /+n option. This switch allows you to sort by any column (indicated by the n in the command). You want to sort by year, which begins in column 23, so enter this command:

```
A:\>sort /+23 <b:wines<Enter>
```

Immediately you have your new listing:

```
Lafite                  45   Bordeaux              France
Y'Quem                  58   Sauterne              France
La Mission Haut Brion   64   Bordeaux              France
Ridge Gyserville        73   Zinfandel             U.S.A.
Phelps Insignia         74   Cabernet Sauvignon    U.S.A.
```

And there you go, from oldest to youngest.

You'll probably also want to keep a listing of your wines by appellation. That's the information that begins in column 28. Again, you use the *+n* switch:

```
A:\>sort /+28 <b:wines<Enter>
```

Voilà!

```
Lafite                  45   Bordeaux              France
La Mission Haut Brion   64   Bordeaux              France
Phelps Insignia         74   Cabernet Sauvignon    U.S.A.
Y'Quem                  58   Sauterne              France
Ridge Gyserville        73   Zinfandel             U.S.A.
```

Do I hear you murmur about a list by countries? Right away!

```
A:\>sort /+50 <b:wines<Enter>
Lafite                  45   Bordeaux              France
La Mission Haut Brion   64   Bordeaux              France
Y'Quem                  58   Sauterne              France
Phelps Insignia         74   Cabernet Sauvignon    U.S.A.
Ridge Gyserville        73   Zinfandel             U.S.A.
```

And when I think of all the years I spent alphabetizing by hand as I slowly muttered the alphabet under my breath. The beauty of SORT is that it is fun and functional.

The key to successful sorting is to make sure that each part of each entry on your list starts at the correct column position. For example, the appellation data must always begin in column 28 if you expect sort /+28 to sort your wines properly by appellation.

Just as you can use a file as the input for the SORT command, you can also redirect the output to a file. For clarity's sake you would like to keep each sort in a separate file. This makes referencing your collection much quicker. To output the results of a sort to a file, just include the output-reassignment character ">" in the command:

```
A:\>sort <b:wines >b:vintners<Enter>
```

This command translates into MS-DOS as follows: sort on column one the information in the "wines" file and put the output in a file called "vintners." When you perform a sort that redirects the output, you have assigned a new standard output device. Therefore, it follows that you will no longer see the sort on your regular standard output device, the screen. Once SORT has transferred the results to a file, it returns you to the prompt:

```
A:\>
```

You can verify the new file by using DIR:

```
A:\>dir b:vintners<Enter>

Volume in drive B is WINE CELLAR
Directory of B:\

VINTNERS        29   12-17-90   2:15p
        1 File(s)         29 bytes
                      36448 bytes free
```

Since you probably want only the latest version of your list, it's OK that the > redirection symbol throws out the old contents of the file each time you run the command. If you want to add each new sorted list to the previous ones, you would need to use >> so that the output of the new SORT is appended to the contents of the "vintners" file:

```
A:\>sort <b:wines >>b:vintners<Enter>
```

Using redirection, you can also create individual files to hold your other sorts:

```
A:\>sort /+23 <b:wines >b:years<Enter>

A:\>sort /+28 <b:wines >b:type<Enter>

A:\>sort /+52 <b:wines >b:country<Enter>
```

When you have done all this, your directory will look like the following:

```
A:\>dir B:<Enter>

Volume in drive B is WINE CELLAR
Directory of B:\

WINES           29   12-17-90   2:07p
VINTNERS        58   12-17-90   2:16p
YEARS           29   12-17-90   2:16p
TYPE            29   12-17-90   2:16p
COUNTRY         29   12-17-90   2:17p
        5 File(s)        174 bytes
                     357376 bytes free
```

The possibilities of SORT are intriguing. Not only does it rearrange your data very quickly, but, in conjunction with input and output redirection, it becomes a really powerful tool as well.

But you don't have to limit the use of SORT to files. Like all filters, it is really most useful in piping. You can use the output of a command as input to the SORT filter.

You create a piping sequence by separating the various commands, filters, and files with the vertical-bar character (|). For example:

```
dir | sort >b:alphadir
```

When using piping, you leave a space before and after each vertical bar. The previous command goes to the current directory, sorts the directory on the first column (since no options are included in the SORT command), and then puts the sorted directory in a file called "alphadir" on the disk in drive B.

Let's try it, using your system disk:

```
A:\>dir | sort >b:alphadir<Enter>
```

The directory won't be listed on the screen, but you will hear the drive working and the indicator light will be on. This is PIPE creating the temporary file that holds the output of DIR and the output of SORT. When the sorted directory is completed, it will be redirected to the file "alphadir." If you want to see the sorted display, enter the command without output redirection:

```
A:\>dir | sort<Enter>
```

In a few seconds the sorted listing will appear on the screen:

```
                          153600 bytes free
            28 file(s)    496036 bytes
      Directory of A:\
      Volume in drive A is DOSBOOT
      Volume Serial Number is 1404-76AC
      %PIPE1   $$$          0 12-03-90   2:38p
      %PIPE2   $$$          0 12-03-90   2:38p
      4201     CPI       6404 08-15-90   3:33a
      4208     CPI        720 08-15-90   3:33a
      5202     CPI        370 08-15-90   3:33a
      APPEND   EXE      11746 08-15-90   3:33a
      ASSIGN   COM       6169 08-15-90   3:33a
      ATTRIB   EXE      16223 08-15-90   3:33a
      BACKUP   EXE      35911 08-15-90   3:33a
      DEBUG    EXE      22028 08-15-90   3:33a
      DOSKEY   COM       4986 08-15-90   3:33a
      EDLIN    EXE      13929 08-15-90   3:33a
      EMM386   EXE      61058 08-15-90   3:33a
```

```
FASTOPEN EXE     12308 08-15-90    3:33a
FDISK    EXE     55896 08-15-90    3:33a
FORMAT   COM     29545 08-15-90    3:33a
GRAFTABL COM     10033 08-15-90    3:33a
GRAPHICS COM     19230 08-15-90    3:33a
GRAPHICS PRO     21226 08-15-90    3:33a
JOIN     EXE     17991 08-15-90    3:33a
KEYB     COM     10481 08-15-90    3:33a
LCD      CPI     10703 08-15-90    3:33a
MIRROR   COM     15897 08-15-90    3:33a
NLSFUNC  EXE      7254 08-15-90    3:33a
REBUILD  COM     17504 08-15-90    3:33a
RESTORE  EXE     38701 08-15-90    3:33a
SETVER   EXE      8282 08-15-90    3:33a
SHARE    EXE     13436 08-15-90    3:33a
SYS      COM     12080 08-15-90    3:33a
UNDELETE EXE     15925 08-15-90    3:33a
```

Note the first two files in the listing. These are the temporary "piping" files created during the SORT procedure. (MS-DOS version 5.0 uses a different scheme for naming these files: they will have mysterious names like "anaccmgb" or "anaccnad.") It is important to remember that when you SORT a file, it does not change the contents of the file. The file remains in the same order as it was prior to the sort. For instance, if you performed the previous sort on your system disk, the sorted listing would not appear the next time you entered DIR. Instead, you would get the normal directory listing. This is why you should redirect the output of a SORT to a file if you want to use the sorted information again.

Of course the kinds of commands we have been using—which include redirection symbols, pipes, and switches such as /+28—can be hard to remember and hard to type. As you know from Chapter 8, you can put complicated commands in easy-to-use batch files. For example, if you have a version of MS-DOS earlier than 5.0 and you want to be able to sort directories, you can create a batch file as follows:

```
A:\>copy con sdir.bat<Enter>
dir %1 | sort<Enter>
^Z<Enter>
1 file(s) copied
A:\>
```

Now, when you run "sdir.bat," the dir %1 part gets a listing of whatever directory name you put on the command line, thanks to the replaceable parameter %1. The listing is then piped to the SORT command and, since we didn't redirect the output, the sorted listing goes to the screen. (MS-DOS 5.0 users should just put the command dir /o:n %1 in a batch file, or put the command set DIRCMD = /o:n in AUTOEXEC.BAT, since using DIR with the sort switch avoids the need for creating a pipe file and running the separate SORT command.)

Similarly, you can save frequently used wine-cellar sorting operations in batch files such as:

```
A:\>copy con appel.bat<Enter>
sort /+28 < wines<Enter>
^Z<Enter>
1 file(s) copied
```

Now just type "appel" to get your wine list sorted by appellation.

The FIND Filter

Use:	Locates strings within a file

Switches:

/v	Display lines not containing the string
/c	Display a count of the lines containing the string
/n	Display the line number of each line containing the string

Examples:

```
find "France" b:wines
find /v "France" b:wines
find /c "France" b:wines
find /n "France" b:wines
dir | find "EXE"
```

FIND is a fast and easy way to locate specific items in a file. FIND works with strings. A string is simply a group of characters enclosed in quotation marks. Like the SORT filter, FIND can receive input from a file or command and send it to any designated standard-output device such as the screen, another file or program, or the printer.

Okay, now let's put FIND to work. One note of caution about the use of strings. Strings within a file will be found only when they exactly match the enclosed string in the command. This includes the use of upper- and lowercase letters and all punctuation marks.

Suppose we want to find out which of our recent purchases were from France. Enter this command:

```
A:\>find "France" b:wines<Enter>
```

Note that you enter the command first, followed by the string, which must be enclosed in quotation marks (see fig. 11-5). The name of the file to search is entered last. Every line containing the string will appear on the screen:

```
------------- b:wines
Lafite                    45    Bordeaux             France
La Mission Haut Brion     64    Bordeaux             France
Y'Quem                    58    Sauterne             France
```

Yes, there are our three French wineries.

Suppose you want a list of French wines, and you want them in alphabetical order. To get such a list, simply combine FIND in a pipeline with SORT:

```
A:\>find "France" b:wines | sort<Enter>

-------------- b: wines
La Mission Haut Brion     64    Bordeaux           France
Lafite                    45    Bordeaux           France
Y'Quem                    58    Sauterne           France
```

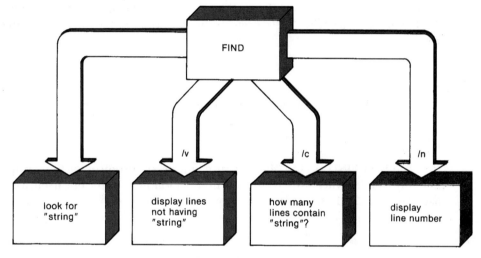

Fig. 11-5. The FIND command.

Or, you can put this sorted French list into its own file for later reference:

```
A:\>find "France" b:wines | sort >b:french<Enter>
```

The last command would not produce any display, of course, because you reassigned the output to be sent to the file "French."

There may be times when you want to FIND in a file lines that do not contain a specified string. FIND allows you to do this with the /v option. You want to list your American purchases:

```
A:\>find /v "France" b:wines<Enter>
```

FIND works for a few seconds and produces this display:

```
-------------- b:wines
Phelps Insignia       74    Cabernet Sauvignon    U.S.A.
Ridge Gyserville      73    Zinfandel             U.S.A.
```

But now you are reaching new, even more esoteric requirements. You want all non-French wines, and you want them in alphabetical order:

```
A:\>sort <b:wines | find /v "France"<Enter>
```

Don't let the length of this command confuse you. Just take it one step at a time. It tells DOS: sort the items in the "wines" file (on the first column, because no options are listed), and then find all lines that do not include the string "France." See, it's not really confusing at all, although you might want to put this command in a batch file for future use!

Now let's suppose that you are not particularly interested in the names of the French wines; you just want to know how many are in the file. Then you would use FIND with the /c switch. The /c switch returns a count of the lines containing the string:

```
A:\>find /c "France" b:wines<Enter>
```

The response is the name of the file, followed by a number:

```
-------------- b:wines: 3
```

The final FIND option allows you to locate occurrences of the string very precisely. The /n switch displays the line number followed by the line itself, for every instance of the indicated string:

```
A:\>find /n "France" b:wines<Enter>

-------------- b:wines
[1]Lafite                45   Bordeaux          France
[4]La Mission Haut Brion 64   Bordeaux          France
[5]Y'Quem                58   Sauterne          France
```

The line numbers indicate the position of the entries in the original file. For example, there are only three items in our display. Yet "Y'Quem" is assigned a line number of 5. This is because "Y'Quem" was the fifth entry in our original b:wines file.

Locating a string by line number can be very useful in large files. It is a fast and easy way to locate any type of string.

Just like the SORT filter, you don't need to limit the use of FIND to a display on the screen or a redirection to a file. You can also use it with other commands. Try this combination on your system disk:

```
A:\>dir | find "EXE"<Enter>
```

Just ask and you shall receive:

```
FDISK     EXE     55896 08-15-90    3:33a
SETVER    EXE      8282 08-15-90    3:33a
DEBUG     EXE     22028 08-15-90    3:33a
EDLIN     EXE     13929 08-15-90    3:33a
EMM386    EXE     61058 08-15-90    3:33a
FASTOPEN  EXE     12308 08-15-90    3:33a
JOIN      EXE     17991 08-15-90    3:33a
NLSFUNC   EXE      7254 08-15-90    3:33a
SHARE     EXE     13436 08-15-90    3:33a
UNDELETE  EXE     15925 08-15-90    3:33a
BACKUP    EXE     35911 08-15-90    3:33a
RESTORE   EXE     38701 08-15-90    3:33a
APPEND    EXE     11746 08-15-90    3:33a
ATTRIB    EXE     16223 08-15-90    3:33a
AUTOEXEC  BAT       389 12-03-90    4:47p
```

FIND will take your request very literally. It will list not only the files with the extension EXE, but also any files that contain the string "EXE" within their filenames (e.g., AUTOEXEC.BAT).

Neither the SORT nor the FIND filter allows the use of wildcard characters. Wildcard characters get the filters hopelessly confused, and the machine will just roll over and play dead if they are used in the filter command. One other unusual trick: in FIND, a quotation mark (") is interpreted as a search for an apostrophe ('). Well, everybody has little quirks.

At this point, you are probably realizing just how useful these filters are, and you're shouting, "More, more." No sooner said than done.

The MORE Filter

Use:	Pauses in a display when the screen is filled
Examples:	`more <b:wines`
	`dir	more`

Is a small voice in the back of your head telling you that stopping a scroll at the bottom of a filled screen is not totally unfamiliar? If so, give yourself a pat on the back. You saw this action when you used the /p (pause) switch with the DIR command (only in that case the message from MS-DOS was "Strike any key when ready" or "Press any key to continue").

MORE does the same thing in a filter form; it pauses at the bottom of the screen to make reading displays easier. This is how MORE would apply to our "wines" file:

```
A:\>more <b:wines<Enter>
```

But stop. It's not really worthwhile to enter this command because our "wines" file is less than one screen long in its entirety.

Let's use MORE in a more realistic situation. Switch back to your system disk (unless you're there now) and try this command:

```
A:\>dir | more<Enter>
```

This directory contains many files, so it will take MS-DOS a few seconds to construct the temporary pipe files. But when it's finished, you should see the contents of your system disk displayed until the screen is filled. The last line reads `-- More --`. To get the remainder of the directory, just press any key.

To FIND and SORT Still MORE

Now that you've learned about the SORT, FIND, and MORE filters and have examples of how they are used in piping and redirection, let's use them as building blocks to show how they can interact. You have come to the conclusion that it would really be easier to read your system disk directory if the files were listed alphabetically and the display stopped scrolling automatically when the page was full. This is an eminently reasonable request:

```
A:\>dir | sort | more<Enter>
```

And here is the answer to your needs:

```
                          153600 bytes free
        28 file(s)        496036 bytes
 Directory of A:\
 Volume in drive A is DOS5BOOT
 Volume Serial Number is 1404-76AC
 4201     CPI      6404 08-15-90    3:33a
 4208     CPI       720 08-15-90    3:33a
 5202     CPI       370 08-15-90    3:33a
 APPEND   EXE     11746 08-15-90    3:33a
 ASSIGN   COM      6169 08-15-90    3:33a
 ATTRIB   EXE     16223 08-15-90    3:33a
 BACKUP   EXE     35911 08-15-90    3:33a
 DEBUG    EXE     22028 08-15-90    3:33a
 DOSKEY   COM      4986 08-15-90    3:33a
 EDLIN    EXE     13929 08-15-90    3:33a
 EMM386   EXE     61058 08-15-90    3:33a
 FASTOPEN EXE     12308 08-15-90    3:33a
 FDISK    EXE     55896 08-15-90    3:33a
 FORMAT   COM     29545 08-15-90    3:33a
 GRAFTABL COM     10033 08-15-90    3:33a
 GRAPHICS COM     19230 08-15-90    3:33a
 -- More --
 GRAPHICS PRO     21226 08-15-90    3:33a
 JOIN     EXE     17991 08-15-90    3:33a
```

You press a key.

```
KEYB      COM     10481 08-15-90    3:33a
LCD       CPI     10703 08-15-90    3:33a
MIRROR    COM     15897 08-15-90    3:33a
NLSFUNC   EXE      7254 08-15-90    3:33a
REBUILD   COM     17504 08-15-90    3:33a
RESTORE   EXE     38701 08-15-90    3:33a
SETVER    EXE      8282 08-15-90    3:33a
SHARE     EXE     13436 08-15-90    3:33a
SYS       COM     12080 08-15-90    3:33a
UNDELETE  EXE     15925 08-15-90    3:33a
```

Another way to redesign the directory is to group all the same kinds of files together and list them with the extensions in alphabetical order. To do this you need to know that the extension designation begins in column 10:

```
A:\>dir | sort /+10 | more<Enter>
```

Wait a second, and here it is:

```
                        153600 bytes free
            28 file(s)    496036 bytes
DOSKEY    COM      4986 08-15-90    3:33a
ASSIGN    COM      6169 08-15-90    3:33a
GRAFTABL  COM     10033 08-15-90    3:33a
KEYB      COM     10481 08-15-90    3:33a
SYS       COM     12080 08-15-90    3:33a
MIRROR    COM     15897 08-15-90    3:33a
REBUILD   COM     17504 08-15-90    3:33a
GRAPHICS  COM     19230 08-15-90    3:33a
FORMAT    COM     29545 08-15-90    3:33a
5202      CPI       370 08-15-90    3:33a
4208      CPI       720 08-15-90    3:33a
4201      CPI      6404 08-15-90    3:33a
LCD       CPI     10703 08-15-90    3:33a
   Volume Serial Number is 1404-76AC
NLSFUNC   EXE      7254 08-15-90    3:33a
SETVER    EXE      8282 08-15-90    3:33a
APPEND    EXE     11746 08-15-90    3:33a
FASTOPEN  EXE     12308 08-15-90    3:33a
SHARE     EXE     13436 08-15-90    3:33a
-- More --
EDLIN     EXE     13929 08-15-90    3:33a
UNDELETE  EXE     15925 08-15-90    3:33a
ATTRIB    EXE     16223 08-15-90    3:33a
JOIN      EXE     17991 08-15-90    3:33a
DEBUG     EXE     22028 08-15-90    3:33a
BACKUP    EXE     35911 08-15-90    3:33a
```

```
RESTORE   EXE     38701 08-15-90   3:33a
FDISK     EXE     55896 08-15-90   3:33a
EMM386    EXE     61058 08-15-90   3:33a
 Volume in drive A is DOS5BOOT
GRAPHICS  PRO     21226 08-15-90   3:33a
 Directory of A:\
```

You could attempt to SORT by date and/or time, but this is pretty useless. Why? Because SORT is very literal. If it is presented with these three dates:

09-05-89
05-02-90
07-16-91

it will SORT them like so:

05-02-90
07-16-91
09-05-89

In other words, SORT interprets 09-05-89 as greater than 05-02-90, so it puts it at the bottom of the list. As we demonstrated in our "wines" file when we sorted by year, you can successfully use numbers to SORT, but they must run consecutively. You could sort the system disk by file size, for instance:

```
A:\>dir | sort /+17 | more<Enter>
```

The DOSKEY to Command Performance

You have learned how to amaze and dazzle your friends with complicated and powerful commands. It would be nice, however, not to have to retype these long command lines continually. You can, of course, save frequently used commands in batch files, but sometimes it would be better to edit commands "on the fly," shaping them to suit the needs of the moment. In Chapter 8, you learned how MS-DOS keeps a "template" based on the last command you entered. By recalling and editing the template, you can save a considerable amount of typing. Unfortunately, you can only go back to the previous command, not that beautiful SORT /+28 < WINES | FIND "Cabernet" | PRINT command you used a few minutes ago. Also, the ability to edit the command line is rather limited.

Well, if you have MS-DOS 5.0, you can take advantage of yet another bag of tricks for reusing and combining commands. The DOSKEY command loads into memory a small program that adds the following capabilities to standard MS-DOS command-line processing:

❑ A list of previously used commands you can retrieve, edit, and reuse

❑ Improved command editing, using keys like those found in word processors

❑ The ability to issue more than one separate MS-DOS command on the same command line

❑ The ability to define your own command combinations and save them for later use

To run DOSKEY, make sure that the file DOSKEY.COM is on the current disk (if you are running MS-DOS from a floppy disk). Now type

```
A:\>doskey<Enter>
DOSKey installed.
```

The DOSKEY Command

Use:	Lets you reuse and edit previous commands and define command macros
Example:	`doskey` `doskey sdir=dir /o:n $1`

Recalling Previous Commands

Once DOSKEY is installed, it makes a "recording" of each command you use. It can store as many as several dozen commands, depending on how long your commands are. If you want to increase DOSKEY's recording capacity, run DOSKEY as follows:

```
A:\>doskey /bufsize=512<Enter>
```

In this case DOSKEY will have room for 512 characters of commands—but the default setting is enough for most people.

Now suppose that you're busy examining and sorting your wine list. Issue the following three commands (don't worry about their output):

```
A:\>dir wines<Enter>
A;\>sort /+28 < wines<Enter>
A:\>sort /+50 < wines<Enter>
```

(We've left out the output of these commands to save space.) Any time you want DOSKEY to show you the list of commands it has recorded, just press <F7>:

```
A:\><F7>
1: dir wines
2: sort /+28 <wines
3:>sort /+50 < wines
A:\>
```

After pressing a function key such as <F7> or an arrow key, you don't need to press <Enter>. Note that each command is given on a numbered line. The numbers are not part of the commands; like the line numbers in EDLIN, they're just there to keep track of things.

You can go back to any recorded command by pressing the <Up Arrow> key to move back up the list. The line next to your MS-DOS prompt scrolls to show you the commands one at a time as you press the key. Suppose, for example, that you want to sort your wines by year. You recall that the command you need is "sort /+23 < wines". Hmm. You just used a similar command a few moments ago when you sorted your wines by appellation: "sort /+28 < wines".

You can go back to this similar command, edit it, and reissue it to get the listing you need. Press <Up Arrow> once, and you see

```
A:\><Up Arrow>
A:\>sort /+50 < wines
```

You need to go one command farther back, so press <Up Arrow> again. Now you see

```
A:\>sort /+50 < wines<Up Arrow>
A:\>sort /+28 < wines
```

There are several other ways to go back to earlier commands, as shown in the accompanying box. We'll leave the experimentation to you.

Working With The DOSKEY Command List

To	Press
Display the list of recorded commands	<F7>
Go back one command	<Up Arrow>
Get the next command in the list	<Down Arrow>
Get the first (oldest) command on the list	<Pg Up>
Get the last (newest) command on the list	<Pg Down>
Go back to the command that has a particular number	<F9>, type the number, <Enter>
Find the last command that begins with a particular string	<F8>, type the string, <Enter>
Repeat search	<F8>

Editing Commands

Now that you have the command you want, you need to edit it so that the "28" becomes a "23".

As shown in the next box, DOSKEY provides you with several useful keys for editing commands. As a bonus, these keys work the same way they do in Edit, the only difference being that you are confined to working with one command line rather than a screenful of text. Again, you should experiment with these keys to see how easy they are to use.

DOSKEY Command Editing Keys

To	*Press*
Move the cursor one character to the left	\<Left Arrow\>
Move the cursor one character to the right	\<Right Arrow\>
Move the cursor one word to the left	\<Ctrl\>\<Left Arrow\>
Move the cursor one word to the right	\<Ctrl\>\<Right Arrow\>
Move the cursor to the beginning of the command	\<Home\>
Move the cursor to the end of the command	\<End\>
Delete the character over the cursor	\<Del\>
Delete the character to the left of the cursor	\<Backspace\>
Delete from the cursor to the end of the line	\<Ctrl\>\<End\>
Delete from the cursor to the beginning of the line	\<Ctrl\>\<Home\>
Delete the entire command line	\<Esc\>
Insert characters at the cursor (not needed in insert mode)	\<Ins\>, the characters

---

Right now the command line reads:

```
A:\>sort /+28 <wines<Enter>
```

So, one way to edit our command is to press \<Ctrl\>\<Left arrow\> to move the cursor to the "\<" in "\<wines", then press \<Left Arrow\> twice to move the cursor to the 8. Now press \<Del\> to remove the "8", and press "3" to change "28" to "23". (By default DOSKEY's command editor is in Insert mode, so you don't have to press \<Ins\> before inserting text.)

That's it—your command is now:

```
A:\>sort /+23 < wines
```

Now all you have to do is press <Enter> to get your list of wines sorted by year. At first, this editing process may seem too tedious to bother with, but if you try it you'll find that it becomes quick and easy.

Using More Than One Command at a Time

DOSKEY can speed up your work with MS-DOS by letting you send several commands to your PC simultaneously. To do so, simply separate the commands by pressing <Ctrl>T. (When you do this, DOSKEY will display a "paragraph" symbol (¶) where you pressed <Ctrl>T.)

For example, when you check your disk you often have to change directories and get a listing of what you've got. Of course, you can do it as follows:

```
A:\>cd farming<Enter>
A:\>dir farming<Enter>
```

But with DOSKEY, you can type the CD command, press <Ctrl>T, and type the DIR command all on one line:

```
A:\>cd farming <¶> dir
```

When you press <Enter> to execute the CD command, you change to the FARMING directory. The DIR is then immediately executed, giving you a listing of that directory. You're now ready to work from the farming directory.

Here's another example. As you know, you have to delete any files in a directory before you can remove the directory. If you're *sure* that you don't want anything in the OLDSTUFF directory any more, you can issue the DEL and RD commands in one shot, like this:

```
A:\>del temp\*.* <¶> rd temp<Enter>
A:\>del temp\*.*
All files in directory will be deleted!
Are you sure (Y/N)?y

A:\>rd temp
```

First, MS-DOS echoes your DEL command. The DEL command issues its warning as usual, so you must press *y*. The RD command, which is then echoed, then removes the directory.

Holy Macro, DOS Man!

The last DOSKEY feature we'll look at is its ability to help you define *macros*. A macro is similar to a batch file—it is a combination of predefined commands that are executed all at once when you type its name. Macros and batch files, differ, however. A macro is stored in memory; therefore, it can be executed without reading a file from the disk. A macro can hold several commands in a single line, but it can't hold more than 128 characters. Nevertheless, macros are very useful for issuing complex command combinations.

You define a macro by typing "DOSKEY," the name of the macro, an equal sign, and the command line to be run. For example, suppose you want to get sorted directories without having to remember to use the /o:n switch with DIR. You can define a macro called SDIR:

```
A:\>doskey sdir=dir /o:n<Enter>
```

Now suppose that you are in a directory, called CELLAR, that has various wine-related files in it. To get a sorted directory, just type:

```
A:\CELLAR>sdir<Enter>
A:\CELLAR>dir /o:n
```

Note that, as with batch files, the actual command being executed is echoed. Soon you see the directory listing:

```
Volume in drive A is WINE CELLAR
Volume Serial Number is 13F7-2C2C
Directory of A:\CELLAR

.            <DIR>      10-03-90   12:27p
..           <DIR>      10-03-90   12:27p
FORTRAD      18853 08-15-90    3:33a
PRICES        6719 08-15-90    3:33a
PURCHASE     11746 08-15-90    3:33a
WINES          287 10-03-90   11:01a
        6 file(s)       37605 bytes
                       320512 bytes free
```

The only problem with our macro is that it won't take a pathname; it will only list the current directory. (In fact, it will list the current directory and ignore any pathname you give it.) To fix this, you need to put a replaceable parameter in your macro. Sound familiar? Yes, these replaceable parameters work the same way as the ones you used in batch files, except that the parameter number is preceded by a dollar sign ($) rather than a percent sign (%):

```
A:\>doskey sdir=dir /o:n $1<Enter>
```

Now you can type:

```
A:\>sdir cellar<Enter>
```

without being in the CELLAR directory, and get the correct listing.

You can set up DOSKEY macros that issue more than one command. Instead of pressing <Ctrl>T to separate commands, you put a $t between the commands.

For example, suppose you'd like to "delete" files without actually removing them from your disk. To do this, you could copy the file into a directory called TRASH and then delete the original file. At the end of the day you could go through your "trash can" and review each file to determine whether to throw it away for good. To do this, use MD to create your TRASH directory, and then define a macro called "dump":

```
A:\>doskey dump=copy $1 trash $t del $1<Enter>
```

Now, when you type "dump", the file or group of files you specified on the command line will be copied into the TRASH directory and deleted from their original location. For example, here's how to dump your wines if the Revenuers are on your tail:

```
A:\>dump wines<Enter>
A:\>copy wines trash
        1 file(s) copied

A:\> del wines
```

Once you have defined several macros, you may want to get a list of them. To do so, type DOSKEY followed by the /dmacs switch:

```
A:\>doskey /dmacs<Enter>
SDIR=dir /o:n $1
DUMP=copy $1 trash $t del $1
```

Of course, macros wouldn't be very useful if you had to redefine them at the start of each session. To save your macros, put them into a batch file and run both DOSKEY and the batch file from your AUTOEXEC.BAT file. This way, everything will be set at the start of each session. Once you've defined some macros, you can use redirection to put them in a batch file:

```
A:\>doskey /dmacs > mymacs.bat<Enter>
```

Now you can run "mymacs.bat" to install your macros automatically.

DOSKEY has a number of other interesting features, but they're beyond the scope of this book. Look in your MS-DOS manual for more details.

In this chapter you learned about the various ways to use the redirection, piping, and sort features of MS-DOS. These are skills that will stand you in good stead as you use MS-DOS more and more. The SORT, FIND, and MORE filters are very useful in reorganizing and using your data. If you have MS-DOS 5.0, you learned how DOSKEY can make even complicated MS-DOS commands easy to use. In the next chapter, you will learn about a different approach to ease of use: the DOS shell.

12

What's on the Menu?

- Getting Started
- Playing the Shell Game
- Climbing the File Tree
    - Menus and Options at Your Command
    - Let's Have a Dialog
    - I've Got a Little List...
- Working with Files
    - Doing the Chores, DOSSHELL Style
    - A Handy Helper
- Working with Multiple Directories and Files
    - Using Path Names with DOSSHELL
    - Working with More Than One File
    - Where's That File?
- Running Programs from DOSSHELL
    - Getting Prompt Service
    - Running a Program from the File List
    - Using the Program List
    - Adding Your Own Program Groups
    - Adding Programs to a Group
    - Switching Between Programs
    - Associating Data Files and Programs

12 What's on the Menu?

You've come a long way toward mastering MS-DOS and its many features. The journey started with computer terminology and the layout of the keyboard and continued through the lore of drives, disks, and files. Finally, you ventured into directories and files, and you learned to use precise path names to find your way among them. You even learned how to write batch files that automate some routine tasks, such as formatting and backing up disks.

Perhaps, however, you wished for an easier way to manage files and run programs. After all, working with MS-DOS is sometimes an awkward undertaking. For example, while the TREE command gives you a nice outline of your file structure, you still have to remember specific MS-DOS commands when you want to copy, delete, or otherwise work with a file. And when you spot in the distance the file you want, you have to change directories to bring it into reach or use path names to go out and grab it. While you're doing this, however, that nice tree diagram is scrolling off the screen so you can't refer to it any more. Suppose that you could just point at the tree, choose a directory, and get a list of its files. Suppose you could select the files you wanted from the list and pick from a handy menu the operation you wanted to perform.

Well, if you have MS-DOS version 4.0 or later, your dream can be a reality. The DOSSHELL program that comes with the latest versions of MS-DOS lets you work with lists of directories, files, and programs in separate areas or *windows* on the screen. You can make selections with the keyboard or the mouse.

The menus, dialog boxes, lists, and buttons found in Edit are very similar in appearance and operation to those in the DOSSHELL program. If you read Chapter 6 on Edit, you've already used many of the basic techniques found in DOSSHELL. If you are still a bit hazy about the use of these techniques, you may wish to review Chapter 6. All set? Let's get started.

Getting Started

DOSSHELL doesn't require you to use a mouse, but selecting items from menus and lists, operating dialog boxes, and scrolling text is often easier to do with a mouse than from the keyboard. We will give both keyboard and mouse techniques throughout this chapter, and we recommend that you try both. Make sure that your mouse has been installed according to the directions in its manual.

If you installed MS-DOS to a hard disk, you start DOSSHELL simply by typing its name at the MS-DOS prompt:

```
C:\>dosshell<Enter>
```

If you installed MS-DOS to floppy disks, start the system with the disk marked Startup (if you have 5 1/4" disks) or Startup/Support (if you have 3 1/2" disks) in drive A. When MS-DOS has started up, replace the disk in drive A with the disk marked Shell (for 5 1/4" disks) or Shell/Utility (for 3 1/2" disks).

Of Shells and MS-DOS Versions

MS-DOS introduced DOSSHELL with version 4.0. This chapter, however, discusses the improved version that comes with MS-DOS 5.0 or later. If you are using version 4.0's DOSSHELL, most of the concepts and techniques discussed here will still be applicable, but the appearance and organization of the screen displays will be different. Some features, such as program switching, are not available in the MS-DOS 4.0 version of DOSSHELL. We suggest upgrading to version 5.0.

Numerous companies, such as Symantec (Norton Utilities) and Central Point (PC Tools), offer their own DOS shell programs. These third-party programs are similar to the MS-DOS DOSSHELL and they often include additional features and utility programs. Also, the very popular Microsoft Windows program offers a kind of super DOS shell that allows you to work with several programs at a time and to cut and paste data between programs. Third-party DOS shells and Microsoft Windows generally work with MS-DOS versions 3.0 or later.

DOSSHELL displays information in either *graphics mode* or *character mode*. Graphics mode allows a slightly more detailed and attractive representation of the mouse pointer and the symbols indicating files and directories. DOSSHELL will use whatever graphics display your PC has—CGA, EGA, or VGA. On the other hand, if your PC doesn't have a graphics adapter, the mouse pointer and symbols will be displayed with combinations of text characters. There is no real difference in features or operation between graphics and text modes. The number of items that can fit in the various screen windows depends on the *resolution* of your video display. Typically, a video screen can display 25 to 60 or more lines. (The screen illustrations in this chapter use graphics mode with 25 lines per screen.)

In most cases, you should let DOSSHELL set the display characteristics according to the video hardware it finds in your system. If you have trouble seeing the display or you simply wish to experiment with other displays, you can start DOSSHELL with the /t: switch to force DOSSHELL to run in text mode. You follow the /t: with the letter l, m, or h (for low, medium, or high resolution). To force DOSSHELL to run in graphics mode, use the /g: switch followed by l, m, or h. For additional DOSSHELL option switches, see your MS-DOS manual.

Playing the Shell Game

As shown in figure 12-1, the DOSSHELL screen has several parts. From the top of the screen to the bottom, they are:

❏ The *title bar*, which displays the name "DOS Shell"

❏ The *menu bar*, with menus, or lists of commands. The menu bar in DOSSHELL works just like the one in Edit.

❏ The *drive selector*, which is used to pick the disk drive whose files are to be displayed. In this example, drive C has been selected.

❏ A set of windows for displaying the *Directory Tree* and a *file list*. In the illustration, the Directory Tree shows the root directory of drive C, and the file list shows the files in that directory.

❏ A *program list* window. In figure 12-1 this window shows the Main *program group*. You will learn more about program groups later.

❏ A *status line* at the bottom of the screen. Depending on circumstances, this lists useful keys, the current time, or other messages.

In figure 12-1, note the arrow-shaped *mouse pointer* near the upper left corner of the screen. (The mouse pointer appears only if you have installed a mouse.) Each window has a set of *scroll bars* on its right edge. As with Edit, you can use the scroll bars to change the portion of the text displayed in the window.

Climbing the File Tree

In Chapter 10 you were an industrious agriculturalist trying to manage information about your fruit and lumber crops. We are going to ask you to pick up this role again, but this time there will be some new twists. Having been a bit frustrated with the effort involved in keeping your file tree in good order, you've obtained the latest in farm tools, namely DOSSHELL. You will use it to check your file tree, take care of some pruning and grafting, and even use it to set up some programs so that your young assistant can learn to perform routine tasks. With that done, you will be able to sit on the porch and sip a tall, cool glass of lemonade. Start by putting the disk you used in Chapter 10 (the one with the FRUITS and LUMBER directories and their subdirectories) in drive B.

Before you can use DOSSHELL to examine a disk, you must tell it to read the disk's directory. You do this by selecting the drive (B in this case) from the drive selector. Depending on whether you have a hard disk, right now either drive C or drive A will be selected—you can tell because its symbol is highlighted. Use the arrow keys to select drive B, and press <Enter>. There is a shortcut for selecting drives: press <Ctrl> followed by the letter of the drive you want. Thus you can select drive B directly by pressing <Ctrl>B. Or, if you have a mouse, select items with the mouse by clicking on them (moving the mouse pointer over the item and pressing the left mouse button). Thus, to select drive B, click on its symbol. Once you have selected a drive, DOSSHELL will display a brief message that shows its progress in reading the directories from the disk.

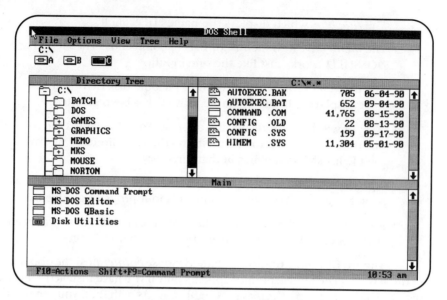

Fig. 12-1. Opening DOSSHELL screen.

Whenever you perform an operation that changes the contents of the selected disk, such as copying or deleting files, select that drive again. This lets DOSSHELL reread and update its directory. It also keeps the lists you are viewing and the actual disk contents "in sync."

After the message, you'll see a `Directory Tree` window with a representation of the root of the file tree on drive B (see fig. 12-2.) Meanwhile, the window to the right will show a list of files in the root directory.

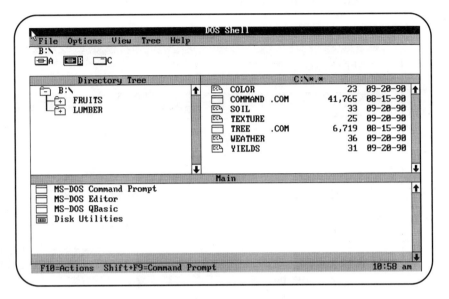

Fig. 12-2. Changing to drive B.

Next, press <Tab> to move from the drive-selector area to the `Directory Tree` area. As with Edit, you press the <Tab> key to move from one area of the screen to the next and <Shift><Tab> to move backwards. Alternatively, you can use the mouse and just click on the item you want—a directory in this case.

In the `Directory Tree` display, directories are indicated by a folder symbol in graphics mode or a set of brackets in text mode. Note that the symbols for the FRUITS and LUMBER directories include a plus sign (+). The plus sign tells you "there's more"—these directories have subdirectories.

Now press the <Down Arrow> key or click the mouse to select the FRUITS directory in the Directory Tree window. That done, press the <+> key. Pressing the <+> key tells DOSSHELL to expand a directory and list its subdirectories. Figure 12-3 shows the FRUITS directory expanded to list its CHERRIES subdirectory. Now select the CHERRIES subdirectory by pressing the <Down Arrow> key and <Enter>. Note that the file-list window to the right now lists only the files in this subdirectory, namely "yields."

The CHERRIES folder symbol is blank, indicating that it can't be expanded further. Note that the FRUITS folder now has a minus sign (-) in it. This means that you can *collapse* this directory to hide the symbols for its subdirectories. By using the plus and minus keys you can control the amount of directory-structure detail you see. This is similar to viewing topics and subtopics with an outlining program. (Alternatively, you can use the `Tree` menu and select the appropriate item. You will learn more about using menus in a moment. The Expand All item is particularly useful in that it expands your directory tree to the maximum possible extent, showing all directories, subdirectories, sub-subdirectories, and so on.) Now select the B:\ directory to return to the root.

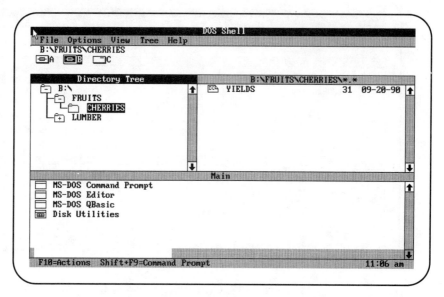

Fig. 12-3. Expanding the FRUITS directory.

Being an adventurous sort, you decide to put in a fish pond and try to raise some trout. You'll need to create a new directory called FISH to hold information about these critters. To do so, you will issue the Create Directory command on the DOSSHELL File menu. First, though, you will have to open the File menu.

Menus and Options at Your Command

As with Edit, you select, or open, a menu by pressing <Alt> followed by the first letter of the menu name. Alternatively, you can press <F10> to activate the menu bar and use <Left Arrow> or <Right Arrow> followed by <Enter> to select a menu. With the mouse, just click on the name of the menu you want.

Use any of these techniques to open the File menu, which is shown in figure 12-4. Note that many of the items listed are shown in dim characters: *dimmed* commands are unavailable because they aren't relevant to what you are currently doing. In this case, most of the dimmed commands refer to operations performed on individual files. Since you haven't selected any files yet, these commands aren't available. Note that some command names (such as Create Directory) are followed by ellipses (...). The ellipsis indicates that selecting this command will display a dialog box requesting further information.

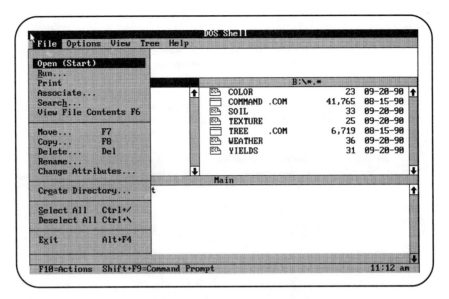

Fig. 12-4. The `File` **menu.**

As with Edit, you select a command from an open menu by pressing the arrow keys and pressing <Enter> or by pressing the highlighted letter in the command you want. Press "e" now to select `Create Directory`, or click on `Create Directory` with the mouse.

Working with DOSSHELL Windows and Menus

To:	*Do:*
Highlight the desired window	Press <Tab> or <Shift><Tab>
Select an item such as a directory or file	Press <Up Arrow> or <Down Arrow>, then press <Enter> or click on the item with the mouse
View an item that is not visible	Scroll the list with the <Pg Down> or <Pg Up> keys, or click the mouse on the scroll-bar arrows, or drag the scroll-bar slider with the mouse
Open a menu	Press <Alt> and the first letter of the menu name, or press <F10> and use the arrow keys and <Enter>, or click on the menu name with the mouse
Choose a menu item	Press the underlined letter in the item name, or press the arrow keys and <Enter>, or click on the item name with the mouse

Let's Have a Dialog

Figure 12-5 shows the `Create Directory` dialog box. The cursor is already in the list box entitled "New directory name", so enter "fish".

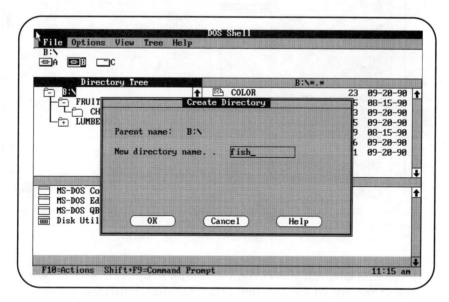

Fig. 12-5. The `Create Directory` **dialog box.**

Just as with the dialog boxes used in Edit, you move from one part of a dialog box to another by pressing the <Tab> or <Shift><Tab> keys or by clicking with the mouse on the area you want. Like most dialog boxes, this one has three buttons at the bottom: `OK`, `Cancel`, and `Help`. You press the `OK` button when you're finished with the dialog box and want to go ahead and perform the current operation. You press the `Cancel` button to terminate the operation without performing it. The `Help` button, as you will see later, provides a screen that describes the commands and options in the dialog box. Since you want to go ahead with the operation, and the `OK` button is already highlighted, simply press <Enter> or click the mouse on the `OK` button to create the FISH directory. As you can see in figure 12-6, the FISH directory has now been added to the root directory of drive B, as shown in the `Directory Tree` window.

I've Got a Little List . . .

Have you noticed the file-list window to the right of the `Directory Tree` window? As you select different directories, the list of files in the window to the right changes automatically, to show you the contents of the currently selected directory. Three basic pieces of information are provided about each file: its name (including its extension, if there is one), its size in bytes, and the date it was created or last modified. In other words, this display is a kind of abbreviated form of the DIR command.

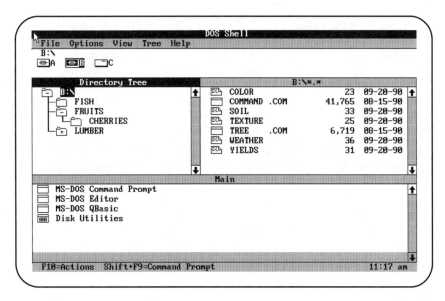

Fig. 12-6. FISH directory added to tree.

You can sort the directory listing in various ways. To see how this is done, select Display Options from the Options menu, and the Display Options dialog box appears, as shown in figure 12-7.

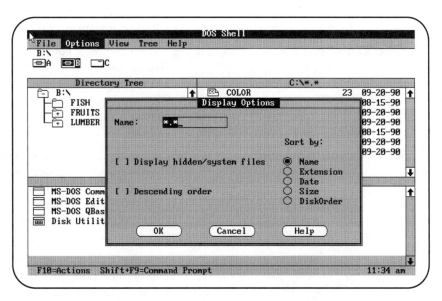

Fig. 12-7. The File Display Options **dialog box.**

This dialog box gives you many options for sorting your directory displays. Suppose, for example, that you want to see only files whose names meet certain specifications. You could enter a filename with the appropriate wild cards in the Name text box. For example, entering *.txt would select only those files that have a TXT extension.

Look at the two check boxes below the Name text box. Display hidden/ system files tells DOSSHELL to include in the listing those files that are normally hidden from DIR listings, such as the MS-DOS system files. Descending order reverses the order in which files are sorted in the listing. By default, files are sorted alphabetically by name from A to Z, but checking this box makes the order go from Z to A.

Finally, there are five options under the heading Sort by. Note the circular buttons beside each option. This type of button is often called a *radio button*, because, like the tuning buttons on a car radio, only one can be "on" at a time. Selecting a different button "unselects" the button that was previously on. As you can see, as an alternative to sorting by name, you can sort by extension, date, size, or disk order. Sorting by disk order means to list the files in the order they are physically stored on the disk.

Working with Options in Dialog Boxes

To:	*Do:*
Highlight an area of the dialog box	Press <Tab> or <Shift> <Tab>, or click directly on the item you want with the mouse
Select a check-box item	Press an arrow key to move to the item you want, then press <Spacebar> to select it, or click in the check box with the mouse. (You can select as many check boxes as you wish.)
Select a radio-button item	Press an arrow key until the item you want has been selected, or click on the radio button with the mouse. (You can only select one radio button at a time.)
Select a command button	Press <Tab> or <Shift><Tab> to highlight the button, then press <Enter>; or click on the button with the mouse

Working with Files

Most of your actual work with files involves finding the file you want on the list, selecting it, and then using a command from the File menu to perform an operation such as copying, deleting, or moving. Since the file list changes with the directories you select, you must first select the correct directory. Fortunately DOSSHELL makes it easy to browse through directories until you find the file or files you want.

You select a file from the file list by highlighting the filename with the arrow keys or clicking on the filename with the mouse. If the file list is too long to fit in the window, use the <Pg Down> and <Pg Up> keys or the mouse and scroll bar to scroll the list until you find the file you want.

Have you ever wished that you could take a quick peek into a file in one of your DIR listings? It would be nice not to have to run Edit or some other program just to check a file's contents. With DOSSHELL, you can look at the selected file without having to run a separate program. For example, do you remember what you put in the "weather" file? No, we don't either, so let's view this file.

You should now be looking at the file list for the root directory of drive B. (If not, select the B:\ directory in the Directory Tree window, and then return to the File List window.) Select the "weather" file and open the File menu.

Once you have selected a file, a number of new commands become available on the File menu. For example, we could select the View File Contents command. Look at this command name and note the shortcut key, F6, listed to the right. (You can press F6 to view the currently selected file, without having to open the File menu first.) To see how this works, press <F6>.

Figure 12-8 shows the file-viewing screen. You press <Pg Dn> or <Pg Up> to scroll through this file if it is too long to fit on one screen. Since your file has only one line of text, you don't have to do this. Press <Esc> to exit the file-viewing screen.

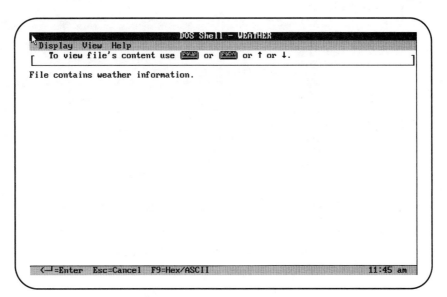

Fig. 12-8. Viewing file contents.

Steps for Working with Files

1. Select the drive to be used

2. Use the directory tree to find the appropriate directory or subdirectory

3. View the directory's file list

4. Select one or more files

5. Open the File menu and choose the appropriate command for the operation you want to perform

---

Doing the Chores, DOSSHELL Style

The File menu includes many other helpful options. For example, suppose you decide that day-to-day forecasts in the "weather" file aren't worth storing on disk. You're more interested in long-term weather trends, or "climate." While the "weather" file is still selected, can you use DOSSHELL to change its name from "weather" to "climate"? Open the File menu and look it over again. You see that it includes a Rename command. Select this command now.

   Figure 12-9 shows the Rename File dialog box. It's certainly simple enough: just type the new name, "climate," and press <Enter> or click on OK, and you're done. "Weather" is now called "climate."

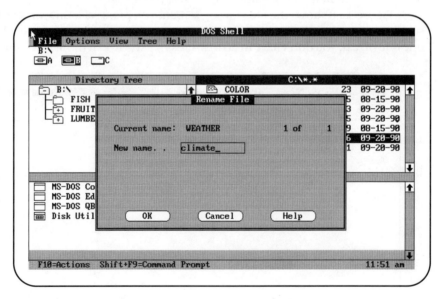

Fig. 12-9. The Rename File **dialog box.**

Some Common File Operations

The File menu includes four commonly needed operations: move, copy, delete, and rename. You have already learned how to perform these operations at the command line with the COPY, DEL (or ERASE), and REN commands. You also know how to use a batch file to move a file (copying it and deleting the original.) With DOSSHELL, however, you don't have to remember the exact command line to use, and you can select the file directly rather than having to change directories manually or use a long pathname. DOSSHELL will ask you to confirm any operation that would delete a file or replace one file with another. Although you can turn off these warnings by selecting Confirmation from the Options menu, it's probably a good idea to leave them on as an extra measure of safety.

A Handy Helper

If you're confused or uncertain at any point while using DOSSHELL, you can dispel the confusion quickly with the program's on-line Help feature, and in the process, you'll learn more about the shell and its capabilities. DOSSHELL provides context-sensitive help tailored for your situation.

For example, suppose you've opened the File menu and you're searching for a way to change a file's name. You're pretty sure that Rename will do the trick, but exactly how does it work? Use the arrow keys to highlight Rename on the menu, and then press <F1> to get the help display, which is shown in figure 12-10.

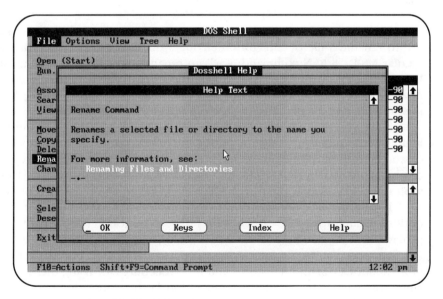

Fig. 12-10. Using Help **on a menu command.**

The Help text box briefly describes the Rename command. It also gives the name of a related topic you can go to for more information. In this case, there is only one topic, Renaming Files and Directories, but some Help text boxes list several related topics. To explore this particular topic, press <Tab> to highlight it and then press <Enter>, or just click on the topic with the mouse. The resulting display is shown in figure 12-11.

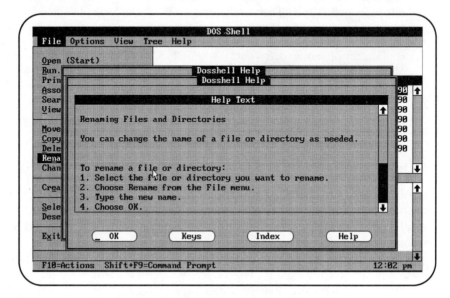

Fig. 12-11. Getting help on a subtopic.

This Help text box is more specific—it gives you a detailed set of steps that you use to rename a file or directory. Rename a directory? Yes, by contrast with the regular MS-DOS REN command, you can rename directories as well as files with DOSSHELL. This is a much less tedious procedure than creating a directory with a new name, copying all the files from the old directory to the new one, deleting all the old files, and, finally, deleting the old directory.

Since you're done with this Help text box and the OK command button is highlighted, you can press <Enter> to get rid of it. Note the three additional buttons on the bottom of the help box: Keys gives you a list of the special keys and key combinations used by DOSSHELL; Index displays an alphabetical index of DOSSHELL topics; and Help displays help on using the help facility itself. Try these on your own.

Finally, if you're not sure how to respond to a dialog box, or what the various options mean, press <F1> or click on the Help button in the dialog box, and the program will provide help for using the dialog box, as shown in figure 12-12.

Suppose you're not "stuck" on any particular matter, but you want to learn more about DOSSHELL's features and the procedures for using them. At any time when you're not in the middle of an operation, you can open the Help menu shown in figure 12-13, select the kind of information you want, and browse among the topics provided. The Shell Basics item is particularly useful for reviewing the basic techniques for manipulating the windows, menus, and lists. The Commands and Procedures items provide you with more information about accomplishing specific tasks.

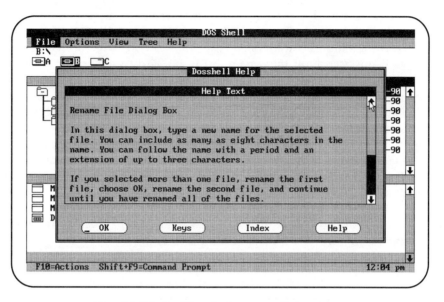

Fig. 12-12. Getting help on a dialog box.

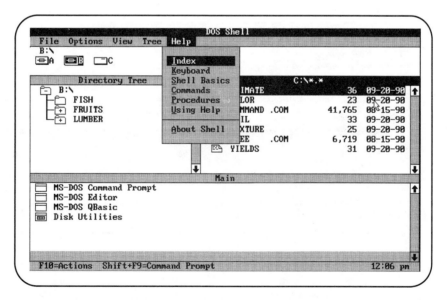

Fig. 12-13. The Help menu.

Working with Multiple Directories and Files

Here's a common situation in file management: you want to compare the contents of two directories. For example, suppose you want to check whether the "soil" and "weather" files are in both the FRUITS directory and the LUMBER directory on drive B.

The traditional DIR command will only show one directory listing at a time, and since listings scroll off the screen, it can be hard to remember what was in one directory while you're looking at another. With DOSSHELL, however, you can list two directories and their files on the same screen. You do this from the View menu, which controls how DOSSHELL divides up the space on the screen. The default arrangement—the one we have been using—has one set of directory-tree and file-list windows and a program-list window. By selecting Dual File Lists from the View menu, you can change this display to make it show two directory-tree windows, each with its corresponding file list. (The program list goes away, but you can get it back by selecting File/Program List from the menu.)

To solve your problem of comparing directories, select Dual File Lists from the View menu now. Next, select FRUITS from the top directory tree and check the accompanying file list. Next, press <Tab> to go down to the second directory tree, and select LUMBER. You can see that the same two files are there, as shown in figure 12-14.

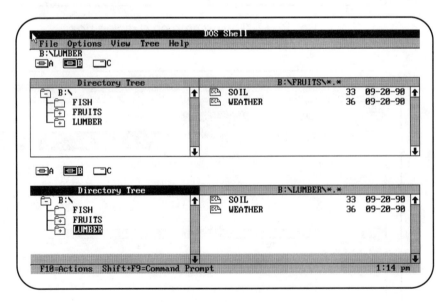

Fig. 12-14. Dual file lists.

Note that the drive selector also appears twice; this means that you can select different drives as well as different directories for the two lists.

When you are looking at an extensive directory tree or file list, you may find it convenient to select Single File List from the View menu. This option dedicates the entire screen to displaying the directory and file lists, making room for more items and allowing faster scrolling.

Options for Changing List Arrangements in the View **Menu**

Choose: | *To display:*

Single File List   One large directory tree and file list

Dual File Lists   Two smaller directory trees and file lists

All Files   A list with all the files on the disk but no directories. (This is useful for looking for specific files.)

Program/File List   A directory tree and file list at the top and a program list at the bottom. (This is the default.)

Program List   One large program list

Using Path names with DOSSHELL

In the DOSSHELL program, you don't have to write a pathname to specify the directory and file you will be working with, but you do have to write path names to specify the destination for operations such as move and copy. Suppose, for example, that you want to copy the "yields" file from the root of drive B into the new FISH directory you created earlier. That way you can use the file as a pattern or *template* for recording the success of your fish pond. Select yields and then select Copy from the File menu. The dialog box that appears is shown in figure 12-15.

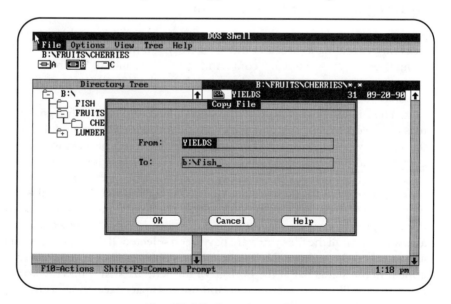

Fig. 12-15. Copying a file.

The name of the source file—the file you are copying from—already appears in the `From` box. You must fill in the destination in the `To` text box and let DOSSHELL know where to copy the file. In figure 12-15, we entered `b:\fish` to copy the file into the FISH directory.

You may have noticed, by the way, that DOSSHELL actually helps you become more familiar with path names. When you select a file from the file list, the appropriate pathname is displayed in the list's title bar. Thus, one way to make copying files easier is to use `Dual File Lists` as mentioned earlier and use the second directory tree to find the correct pathname for the destination directory.

Copying and Moving Files with the Mouse

If you have a mouse, you can also copy or move a file without using the `File` menu. First click on the file's name in the file list. While holding the mouse button down, press the <Ctrl> key (for copying) or the <Alt> key (for moving) and drag the file name toward the directory list. The mouse pointer will change into a circle and then into a file icon. Drag the icon to the name of the directory to which you wish to copy or move the file, and release the mouse button. DOSSHELL will prompt you for confirmation unless you have turned the `Prompt on Mouse Action` option off. Note that you can only copy or move one file at a time using this method.

Working with More Than One File

As a progressive farmer, you want to cultivate organic vegetables. Start this new sideline by creating a directory called VEGGIES in the root directory of drive B by using the `Create Directory` command in the `File` menu. You now want to copy three files—"climate," "soil," and "texture"—to the VEGGIES directory so that you can start your record keeping.

You can use wild cards with the COPY command to specify a group of related files to be copied, but this command can't copy several unrelated files such as the three we're working with here. Fortunately, this is yet another case where DOSSHELL goes beyond the capabilities of the ordinary MS-DOS command line.

In the `File` menu, you can use commands such as `Move`, `Copy`, and `Delete` with more than one file. To do so, first go to the file list and select all the files you will be working with. To select a group of files that are listed consecutively, use the arrow key to highlight the first file, then hold down the <Shift> key while pressing the arrow key until all the files you want have been selected. If the files you want to select are scattered throughout the file list, press <Shift><F8> and the word ADD will appear in the status bar at the bottom of the screen. Next, press the arrow keys to move to each file you want to select, and press <Spacebar> to select that file. When you are done, press <Shift><F8> again.

With the mouse, you can select a consecutive group of files by clicking on the first file name and then clicking on the second file name while holding the <Shift> key down. If the file names you wish to select aren't consecutive, click on each file name while holding the <Ctrl> key down.

In our example, "climate," "soil," and "texture" aren't consecutive. Use the <Shift><F8> keyboard method or the mouse method with the <Ctrl> key. Now select Copy from the File menu. The Copy File dialog box is shown in figure 12-16.

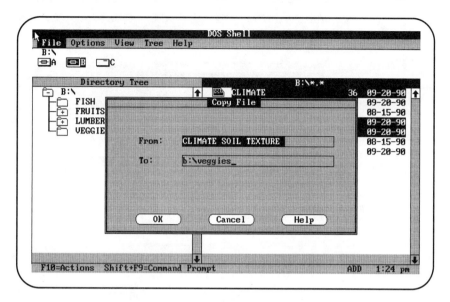

Fig. 12-16. Copying multiple files.

DOSSHELL fills in all three source file names in the From text box of the Copy File dialog box. Type b:\veggies in the To text box and press <Enter> to copy all three files to the VEGGIES directory.

Just as DOSSHELL lets you look at more than one directory at a time, you can also select files from more than one directory. To do so, first choose Select Across Directories from the File menu, and make your selections as usual, using the <Tab> key or mouse to move between file lists.

Where's That File?

Just as you sit there contemplating a socially correct and financially profitable future as an organic farmer, the phone rings. It's your insurance agent, and she wants to make an appointment to look over your various insurance policies. You recall that you have stored some notes about insurance on your hard disk, but where might they be squirrelled away among dozens of directories and several layers of subdirectories?

DOSSHELL offers handy features for those of us who don't know where everything is on our hard disk. To see how these features work, change drives to C (the hard disk) if you have one. Select Search... from the File menu, and you get the Search File dialog box shown in figure 12-17.

It seems likely that at least a few of your insurance files will have some form of the word "insurance" in their names, so type insur*.* (note the wild cards) in the Search for text box, and press <Enter> or click on OK. DOSSHELL will display the results of your search. What *you* see on your own PC will of course depend on whether any files on your hard disk match the wild-card specification. Most likely, none do. But look at figure 12-18 to get an idea of the files that insur*.* uncovers.

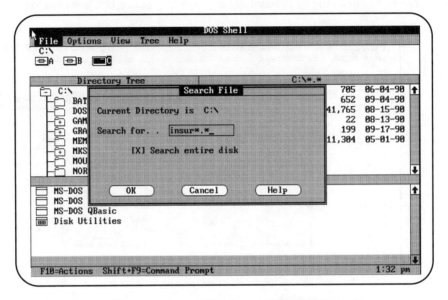

Fig. 12-17. Searching for a file on disk.

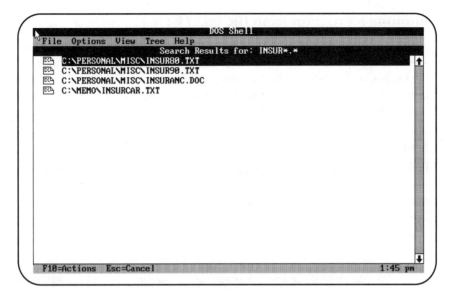

Fig. 12-18. Results of a disk search.

Looking at the illustration, you can see that four different matching files were found: three of them are in the PERSONAL\MISC directory, and one is in the MEMO directory. The search results make up a file list just like the ones shown with directory-tree windows, so you can select one or more of these files and use the View File Contents command in the File menu to see what is in them. When you are done working with the retrieved files, press <Esc> to return to the regular DOSSHELL screen.

Running Programs from DOSSHELL

As you've seen, DOSSHELL is a useful and versatile filing assistant which lets you simplify many file-management tasks. But working with a PC also involves running programs and keeping track of them. DOSSHELL offers several different ways to run your programs, and you can even run several programs at once!

Getting Prompt Service

If you've become familiar with the MS-DOS command prompt, commands, and switches, rest assured that you can use DOSSHELL without abandoning what you've already learned. Simply press <Shift><F9> and the screen will clear and show you a standard MS-DOS prompt, such as C:\>. You can type whatever MS-DOS commands you wish, run utilities or other programs by typing their names as usual, and so on. When you want to return to the shell, type "exit."

Running a Program from the File List

Another way to run a program is to find it in a file-list window, select it, and press <Enter>. With the mouse, you can select and run a program all at once by pressing the button twice (this is called *double clicking*). The program will run as usual. The only disadvantage of this method of running programs is that you can't specify command switches or filenames for the program.

Using the Program List

In many ways, the easiest and most versatile way to run programs is to use the program list, which by default is at the bottom of the screen. A sample program list is shown in figure 12-19. Note that the programs shown and their order may differ from one system to another—this doesn't matter, since we'll soon show you how to add the programs of your choice to the program list.

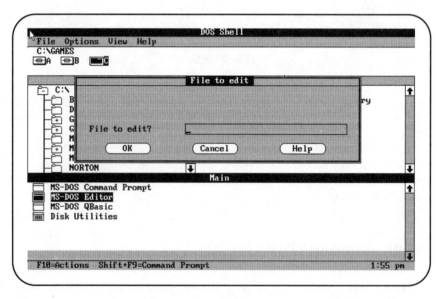

Fig. 12-19. Running Edit from the program list.

Just as a directory can contain subdirectories as well as files, the program list can contain additional program lists as well as individual programs. Programs are organized into *program groups*, each of which may have many programs. When you start working with the program list, you are in the Main program group. In our example this group contains three programs: MS-DOS Command Prompt (that is, the COMMAND.COM program), the MS-DOS Editor (Edit), and the BASIC language (MS-DOS QBasic). The Main group also includes a subgroup, Disk Utilities. You can tell that Disk Utilities is a group because its folder symbol includes several tiny squares representing items within the group.

To run a program from a group's program list, use the arrow keys to highlight the program's name, and press <Enter>; or choose Run from the File menu. With the mouse, simply double-click on a name in the program list to run the program. Many programs, such as Edit in this example, are set up to ask you for information before they start. With Edit, a dialog box asks you to enter the name of the file to edit. Type a filename and press <Enter>, or just press <Enter> to start Edit with a new, empty file.

To select programs from a subgroup, you first open the subgroup (by pressing the arrow keys and <Enter> or clicking the mouse on the group name.) Open the Disk Utilities subgroup. Figure 12-20 shows the program list for this group.

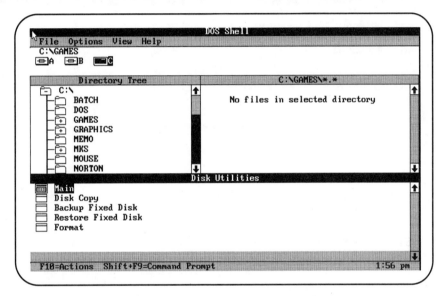

Fig. 12-20. The Disk Utilities **program group.**

As you might expect, the Format item runs the now-familiar Format command. Select Format, and you will see the box shown in figure 12-21.

The box asks you for the parameters (switches) you wish to use. For example, you might use /f:720 to format a 720K disk. Or you could change the supplied drive letter to format a disk in drive B instead of drive A. Unless you actually want to format a disk (and have put a blank disk in the appropriate drive), choose the Cancel button to abandon the formatting operation.

Adding Your Own Program Groups

The nice thing about DOSSHELL's program lists is that you can customize them—you can set up your own program groups according to the kinds of work that you do, or set up a group for each user in your office, or set up any other kind of organization that makes sense to you.

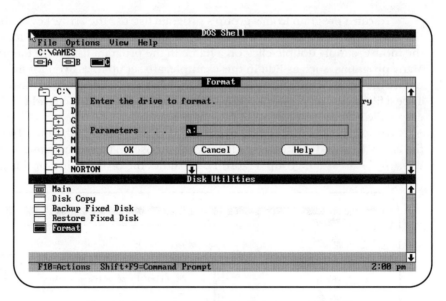

Fig. 12-21. Running FORMAT from DOSSHELL.

Running Programs

To run a program from:	Do the following:
The MS-DOS command line	Press <Shift><F9>; *or* choose MS-DOS Command Prompt from the Main program group, then type the command line and <Enter>
A file list	Highlight the program's file name and press <Enter>; *or* double-click the mouse on the file name
A program group	Open the program group (if necessary), highlight the program name, and press <Enter>; *or* select Run from the File menu; *or* double-click the mouse on the program name

---

Perhaps you've been spending too much time sitting at your PC rather than riding a tractor out on the farm, and you'd rather delegate your routine record-keeping chores to your assistant. Why not set up for your assistant a program group that has only the farming-related programs he or she needs?

If necessary, select the Main program group again from the program list. Now choose New from the File menu. Since the program list is active, DOSSHELL "knows" that you want to work with programs, not files, and the File menu's list of commands reflects this. The first box you see, called New Program Object, is shown in figure 12-22.

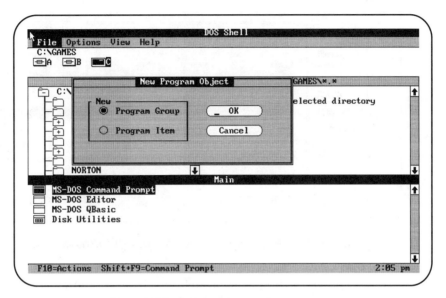

Fig. 12-22. Adding a program group.

Note that you can add either a program group or a program item (an individual program) by choosing the appropriate radio button. Program Item is the default; use the arrow key or mouse to select Program Group, then press <Enter> or click on OK.

Next, the Add Group dialog box shown in figure 12-23 asks for some information about the new group. You must give the group a title that will appear in the program list. We quite logically used "Farming." You can also add some help text to help users understand the purpose of the program group. The text you type here will be displayed if <F1> is pressed while the program group is selected. We entered, "This group is for managing our farm holdings." Text in this box scrolls toward the left as you type it in. Finally, we added a password so that only authorized assistants can use this program group. (Whether to add a password is your decision, though DOSSHELL passwords aren't really intended to keep out the criminally inclined.) The Save button is highlighted, so press <Enter> to create the new program group.

Adding Programs to a Group

Since a program group isn't much good without programs, you will want to add some programs for your assistant to use. Let's suppose that you've written a BASIC program called "farm.bas" that keeps track of farm information and performs useful calculations. This program is in the DOS directory on your hard disk.

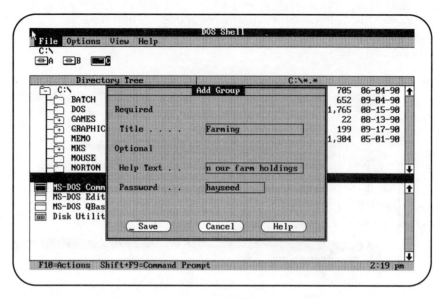

Fig. 12-23. Specifying information for the farming group.

To add a program, choose New again from the File menu, and press <Enter> or click on <ok> to accept the default. You will see the Add Program dialog box, as shown in figure 12-24.

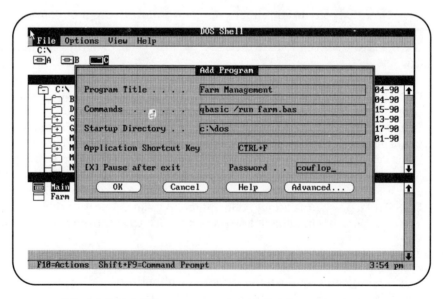

Fig. 12-24. Adding a program to the farming group.

Beginning with the first text box, add the program title, which is "Farm Management" in our case. Next add the actual command that will be used to start the program. In this example we are using a QBASIC program; therefore, the command runs QBASIC and tells it to run the program "farm.bas." In the Startup Directory text box, give the pathname of the directory the program should use. You can also specify an Application Shortcut Key—a <Ctrl>-, <Alt>-, or <Shift>-key combination that will start the program instantly without the user having to select it first. Check Pause after Exit if you want the "Press any key to continue" message displayed after you exit the program and before you return to the shell. Finally, we added a password.

To run this program, the user will need both the group password and this program's password. Press <Enter> when you have completed the information, and the Farm Management program will be added to the Farming program group. When it is selected, "farm.bas" will be run, but the user doesn't need to know that—the program can be selected from a list of descriptive names, which is another advantage of using DOSSHELL to organize your programs.

Note the Advanced button on the Add Program dialog box. This button leads you to further options you can use to control how a program runs. The details of these options are beyond the scope of this book, but you may want to read about them in your MS-DOS manual or consult the on-line help system. We encourage you to experiment with program groups by practicing creating and arranging them.

Switching Between Programs

The MS-DOS version 5.0 DOSSHELL gives you an exciting new capability: you can have several active programs and switch among them as the need arises. For example, suppose you are working on improving "farm.bas" and want to make some notes while working in QBASIC. QBASIC, however, won't let you edit more than one file at a time, so you'd like to have Edit handy for making notes while you work.

To use more than one program at a time, choose Enable Switcher from the Options menu. As shown in figure 12-25, the program list now has a second window to the right, called Active Task List.

Now, whenever you select and run a program, instead of exiting the program as usual, press <Alt> <Esc> and you will be returned to the DOSSHELL screen, where the program's name will appear on the Active Task List. You can now run another program or switch to one that is already running by selecting it from the Active Task List.

Alternatively, you can switch directly from one program to another by pressing <Alt><Tab> and proceeding through your programs in the order you've used them.

Thus, while developing your improved farm program, you can press <Alt><Tab> to switch to Edit, make some notes, and press <Alt><Tab> to get back into QBASIC and continue your programming.

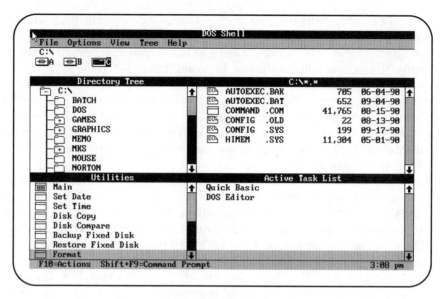

Fig. 12-25. Switching among programs.

Associating Data Files and Programs

DOSSHELL offers one more trick to make it easier for you to work with your programs. As you know, you can select a program from a file list and run it. You can't "run" a text file, however. You have to run a program such as Edit and then specify the name of the text file. Wouldn't it be nice to be able to run Edit automatically whenever you select a text file? In fact, this is easy to do: DOSSHELL lets you *associate* a program with a file extension. This way, whenever a file with that particular extension is selected, the specified program is run automatically and calls up that file.

To see how this works, choose from the file list a file that has the appropriate extension. In our example, we found the file "organic.txt" on drive B and selected it. Now choose `Associate...` from the `File` menu. You will see the `Associate File` dialog box shown in figure 12-26. Enter the name of the program to be associated with the files that have the .TXT extension. In our example, we used `c:\dos\edit.com`. Be sure to give the complete pathname and extension for the program, so that DOSSHELL will always know where to find it.

Now if you select *any* file with the .TXT extension and press <Enter> or double-click on the file name with the mouse, Edit will be run and the file will be ready for you to view and edit. Pretty nifty!

This concludes your tour of DOSSHELL. You have managed directories and files, run programs, and added new groups and programs to DOSSHELL's lists. You have seen how DOSSHELL offers some capabilities that aren't available from the command line and makes many tasks easier to perform.

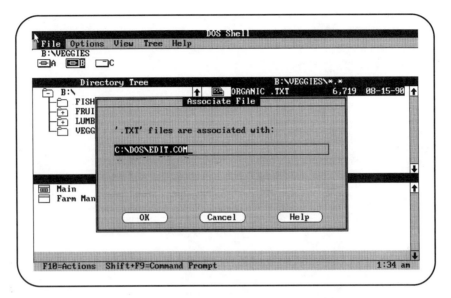

Fig. 12-26. Associating a file type with a program.

There are many DOSSHELL features we couldn't cover due to lack of space, but now that you know your way around the menus, dialog boxes, and help screens, you can explore them on your own. You may well find that DOSSHELL makes your work easier and increases your productivity.

13

Tooling Around DOS

- It Slices, It Dices . . . Introducing Utility Packages
    - Norton Utilities
    - PC Tools
- Making Backup Easy
- The Doctor Is In
- Recovery Room
    - Backing Up Directory Information
    - Restoring Erased Files
    - Restoring Accidentally Formatted Disks
- Revving Up Your Disk
    - Device Drivers
    - Cache-ing in on Speed
    - Buffing Up Your BUFFERS
    - Speedy Navigation with FASTOPEN
    - Defragmentation
    - Interleaving
- Tools for File Management
    - Where's That File?
    - Where's That Letter About…
    - What Does "gb99zrkl.txt" Mean, Anyway?
- Devising with Devices

- Speaking in Tongues
- Using Your Resources
    - FILES
    - FCBS
    - LASTDRIVE
    - STACKS
- Thanks for the Memories
    - Memory Lane
    - Which Kind of Memory Should You Use?
    - Freeing Up More Memory

13 Tooling Around DOS

You should now be comfortable with everyday use of MS-DOS: backing up disks, copying files, organizing directories, and running programs. This chapter introduces some utility programs and customizing techniques. You will learn how to back up files easily, apply first aid for disk problems, improve the performance of your hard disk, ease your file-management problems, configure MS-DOS features to extend your PC's capabilities and suit your needs, and speed up your applications by improving their use of memory. By mastering the tools and techniques in this chapter, you can be confident that you are getting the most productivity from your hardware and software.

This chapter covers tools and techniques from several sources. You'll learn about additional MS-DOS commands you can use to reconfigure your system. For example, you can change the amount of memory MS-DOS uses to keep track of directories and files. You can also install programs called *device drivers* that are loaded into memory, to accommodate add-on hardware or extend the capabilities of your screen display, keyboard, or other built-in devices. Most of these commands and device drivers are loaded by the CONFIG.SYS file; others are run from the AUTOEXEC.BAT file. These two files control the automatic setup and configuration of your system; you have already seen some examples of how AUTOEXEC.BAT can be used. Recent versions of MS-DOS, particularly versions 4.0 and later, have added many new features to enhance performance and increase flexibility.

This chapter also presents techniques for managing *utility programs*. These are special programs designed to improve the ease of use and performance of your system. Take a look on any large dial-up bulletin board or information service or the disk library kept by a PC user group, and you'll see hundreds of utility programs to help you find and manage files, check the condition of your hard disk, recover lost data, and so on. These utility programs vary in completeness and quality. They are offered either free of charge or as *shareware*, a pay-as-you-go arrangement that requires you to pay for the program only after you've tried it and decided that it suits your needs.

For added professional polish and the convenience of having many different utilities in the same package, you can buy a utility package such as Central Point Software's PC Tools or Symantec's Norton Utilities. Throughout this chapter we will illustrate some of the useful features of these two software packages. Such utility packages can be excellent investments. Their modest cost of about $75 to about $150 will be repaid quickly in added security and productivity.

Don't worry about mastering all the details of each MS-DOS command or utility package feature in this chapter. Indeed, we don't have the room to list all the switches and other parameters included in many commands. The important thing is to get a sense of what is available and how to go about using it. We can only give a few examples to show typical use, and the settings shown may not be the best for your situation. To get the most out of each command or program, consult your MS-DOS manual (for MS-DOS commands) or the documentation that comes with your utility package. (Both PC Tools and Norton Utilities also have extensive on-line documentation.) You may also want to read more about MS-DOS configuration and customizing in our book *The Waite Group's MS-DOS Bible*.

This chapter introduces a number of new concepts in the course of explaining how to customize and fine-tune your system. Don't worry about mastering them all at once. Move at your own pace. Take the time to try out the features that most interest you and seem to make your system easier to use, more secure from data loss, or faster.

It is often said that MS-DOS systems are harder to use than systems that are neatly packaged with hardware and software ready to run "out of the box." In fact, life is continually getting easier for MS-DOS users, because MS-DOS versions 4.0 and later perform automatic installation and configuration and because DOSSHELL and other graphical interfaces such as Microsoft Windows make MS-DOS more accessible. And the big advantage of MS-DOS systems continues to be your ability to "mix and match" hardware and software to suit your needs. You aren't limited by what one manufacturer chooses to provide; you have all the fruits of a highly competitive marketplace to choose from.

It Slices, It Dices . . . Introducing Utility Packages

What kinds of things do utility packages do? How do you use them? Let's look at Norton Utilities and PC Tools, two of the most popular ones. Remember, however, that there are other utilities available. Also, most utility packages are revised frequently, with new features constantly being added.

Norton Utilities

The Norton Utilities package consists of about 25 different utility programs. You can run these programs directly from the command line (like regular MS-DOS commands), or you can select them from a menu using a program called the Norton Integrator. As shown in figure 13-1, this program presents a menu of utilities on the left side of the screen. The right side is devoted to a help window that gives information about the currently selected utility (FR, or Format Recover, in this illustration.) The help window briefly describes the purpose of the utility, gives the format for the command line, and lists the switches you can use. To run the highlighted utility, type any command-line parameters you need, and then press <Enter>.

Nearly all the utilities have simple two-letter abbreviations; for example, Format Recover is FR. This makes them easy to remember, even without the Norton Integrator. Since the utilities are really stand-alone programs, you can include them in batch files and even run appropriate ones from your AUTOEXEC.BAT file.

The utilities focus on disk maintenance and repair and on file management. Table 13-1 lists some of the more important ones:

Table 13-1. Selected Norton utilities.

Utility	*Purpose*
	Disk Diagnosis and Repair
Disk Information (DI)	Gives detailed information about disk organization
Disk Test (DT)	Tests disk surface for problems; moves data out of problem areas
Norton Disk Doctor(NDD)	Tests, diagnoses, and automatically fixes problems with disk structure
Norton Utility (NU)	Inspects and edits data in disk sectors
	Recovering Lost Data
Format Recover (FR)	Restores an accidentally formatted hard disk
Safe Format (SF)	Formats a floppy disk without destroying data, allows recovery from accidental floppy disk format
Quick Unerase (QU)	Automatically restores an accidentally deleted file
Unremove Directory (UD)	Recovers a directory that was accidentally removed, restoring its file information
	Security
Wipedisk (WD)	Physically overwrites all data so that someone can't "undelete" it and learn your secrets
Wipefile (WF)	Overwrites selected files
	Improving Disk Performance
Speed Disk (SD)	Reorganizes fragmented files to speed up disk access
	Improving File Management
Directory Sort (DS)	Sorts directories by name or other criteria
File Attribute (FA)	Make files read-only, hidden, etc., or makes hidden files visible
File Find (FF)	Searches all directories on the disk for a file
File Info (FI)	Attaches descriptive comments to files (comments can be viewed in a special directory format)
Text Search (TS)	Searches specified files for text string (can search entire disk)

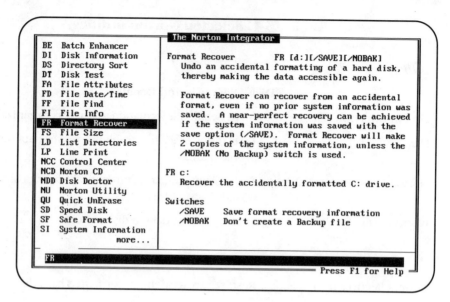

```
BE  Batch Enhancer        ┌──── The Norton Integrator ────┐
DI  Disk Information       Format Recover        FR [d:][/SAVE][/NOBAK]
DS  Directory Sort           Undo an accidental formatting of a hard disk,
DT  Disk Test                thereby making the data accessible again.
FA  File Attributes
FD  File Date/Time           Format Recover can recover from an accidental
FF  File Find                format, even if no prior system information was
FI  File Info                saved. A near-perfect recovery can be achieved
FR  Format Recover           if the system information was saved with the
FS  File Size                save option (/SAVE). Format Recover will make
LD  List Directories         2 copies of the system information, unless the
LP  Line Print               /NOBAK (No Backup) switch is used.
NCC Control Center
NCD Norton CD              FR c:
NDD Disk Doctor              Recover the accidentally formatted C: drive.
NU  Norton Utility
QU  Quick UnErase         Switches
SD  Speed Disk              /SAVE    Save format recovery information
SF  Safe Format            /NOBAK   Don't create a Backup file
SI  System Information
              more...

FR
                                            Press F1 for Help
```

Fig. 13-1. Norton Integrator.

In addition to those listed, Norton includes utilities that enhance the MS-DOS batch commands, provide statistics about system performance, and so on. New features come along with each version.

PC Tools

Although PC Tools provides many of the same features as Norton Utilities, it has a distinctly different "feel." The Norton Utilities is like a chest of finely crafted, specialized tools; PC Tools is a diverse smorgasbord with a mind-boggling variety of utilities and accessories. You can run the individual tools from the MS-DOS command line, but they are really designed to be used as part of an integrated working environment.

The key to this working environment is PC Shell, shown in figure 13-2. If you've read Chapter 12 and have used DOSSHELL, you'll immediately recognize many similarities between PC Shell and DOSSHELL. For example, PC Shell also has a directory-tree window and a file-tree window. You select a directory and files to work with and then select the command you want.

Like Norton, PC Tools provides an assortment of utility programs. You can run the utilities from the MS-DOS command line or from PC Shell, which includes them in an Applications menu. Table 13-2 summarizes these programs.

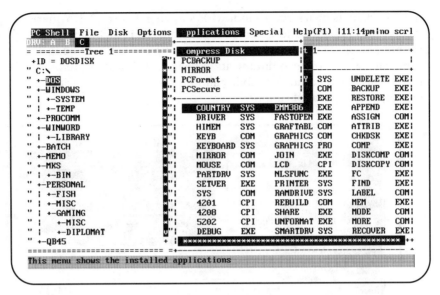

Fig. 13-2. PC Tools shell.

Table 13-2. PC Tools utility programs.

Program	Purpose
Compress	Speeds up disk access by reorganizing fragmented files
Mirror	Records disk structure for emergency restoration
PC Backup	Backs up a hard disk, letting you choose directories to be backed up directly from a directory-tree display
PC Cache	Speeds up disk access by keeping recently accessed disk sectors in memory
PC Format	Replaces the MS-DOS format command with a formatting program that does not wipe out existing data; allows recovery from an accidental format
PC Secure	Scrambles data so that it cannot be read without a password; compresses data so that more of it fits on the disk
Rebuild	Restores disk contents by using the information recorded by the Mirror program, or uses the remaining structure to restore disk contents

In addition to PC Shell and the utility programs, PC Tools also provides a complete "desktop" with many applications such as a text editor, outliner, database, appointment calendar, and phone dialer. You can run several of these programs at once, each in its own screen window, as shown in figure 13-3. Your desktop can be loaded into memory and accessed even while your main application program is running. Desk-accessory programs aren't comparable to full-fledged word processors, databases, or telecommunication programs, but they are quite adequate for many tasks. Their instant availability allows you to perform a variety of tasks without leaving your main application.

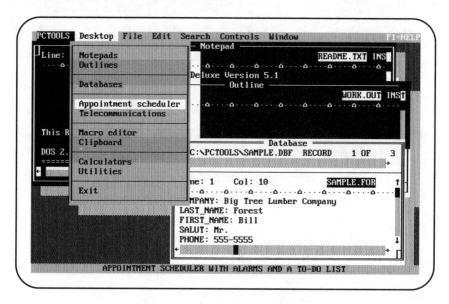

Fig. 13-3. PC Tools desktop.

Which utility package should you get? There is no one answer. The more-focused Norton Utilities may be more to your taste if you are already running a DOS shell or Microsoft Windows, and you have or don't need desk-accessory programs. Norton's disk utilities tend to be more thorough; in particular, the Norton Disk Doctor can diagnose and fix highly technical problems without your having to know what is going on. On the other hand, if you want one package that does almost everything but make you a cup of coffee and does most everything well, choose PC Tools. As you'll see next, a program such as PC Backup (a part of PC Tools) is itself worth the price of admission. Of course, you could buy both or investigate other utility or accessory software. We suggest that you read comparative reviews in the PC magazines to help you choose the package with the features you want.

Now that you have some idea of what utility programs are good for and why you might want one, let's investigate specific areas where utilities and MS-DOS commands can improve the security, efficiency, and ease of use of your PC. We'll start by looking again at the need to make backups.

Making Backup Easy

In Chapter 10 you learned how to use the MS-DOS BACKUP command to save on floppy disks all or part of the contents of your hard disk. The MS-DOS BACKUP program certainly works, and since you already own DOS, it's free. So why would you want to buy a separate backup program? There are two answers to the question: speed and ease of use. Backing up a large hard disk with MS-DOS BACKUP can take more than an hour. Furthermore, the MS-DOS BACKUP program requires you to remember which command switches to use for a complete backup, a partial (incremental) backup, or a backup that includes subdirectories. You must also include path names to specify what you want backed up. While many of these steps can be automated by putting your BACKUP command in a batch file, you still don't have much flexibility. Because backing up a hard disk is time-consuming and hard to do, many people put off making backups—and that can lead to an expensive disaster.

To meet the need for a better BACKUP, a number of backup utilities have come on the market. A good, representative example is PC Backup, a part of PC Tools. The main PC Backup screen is shown in figure 13-4.

Like PC Shell, this screen has a directory-tree window and a file-list window. You can choose the directories and files to be backed up from the Backup menu, or you can choose directories directly from the directory tree using the keyboard or mouse. You can select all the files in a particular directory, or just certain ones. Suppose that you also want to back up subdirectories of the selected directories. You just select the "Subdirectory Inclusion" item on the Backup menu.

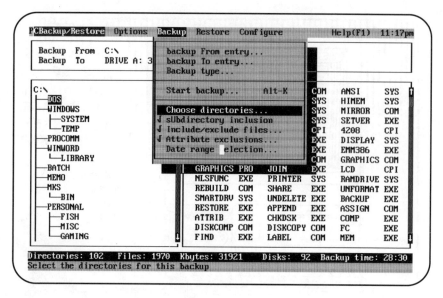

Fig. 13-4. PC Backup screen.

The "Include/Exclude files" option is one of the most interesting and powerful features of PC Backup. You use it to specify the extensions of files that are to be included (backed up) or excluded (not backed up). For example, suppose your work involves a word processor that makes files with an extension of .DOC, a text editor that uses files with a .TXT extension, and a spreadsheet that uses the extensions .WKS and .MAC. In most cases, only your work files (documents, spreadsheets and databases) change from day to day. Your program files (with .EXE or .COM extensions) would not change. It wouldn't make sense to spend half an hour backing up your program files each day when they haven't changed. Using the Include/Exclude facility, you can set up a list like the following:

```
C:\WORD\*.DOC
C:\NOTES\*.TXT
C:\ACCTNG\*.WKS
C:\ACCTNG\*.MAC
```

This list specifies that only the files in the WORD, NOTES, and ACCTNG directories with the specified extensions be backed up when the backup is run. This type of list speeds up the backup process tremendously. Still, some files in other directories that you would want to back up might be left out. Also, many programs maintain initialization files for storing settings you have selected, and these wouldn't be backed up either.

A more conservative approach is to tell PC Backup to back up everything *except* program files, as shown with the following specifications:

```
*.*
-*.*
-*.COM
-*.EXE
```

Here, the *.* means "include all files on the disk." But the specifications that follow, preceded by minus signs, indicate exclusions or exceptions. -*.* means exclude all files in the root directory (most well-organized PC users don't keep data files there, anyway.) The specifications -*.COM and -*.EXE exclude all program files from the backup.

In addition to inclusion or exclusion specifications, you can also specify backup of all files created or modified after a certain date, all files except hidden or system files, and so on. By using switches, you can use many of these specifications with MS-DOS BACKUP, but PC Backup lets you specify them all with menus. Finally, you can save sets of specifications to disk and reuse them for later backups.

Restoring files from your backup disks is done with similar ease. PC Backup includes special techniques that allow it to simultaneously read data from one disk while copying it to another. This makes the backup process considerably faster than that used by MS-DOS.

The Doctor Is In

Having secured your peace of mind with regular backups, what do you do if you issue the DIR command and get an MS-DOS message such as "General Failure" or "Sector Not Found?" How do you find out what is wrong with the disk? How do you fix it?

You don't need to know all the gory details of disk organization to manage your disks effectively. Take a look at figure 13-5, which will help you visualize what is going on when disk utilities are used. The organization of a disk (floppy or hard) basically consists of the following parts (the actual number of disk sectors used for each of these areas varies and depends on the capacity of the disk):

❏ The *boot record*, which has information describing the structure of the disk. It includes the *partition* table, which describes how the disk is divided into parts that can be assigned their own drive letters. If the disk is bootable, the boot record also includes program codes that MS-DOS needs to boot from the disk.

❏ The *file allocation table*, or FAT. This is a list of the *clusters*—groups of physical disk sectors—that contain data, showing which clusters belong to each file. A second copy of the FAT immediately follows. Most versions of MS-DOS don't actually use this copy, but MS-DOS 5.0 and some utility programs do.

❏ The *directory area*, which contains the root directory of the disk

❏ The *data area*, which contains the actual data in your files and makes up most of the disk surface

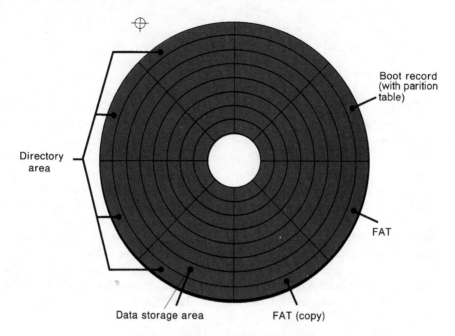

Directory area

Boot record
(with parition
table)

FAT

Data storage area　　　FAT (copy)

Fig. 13-5. Key areas of a disk.

As you have seen, MS-DOS offers the CHKDSK command for finding problems such as a garbled FAT (discrepancies between the list of disk clusters and the actual areas occupied by files on the disk). It certainly doesn't hurt to run CHKDSK and see if it can fix the problem. (For a more detailed explanation of what the messages from CHKDSK mean, see your MS-DOS manual or one of the Waite Group books mentioned earlier in this chapter.) CHKDSK can only fix a limited range of problems, and it can't perform a "preventative" examination of the disk surface. Both PC Tools and Norton Utilities offer programs that can do a much more thorough job of disk doctoring. We will look at the Norton Disk Doctor here.

Although Norton includes an excellent "everything you ever wanted to know about disks" guide in its package, the Norton Disk Doctor doesn't require you to have any special knowledge of the details of disk structure. Run the Disk Doctor by typing NDD at the MS-DOS command line or from the Norton Integrator, and then select Diagnose Disk and specify the disk to be examined. The doctor will get out a stethoscope and flashlight and go to work. As shown in figure 13-6, the various characteristics of the disk (a large hard disk in this case) are ferreted out and listed.

The scanning process includes inspection of the partition table, the boot record, the FAT, and the structure of the root directory and all subdirectories. You will be informed of any problems, given appropriate cautions, and asked whether to have NDD fix the problem.

Having looked at the "logical" structure of the disk, the Disk Doctor asks if you want to test the whole physical surface of the disk. As shown in figure 13-7, NDD shows you a map of the disk indicating the used and unused blocks (areas) and the locations of any bad clusters. (A *cluster* is the actual unit of disk space MS-DOS uses for storing files. The number of physical sectors per cluster depends on the disk format; most hard disks have four 512-byte sectors per cluster.) NDD also asks whether bad clusters should be fixed automatically.

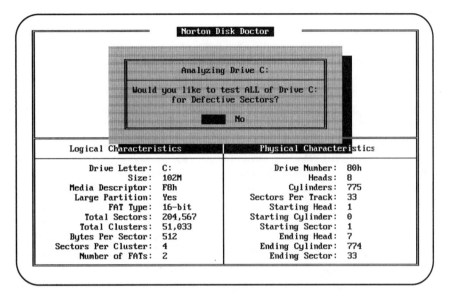

Fig. 13-6. Norton Disk Doctor disk scan.

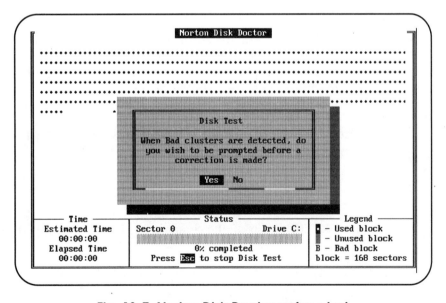

Fig. 13-7. Norton Disk Doctor surface test.

Recovery Room

Disks do develop physical problems, but the most common cause of disk problems is human error. If you were distracted and typed "del datafile" instead of "dir datafile," your "datafile" would be erased. Or would it? Suppose you accidentally format a floppy disk that has important data on it or—horror of horrors—reformat a whole hard disk. Can you restore your disk organization to its original condition? Can you get the data in a deleted file back? Only a few years ago the answer was "probably not." Today, both MS-DOS (starting with version 5.0) and utility programs (for all versions of MS-DOS) enable us to answer "probably yes."

Keep two important things in mind to maximize the chances of full recovery. First, and most importantly, *never copy any files to a disk from which you want to recover data.* When MS-DOS deletes a file, it updates its list of file locations on the disk and marks the file's clusters as being "free" and available for storing new files. The data in the deleted file is still there, so it is potentially recoverable; however, if you then copy another file to the disk (or add to an existing file), MS-DOS may put the new data in the newly freed clusters and obliterate the old data for good.

Second, you should regularly run whatever utilities are provided for backing up crucial directory and file sector information. For example, you would run the MIRROR command in MS-DOS 5.0 or in PC Tools. Doing so improves the chances that your data can be recovered, because MS-DOS or the utility will know where to look for the file's clusters on the disk. Let's look at these recovery utilities next.

Backing Up Directory Information

MS-DOS 5.0 includes a new command called MIRROR. This command makes a backup copy of the FAT and, optionally, the partition table. If something garbles one of these areas, you can use the backup copy to restore the organization of the disk and access to your data.

The MIRROR Command (MS-DOS 5.0 and later)

Use: Back up the FAT and partition table of a disk

Example: `mirror c: /tc`

If you type MIRROR by itself, the command makes a copy of the FAT of the current disk:

```
C:\DOS>mirror<Enter>

Drive C being processed.

MIRROR successful.
```

To save the partition table as well, add the /partn switch. You will be prompted to insert a disk into another drive to receive a file containing this information. (If the partition table goes bad, you can't access the disk at all until it is fixed. Therefore, there would be no point in saving the partition information on the same disk.)

```
C:\DOS>mirror /partn<Enter>
Disk Partition Table saver.

The partition information from your hard drive(s) has been read.

Next, the file PARTNSAV.FIL will be written to a floppy disk.
Please insert a formatted diskette and enter the name of the
diskette drive.
What drive? A<Enter>
Successful.
```

MIRROR can also install in memory a small program called "delete tracking" that keeps track of all the files you delete. This program is important because it gives the UNDELETE command (which you will learn about later) more information to use when recovering a file, thus allowing you a better chance of making a full recovery. To install the "delete tracking" feature of MIRROR, add the /t switch followed by the letter of the drive on which deletions will be tracked. You can repeat the /t switch for as many drives as you wish to track:

```
C:\DOS>mirror /tb /tc<Enter>
WARNING!  Unrecognized DOS INT 25h/26h handler. Some other TSR
programs may behave erratically while Delete-Tracking is resident!
Try installing Mirror BEFORE your other TSR's.
```

What happened? MIRROR is warning us that another program already resident in memory—a *terminate and stay resident* (TSR) program—may have problems interacting with the MIRROR delete tracking. It is a good idea to run MIRROR *before* you load other memory-resident programs such as the MS-DOS PRINT command, the PC Tools desktop, and Borland's SideKick. In fact, you will probably want to put the MIRROR command near the beginning of your AUTOEXEC.BAT file so that it will load early and automatically.

Despite the possible problem, MIRROR continues:

```
The following drives are supported;
Drive B - Default
Drive C - Default

Installation complete.
```

Since we used the /tb and /tc switches, drives B and C now have delete tracking.

If delete tracking causes problems or you need to free up some memory, you can remove it by typing:

```
C:\>mirror /u<Enter>
```

See your MS-DOS manual for more information about the MIRROR command. By the way, PC Tools includes a very similar MIRROR utility you can use with versions of MS-DOS prior to 5.0.

Restoring Erased Files

MS-DOS 5.0 also includes the UNDELETE command, which attempts to restore an accidentally deleted file. If you haven't copied any files to the disk following the accidental deletion, the chances of recovery are good. For best results, run MIRROR with the delete tracking option at the start of each session, so that UNDELETE will be able to get complete information about the deleted file.

Suppose one bleary-eyed night you are working on your farming files, and you can't remember whether CLIMATE is a file or a directory. You decide to do a DIR to find out, and you type:

```
C:\DOS>del b:climate<Enter>
```

Whoops! You meant DIR, not DEL. Fearfully, you try the DIR command:

```
C:\DOS>dir b:climate<Enter>

 Volume in drive B has no label
 Volume Serial Number is 1338-16D3
 Directory of B:\

File not found
```

The file is gone—or rather, the DIR command can't find it because it is no longer listed in the directory. Before you do anything else with this disk, use the UNDELETE command to bring back the "climate" file:

```
C:\DOS>undelete b:climate<Enter>
Directory: B:\
File Specs: CLIMATE.*

    Delete Tracking file contains    1 deleted files.
    Of those,    1 files have all clusters available,
                 0 files have some clusters available,
                 0 files have no clusters available.

    DOS Directory contains    1 deleted files.
    Of those,    1 files may be recovered.
```

```
Using the Delete Tracking file.

      CLIMATE            36  9/20/90  9:38a  ...A Deleted:
9/28/90  1:07a
All of the clusters for this file are available.
Do you want to recover this file? (Y/N)y
File successfully undeleted.
```

Whew! It's back. Don't believe it? Try another DIR command:

```
C:\DOS>dir b:climate

 Volume in drive B has no label
 Volume Serial Number is 1338-16D3
 Directory of B:\

CLIMATE              36 09-20-90   9:38a
        1 file(s)          36 bytes
                      575488 bytes free
```

The UNDELETE Command (MS-DOS 5.0 and later)

Use: Restores files accidentally deleted with the DEL command

Example: undelete climate

Again, users of versions of MS-DOS prior to 5.0 can resort to the PC Tools version of UNDELETE (which you can run from PC Shell). Norton Utilities includes the similar Quick Unerase (QU) program, as well as the more elaborate Unerase which you can use to rebuild files sector by sector if QU doesn't work.

Restoring Accidentally Formatted Disks

If accidentally deleting a file is every PC user's bad dream, accidentally formatting a disk (particularly a hard disk) counts as a nightmare. It's actually possible in most cases to recover all or most of the data on a newly formatted disk, however, because existing data on a hard disk isn't actually written over when the disk is formatted. Instead, only the FAT and the root directory are cleared out. (A few versions of MS-DOS, such as Compaq DOS through version 3.2, do remove the data, however.)

To restore an accidentally formatted hard disk, run the UNFORMAT command (with MS-DOS 5.0 or later). However, because this command relies on the information saved by the MIRROR command to restore the FAT and your disk organization, you will probably not be able to restore files that changed since the last time you ran MIRROR (another good reason to run MIRROR from AUTOEXEC.BAT at the start of each session).

The UNFORMAT Command (MS-DOS 5.0 or later)

Use: Restores an accidentally formatted hard disk

Example: `unformat c:`

UNFORMAT can also help you restore a hard disk that is so badly garbled that MS-DOS doesn't even acknowledge its existence. Recall that you can use MIRROR to save a copy of the disk-partition table. Suppose you have done so and later get an error message such as "Invalid Drive Letter" telling you that MS-DOS can no longer access your hard disk. To restore the disk-partition table, boot from a floppy disk that has the UNFORMAT command on it and type:

```
unformat c: /partn
```

UNFORMAT will read the partition information from the floppy on which you saved it with the MIRROR command and rebuild the partition table of your hard disk. PC Tools includes a similar UNFORMAT command. The Norton Utilities equivalent is called Format Recover (FR).

The recovery situation with floppy disks is a bit more complicated. Most versions of FORMAT do write over the existing data. The FORMAT command in MS-DOS version 5.0 doesn't write over data, however, unless you specify the /u switch. PC Tools provides its own improved FORMAT program, PC Format, which again preserves existing data. Norton's equivalent is the Safe Format (SF) program. If you are using a version of MS-DOS earlier than 5.0 and have one of these utilities, it is a good idea to rename the MS-DOS format as something like DOSFMT and rename the utility format as FORMAT. That way, you will run the "safe" format instead, and you should be able to recover from an accidental format.

With MS-DOS version 5.0 or later, use the REBUILD command to restore an accidentally formatted floppy disk. To test this command, we used the FORMAT command to reformat our floppy disk with the farming file examples on it. Before we formatted it, the root directory of the disk looked like this:

```
C:\DOS>dir b:<Enter>

 Volume in drive B has no label
 Volume Serial Number is 1338-16D3
 Directory of B:\

TREE     COM      6719 08-15-90   3:33a
COMMAND  COM     41765 08-15-90   3:33a
CLIMATE            36 09-20-90   9:38a
SOIL               33 09-20-90   9:39a
YIELDS             31 09-20-90   9:39a
TEXTURE            25 09-20-90   9:39a
```

```
COLOR                  23 09-20-90    9:40a
FRUITS        <DIR>       09-20-90    9:42a
LUMBER        <DIR>       09-20-90    9:43a
FISH          <DIR>       09-20-90   11:17a
VEGGIES       <DIR>       09-20-90    1:21p
PCTRACKR DEL         9104 09-28-90    1:08a
       12 file(s)       57736 bytes
                       575488 bytes free
```

After the formatting, all the data on the disk appears to have gone away:

```
C:\DOS>dir b:<Enter>

Volume in drive B is WHOOPS
Volume Serial Number is 217A-08D4
Directory of B:\

File not found
```

Let's assume that we've been using MIRROR faithfully with drive B. We run REBUILD and go through the following dialog:

```
C:\DOS>rebuild b:<Enter>

The LAST time MIRROR was used was at 13:27 on 9/28/90
The PRIOR time MIRROR was used was at 14:11 on 9/27/90

If you want to use the LAST file as indicated
above, press 'L'. If you wish to use the PRIOR
file as indicated above, press 'P'. Press ESCAPE
to terminate REBUILD 1

The MIRROR image file has been validated.
Are you SURE that you want to update the SYSTEM area
of your drive B (Y/N)? y<Enter>
The SYSTEM area of drive B has been rebuilt.
You may need to reboot the system.
```

Issuing a DIR command should reveal that everything has been restored. (It *is* a good idea to reboot, though, because information about drive B held in memory may no longer match the actual structure of the disk.)

REBUILD will attempt to restore a disk even if MIRROR hasn't been run or hasn't been run recently. To do so, it will scan the directory sectors and try to determine where existing files are on the disk. Here's what happens if we run REBUILD on a disk that doesn't have a reasonably current MIRROR file:

```
C:\DOS>rebuild b: /test<Enter>

   CAUTION !!
This attempts to recover all the files lost after a
FORMAT, assuming you've NOT been using MIRROR. This
method cannot guarantee complete recovery of your files.

The search-phase is safe: nothing is altered on the disk.
You'll be prompted again before changes are written to the disk.

Using drive B:

Are you SURE you want to do this?
If so, type in YES; anything else cancels.
yes<Enter>
100% searched, 6 subdirs found.
Files found in the root: 0
Subdirectories found in root: 4

Walking the directory tree to locate all files...
Path=B:\
Path=B:\SUBDIR.1\
Path=B:\SUBDIR.1\CHERRIES\
Path=B:\SUBDIR.1\
Path=B:\SUBDIR.2\
Path=B:\SUBDIR.2\REDWOOD\
Path=B:\SUBDIR.2\
Path=B:\
Path=B:\SUBDIR.3\
Path=B:\
Path=B:\SUBDIR.4\
Path=B:\

Files found: 9
```

REBUILD has found some subdirectories, but their names are gone, so they're referred to as SUBDIR.1, SUBDIR.2, and so on. The names are gone because formatting removes the entries in the root directory. Note that the lower-level subdirectories CHERRIES and REDWOOD are also found. Since these subdirectories aren't in the root directory, the formatting process hasn't written over them.

```
Warning!  The next step writes changes to disk.

Are you SURE you want to do this?
If so, type in YES; anything else cancels.
? yes<Enter>
```

```
Checking for file fragmentation...
Path=B:\
Path=B:\SUBDIR.1\
Path=B:\SUBDIR.1\CHERRIES\
Path=B:\SUBDIR.1\
Path=B:\
Path=B:\SUBDIR.2\
Path=B:\SUBDIR.2\REDWOOD\
Path=B:\SUBDIR.2\
Path=B:\
Path=B:\SUBDIR.3\
Path=B:\
```

REBUILD scans the cluster list. If a file is not fragmented—that is, scattered in several groups of clusters in different areas of the disk—it can usually be completely recovered. If it is fragmented, however, REBUILD can't find all of it, so you're asked to accept a truncated version:

```
Path=B:\SUBDIR.4\
ORGANIC.TXT         6719  8-15-90   3:33am
Only 1024 bytes are recoverable
Truncate or Delete this file?t<Enter>
File size truncated.
```

We decided to accept the truncated file, since we'll get at least some of our data back. Finally, REBUILD summarizes its efforts:

```
Path=B:\
9 files recovered.

Operation completed.
```

Now, suppose you issue a DIR command. You'll see the following:

```
C:\DOS>dir b:<Enter>

 Volume in drive B has no label
 Volume Serial Number is 217A-08D4
 Directory of B:\

SUBDIR   1   <DIR>      09-28-90   12:00a
SUBDIR   2   <DIR>      09-28-90   12:00a
SUBDIR   3   <DIR>      09-28-90   12:00a
SUBDIR   4   <DIR>      09-28-90   12:00a
        4 file(s)            0 bytes
                      713728 bytes free
```

While you've lost the actual subdirectory names, most of the files are intact.

For versions of MS-DOS earlier than 5.0, you can use the very similar PC Tools REBUILD program. With Norton Utilities, this service is provided by Format Recover (FR).

Revving Up Your Disk

The performance of your disk drives, particularly your hard disk, often determines the performance of your system as a whole. In many cases it does little good to have a speedy new 80286 or 80386 processor if your program seems to take forever to get data from the disk or to return it there when you are done processing. Fortunately, revving up your hard disk doesn't have to mean scrapping the old drive and paying hundreds of dollars for a new, faster one. You can speed up your disk by using free or inexpensive software to "index" it for faster file finding, reorganize your disk contents for faster retrieval, and use memory (RAM) to hold data for ready access.

Device Drivers

One way to speed access to your programs and data files considerably is to use a portion of RAM to hold them. You can copy files to and from this memory, use DIR to list the names of files stored there, and in most ways treat the memory just like a disk drive.

How do you do this? Well, one of the remarkable features of MS-DOS is its flexibility. The work of hardware devices such as memory chips, disks, video displays, and keyboards isn't "set in stone." By installing an appropriate *device driver* in memory, you can change the way the hardware works and give your programs access to new capabilities such as the ability to use fast memory to substitute for a slow disk drive. MS-DOS comes with about a dozen device drivers, and hardware manufacturers provide many more.

To create a virtual disk out of memory, put a statement like this in your CONFIG.SYS file:

```
DEVICE=C:\DOS\SYS\RAMDRIVE.SYS 360 512    (MS-DOS version 5.0)
DEVICE=C:\DOS\SYS\VDISK.SYS 360 512       (earlier versions)
```

The DEVICE command loads a device driver. It is always followed by an equals sign and a full path name that tells MS-DOS where to find the driver. In our well-organized system, all device drivers are stored in the SYS subdirectory of the DOS directory. If yours are somewhere else (such as C:\DOS), substitute the appropriate path name.

Just as regular MS-DOS commands often include switches and other command-line parameters, most device drivers also have such specifications, which you can read about in detail in your MS-DOS manual. In this example, the numbers 360 and 512 specify that the virtual drive will hold up to 360K worth of files and that it will use a sector size of 512 bytes. (The default sector size is 128 bytes. If you are going to have a large number of files on your virtual disk, a value like 128 is better because it reduces the minimum file size.)

The DEVICE command

Use: Loads a device driver from your CONFIG.SYS file

Example: `device=c:\dos\sys\ansi.sys`

VDISK.SYS may also give you an opportunity to take advantage of your add-on extended or expanded memory. (We will explain the difference between these two types of memory later.) Starting with DOS 3.0, you can use extended memory by adding the /E switch with RAMDRIVE.SYS or VDISK.SYS as follows:

```
DEVICE=C:\DOS\RAMDRIVE.SYS 1024 512 /E   (MS-DOS 5.0)
DEVICE=C:\DOS\SYS\VDISK.SYS 1024 512 /E  (earlier versions)
```

Here we have a system that has memory to burn. We've designated 1024K (1 MB) of memory for use with the virtual disk with 512 bytes per sector and using extended memory.

With MS-DOS version 4.0 and later you can also use expanded memory for a virtual disk:

```
DEVICE=C:\DOS\SYS\RAMDRIVE.SYS 1024 512 /A (MS-DOS 5.0)
DEVICE=C:\DOS\SYS\VDISK.SYS 1024 512 /X    (earlier versions)
```

This allocates 1024K of expanded memory to your virtual disk. (Use of extended or expanded memory requires some additional device drivers, which we'll discuss later.)

A virtual disk drive and a physical disk drive differ in two substantial ways. First, the virtual drive is much faster than a physical floppy drive (or even a fast hard drive) because it has no physical parts like motors, switches, or read/write heads; it only has electronic signals. The other difference is that the virtual drive, unlike the physical drive, doesn't store its contents permanently. When you turn off the power or reboot your system, everything in the virtual drive is lost. Therefore you have to be sure to save any changed files to a physical disk before ending your session!

Should you use a virtual disk? If your system has only floppy disk drives, copying programs and files to a virtual disk will speed things up immensely—but only if you can spare the memory. In particular, programs that create many temporary files will be sped up if they can use a virtual disk.

Most applications use 400K or more, so you will probably need expanded or extended memory. If you have a fast hard disk, however, the gain in speed probably doesn't justify using memory for a virtual disk. That same memory can be used for BUFFERS, FASTOPEN, and a disk cache (all discussed later in this chapter). The rest of the expanded or extended memory can be used directly by your applications where possible. This strategy gives you an impressive increase in speed with the security of keeping all data on physical disks.

Cache-ing in on Speed

A device driver can also be used to set up a *cache*, an area of memory to hold data that has been read from the disk or will eventually be written to the disk. Like the virtual disk, a cache takes advantage of the fact that operations performed within memory are much faster than operations involving physical disk drives. Unlike the virtual disk, however, the disk cache works automatically as your MS-DOS commands or other programs access the disk. You won't need to copy files back and forth to memory, and caching reduces the chance of losing data in a power failure.

To understand how caches work, consider what happens when your program asks MS-DOS to read, for example, 128 bytes from the disk; MS-DOS has to read a whole 512-byte sector because of the way the disk drive controller is designed. If there is no provision for saving the whole sector in memory, and the program requests the next 128 bytes of data, the sector has to be read again. Time is wasted positioning the recording head, waiting for the sector to arrive at the head, and rereading the data. With a cache, however, a whole 512 byte sector (or more) is stored in memory the first time it is requested. On subsequent requests, the driver first checks memory to see if the sectors containing the data the program needs are already there, as shown in figure 13-8. If they are, the data is transferred from memory, not read from the disk again. Similarly data to be written can be accumulated and then written all at once, an operation called *write caching*. (Not all cache software does write caching, and it isn't a good idea for some critical operations, since a power failure would lose data waiting to be written. This could put your database "out of sync.")

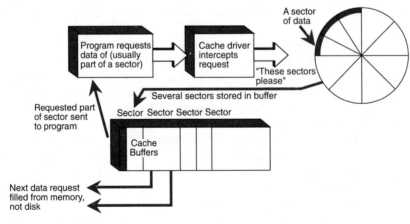

Fig. 13-8. How a disk cache works.

Many different disk-caching programs are available; PC Tools has one called PC Cache. IBM provides a cache driver called IBMCACHE.SYS with its PS/2 models, and MS-DOS (starting with version 5.0) comes with a cache program called SMARTDRV.SYS. If your system has 1MB or more of memory, you should use extended or expanded memory for the disk cache. This way, you conserve as much of the standard 640K memory for your applications as possible.

To determine the appropriate settings for the DEVICE statement in your CONFIG.SYS file, read the documentation for your cache program. (PC Cache and IBMCACHE have their own installation programs to help you.) The following statement lists the settings for SMARTDRV.SYS, the cache program that comes with MS-DOS version 5.0:

```
DEVICE=C:\SYS\SMARTDRV.SYS 1024 512
```

This statement says to make the cache size 1024K (1MB) and never reduce it below 512K. (SMARTDRV.SYS allows the cache size to be reduced when a running program asks for more memory). With SMARTDRV.SYS, the cache is placed in extended memory by default. If you want to use expanded memory instead, add the /A switch.

Buffing Up Your BUFFERS

Prior to disk caches, MS-DOS relied on *buffers* to hold data being read from the disk. The BUFFERS setting is included in the CONFIG.SYS file to allocate blocks of memory for the buffers. Buffers, like caches, allow programs to access data directly from memory without having to reread the disk. Since most caches are much more efficient than BUFFERS, you should only use this setting if you don't have a cache or don't have room in memory to install one.

The simple form of the BUFFERS setting, usable in all versions of MS-DOS, is shown below. Note that BUFFERS is followed by an equals sign and the number of 512-byte buffers to be allocated:

```
BUFFERS=10
```

This sample listing allocates ten 512-byte buffers, or about 5K. An allocation of 20 buffers is sufficient for most applications.

Starting with MS-DOS version 4.0, you can specify how many sectors MS-DOS will read each time it goes to the disk for data. Make this specification by adding a second number in your BUFFERS setting. For applications such as word processors, most spreadsheets, and database programs that read the whole database into memory, it is more efficient to read several sectors at a time, since the data is arranged sequentially rather than scattered about at random. A typical BUFFERS setting for MS-DOS version 4.0 or later follows:

```
BUFFERS=20, 4
```

This setting specifies that twenty buffers will be allocated, and data will be read from the disk 4 sectors at a time. With MS-DOS version 4.0 you can add the /x switch to put the buffers in expanded memory (if available). Version 5.0 doesn't provide this option, because it automatically puts buffers in the high memory just above 640K if MS-DOS is installed there. (We'll talk more about this later in this chapter).

Speedy Navigation with FASTOPEN

Besides speeding up access to the actual data in your files, you can also speed up the process by which MS-DOS finds the files that hold the data. Do this with the FASTOPEN command, which is available starting with MS-DOS version 3.3 and improved in later versions. FASTOPEN allocates memory buffers to hold file directory information, in effect creating a kind of speedy index to your disk contents.

Every time MS-DOS is asked to find a file, it must search directories on the disk. On a hard disk, where a file may have a path as long as `C:\OFFICE\CORRES\JULY\LETTER4`, this means searching the root directory for the location of the OFFICE directory, searching that directory for the CORRES subdirectory, then searching that subdirectory for the JULY subdirectory, and finally finding the entry for the file LETTER4 and noting which cluster contains the beginning of the file's data, as shown in figure 13-9. If you were working with that file in your word processor, you might have to access it repeatedly during a session in order to save it to disk or view a different part of it.

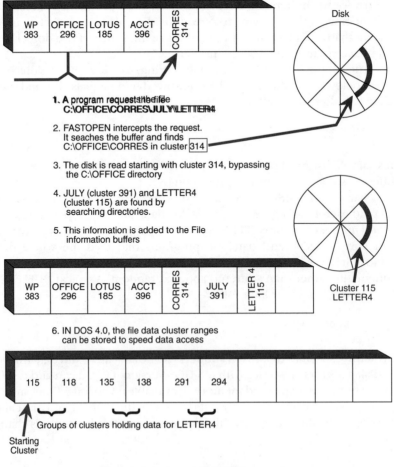

Fig. 13-9. How FASTOPEN works.

With FASTOPEN installed, the actual location of the first cluster for each directory along the path to the file is stored in a file-information buffer. When the file is needed again, FASTOPEN checks whether its "address" is already in a buffer; if it is, MS-DOS can go directly to the file on the disk, bypassing all the directories and subdirectories. Even if the file hasn't been referred to before in the current session, some of the directories on its path may already have been used. If so, FASTOPEN can take a "short cut" to the last-remembered directory in the path.

If you have MS-DOS 3.3, use your AUTOEXEC.BAT file to run FASTOPEN:

```
FASTOPEN C:=50
```

This FASTOPEN command sets up the FASTOPEN buffer for drive C: with room for 50 pieces of file or directory information. (You must specify a hard drive: FASTOPEN won't work with floppies). Fifty should be enough for most users, though if you work with a lot of files (or you have many deeply nested subdirectories), you might try 100. Don't use too many FASTOPEN buffers, however. Doing so ties up memory and may slow down your system because of the time needed to search through all the buffers.

FASTOPEN can be used with the INSTALL command, available starting with MS-DOS version 4.0. The INSTALL command is an alternative way to install many memory-resident programs. INSTALL uses the CONFIG.SYS file rather than AUTOEXEC.BAT. Where it works, it is preferable to use DEVICE because it loads programs more efficiently. Take a look at the INSTALL command below:

```
INSTALL=C:\DOS\FASTOPEN.EXE C:=(100,200) /X
```

This example specifies 100 file information buffers and 200 cluster information buffers; the /X specifies that expanded memory will be used for these buffers.

What is a cluster-information buffer? Well, you already know that each disk has a file-allocation table (FAT) that tells MS-DOS which clusters are holding the data stored in a particular file. When enough continuous space is available on the disk, a new file will be stored in consecutive clusters. However, as disk space is used and existing files are expanded, many files end up stored in separate groups of clusters.

The second number used with the FASTOPEN reserves a number of buffers (200 in the example) to hold the starting and ending cluster numbers for each segment of the file. As with the directory information, this means that FASTOPEN can often take a "shortcut" to find the next part of the file needed, speeding up access to your data.

For fast disk access, use FASTOPEN with your disk cache or BUFFERS setting. The cache or buffers store the actual file data, while FASTOPEN stores the information needed to get at that data. This increases the effective speed of your hard disk considerably.

The INSTALL command

Use:	Installs memory-resident programs in CONFIG.SYS
Example:	`install=c:\dos\fastopen.exe c:=(100, 50)`

Defragmentation

In the previous section we showed how FASTOPEN could record the list of separate clusters containing a file's data. A file whose data is stored in separate groups of clusters is said to be *fragmented*. FASTOPEN can help MS-DOS find the cluster locations more quickly, but the physical reading of the disk necessarily slows down when a file is fragmented. The disk head has to move and reposition itself repeatedly to read each part of the file. On a hard disk that stores hundreds of constantly changing files, fragmentation tends to get worse over time, slowing down disk access.

The answer to the fragmentation problem is to run a utility program that rearranges the files on your disk and stores all of the clusters for each file together. In other words, the answer is to "defragment" the disk. One way to defragment a disk is to run BACKUP, reformat the disk, and then use RESTORE to put your files back on the disk. RESTORE will put the files on the disk one at a time without fragmenting them. The problem is that this process is very slow, so it isn't practical for frequent use.

Practical alternatives include the Speed Disk (SD) program in Norton Utilities and the PC Compress program in PC Tools. Both of these programs analyze your hard disk for fragmentation. Figure 13-10 shows a screen from PC Compress.

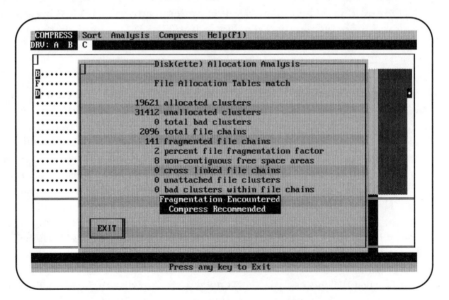

Fig. 13-10. PC Compress fragmentation analysis.

If the program says you have fragmented files, run the compress feature and the files will be rearranged on your disk so that they are no longer fragmented. (It is a good idea to have a current backup before running the compress program. Then again, it is always a good idea to have a current backup....) The first time you run a defragmentation program the process may take twenty or more minutes, depending on the size of your hard disk. After the first time, however, run the utility perhaps once a week, and it will only require a few minutes.

Interleaving

The final disk-speedup technique we will look at involves the order in which sectors are recorded on the disk. You might logically assume that sectors on a disk are arranged in simple numerical order: 1, 2, 3, 4, 5, 6, 7, 8, 9. In many cases, however, this is not true. To see why, let's suppose that the disk controller takes a certain number of milliseconds to process the data that has been read from sector 1. While this data is being processed, the hard disk continues to spin at 3600 RPM. When the controller has finished dealing with sector 1, it goes to read sector 2. Unfortunately, by now the disk has spun past sector 2 and is at sector 3 or 4. This means that the controller has to wait until the disk has completed its revolution and *then* position at sector 2 and read it. This waiting slows down disk access considerably, because only one sector can be read per disk revolution.

To avoid the wait, many hard disks use *interleaving*. With interleaving, the sectors are recorded in an order like the following: 1, 6, 2, 7, 3, 8, 4, 9, 5. While sector 1 is being processed, sector 6 moves by without being read; when sector 1 is finished being processed, sector 2 is in position to be read, and so on. With this arrangement, sectors 1, 2, 3, 4, and 5 can be read during the first revolution of the disk, and the remaining sectors (6, 7, 8, and 9) can be read during the second revolution. Since the whole track can be read in only 2 revolutions instead of 9, disk access is sped up considerably. (The arrangement we have illustrated in figure 13-11 is called a 2:1 interleave because every other sector is read.)

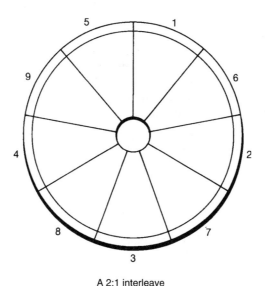

A 2:1 interleave

Fig. 13-11. A 2:1 interleave, with every other sector read.

In fact, many modern disk controllers *are* fast enough to work efficiently with a 1:2 interleave or even with a 1:1 interleave (in other words, no interleave at all, with sectors arranged consecutively). You can buy a utility program that analyzes your controller and disk, recommends an optimum interleave, and rearranges the data on your disk to use that interleave. Probably the most comprehensive utility for this purpose is SpinRite from Gibson Research, which also performs extensive "refurbishing" of your physical disk format to prevent gradual deterioration of data.

Tools for File Management

Utilities can also make it easier to find files, to find text in files, and to remember the purpose of each file. Of the many file-related utilities, we will show you three examples from the Norton Utilities. Of course, many more kinds of file-management utilities are available.

Where's That File?

File Find (FF) in Norton Utilities lets you find a file anywhere on the disk. You can also use wild cards to look for files whose names match certain specifications. (MS-DOS version 5.0 provides a similar service through DOSSHELL).

Let's say you want to collect the on-line documentation for all your software in one place. Usually these files have a name such as "read.me" or "readme." You could use FF with a wild-card specification to find the location of all of these files, like so:

```
C:\>ff c: read*.* > doclist<Enter>
C:\>copy doclist lpt1:<Enter>
```

By default, FF searches the entire current disk, though you can have it search all disks on your system if you wish. Here you use the > redirection symbol to direct FF to put the list in the file "doclist", and then copy that file to lpt1: (the printer) to get a printed list. The list will look something like this:

```
FF-File Find, Advanced Edition 4.50, (C) Copr 1987-88, Peter Norton

C:\WINDOWS
        readme.txt        33,407 bytes    3:00 am  Tue May  1 90

C:\WINWORD\LIBRARY
        readme.doc        24,555 bytes   12:00 pm  Wed Nov 15 89

C:\QC25\BIN
        readme.doc        10,376 bytes    4:50 pm  Wed Apr  4 90

C:\UTILS
        read.me            1,987 bytes    7:22 pm  Mon May 30 88
```

```
C:\GAMES\BOB1940
        read.me           6,374 bytes    4:08 am   Mon Oct  2 89
        readme.bat           17 bytes    4:48 am   Mon Oct  2 89

C:\GRAPHICS\INSET
        readme.doc        2,880 bytes   11:05 am   Mon Jun 22 87

C:\GRAPHICS\HIJAAK
        read.me          10,367 bytes   11:59 am   Mon Jul 17 89

C:\NORTON
        read.me           5,553 bytes    4:51 pm   Tue Jan  3 89

C:\PCTOOLS
        readme.bak       16,718 bytes   11:32 pm   Tue Sep 25 90
        readme.txt       16,718 bytes   11:35 pm   Tue Sep 25 90
```

```
11 files found
```

Now that you know where to find the files, you can use the MS-DOS PRINT command to print each one.

Where's That Letter About...

The Text Search (TS) program in Norton Utilities represents another useful type of file utility; it looks at all the files on your disk and finds those that contain a particular word or phrase. Not only will the utility tell you the name of each file that has the text, it will also display a few lines before and after the key text so that you'll have some idea of the context in which the word or phrase is used. (This improved display and the ability to use wild cards to search multiple files makes TS more versatile and useful than the MS-DOS FIND command you saw in Chapter 11).

Let's suppose you're a writer who keeps in touch with your editors by electronic mail. You remember that your managing editor sent you a list of deadlines for your book *Surfing with MS-DOS*, but you can't remember which letter contains the information. You have a directory called \BOOK\CORRES that has about thirty letters in it, and you don't want to go through them one at a time. With TS, you simply specify the pathname to be searched and the text to be searched for:

```
ts \book\corres "Surfing"
```

TS starts going through the files in \BOOKS\CORRES. Eventually you see:

```
Searching C:\BOOK\CORRES\edit1214.txt

Found at line 241, file offset 8,269

        Please let me know. Thanks!\

Scott
```

```
(cc Joel)
From: scalamar
Subject: Re:  Deadlines

We would like you to have the first draft of Surfing with
MS-DOS in to us by April 1, 1991. Will this work out
OK with you, or do you need more time? Also, what do you
think of my idea of having the book include an assemble-it-
yourself cardboard minisurfboard with all the MS-DOS commands
listed on it?
Regards,
Scott
```

TS then asks you if you want to search through more files, and you press "y" to continue the search:

```
Search for more (Y/N) ?y
Searching C:\BOOK\CORRESS\edit0108.txt

Search Complete

1 file found containing the text "Surfing"
1 occurrences
```

TS didn't find any more files that had your text. A glance at the calendar tells you it's already February. Better get to work on the book!

What Does "gb99zrkl.txt" Mean, Anyway?

Our last file-utility example addresses a problem that people have had with MS-DOS ever since it came out: the limiting of filenames to eight characters and a three-character extension. No matter how hard you try, it's often hard to come up with a filename descriptive enough to make you remember why you made the file.

The Norton Utilities File Info (FI) program lets you attach descriptive comments to your filenames. You can then use it to display a directory with both the MS-DOS filenames and your own comments attached.

Consider the following standard MS-DOS directory:

```
C:\REPORTS>dir<Enter>

 Volume in drive C is DOSDISK
 Volume Serial Number is 9627-2781
 Directory of C:\REPORTS
```

```
    .              <DIR>      09-28-90   10:43a
    ..             <DIR>      09-28-90   10:43a
  Q1FR1990            41765 08-15-90    3:33a
  Q1SR1990             6719 08-15-90    3:33a
  Q1TR1990            11746 08-15-90    3:33a
          5 file(s)         60230 bytes
                         64260096 bytes free
```

All right, just what *is* Q1FR1990? How is it different from the other two files listed? Now suppose you used FI at the time you created these files and attached comments to their names. You could do this simply by typing FI followed by the filename and your comment, like this:

```
C:\REPORTS>fi q1fr1990 Financial Report, 1st Qtr 1990<Enter>
FI-File Info, Advanced Edition 4.50, (C) Copr 1987-88, Peter Norton

 Directory of C:\REPORTS

q1fr1990        41,765    8-15-90    3:33a   Financial Report 1st Qtr 1990

1 comment added
```

"Financial Report 1st Quarter 1990" certainly tells you a lot more than "q1fr1990." Let's say you add similar comments to the other two files. Now when you want to view the directory with descriptive comments attached, you just type FI followed by the directory name (if it's not the current directory):

```
C:\>fi c:\reports<Enter>
FI-File Info, Advanced Edition 4.50, (C) Copr 1987-88, Peter Norton

 Directory of C:\REPORTS

.              <DIR>      9-28-90   10:43a   Quarterly Reports by Type and Year
..             <DIR>      9-28-90   10:43a
q1fr1990        41,765    8-15-90    3:33a   Financial Report 1st Qtr 1990
q1sr1990         6,719    8-15-90    3:33a   Sales Report 1st Qtr 1990
q1tr1990        11,746    8-15-90    3:33a   Tax Report 1st Qtr 1990
fileinfo fi        445    9-28-90   10:49a

6 files found   64,258,048 bytes free
```

The last file shown, "fileinfo.fi," is used by File Info to hold your comments and link them to the corresponding filenames.

Devising with Devices

You have already seen how device drivers add capabilities to your hardware; for example, in MS-DOS version 5.0 SMARTDRV.SYS adds a disk cache, and RAMDRIVE.SYS turns part of your memory into a virtual disk drive. Device drivers enhance the performance and versatility of PCs using MS-DOS. Table 13-3 lists the device drivers that come with MS-DOS (note that many are found only in later MS-DOS versions):

Table 13-3. MS-DOS device drivers.

Driver	Purpose	Versions
ANSI.SYS	Adds screen and keyboard functions	2.0-
DISPLAY.SYS	Provides screen display for foreign languages	3.3-
DRIVER.SYS	Adds disk drives	3.2-
EMM386.EXE*	Simulates expanded memory for 386 systems	5.0-
HIMEM.SYS	Manages expanded and high memory	5.0-
PRINTER.SYS	Prints foreign-language characters	3.3-
RAMDRIVE.SYS	Creates virtual (RAM) disk	5.0-
SMARTDRV.SYS	Creates disk cache	5.0-
VDISK.SYS	Creates virtual (RAM) disk	2.0-4.0
XMAEM.SYS*	Simulates expanded memory for 386 systems	4.0
XMA2EMS.SYS*	Allows use of expanded memory	4.0

* The drivers XMA2EMS.SYS and XMAEM.SYS used in MS-DOS version 4.0 were replaced in version 5.0 with EMM386.EXE and HIMEM.SYS

The important thing to remember about device drivers for now is that they're there if you need them. We don't have room to show you in detail how to use these drivers; consult your MS-DOS manual or one of the reference books mentioned earlier in this chapter.

Speaking in Tongues

One illustration of the versatility of device drivers, at least with MS-DOS version 3.0 or later, is that you can change the character set used on your keyboard, screen, and printer to a language other than English.

Suppose, for example, you want to set up a PC for use with the German language. First, put the COUNTRY command in your CONFIG.SYS file to tell MS-DOS which country's format you will be using:

```
COUNTRY=049,437,C:\SYS\COUNTRY.SYS
```

The first number (049) is the country ID for Germany, and the second (437) is the number for the *code page* or character set that can be used with that language. The COUNTRY.SYS file contains the information that MS-DOS needs to format dates, times, and other information according to the country you select.

Next, put the KEYB (keyboard) command in your AUTOEXEC.BAT file to change the way MS-DOS interprets the character codes you generate when pressing keys. Since different languages use the various letters of the alphabet with a different frequency than English does, each language has its own keyboard layout. You set up the German keyboard layout as follows:

```
keyb gr,437,c:\sys\keyboard.sys
```

That takes care of the keyboard. You also have to set up the video to display the foreign language correctly. A sample setting for a German EGA display is:

```
device=c:\sys\display.sys con:=(ega,437,2)
```

Finally, if you have an IBM printer you can set it up to print the foreign-language character set. (Unfortunately, foreign-language printer support is limited to certain models of IBM printer only.) For example, for an IBM 4201 Proprinter you specify:

```
device\c:\sys\printer.sys lpt1:=(4201,437,1)
```

If you'd rather "parlez-vous Française" than "sprechen Sie Deutsch," no problem—just check your MS-DOS manual for the appropriate codes for French (or Spanish, Norwegian, or one of about a dozen other languages) and use them in place of the German ones. You can also read about other options for the display and printer setup.

Commands for Foreign-language PCs

COUNTRY	Specifies the country whose format is to be used
KEYB	Reconfigures the keyboard for another language
DISPLAY.SYS	Reconfigures the video display
PRINTER.SYS	Reconfigures some IBM printers

Once you've set up your foreign-language PC, you will notice some differences. Some keys will type different letters from those on the English keyboard; you may want to move the keycaps or attach labels to the keys. Directory listings will show dates and times in a different format. If you want to go back to English, simply remove from AUTOEXEC.BAT and CONFIG.SYS the commands given above, or put the word REM in front of each command to make it nonexecutable.

Using Your Resources

This section discusses the commands you can add to your CONFIG.SYS file to increase the number of "resources" that MS-DOS provides to your program. In most cases your application's documentation will tell you what to put in your CONFIG.SYS file.

MS-DOS is designed to provide enough room to store information about files and disk drives for "normal" use. But as you run more and bigger programs, you may exceed the built-in limits. When the default settings provided by MS-DOS don't give your applications programs or MS-DOS commands enough access to files, disk drives, or special memory areas called *stacks*, your program may stop running.

FILES

MS-DOS keeps information about all open files in memory. By default, MS-DOS allows up to eight files to be open at one time. But many applications, especially databases, need to have more files open. For example, if you use memory-resident programs such as SideKick or run the MS-DOS PRINT command "in background," these utilities use additional files. You may exceed the default limit of eight and get an error such as "unable to open file." To keep this from happening, put a statement such as FILES=20 in your CONFIG.SYS. You can use a number up to 255, though any given program cannot use more than 20 files.

FCBS

You probably won't need the FCBS command unless you are running an older program that uses something called a *file-control block* to keep track of its files. (Most programs use "file handles" instead, and those are taken care of by the FILES command.) If you get error messages referring to FCBs, try a statement such as FCBS 12,6. This means "allow space for up to 12 file-control blocks, and don't close the first 6 of these to make room for new files." Up to 255 FCBS can be specified. You may have to experiment with this setting—check your program documentation.

LASTDRIVE

You need the LASTDRIVE command if you have more than 5 disk drives (or you want to have more than five letters to use to refer to disk drives). Most people don't have five physical disk drives attached to their PCs; instead, they use "logical drives" created with the FDISK utility when the hard disk was partitioned, virtual disks created with VDISK.SYS or RAMDRIVE.SYS, or drives created with the ASSIGN and SUBST commands, which all require additional drive letters. Suppose you've used some of these commands, and you expect to be able to access a drive G, but you get an error message instead. In this case, include a command such as LASTDRIVE=G in your CONFIG.SYS. (This allows for 7 drives with letters A through G.) You can have up to 26 drives (LASTDRIVE=Z).

STACKS

Finally, the STACKS command refers to *memory stacks*, which are blocks of memory that the processor uses to temporarily store information when it is interrupted, for example, by a signal sent by a hardware device. Some devices interrupt the processor so frequently that it runs out of stacks. When this happens, you get a message referring to "internal stack failure," the system is halted, and you have to reboot. To prevent this, try a statement such as STACKS = 16 in your CONFIG.SYS. (The STACKS command is available starting with MS-DOS 3.2.) You can also specify a second number that increases the size of each stack from its default, which is usually 128 bytes. Thus STACKS = 12,256 designates up to 12 stacks of up to 256 bytes each. You probably won't have to specify the stack size unless told to by your program or hardware-device documentation.

Commands That Provide Additional Resources	
Use	**To Increase**
FILES	Number of files your programs can use
FCBS	Number of file control blocks for programs
LASTDRIVE	Number of drive letters
STACKS	Number of stack areas for processing interrupts

The FILES, FCBS, LASTDRIVE, and STACKS commands all consume memory according to how many of each you specify. In most cases the amount of memory involved is small. Still, it is a good idea to set these and other settings no higher than is needed by your applications. Although keeping your settings low requires some experimentation to be effective, it allows more of that precious 640K of MS-DOS memory to be available for processing your data, usually at a higher speed.

Thanks for the Memories

The matter of memory and how to save it will be the last topic covered in this chapter. Improving disk performance can make a big difference in the speed of many applications, but the other key to improved performance is providing your applications with as much usable memory as possible. While some older programs are designed to use a relatively small amount of memory, modern programs usually want all the memory they can get. If your word processor takes "forever" to scroll to the end of a long file, you should look for ways to provide more memory. Depending on the design of your PC you can do this by adding more chips to the main system board, plugging in a memory-expansion card, or both. But the next question is "what kinds of memory are there, anyway?"

Memory Lane

If you've been involved with PCs for some time, you've probably heard a number of confusing terms such as "conventional memory," "extended memory," and "expanded memory." These terms refer not to different kinds of memory chips but different ways that your PC accesses and uses memory. Figure 13-12 shows the kinds of memory that can be installed in your system.

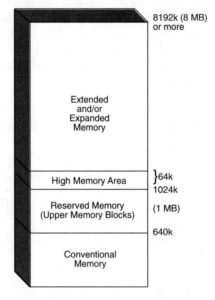

Fig. 13-12. Types of memory.

Until a few years ago, conventional memory was the only kind of memory MS-DOS and your applications could use. A PC can have up to 640K of conventional memory. Unless you tell them otherwise, MS-DOS and most programs load into conventional memory. Unfortunately, when you want to load MS-DOS, some "pop-up" memory-resident programs, and your main application, you're likely to find out that 640K isn't enough. Indeed, many PCs sold today come with a minimum of 1MB of physical memory in order to give you additional memory resources.

As shown in figure 13-12, there is a 64K chunk of memory called the *high memory area*. MS-DOS 5.0 and a few programs can load into this high memory. Loading MS-DOS 5.0 into this memory frees up more of the 640K of conventional memory for use by your programs.

The area of memory from 640K up to 1024K (1 MB) is called *reserved memory* because MS-DOS reserves certain parts of it for use by the video display and other devices. In most cases some of this memory is actually free, and MS-DOS 5.0 can use these *upper memory blocks* to load device drivers that would otherwise have to go in lower memory.

Finally, memory starting at the 1024K (1MB) address can be accessed as either *extended memory* or *expanded memory* (see fig. 13-13). Extended memory involves the processor "extending" its ability to access memory so that it can use these higher memory addresses. Expanded memory is an alternative approach. Rather than letting the processor reach directly into the upper memory, the processor moves chunks of upper memory in and out of lower memory where programs can get to it easily.

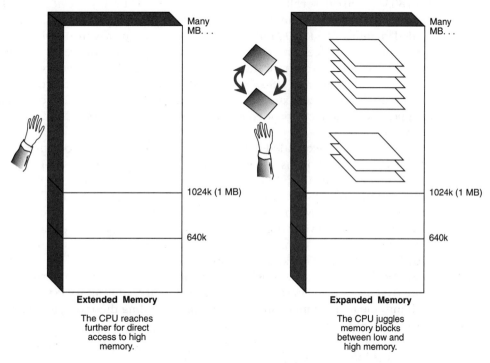

Many MB. . .

1024k (1 MB)

640k

Many MB. . .

1024k (1 MB)

640k

Extended Memory

The CPU reaches further for direct access to high memory.

Expanded Memory

The CPU juggles memory blocks between low and high memory.

Fig. 13-13. Extended vs. expanded memory.

Which Kind of Memory Should You Use?

The obvious question is "what kind of memory do I have, and what kind *should* I have?" This depends on three things: the kind of processor (CPU) your system is running, your application program or programs, and the version of MS-DOS you are running.

First, if your system is using an 8088 or 8086 processor (such as the original IBM PC and most models of the PC XT), you don't have to worry about extended versus expanded memory because extended memory is available only with 80286, 80386, or later-model processors.

But if you can choose between them, which will it be, expanded or extended? If you have an 80286 processor, you must physically set your memory board to extended memory or expanded memory or some combination of both. This setup is either done by pushing tiny switches called *DIP switches* on the board itself, or—in the case of IBM PS/2 systems with "Micro Channel"—by running a menu-driven configuration program. Check the documentation for your main application programs. If it specifies that they can use expanded memory but doesn't mention extended memory, set your board to "expanded." One exception is Microsoft Windows, which works better with extended memory.

If you have an 80386 or later processor, however, you have more flexibility. With an 80386, you can set all your memory to extended but run a device driver that will convert memory to expanded "on the fly" as requested by programs that want expanded memory. The HIMEM.SYS device driver that comes with MS-DOS version 5.0 performs this service. Therefore, it is usually best to configure all additional memory as extended if you have such a driver and an 80386 or later processor.

Finally, your version of MS-DOS also makes a difference. Versions of MS-DOS before 4.0 don't recognize extended or expanded memory, although you can still run applications that use expanded memory, by using a driver supplied with your memory board.

MS-DOS 4.0 uses expanded (and occasionally extended) memory for a limited number of commands. You install the XMA2EMS.SYS driver to enable MS-DOS to use expanded memory. On 80386 systems you must first install the XMAEMS.SYS driver. The installation program takes care of setting up the statements in the CONFIG.SYS file for you. Unfortunately, however, the drivers don't work with all memory boards, so you may have to use your board's own driver instead. In this case you won't be able to run MS-DOS commands in expanded memory, but you can still run application programs in expanded memory.

MS-DOS 5.0 provides a much more complete facility for using extended or expanded memory. If you have extended memory, you can tell MS-DOS to load most of itself into the high memory area. You do this by adding these two statements to your CONFIG.SYS file:

```
device=c:\sys\himem.sys
dos=high
```

Now, instead of having perhaps 530 or 540K of conventional memory available, you will have around 600K. Starting with MS-DOS 4.0 you can use the MEM command to get a quick report on what kinds of memory you have and how much, as follows:

```
C:\>mem<Enter>
    655360 bytes total conventional memory
    655360 bytes available to MS-DOS
    602608 largest executable program size

   3145728 bytes total contiguous extended memory
         0 bytes available contiguous extended memory
   2031616 bytes available XMS memory
           MS-DOS resident in High Memory Area
```

Freeing Up More Memory

As you have seen, on the one hand you get better disk performance by allocating memory for various features such as a disk cache or buffers, FASTOPEN, or a virtual disk. On the other hand, your applications will probably run faster if they have access to more memory. This means that you may have to make a trade-off between memory devoted to disk operations and memory used for the actual data processing performed by your applications. Everyone's circumstances are different, but there are some general rules to follow.

Check your applications to see if they can use expanded or extended memory instead of conventional memory. In many cases you can add a command-line switch that tells the program what kind of memory to use. Some modern programs automatically look for and take advantage of your add-on memory.

Review your CONFIG.SYS and AUTOEXEC.BAT files periodically. Remove any device drivers or memory-resident programs you no longer need. For example, if none of your programs use extended screen functions or a mouse, you don't need to install ANSI.SYS or a mouse driver.

Fine-tune your cache or buffers and FASTOPEN by starting with high values and reducing them until a noticeable slowdown in disk performance occurs. You might time how long it takes for a program to find or load a file at various settings. Reboot after each test to start with a clean slate.

If you have MS-DOS version 5.0, you may be able to load many device drivers with the LOADHIGH command in place of DEVICE or INSTALL. LOADHIGH attempts to load the driver into upper memory rather than conventional memory. See your MS-DOS manual for more details. The ability to run MS-DOS and many device drivers in high memory is a good reason to upgrade to version 5.0.

Starting with MS-DOS 4.0, you can use expanded memory for the BUFFERS and FASTOPEN commands.

If you have some extended memory—such as the 384K of extended memory that is built in on many PCs with 1MB of total memory—and you aren't using it for anything else, try setting your disk cache to use it instead of conventional or expanded memory. Also, if you are using a disk cache, use the statement BUFFERS=3 to avoid wasting memory on unnecessary MS-DOS buffers.

Check your memory-resident programs such as "desktop accessories." You may be able to get a version that loads into expanded memory rather than conventional memory. Also, with some of these programs you can install just the functions you need—the ones not already found in your main application.

Reading this chapter has considerably increased your knowledge of MS-DOS, and you have learned about many utility programs that can help you get the most out of your PC. We suggest that you review this chapter periodically as you gain more experience with your PC or after you add new devices or memory to your system.

Appendix

Error Messages

- Device Error Messages
- Additional Error Messages

Appendix
Error Messages

Learning to use MS-DOS is a trial-and-error process. No matter how conscientious or diligent you are, you will make mistakes. Making and correcting your mistakes is one of the most effective means of learning.

The designers of MS-DOS are no different from you in that respect. They make mistakes sometimes. To make things easier for you, they have documented many of the most common errors. These error messages are provided to help you correct your mistakes.

The most frequently encountered error messages are covered in this appendix; some messages, however, are not included. If you receive a message that isn't listed here, see your user's manual for a complete list of messages found on your computer system.

This appendix divides error messages into two categories: those that refer to devices such as disk drives or printers, and those that refer to MS-DOS commands or MS-DOS itself, though they may also involve a device. The messages are listed in alphabetical order.

The wording of some messages varies with the version of MS-DOS you are using. In most cases you should have no problem understanding the essentials of the message.

Device Error Messages

Device error messages are displayed if MS-DOS finds an error when it tries to use a device attached to the computer. These messages have a common format; once you understand the format, the messages will be easy to follow.

This format has two variations. The first is displayed when MS-DOS has a problem "reading" (trying to get information from) a device:

```
type error reading device
Abort, Ignore, Retry, Fail??
```

The second variation is displayed when MS-DOS has a problem "writing" (trying to put information on) a device:

```
type error reading device
Abort, Ignore, Retry, Fail?
```

(Versions of MS-DOS before 4.0 say "Abort, Retry, Ignore" for both variations.)

"Type" defines the nature of this specific error and will vary with each instance. "Device" refers to the piece of hardware involved in the error, such as a disk drive or a printer.

The second line of our format offers you four options for recovering from the error: Abort, Ignore, Retry, and Fail. MS-DOS waits for you to enter the first letter of one of these options from the keyboard.

Before responding, check the obvious causes for the error. For instance, if the error concerns a disk drive, you may have left the door open or failed to insert the correct disk. If the error indicates trouble with the printer, you may need to turn on the printer, push its "on-line" button, or insert paper.

When you have checked all the obvious causes, enter one of the four options:

A (Abort)	Causes MS-DOS to stop the operation in progress. Enter this response if R or F fails to correct the error.
I (Ignore)	(Not found in some messages) Causes MS-DOS to retry the operation but ignore any errors it may encounter. It is not recommended that you use this response, because it can result in losing data being read or written. It may enable you, however, to retrieve part of a damaged file from a disk.
R (Retry)	Causes MS-DOS to try to perform the command or program again. This sometimes works even if you have not adjusted anything, because the error might be minor and might not recur on the next try. It may be worth repeating this option a few times if the error recurs.
F (Fail)	(MS-DOS version 4.0 or later) Sends to MS-DOS or your application program a message that says that the read or write operation has failed. This option may enable your application to continue processing and activate its own error-handling procedures.

The following messages might appear in the "type" section of the error message.

Bad call format. A driver is part of the operating system; it controls a specific input/output device; for instance, a modem or printer. Each driver has specific codes in MS-DOS. One such identifier is a "length request header." This message means an incorrect length request header was sent to the driver for the specified drive. Consult your dealer.

Bad command. The command issued to a device is invalid.

Bad unit. An incorrect "subunit number" (another driver code) was sent to the driver for the specified drive. Consult your dealer.

Data. An error was detected while reading or writing data. Use CHKDSK or a utility program to see whether your disk has a defective area.

Disk. After three tries, a disk read or write error is still occurring. You may have inserted the wrong type of disk (high-density disk in a low-density drive) or your disk may be inserted wrong. If neither is true, you may have a bad disk.

If you receive the Disk message, try the standard corrective procedures and available utilities before removing the disk. You may be able to salvage the data on the disk.

File allocation table bad, drive *d*. This message always refers to a specific disk drive. It tells you that the file allocation table (FAT) on the indicated drive is faulty. If you receive this error frequently, the disk is probably defective. You may be able to "rebuild" the FAT using a utility program.

No paper. This one is easy to solve. There isn't any paper in your printer, or the printer is not turned on. Correct the problem and press "R."

Non-DOS disk. Invalid data appears on the allocation table of the specified disk in the indicated device. The disk needs to be reformatted, or the entire disk may be wiped out.

Not ready. The device is not ready to read or write data. This may mean the power is not turned on, or no disk is in the indicated drive, or the drive door is open.

Read fault. For some reason the device cannot receive or transmit data. The power may not be on, the drive may not contain a disk, or the device is not properly configured for MS-DOS use.

Sector not found. The sector holding the data you want cannot be located. The disk may be defective or you may be using a high-density disk in a low-density drive.

Seek error. MS-DOS cannot locate the proper track on the disk in the indicated drive.

Write fault. For some reason the device cannot receive or transmit data. The power may not be on, the drive may not contain a disk, or the device is not properly configured for MS-DOS use.

Write protect. You have instructed MS-DOS to write to a disk that is write-protected (either temporarily by you or permanently by the manufacturer). Either insert a new disk or remove the write-protect tab (or move the slide on a 3 1/2" disk). First, make sure that you want to write to the disk. If there is no write-protect notch, you are out of luck.

Additional Error Messages

Again, this is not a complete listing of all other error messages that may be received from MS-DOS. Check your system manual if you cannot locate the message either in the "Device Error Messages" section or in this section.

Some error messages are associated with a specific command. When this is the case, the command has been written in parentheses following the error message.

Access denied. You tried to access a write-protected, read-only, or (on a network) locked file. This message can also appear if you use the CD command with a file instead of a directory or the TYPE command with a directory instead of a file.

All specified file(s) are contiguous (CHKDSK). All the files you requested to write are on the disk sequentially. This is good news.

Allocation error, size adjusted (CHKDSK). An invalid sector number appeared in the file-allocation table. The indicated file was truncated at the end of the previous good sector.

Attempted write-protect violation (FORMAT). You attempted to FORMAT a write-protected disk. Remove the disk and insert a new one (or remove write protection).

Bad command or filename. You entered the command or filename incorrectly. Check the spelling and punctuation and make sure that the command or file you specified is on the disk in the indicated drive. You may be calling an external command from a disk that does not contain the command.

Bad or missing command interpreter. MS-DOS needed to reload its instructions but was unable to find the COMMAND.COM file on disk. Restart the system from a bootable disk that has COMMAND.COM. If you are using a hard disk and COMMAND.COM is not in the root directory, copy COMMAND.COM to the root directory or use the COMSPEC command in your CONFIG.SYS file to tell MS-DOS where to find it. For more details, see your MS-DOS manual under "COMSPEC."

Cannot edit .BAK file - rename file. To protect your data, you cannot access a backup file that has a .BAK extension. Rename the file using REN, or copy the file, giving it a new name.

Cannot load COMMAND, system halted. While attempting to load the command processor, MS-DOS found that the area in which it keeps track of available memory is destroyed. Try booting MS-DOS again.

Contains xxx noncontiguous blocks (CHKDSK). The indicated file has been written in sections on different areas of the disk (rather than in sequential blocks). Fragmented files take longer to read, so run a file defragmentation utility (if available).

Disk boot failure. While trying to load MS-DOS, an error was encountered. If this continues, use a backup MS-DOS disk.

Disk error writing FAT x (CHKDSK). There was a disk error while CHKDSK was trying to update the FAT on the indicated drive. X will be a 1 or a 2, depending on which of the allocation tables could not be written. If both allocation tables are indicated, the disk is unusable.

Duplicate filename or file not found (RENAME). The name you indicated in a RENAME command already exists on the disk, or the file to be renamed is not on the disk in the specified drive.

Entry error (EDLIN). Your last command contains a syntax error.

Error in EXE file. The .EXE (program) file you tried to run had the wrong format. You may need a later version of MS-DOS.

Error loading operating system. An error was encountered while trying to load the operating system from the fixed (hard) disk. If the problem persists, load MS-DOS from a disk and use SYS to copy MS-DOS to the fixed disk.

EXEC error. MS-DOS found an error while reading a command or couldn't open a new file. Try raising the value of FILES in your CONFIG.SYS file.

File cannot be copied onto itself. You tried to give an already existing filename to a new file in the same directory.

File Creation Error. You may have tried to add or replace a file whose name already exists on the disk and is read-only. This error can also occur if you try to add a file to a root directory that is filled to capacity. Try a different filename or reorganize your disk.

File is READ-ONLY. The file has the "read only" attribute, so you can't remove it or change its contents. If you really want to change the file, use the ATTRIB command (or DOSSHELL) to remove the read-only attribute.

File not found. The file named in a command parameter could not be found, or the command could not be found on the specified drive.

Incorrect DOS version. You attempted to run an MS-DOS command that requires a different version of MS-DOS. When upgrading your MS-DOS version, always replace all system and utility command files.

Incorrect number of parameters. You didn't use the correct number of command-line parameters (path names and/or switches). Check the command in your manual or (for MS-DOS 5.0 users) reissue it with the /? switch to get help.

Insufficient disk space. There is not enough free space on the disk to hold the file you are writing. If you think that there should be enough space, use CHKDSK to get a disk-status report.

Intermediate file error during pipe. This message may mean that the intermediate files created during a piping procedure cannot be accommodated on the disk because the default drive's root directory is full. Other possible causes are that your disk is too full to hold the data being piped, or the piping files cannot be located on the disk.

Invalid COMMAND.COM in drive *d*. While trying to reload the command processor, MS-DOS found that the copy of COMMAND.COM on the disk is a different version. Insert a disk containing the correct version of MS-DOS.

Invalid directory. One of the directories in the specified pathname does not exist.

Invalid number of parameters. The specified number of parameters does not agree with the number required by the command.

Label not found (GOTO #). In a GOTO command, you have named a label that does not exist in the batch file. Use a text editor to review the batch file and make sure that all GOTO statements contain valid labels.

No room for system on disk (SYS). The specified disk does not contain the required reserved space for the system. (Is the system already on the disk?) You can solve this problem by using FORMAT /s to format a new disk and then copying your files to this disk, but doing this will destroy any existing data on the disk.

Nonsystem disk or disk error. Replace and strike any key when ready. You probably tried to boot from a disk that doesn't contain the system files. Replace the disk with a bootable system disk (or boot from the hard drive if present).

Out of environment space. This probably means that a program or batch file is trying to create environmental variables (values like PATH that are stored in memory for programs to access), but there isn't enough room. See the SHELL and COMMAND commands in your MS-DOS manual for details on how to fix this problem.

Syntax error. The command was entered incorrectly. Check the format in your MS-DOS manual or (for MS-DOS 5.0 users) reissue it with the /? switch to get help.

Terminate batch job (Y/N)? You have pressed <Ctrl><Break> or <Ctrl>C during the processing of a batch file. Press "Y" to end processing. Press "N" to stop the command that was executing when you pressed <Ctrl><Break> or <Ctrl>C; processing will continue with the next command.

Too many parameters. You specified too many parameters (path names and/or switches) on the command line. Check your MS-DOS manual or (for MS-DOS 5.0 users) reissue it with the /? switch to get help.

Unable To Create Directory (MKDIR). You tried to create a directory using a name that is already being used for a file or directory, or the disk is full.

Unrecognized command in CONFIG.SYS. A command in your CONFIG.SYS file is invalid, possibly misspelled. Check your MS-DOS manual.

Index

A

A (Append) command, 87
A:\> symbol, 56
Active Task List, 333
Add Group dialog box, 331
Add Program dialog box, 332-333
Advanced button, 333
American Standard Code for Information
    Interchange, *see* ASCII
APPEND command, 267
Apple Macintosh, 48
application program, 8
ASCII files, 66-67, 93
ASCII text files, 196
ASSIGN command, 372
asterisk (*) wild-card symbol, 68-69,
    168-170
auto-indent feature, 107
AUTOEXEC.BAT file, 223-224
    "automating" SUBST commands, 261
    moving directly to BASIC program, 224

B

\<Backspace\> key, 151-152, 160
backup (.BAK) files, 65-66
BACKUP command, 137, 270-272
    comparing to COPY, DISKCOPY,
        XCOPY, 275
    using with batch files, 273
backup utilities, 345-347
BASIC program, 102, 159
    listing categories by extension, 175
    moving directly to using
        AUTOEXEC.BAT, 224
BASIC programming language, 9
BASICA interpreter, 224
batch commands, 342
batch files, 195-196
    adding comments, 210-211
    "chaining", 221
    creating, 196-197
        sharing particular specifications,
            220-221
        using COPY.CON, 199

    using EDLIN, 198-199
    echoing commands, 208-209
    executing under specified
        conditions, 214-216
    formatting disk with lower capacity than
        disk drive, 201-203
    increasing replacable parameters, 219
    inserting built-in stop, 212-213
    pre-named, 223
    removing from current working
        disk, 207-208
    running, 200-201
        second batch files, 222-223
    safety device, 213
    saving macros, 302
    sorting directories, 289-290
    starting, 199-200
    stopping, 203-205
    transferring processing using labels,
        216-218
    using replaceable parameters, 204-208
    using with BACKUP command, 273
boot record, 347
booting, 21-24
    temperatures, 30
Borland's SideKick, 91
buffers, 361
    allocating to hold file directory
        information, 362-363
BUFFERS setting, 361
buttons
    Advanced, 333
    Help, 314
    radio, 316, 331
    save, 331
bytes, 6

C

C (Copy) command, 85-86
C programming language, 9
caches, 360-361
calendar, setting, 28-29
CALL command, 221-223
\<Caps Lock\> key, 153, 158

Central Point (PC Tools), 308
Central Point Software's PC Tools, 91, 339
central processing unit, *see* CPU
CGA (Color Graphics Adapter), 157
CHange DIRectory command, *see* CHDIR command
character mode, 308
characters
    copying one at a time, 162
    global, 168
    inserting into templates, 164
    set, changing language, 370-372
CHDIR command, 238-239
    going to root directory, 239, 241
CHKDSK command, 186-188, 348
    using with /f switch, 189-190
    using with /v switch, 189
CLear Screen command, *see* CLS command
clicking, 93, 101
clocks, 26
    setting, 26, 28-29
        automatically, 224
CLS command, 35-36
clusters, 348
code page, 371
codes
    ASCII, 66
    deciphering, 27
"cold" boot, 30
command buttons, 105
command mode, 73
COMMAND.COM file, 183, 185
commands
    A (Append), 87
    activating within subdirectories, 235
    APPEND, 267
    ASSIGN, 372
    BACKUP, 137, 270-272
        using with batch files, 273
    batch, 342
    C (Copy), 85-86
    CALL, 221-223
    CHDIR, 238-239
        going to root directory, 239, 241
    CHKDSK, 186-188, 348
        using with /f switch, 189-190
        using with /v switch, 189
    CLear Screen, *see* CLS
    CLS, 35-36

comparing
    COPY, DISKCOPY, XCOPY, BACKUP, 275
    I (Insert) to D (Delete), 81
COPY, 131, 138-140, 324-325
    creating files, 198
    moving files to subdirectory, 242-246
    understanding tree-structure directories system, 252-254
    using with wild card symbols, 254-255
    versus RENAME, 144
COUNTRY, 371
Create Directory, 312-313, 324
D (Delete), 80-81
definition, 31
DEL (Delete), 145
DEVICE, 358-359
"dimmed", 312
DIR, 32, 140-141
    deciphering display, 34
    listing specific files, 34-35
    using with switches, 171-173
    verifying file erasing, 146
directing to files on correct path, 249-250
DISKCOPY, 53-56
Display Options, 315
DISPLAY.SYS, 371
displaying on screen, 208-209
DOSKEY, 279, 296-298
    command list, 298
    defining macros, 301-302
    editing keys, 299-300
    sending command to PC simultaneously, 300
Dual File Lists, 322
E (END), 73-74
ECHO, 198, 208-209
    versus REMark, 211
ECHO OFF, 224
EDLIN, 68
Enable Switcher, 333
ERASE, 144-147
    using with wild-card symbols, 170
external, 131-133, 230, 258-261
FASTOPEN, 362-363
FCBS, 372-373
File Find (FF), 366-367

FILES, 373
Find, 115
followed by ellipsis (...), 312
FOR, 220-221
FORMAT, 47-52, 132, 180
   cautionary note, 52
   using with /s switch, 182-184
   using with /v switch, 180-182
Format, 329
getting on-line help, 176-179
GOTO, 216-218
GRAPHICS, 157
HELP, 176
hints for entering, 133
I (Insert), 78
IF, 214-216
INSTALL, 363
instructions for specified command,
   179-180
internal, 131, 236
KEYB, 371
L (List), 75-79, 81
LABEL, 182
LASTDRIVE, 372-373
lastdrive=, 262
list of all DOS commands, 176-179
list of MS-DOS options, 180
M (Move), 84-85
MIRROR, 350-352
MKDIR, 235-237
   creating subdirectories within
      subdirectories, 247
MODE, 190-191
New, 330-332
PATH, 133, 266-267
PAUSE, 212-213
PRINTER.SYS, 371
PROMPT, 240
Q (Quit), 75
R (Replace), 83-84
REBUILD, 354-357
REM (REMark), 210-211
REMark versus ECHO, 211
RENAME, 66, 137, 142-144
   versus COPY, 144
Rename, 318, 320
RESTORE, 273-275
reusing/editing, 297-298
RMDIR, 256-257
S (Search), 82-83

Save, 102, 104
Search..., 325, 327
selecting
   using keyboard, 104
   using mouse, 103-104
   from menus, 102
sending simultaneously, 300
SHIFT, 218-219
Single File List, 322
STACKS, 373
SUBST, 261, 372
switches, 170
SYS, 185-186
T (Transfer), 86-87
TREE, 258-261
TREE.COM, 230
TRUENAME, 262
TYPE, 74-75, 135-136
   verifying duplicate copies, 142
UNDELETE, 352-353
UNFORMAT
   recovering accidentally formatted
      disks, 354
   recovering accidentally reformatted
      disks, 353
   using FASTOPEN with INSTALL, 363
Verify, 115
View File Contents, 327
W (Write), 87
XCOPY, 262-265
CON, 198
CONFIG.SYS file, 262
   loading device drivers from, 358-359
context-sensitive, 96
control functions, 167
control-key combinations, 167
conventional memory, 374
Copy All <F3> function, 161
Copy All function, 162
COPY command, 131, 138-140, 324-325
   comparing to DISKCOPY, XCOPY,
      BACKUP, 275
   creating files, 198
   moving files to subdirectory, 242-246
   understanding tree-structure directories
      system, 252-254
   using with wild card symbols, 254-255
   versus RENAME command, 144
Copy File dialog box, 325
Copy One Character <F1> function, 162
Copy Up To <F2> function, 162-163

copying
  characters one at a time, 162
  disks, 53-56
    with only one drive, 55
  files, 136-140
    changing file name, 140-141
    eliminating drive indicators, 141-142
    from hard disk to floppy
      diskettes, 270-272
    verifying, 140-141
    without using File menu, 324
  floppy diskettes to hard disk, 274-275
  operating system to disk, 182-186
  portions of template, 162-163
  text within EDLIN files, 85-86
COUNTRY command, 371
COUNTRY.SYS file, 371
CP/M, 7
CPU, 5
Create a New Template <F5>
  function, 164-165
Create Directory command, 312-313, 324
<Ctrl> key, 31
current
  directory, 241-242
  drive, 56-58, 129
  line, 68-69
cursor, 96
  moving in Edit program, 97-98

D

D (Delete) command, 80-81
data
  accessing directly from memory
    using BUFFERS, 361
    using caches, 360-361
    using device drivers, 358-359
  area, 347
  storing on disks, 47
date, setting automatically, 224
default drive, 56
defragmentation program, 365
DEL (Delete) command, 145
deleting
  files (accidentally), 352-353
  lines from EDLIN file, 80-81
  text, 111
destination file, 198
DEVICE command, 358-359

device drivers, 339, 358
  changing language of character set,
    370-372
  listing (that come with MS-DOS), 370
  problems reading/writing, 381
  setting up caches, 360
dialog boxes, 95, 104-106
  Add Group, 331
  Add Program, 332-333
  Copy File, 325
  Display Options, 315
  navigating, 314
  Options, 316
  Rename File, 318
  Search File, 325, 327
"dimmed" commands, 312
DIP switches, 376
DIR command, 32, 140-141
  deciphering display, 34
  listing specific files, 34-35
  using with switches, 171-173
  verifying file erasing, 146
directories
  area allocated on disk, 347
  changing, 238-239
  collapsing, 311
  comparing/viewing two, 322
  copying whole contents, 262-265
  creating, 324
    root, 232-233
    tree-structured, 235
  current, 241-242
    identifying, 238-239
  deciphering display, 34
  holding file information in memory
    buffers, 362-363
  identifying current directory, 238-239
  listing files, 32-34
  navigating, 249-250
    short cuts, 250-252
  parent, 239, 246
  removing, 256-257
  root, 234, 246
    accessing with CHDIR
      command, 239, 241
    finding/listing files in subdirectory
      from, 247-248
  working with, 106
  sorting
    using batch files, 289-290
    filenames, 173-176

source, 243
symbol entries, 250-252
target, 243
tree-structured, 230, 235, 246
    advantages, 254
    understanding system, 252-254
updating DOSSHELL program, 310
Directory Tree window, 311
disk drives, 39-40
disk operating system, *see* DOS
disk-caching programs, 360
DISKCOPY command, 53-56
    comparing to COPY, XCOPY,
        BACKUP, 275
disks
    backing up, 345-347
    basic organization, 347
    changing labels, 182
    copying, 53-56
        files to same disk, 255-256
        with only one drive, 55
        operating system to, 182-186
    creating subdirectories on, 235-237
    diagnosing/repairing, 341, 348-349
    double-density, double-sided, 40
    examining available space, 186-188
    example, 231-232
    exposed surfaces, 42-43
    features, 41
    floppy, 39-40
        copying to hard disk, 274-275
        recovering, 354
    formatting
        error message, 52
        lower capacity than disk
            drive, 201-203
    hard, 21
        accidentally reformatting, 350, 353
        activating MS-DOS, 25-26
        copying entire contents, 271-272
        copying files from to floppy
            diskettes, 270-272
        organizing, 267-269
        recovering, 353-354
        using FORMAT command, 50
    history, 39-40
    identifying, 52
    improving access speed, 365-366
    improving performance, 341
    labeling, 52
    labels, 44

"microfloppies", 41
monitoring status/condition, 186-190
protecting operating system, 39
preparing for use, 47-48
reading directory, 309
reformatting (accidentally), 350
restoring original organization, 350
single-sided, 40
source, 54, 129, 138-139
storing data, 47
target, 54, 129, 138-139
"ten commandments", 46
virtual, creating out of memory, 358
volume labels, 181
write-protect notch, 44
Display Options command, 315
Display Options dialog box, 315
DISPLAY.SYS command, 371
DOS, 14
    installing MS-DOS, 22-23
    shell, 22
86-DOS, 15
DOS shell, 22
DOSKEY command, 279, 296-298
    command list, 298
    defining macros, 301-302
    editing keys, 299-300
    sending command to PC
        simultaneously, 300
DOSSHELL program, 307-308
    clearing screen, 327
    comparing directories, 322
    context-sensitive help system, 319-321
    displaying information, 308
    reading disk's directory, 309
    rereading/updating directory, 310
    screen, 308
    starting, 307
    using pathnames, 323-324
    versus PC Shell, 342
    viewing files without running separate
        program, 317
    working with windows, menus, 313
double clicking, 328
double period (".."") symbol, 250-252
double-density disk, 40
double-sided disks, 40
dragging, 93, 102
drive indicators
    eliminating during file copying, 141-142
    specifying during copying, 139

drive selector, 309
drives, 7, 48
    current, 56-58, 129
    default, 56
    displaying pathnames, 258-261
    increasing accessibility past five
        (drives), 372
    indicators, 56-59
        naming files, 129-130
        specifying during copying, 139
    logical, 372
    physical disks versus virtual disks, 359
    selecting short cut, 309
Dual File Lists command, 322

E

E (END) command, 73-74
ECHO command, 198, 208-209
    versus REMark command, 211
ECHO OFF command, 224
EDIT, 64
EDit LINes, *see* EDLIN
Edit menu, 111
EDIT program
    entering text, 134-135
    viewing files, 135-136
Edit program
    advantages, 92-93
    correcting errors in text, 108-109
    customizing, 118
    cutting text, 110-111
    dialog boxes, 104-106
        working with, 106
    entering more text, 98-99, 102
    entering text, 96-98
    moving cursor, 97-98
    opening screen, 95
    page movement, 98-99, 102
    pasting text, 110-111
    requesting information, 104-106
    saving, 105-106
    searching for string of text, 112-113, 115
    starting, 95-96
EDIT.COM file, 95
editing functions, 166
editing keys, 160-166
    with DOSKEY command, 299-300
editors
    line, 63-65, 91
        activating, 70-72
        current line status, 68-69

line numbering, 67-68
        safety features, 65-66
    screen, 92-93
    text, 63
EDLIN, 63-65, 91
    accessing more memory, 87
    activating, 70-72
    advantages over word-processing
        programs, 66
    command format, 68
    copying text, 85-86
    current line status, 68-69
    entering text, 134-135
    exiting program, 73-75
    files
        adding line to end of file, 79
        checking contents, 74-75
        deleting lines, 80-81
        modifying, 76-80
    inputing data into files, 72-73
    line numbering, 67-68
    moving block of text, 84-85
    replacing lines, 83-84
    returning to program, 74
    safety features, 65-66
    searching files, 82-83
    transferring
        data, 86-87
        files into memory, 87
    viewing files, 135-136
EDLIN.COM file, 198
EDLIN.EXE file, 198
EGA (Enhanced Graphics Adapter), 157
Enable Switcher command, 333
<Enter> key, 151-152
Epson, 157
ERASE command, 144-147
    using with wild-card symbols, 170
error messages, 188
    "access denied", 384
    "all specified file(s) are contiguous", 384
    "allocation error, size adjusted", 384
    "attempted write-protect violation", 384
    "bad call format", 382
    "bad command", 382
    "bad command or filename", 133, 384
    "bad or missing command
        interpreter", 384
    "bad unit", 382
    "cannot edit .BAK file - rename file", 384

"cannot load COMMAND, system
  halted", 384
"contains xxx noncontiguous
  blocks", 384
"data", 382
device, 381-383
"disk", 382
"disk boot failure", 384
"disk error writing FAT", 384
"duplicate filename or file not
  found", 385
"entry error", 385
"error in EXE file", 385
"error loading operating system", 385
"EXEC error", 385
"file allocation table bad, drive", 383
"file cannot be copied onto itself", 385
"File Creation Error", 385
"file is READ-ONLY", 385
"file not found", 239, 385
"incorrect DOS version", 385
"incorrect number of parameters", 385
"insufficient disk space", 385
"intermediate file error during pipe", 385
"internal stack failure", 373
"invalid COMMAND.COM in drive", 386
"invalid directory", 386
"invalid number of parameters", 386
"label not found", 386
"no paper", 383
"no room for system on disk", 386
"non-DOS disk", 383
"nonsystem disk or disk error...", 386
"not ready", 383
"out of environment space", 386
"read fault", 383
"sector not found", 383
"seek error", 383
"syntax error", 386
"terminate batch job (Y/N)?", 386
"too many parameters", 386
"Unable To Create Directory", 386
"unable to open file", 372
"unrecognized command in
  CONFIG.SYS", 386
"write fault", 383
"write protect", 383
<Esc> key, 153-155, 160
Escape <Esc> function, 165
Escape key, 28
expanded memory, 375

extended memory, 375
extensions, 128
external commands, 131-133,
  230, 258-261

F

FASTOPEN command, 362-363
FAT, 186-188, 347
  backing up, 350-352
FCBS command, 372-373
FDISK utility, 372
file allocation table, *see* FAT
file extension (associating with
  programs), 334
File Find (FF) command, 366-367
File Info (FI) program, 368-369
File menu
  command selections, 103
  four common operations, 319
  opening, 312
file-control block, 372
file-list window, 314
  running programs, 328
files
  ASCII, 66, 93
    areas of data entry, 67
    contents, 67
    text, 196
  AUTOEXEC.BAT, 224
    "automating" SUBST commands, 261
    moving directly to BASIC
      program, 224
    purpose, 223-224
  backup (.BAK), 65-66
  batch, 195-196
    adding comments, 210-211
    "chaining", 221
    creating, 196-197
    creating files sharing particular
      specifications, 220-221
    creating with COPY.CON, 199
    creating with EDLIN, 198-199
    echoing commands, 208-209
    executing under specified
      conditions, 214-216
    formatting disk with lower capacity
      than disk drive, 201-203
    increasing replacable parameters, 219
    inserting built-in stop, 212-213
    pre-named, 223

batch, (*continued*)

    removing from current working
        disk, 207-208
    running, 200-201
    running second batch files, 222-223
    safety device, 213
    saving macros, 302
    sorting directories, 289-290
    starting, 199-200
    stopping, 203-205
    transferring processing using
        labels, 216-218
    using replaceable parameters,
        204-208
    using with BACKUP command, 273
COMMAND.COM, 183, 185
CONFIG.SYS, 262
    loading device drivers from, 358-359
copying, 136-140
    changing file name, 140-141
    eliminating drive indicators, 141-142
    from hard disk to floppy
        diskettes, 270-272
    to same disk, 255-256
    using wild card symbols, 324-325
    verifying, 140-141
    without using File menu, 324
COUNTRY.SYS, 371
creating, 134-135, 198
    on example disk, 231-232
    using COPY command, 198
    using EDLIN, 71
definition, 123-124
deleting (accidentally), 352-353
destination, 198
directing commands on correct
    path, 249-250
EDIT.COM, 95
editing, 159
EDLIN
    adding lines to end of file, 79
    checking contents, 74-75
    copying text, 85-86
    deleting lines, 80-81
    modifying, 76-80
    moving blocks of text, 84-85
    transferring data, 86-87
    transferring data to memory, 87
EDLIN.COM, 198
EDLIN.EXE, 198
entering text, 134-135
erasing, 145-147

finding/listing in subdirectory form root
    directory, 247-248
fragmented, 364
"hidden", 185-188
holding data in RAM, 358
improving management, 341
increasing ability to open, 372
inputing data, 72-73
listing, 32-34
    specific files, 34-35
locating strings within, 290-293
moving
    to subdirectory, 242-246
    without using File menu, 324
naming, 124-127
    adding descriptive comments to
        filenames, 368-369
    changing copied files name, 140-141
    drive indicators, 129-130
    exception to rule, 245
    restrictions, 126-127
    samples, good/bad, 129
    using extensions, 128
overlay, 267
PIPE, 281-282
program, excluding from backup,
    346-347
QBASIC.EXE, 95
renaming, 143-144
rules for naming, 125-126
searching, 325, 327
    EDLIN, 82-83
    using wild card symbols, 366-367
sorting
    according to numbers located in
        text, 285
    alphabetically/by column, 283-288
    filenames in directories, 173-176
specifying, 129
standard format, 66
viewing, 135-136
    without running separate
        program, 317
working with, 318
FILES command, 373
filters, 283
    FIND, 290-293
    MORE, 293-294
    SORT, 283-286, 289-290
        outputing results to files, 286-288
    using with piping, 288-290

Find command, 115
FIND filter, 290-293
floppy disks, 39-40
    copying to hard disk, 274-275
    drives, 7
        recovering, 354
    restoring accidentally formatted floppy
        disks, 354-358
FOR command, 220-221
FORMAT command, 47-52, 132, 180
    cautionary note, 52
    using with /s switch, 182-184
    using with /v switch, 180-182
Format command, 329
Format Recover (FR), 358
fragmented files, 364
Framework, 8
full-screen editor, 63-64
function keys, 160-161, 167
functions
    <F3> (Copy All), 161
    control, 167
    Copy All, 162
    Copy One Character <F1>, 162
    Copy Up To <F2>, 162-163
    Create a New Template <F5>, 164-165
    editing, 166
    Escape <Esc>, 165
    Insert a New Character <Ins>, 164
    Skip Over One Character <Del>, 163
    Skip Up To <F4>, 163

G

Gibson Research, 366
global characters, 168
global search, 83
GOTO command, 216-218
graphics
    adapter, 308
    mode, 157, 308
    printing, 157
GRAPHICS command, 157
greater than (>) symbol, 280-281

H

hard disks, 21
    activating MS-DOS, 25-26
    copying entire contents, 271-272
    copying files from to floppy
        diskettes, 270-272
    drives, 7

organizing, 267-269
formatting, 353-354
using FORMAT command, 50
help
    on-line for commands, 176-179
    window, 340
Help button, 314
HELP command, 176
Help screen, 116, 118
Help text box, 320-321
"hidden" files, 185-188
high memory area, 374

I

I (Insert) command, 78
    comparing to D (Delete) command, 81
IBMCACHE.SYS, 360
IF command, 214-216
indicators
    drive, 56-59
        eliminating during file copying,
            141-142
        naming files, 129-130
        specifying during copying, 139
input
    buffer, 159, 162
    redirecting, 281
    standard device, 279-280
Insert a New Character <Ins> function, 164
Insert mode, 73, 108
INSTALL command, 363
instructions
    deciphering, 27
    for specified commands, 179-180
interleaving, 365-366
internal commands, 131, 236

K

KEYB command, 371
keyboards, 151, 279-280
    numeric keypad, 157-158
keys
    <Backspace>, 151-152, 160
    <Caps Lock>, 153, 158
    <Enter>, 151-152
    <Esc>, 153-155, 160
    <Num Lock>, 157-158
    <PrtSc>, 156
    <Scroll Lock>, 158
    common misconceptions, 27
    control, 167

<Ctrl>, 31
editing, 160-166
    with DOSKEY command, 299-300
Escape, 28
function, 160-161, 167
special, 151-156, 167
kilobytes, 6

L

L (List) command, 75-79, 81
LABEL command, 182
labels
    disk, 182
    transferring processing, 216-218
Laserjet, 157
LASTDRIVE command, 372-373
lastdrive= command, 262
less-than (>) symbol, 281
line editor, 63-65, 91
    activating, 70-72
    current line status, 68-69
    line numbering, 67-68
    safety features, 65-66
list box, 105
logical drives, 372
Lotus 1-2-3, 8

M

M (Move) command, 84-85
Macintosh System, 7
macros, 301
    command, 297-298
    defining, 301-302
    inserting replaceable macros, 301-302
    saving, 302
megabyte, 6
memory, 5
    allocating buffers to hold file directory
        informat, 362-363
    cache area, 360
    choosing appropiate type, 375-376
    clearing space, 87
    conventional, 374
    creating virtual disks out of, 358
    expanded, 375
    extended, 375
    freeing up, 377
    high-memory area, 374
    installing device driver, 358
    measuring, 6
    RAM, 7, 131
        holding programs, 358

reserved, 374
stacks, 373
storing type, 159
types, 374-375
upper blocks, 375
memory-resident programs, 374
menu bar, 95, 102
menus
    Edit, 111
    File
        command selections, 103
        four common operations, 319
        opening, 312
    opening
        using keyboard, 104
        using mouse, 103-104
    Options, 315, 333
    Search, 112, 114
    selecting, 102
    View, 322
        options for changing list
            arrangements, 323
messages (error), 188
    "access denied", 384
    "all specified file(s) are
        contiguous", 384
    "allocation error, size adjusted", 384
    "attempted write-protect
        violation", 384
    "bad call format", 382
    "bad command", 382-383
    "bad command or filename", 133, 384
    "bad or missing command
        interpreter", 384
    "bad unit", 382
    "cannot edit .BAK file - rename
        file", 384
    "cannot load COMMAND, system
        halted", 384
    "contains xxx noncontiguous
        blocks", 384
    "copyall failure", 216
    "data", 382
    device, 381-383
    "disk", 382
    "disk boot failure", 384
    "disk error writing FAT", 384
    "duplicate filename or file not
        found", 385
    "entry error", 385
    "error in EXE file", 385

"error loading operating system", 385
"EXEC error", 385
"file cannot be copied onto itself", 385
"File Creation Error", 385
"file is READ-ONLY", 385
"file not found", 239, 385
"incorrect DOS version", 385
"incorrect number of parameters", 385
"insufficient disk space", 385
"intermediate file error during pipe", 385
"internal stack failure", 373
"invalid COMMAND.COM in drive", 386
"invalid directory", 386
"invalid number of parameters", 386
"label not found", 386
"no paper", 383
"no room for system on disk", 386
"non-DOS disk", 383
"nonsystem disk or disk error...", 386
"not ready", 383
"out of environment space", 386
"read fault", 383
"sector not found", 383
"seek error", 383
"syntax error", 386
"terminate batch job (Y/N)?", 386
"too many parameters", 386
"Unable To Create Directory", 386
"unable to open file", 372
"unrecognized command in CONFIG.SYS", 386
"write fault", 383
"write protect", 383
"General Failure", 347
"Sector Not Found", 347
"Volume label", 182
microcomputer system, 3
common features, 4
"microfloppies", 41
protective features, 45
microprocessor, 5
Microsoft Windows, 340
Microsoft Windows program, 308
Microsoft Word, 8
MIRROR command, 350-352
MKDIR command, 235-237
creating subdirectories within subdirectories, 247

MODE command, 190-191
modes
character, 308
command, 73
graphics, 157, 308
insert, 73, 108
modifying
EDLIN files, 76-77
adding lines, 78-80
existing lines, 77-78
MORE filter, 293-294
mouse
features, 93
opening menus, 103-104
pointer, 309
scrolling, 101
selecting
commands, 103-104
text, 110
MS-DOS
activating, 25-26
command options, 180
default feature, 56
entering commands, 133
formatting text, 67
history, 15-16
installing, 22-23
list of device drivers, 370
pipeline, 282
prompts, 240
ready indicators, 24-25
starting computer, 21
versions, 16-17
MS-DOS Bible, 191

N

New command, 330-332
Norton Disk Doctor, 348-349
Norton Integrator program, 340
Norton Utilities, 340
<Num Lock> key, 157-158
numeric keypad, 157-158

O

/o ("order") option, 173-176
operate, 13
operating system, 3, 9
activating, 23
copying to disk, 182-186
definition, 13
displaying messages, 50

operating system (*continued*)
  function, 14
  instructions, 31
  protecting disk, 39
  responsibilities, 14-15
Options dialog box, 316
Options menu, 315, 333
OS/2, 7
output
  redirecting, 280-281
  standard device, 279-280
overlay files, 267

P

pages, moving, 98-99, 102
parameters, 204
  replaceable, 204-208
    placing in macros, 301-302
parent directory, 239, 246
partition table, 347
  backing up, 350-352
  saving, 351
Pascal programming language, 9
passwords, 331
PATH command, 133, 266-267
pathnames, 230, 234-235
  displaying every available on given
      drive, 258-261
  referring to using "shorthand", 261
  using in DOSSHELL, 323-324
PAUSE command, 212-213
PC Backup, 344-345
  backing all except program files,
      346-347
  Include/Exclude files option, 346
PC Cache, 360
PC Shell, 342
PC Tools, 340, 342
  utility programs, 343-344
period (".") symbol, 250-252
physical disk drive, 359
PIPE file, 281-282
piping, 288-290
PRINTER.SYS command, 371
printing, 156
  giving printer operating instructions, 190
  graphics, 157
program groups, 328
  adding programs, 331
  designing customized, 330-333
program list, 309

programming language, 8
programs
  adding to customized program
      group, 331
  application, 8
  associating with file extensions, 334
  automating startup, 281
  BASIC, 102
    listing categories by extension, 175
    moving directly to using
        AUTOEXEC.BAT, 224
  defragmentation, 365
  designing customized program
      groups, 330-333
  disk-caching, 360
  DOSSHELL, 307-308
  EDIT
    entering text, 134-135
    viewing files, 135-136
  Edit
    correcting errors in text, 108-109
    customizing, 118
    cutting text, 110-111
    dialog boxes, 104-106
    entering more text, 98-99, 102
    entering text, 96-98
    moving cursor, 97-98
    opening screens, 95
    page movment, 98-99, 102
    pasting text, 110-111
    requesting information, 104-106
    saving, 105-106
    searching for string of text, 112-115
    starting, 95-96
  File Info (FI), 368-369
  holding in RAM, 358
  memory-resident, 374, 377
  Microsoft Windows, 308
  Norton Integrator, 340
  organizing, 328
  REBUILD, 358
  running, 328-330
  selecting from subgroup, 329
  Text Search (TS), 367-368
  TSR, 351
  using multiple programs, 333
  utility, 339-340
    eliminating file fragmenation, 364
    PC Tools, 343-344
  word-processing, 63
PROMPT command, 240

prompts, 240
<PrtSc> key, 156

Q-R

Q (Quit) command, 75
QBASIC.EXE file, 95
question mark (?) wild-card symbol, 83-84,
   168-169
R (Replace) command, 83-84
radio button, 316, 331
RAM memory, 5, 7, 131, 358
Random Access Memory, *see* RAM memory
Read Only Memory, *see* ROM
REBUILD command, 354-357
REBUILD program, 358
REM (REMark) command, 210-211
REMark command, 211
ReMove DIRectory command, *see*
   RMDIR command
RENAME command, 66, 137, 142-144
Rename command, 318, 320
Rename File dialog box, 318
replaceable parameters, 204-208
   placing in macros, 301-302
reserved memory, 374
resolution, 308
RESTORE command, 273-275
RMDIR command, 256-257
ROM memory, 6, 9
   "bootstrap loader", 21
root directory, 234, 246
   accessing with CHDIR
      command, 239, 241
   creating, 232-233
   finding/listing files in subdirectory
      from, 247-248
root symbol, 237

S

S (Search) command, 82-83
save button, 331
Save command, 102, 104
saving, 102
   in Edit program, 105-106
   macros, 302
   partition table, 351
screen editor, 92-93
screens, 279-280
   clearing, 35-36, 95, 327
   DOSSHELL program, 308
   freezing, 32-34

Help, 116, 118
   opening to Edit program, 95
   pausing display when full, 293-294
scroll bars, 94, 99, 102, 309
<Scroll Lock> key, 158
scrolling, 32-34, 98-99, 101-102
   stopping, 158
Search File dialog box, 325, 327
Search menu, 112, 114
Search... command, 325, 327
searching, 266-267
   EDLIN files, 82-83
   for specified files, 325, 327
   global, 83
   string of text, 112-115
Seattle Computer Products, 15
serial number, 51
set, definition, 220
shareware, 339
SHIFT command, 218-219
Single File List command, 322
single-sided disks, 40
Skip Over One Character <Del>
   function, 163
Skip Up To <F4> function, 163
slider box, 102
SMARTDRV.SYS, 360-361
software, 8
   definition, 3
   function, 13
   tools, 63
SORT filter, 283-286, 289-290
   outputing results to files, 286-288
source
   directory, 243
   disk, 54, 129, 138-139
special keys, 151-156, 167
SpinRite, 366
stacks, 372-373
STACKS command, 373
status line, 309
strings, 112-115
   locating within files, 290-293
subdirectories, 233
   activating commands, 235
   creating, 234-237, 245-246
      within subdirectories, 247
   function, 234-235
   listing files in from root directory,
      247-248
   moving files into, 242-246

naming, 234
paths, 235
separating from other subdirectories, 234
SUBST command, 261, 372
Survival Guide, 95, 116
switches, 170
/? (on-line command help), 176-179
/f (using with CHKDSK command), 189
/p (using with DIR command), 172-173
/s (using with FORMAT command),
182-184
/v (using with CHKDSK command),
189-190
/v (using with FORMAT command),
180-182
/w (with DIR command), 171-172
DIP, 376
formatting disk with lower capacity than
disk drive, 201-202
Symantec (Norton Utilities), 308, 339
symbols
A:\>, 56
asterisk (*) wild-card, 68-69, 168-170
double period (".."), 250-252
greater than (>), 280-281
less-than (>), 281
period ("."), 250-252
question mark (?) wild-card, 83-84,
168-169
root, 237
wild-card, 168-169
using with ERASE command, 170
SYS command, 185-186
systems
booting, 21-24
temperatures, 30
contex-sensitive help, 319-321
definition, 13
microcomputer, 3
common features, 4
operating, 3, 9
activating, 23
copying to disk, 182-186
definition, 13
displaying messages, 50
function, 14
protecting disk, 39
responsibilities, 14-15

T

T (Transfer) command, 86-87

tables
file allocation, 347
partition, 347
backing up, 350-352
saving, 351
target directory, 243
target disk, 54, 129, 138-139
templates, 159, 162
copying portions, 162-163
creating new, 165
inserting characters, 164
skipping over part, 163-164
terminate and stay resident program, *see* TSR
program
text
adding addresses/salutations, 106-107
correcting errors, 108-109
cutting, 110-111
deleting, 111
indenting, 107
pasting, 110-111
searching for string of, 112-115
selecting, 110
text box, 105
text editor, 63
Text Search (TS) program, 367-368
text window, 96
time, setting automatically, 224
title bar, 309
TREE command, 258-261
tree-structured directory, 246
advantages, 254
understanding system, 252-254
TREE.COM command, 230
TRUENAME command, 262
TSR program, 351
TYPE command, 74-75, 135-136
verifying duplicate copies, 142

U

UNDELETE command, 352-353
UNFORMAT command
recovering accidentally formatted
disks, 354
recovering accidentally reformatted
disks, 353
UNIX, 7
upper memory blocks, 375
utilities
backup, 345-347
disk diagnosis, repair, 341

FDISK, 341, 372
packages, choosing, 344
programs, 339-340
eliminating file fragmenation, 364
PC Tools, 343-344

V

Verify command, 115
VGA (Video Graphics Array), 157
View File Contents command, 327
View menu, 322
options for changing list
arrangements, 323
virtual disk drive, 359
volume labels, 51, 181

W-X

W (Write) command, 87
The Waite Group's MS-DOS Bible, 340
2nd edition, 180
3rd ed., 216
"warm" boot, 30
wild card symbols168-169
cautionary measures, 254-255
searching files, 366-367
using to copy files, 324-325
using with ERASE command, 170
windows
Directory Tree, 311
file-list, 314
help, 340
word processor, 91
word wrap, 96
word-processing program, 63
WordPerfect, 8
write caching, 360
write-protect notch, 44
XCOPY command, 262-265
comparing to COPY, DISKCOPY,
BACKUP, 275

The Waite Group

100 Shoreline Highway, Suite 285   Mill Valley, CA 94941   (415) 331-0575

Compuserve: 75146,3515   usenet:hplabs!well!mitch   MCI Mail: The Waite Group

Dear Reader:

Thank you for considering the purchase of our book. Computer users have come to know products from **The Waite Group** for the care and quality we put in them. Let me tell you a little about our group and how we make our books and software.

It started in 1976 when I could not find a computer book that really taught me anything. The books that were available talked down to people, lacked illustrations and examples, were poorly laid out, and were written as if you already understood all terminology. So I set out to write a good book about microcomputers. This was to be a special book—very graphic, with a friendly and casual style, and filled with examples. The result was an instant best-seller.

Over the years, I developed this approach into a "formula" (nothing really secret here, just a lot of hard work—I am a crazy man about technical accuracy and high-quality illustrations). I began to find writers who wanted to write books in this way. This led to coauthoring and then to multiple-author books and many more titles (over seventy titles currently on the market). As The Waite Group author base grew, I trained a group of editors to manage our products. We now have a team devoted to putting together the best possible book package and maintaining the high standard of our existing books.

We greatly appreciate and use any advice our readers send us (and you send us a lot). We have discovered that our readers are detail nuts: you want indexes that really work, tables of contents that dig deeply into the subject, illustrations, tons of examples, reference cards, and more.

Discovering MS-DOS, Second Edition, updates the previous best-selling book to cover DOS 5 and the DOS shell. If you would like to explore MS-DOS/PC DOS even further, look for our other DOS books. *Understanding MS-DOS,* Second Edition, melds The Waite Group's expertise and user-friendly style with the classic approach of SAMS *Understanding* Series. *The Waite Group's Using PC DOS,* a comprehensive book for using DOS in the business environment, includes an extensive reference section, a Quick Primer, and tutorials. *The Waite Group's MS-DOS Bible,* Fourth Edition, combines a command reference section with tutorials. It covers introductory DOS topics for users and explores the inner workings of DOS for beginning programmers.

Power Users will want to see *The Waite Group's Tricks of the MS-DOS Masters,* Second Edition, which covers advanced MS-DOS topics and little-known tricks. If you'd like to program in the MS-DOS environment, check out *The Waite Group's Developer's Guide.* Finally, *The Waite Group's MS-DOS Papers* is a diverse collection of essays for MS-DOS users and programmers. You can find a list of all our titles in the back of this book. In fact, let us know what you want, and we'll try to write about it.

Thanks again for considering the purchase of this product. If you care to tell me anything you like (or don't like) about *The Waite Group's Discovering MS-DOS*, Second Edition, please write or email to the addresses on this letterhead.

Sincerely,

Mitchell Waite
The Waite Group

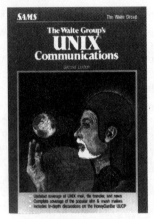

Discovering MS-DOS,
Second Edition

Waite Group Reader Feedback Card   **SAMS**

Help Us Make A Better Book

To better serve our readers, we would like your opinion on the contents and quality of this book. Please fill out this card and return it to *The Waite Group*, 100 Shoreline Hwy., Suite A-285, Mill Valley, CA, 94941 (415) 331-0575.

Name _____

Company _____

Address _____

City _____

State _____ ZIP _____ Phone _____

1. How would you rate the content of this book?

   ☐ Excellent   ☐ Fair
   ☐ Very Good   ☐ Below Average
   ☐ Good   ☐ Poor

2. What were the things you liked *most* about this book?

   ☐ Pace   ☐ Listings   ☐ Appendixes
   ☐ Content   ☐ Design   ☐ Completeness
   ☐ Writing Style ☐ Format   ☐ Price
   ☐ Accuracy   ☐ Cover   ☐ Illustrations
   ☐ Examples   ☐ Index   ☐ Construction

3. Please explain the one thing you liked *most* about this book.

   _____
   _____
   _____

4. What were the things you liked *least* about this book?

   ☐ Pace   ☐ Listings   ☐ Appendixes
   ☐ Content   ☐ Design   ☐ Completeness
   ☐ Writing Style ☐ Format   ☐ Price
   ☐ Accuracy   ☐ Cover   ☐ Illustrations
   ☐ Examples   ☐ Index   ☐ Construction

5. Please explain the one thing you liked *least* about this book.

   _____
   _____
   _____

6. How do you use this book? For work, recreation, reference, self-training, classroom, etc?

   _____
   _____
   _____
   _____

7. Would you be interested in receiving a Pop-Up utility program containing the contents of this book? What would you pay for this?

   _____

8. Where did you purchase this particular book?

   ☐ Book Chain   ☐ Direct Mail
   ☐ Small Book Store ☐ Book Club
   ☐ Computer Store   ☐ School Book Store
   ☐ Other: _____

   _____

9. Can you name another similar book you like better than this one, or one that is as good, and tell us why?

   _____
   _____

10. How many Waite Group books do you own? _____

11. What are your favorite Waite Group books?

    _____

12. What topics or specific titles would you like to see The Waite Group develop?

    _____
    _____
    _____

13. What version of DOS are you using?

    _____

14. What computer are you using with DOS?

    _____

15. Any other comments you have about this book or other Waite Group titles?

    _____
    _____
    _____
    _____

Fold Here

From:

_____

_____

_____

The Waite Group, Inc.
100 Shoreline Highway, Suite A-285
Mill Valley, CA 94941

Staple or tape here   22772